Religion under Siege
I
The Roman Catholic Church in Occupied Europe (1939-1950)

Edited by
Lieve Gevers and Jan Bank

PEETERS

RELIGION UNDER SIEGE
I

ANNUA NUNTIA LOVANIENSIA
LVI

Religion under Siege

Volume I
The Roman Catholic Church in
Occupied Europe (1939-1950)

Edited by
Lieve Gevers and Jan Bank

PEETERS
LEUVEN – PARIS – DUDLEY, MA
2007

A CIP record for this book is available from the Library of Congress.

Cover Illustration: Eucharist celebration and parade organized by the Vlaamsch Nationaal Verbond (Flemish National League) in the Belgian town of Roeselare in commemoration of Reimond Tollenaere, a Flemish-nationalist collaborator who died at the Eastern Front in Russia, 7 February 1942. Collection Cegesoma, Brussels.

*No part of this book may be reproduced in any form,
by print, photoprint, microfilm or any other means without written
permission from the publisher*

© Uitgeverij Peeters, Bondgenotenlaan 153, B-3000 Leuven (Belgium)
ISBN 978-90-429-1932-7
D/2007/0602/75

Contents

Lieve Gevers and Jan Bank
Introduction VII

Idesbald Goddeeris
The Catholic Church in Poland under Nazi Occupation (1939-1945) and the First Years of Communism (1944-1948) 1

Jure Krišto
The Catholic Church in Croatia and Bosnia-Herzegovina in the Face of Totalitarian Ideologies and Regimes 39

Tamara Griesser-Pečar
Staat und Kirche in Slowenien 1941-1950 93

Emilia Hrabovec
Die katholische Kirche in der Slowakei 1939-1945 139

Vilma Narkutė
The Catholic Church in Lithuania under Two Occupying Regimes 173

Lieve Gevers
Catholicism in the Low Countries During the Second World War: Belgium and the Netherlands: a Comparative Approach 205

Lieven Saerens
The Attitude of the Belgian Catholic Church towards the Persecution of Jews 243

Patrick Pasture
Christian Social Movements Confronted with Fascism in Europe: Consistency, Continuity, or Flexibility in Principles, Strategies, and Tactics towards Social and Economic Democracy 283

Johan Ickx
The Roman "non possumus" and the Attitude of Bishop Alois
Hudal towards the National Socialist Ideological Aberrations ... 315

List of Contributors 345

Introduction

The present volume addresses the question of the stance taken by the Catholic Church in occupied Europe during World War II. Although much has been written and published on the subject, it still remains a significant focal point of historical research. In the last ten years we have been confronted with a resurgence of the so-called 'Pius-war', the frequently emotional polemic surrounding the justification or absence thereof of the role of Pope Pius XII who was head of the Catholic Church at the time. The work presented here, however, focuses attention on the role of the local churches rather than that of the pope and the Vatican. Its goal is to shed light more specifically on the position maintained by the Catholic bishops, clergy and faithful in a variety of European countries throughout the war. Indeed, the controversy surrounding *Der Stellvertreter*, the play written by Rolf Hochhuth which appeared in 1963, was not only to call the role of Pius XII into discussion. In fact, the majority of critical commentators have credited the piece with forcing the Catholic Church as a whole and Christianity in the broader sense of the term to accept responsibility for the attitude they maintained during the Second World War.

The studies presented here represent the written results of a research project established under the auspices of the European Science Foundation entitled 'The Impact of National Socialist and Fascist Occupation in Europe' (1999-2005) under the leadership of Wolfgang Benz (Technische Universität, Berlin) and Hans Blom (Niod, Nederlands Instituut voor Oorlogsdocumentatie, Amsterdam). Within the broader framework of the project, research into the aspect of Church and Religion was scribed more specifically to Team 2 'The Continuity of the Churches' under the leadership of the signatories.

It became clear from the beginning that we would not be able to include every country and every denomination and sub-denomination in our study. In establishing our team, we strove nevertheless to reach as broad a spectrum possible, both with respect to the churches and religions in Europe (Catholicism, Protestantism, Orthodoxy, and to a limited degree, Islam) as the various regions of the European continent (North, West, Central and [South] East). The results of the team's research were presented at four workshops held in Leuven (Belgium, 2001), Ljubljana

(Slovenia, 2002), Jachranka (Poland, 2003) and Rome (Italy, 2004). The present volume contains the research results presented in relation to the Catholic Church. A second volume includes the contributions dealing with the other Christian churches and Islam.[1]

In line with the ESF-project, our goal was to focus attention on European countries that were confronted in one way or another with a regime of occupation under the Germans and their allies. We have interpreted the term 'occupation' in its broadest sense, including countries that were not directly subject to a military or civilian government of occupation. From the comparative perspective, we thus considered it appropriate to include satellite states such as Slovakia and Croatia within the range of our research. While the latter were able to maintain a significant degree of autonomy during the war, they were nonetheless obliged at the same time to comply with directives stemming from Berlin or Rome.

Developments in Central and Eastern Europe are given priority in the present collection. They represent the subject of five of the contributions: on Slovenia (Tamara Griesser-Pečar), Croatia (Jure Krišto), Slovakia (Emilia Hrabovec), Poland (Idesbald Goddeeris) and Lithuania (Vilma Narkutė). The team were convinced of the relevance of this option, not only because of the frequently more dramatic character of the events that took place in the said regions during the Second World War but also, and more importantly, because research into the given events is much less advanced when compared with research into the attitude of the Catholic Church in Western European countries. Indeed, it was only after the collapse of communism around 1990 that relevant archives were made available for historical research. In addition, four articles endeavour to shed light on developments in Western Europe. The general situation in Belgium and the Netherlands at the time is presented in a comparative fashion by Lieve Gevers, while Lieven Saerens focuses specifically on the attitude of the Belgian church and of Belgian Catholics to the holocaust. Patrick Pasture provides a panoramic survey of the stance maintained by the Catholic social movements from a European perspective. The volume concludes with the contribution of Johan Ickx on Alois Hudal, which endeavours to shed light on the position maintained by this controversial Austrian prelate. The latter's presence in the Vatican at the time likewise allows for a degree of exploration of Vatican politics during the war.

---

1. Lieve Gevers and Jan Bank (eds.), *Religion under Siege*. Volume II. *Protestant, Orthodox and Muslim Communities in Occupied Europe (1939-1950)*, Annua Nuntia Lovaniensia, 57 (Leuven/Paris/Dudley, MA: Peeters, 2007).

The contributions follow a similar structure. They begin by sketching the situation on the eve of the war, a necessary prerequisite for achieving a clear understanding of the positions adopted and maintained during the war. What was the attitude of the Catholic Church towards the State? What role did the Church play in a given society and how did it manifest itself in the political and social arena? Particular attention is given to the stance adopted by the Church to the emerging fascist and national socialist movements in Europe and the attitude of Catholic opinion towards the nationalist movements. With respect to the war period as such, attention is given in the first instance to the nature of the occupying regime and to the religious and ecclesial politics of the occupying forces. It is evident from the various contributions that this could differ considerably from country to country to another. Light is then shed on the manner with which Catholic opinion and the various Catholic instances reacted to the situation and how their attitude in the matter evolved as the war progressed. What position did they occupy in the highly charged question of accommodation, collaboration and resistance, and what were the motives – ideological or pragmatic – that served as the basis for their position? It goes without saying that the attitude of Catholics and of the Church towards the Holocaust constitutes a particular point of interest in these pages. The contributions conclude with a review of the effect of the war on the position of the Church and of Catholics is the first years following the war. Did the Church and the Catholic population emerge from the war as moral victors? What role did they play or what role was ascribed to them in the purges that took place after the war? To what extent did the Church and the Catholic population contribute to the political and social renewal and/or restoration movements that emerged in the initial post-World War II years? What influence did the war have on post-war relations between Church and State? Each contribution provides a selective list of relevant literature for further research.

It will be evident that the present volume approaches the question at hand from the political-social, institutional and ideological perspective. The concept 'Church' is also interpreted in the broad sense of the term: including the ecclesial leadership, in particular the bishops, the clergy, the religious communities as well as Catholic opinion in general. While it would have been interesting to focus attention on the effect of the war on religious practice and religious life as a whole, it quickly became evident that the project did not offer sufficient scope to pursue such a line of research. Indeed, the latter presupposes a significantly different approach that would require a great deal of additional study. This important aspect thus remains open for exploration and is only touched upon sporadically in the present collection of articles.

The goal of the present volume is thus to stimulate an ongoing comparative study of the attitude of the Catholic Church during the Second World War from a European perspective. Together with the parallel volume that deals with the Protestant and Orthodox churches, this comparative approach can be extended to include other ecclesial denominations and religions in Europe. While significant differences exist between the various countries and denominations, several similar patterns of approach are also strikingly evident. Those who participated in the project consider it an essential task for the future to set about the establishment of such comparative syntheses beyond those found in the present volume and its companion.

Having reached the end of this stage of our research, it now falls to the editors to thank all those who have made a contribution to this volume. Our gratitude extends in the first instance to the authors with whom we worked closely within the framework of our team for a period of five years. This not only lead to fertile academic exchange but also to mutual friendship, which we hope will continue for many years to come. Our gratitude also extends to the European Science Foundation, which was found willing to provide financial support for the stimulating project on 'The Impact of Nationalist and Fascist Occupation in Europe'. We are also extremely grateful to the Netherlands Institute for Advanced Study (NIAS) in Wassenaar (the Netherlands), where we resided as VNC fellows 2004-2005. The institute not only provided a particularly inspiring academic environment for work on the present publication but also important and necessary logistic support for the realisation thereof. We conclude by thanking the Faculty of Theology (K.U.Leuven) for its willingness to publish this collection in its series Annua Nuntia Lovaniensia.

Lieve Gevers (K.U.Leuven, Belgium)
Jan Bank (University of Leiden, the Netherlands)

The Catholic Church in Poland under Nazi Occupation (1939-1945) and the First Years of Communism (1944-1948)

Idesbald Goddeeris

I. Introduction: Polish Historiography and World War II

The Second World War traumatised most European nations but in Poland, it left particularly deep wounds. Both at the beginning as at the end of the war, from the Devil's Pact (August 23, 1939) to the Yalta Conference (February 1945), the Poles were faced with the fact that they had no control over their own fate. This was particularly bitter given the sacrifices Poland made. The Poles had fought fiercely against the Germans. They set up the greatest resistance army on the continent (the 'Armia Krajowa' or Land's Army), started one of the bloodiest insurrections against the Nazis (the Warsaw Rising in August 1944), and participated with two army corps in the liberation of the European continent. The price Poland paid was high. It had more casualties than any other European country. More than 6 million of the 35 million Poles died in the war, i.e. 17% of the total population compared to 12% in the USSR, 11% in Yugoslavia, 8% in Germany and 1.3% in France). Of the 18 million Nazi victims, 11 million died on occupied Polish territory. The more than 3 million Jews that lived in Poland in 1939 were nearly all exterminated: less than a tenth survived, half of them by escaping to the Soviet Union. The Polish capital, Warsaw, lost 850,000 (90%) of its inhabitants and was almost totally destroyed. Altogether, 55% of the Polish jurists perished, 40% of the physicians and more than 30% of the university lecturers as well as Roman Catholic clergymen.[1]

---

1. Standard literature on the Second World War in Poland includes titles as Józef Garliński, *Poland in the Second World War* (London, 1985, originally in Polish); Norman Davies, *God's Playground: A History of Poland* (New York/London, 1980) vol. II, 435-491. The quoted statistics were found in: Jan T. Gross, *Neighbors: The Destruction of the Jewish Community in Jedwabne, Poland* (Princeton, NJ/Oxford, 2001) 6-7; Davies, *God's Playground*, vol. II, 463 and Jerzy Kłoczowski and Lidia Müllerowa, "La guerre et l'occupation (1939-1945)," *Histoire religieuse de la Pologne*, ed. Jerzy Kłoczowski (Paris, 1987) 462, 476. The exact percentage of casualties in other countries is not always clear. On Poland Kłoczowski and Müllerowa made a miscalculation, writing that 6.3 million death people on a population of 35.5 makes 22%.

Indeed, the Catholic Church was greatly affected. Central to the Polish nation, the Church was to disappear for a long period from a country that was considered by the occupier as a *Lebensraum* for *Volksdeutschen*. In Central Poland, where a *Generalgouvernement* (General Government) was founded, the German policy towards the Church was not restrictive in all areas, as maintaining social peace and mobilizing the population against bolshevism was more important while the war lasted. However, in the Western provinces of Poland that had been incorporated in the *Dritte Reich*, almost all clergymen were arrested or banished. In 1939, Łódź, which is currently the second largest city of Poland, counted almost 350,000 Catholics,[2] but only two Catholic priests were allowed to minister. In Poznań, the seat of the Polish Primate at that time, only two churches were open for the 180,000 Catholic Poles.[3]

The traumas wrought by these experiences and other factors, such as the Jewish monopolization of the Holocaust and the position of the Catholic Church in Communist Poland, has led to the intense production of historical studies on the Polish Church in the Second World War. Many sources have been preserved, created (e.g. by numerous interviews) and published. Detailed martyrologies have been made of all the clergymen who were killed by the Nazis or were victims of their repression.[4] A history of female monastic orders, for instance, has been set down in fifteen voluminous tomes in an exhaustive, almost prosopographical way.[5] A lot of this research has been done by clergymen and paid by Catholic institutions. Sometimes, this knowledge is used to give 'scientific' support to social and clerical matters even today: in June 1999, Pope John Paul II beatified 108 martyrs for the faith of World War II.[6] However, not all the studies on the Polish Catholic Church during the Nazi occupation were based on emotional material. Several monographs are the result of profound doctoral or postdoctoral research, and numerous scholars have specialized and published on this subject over the years (e.g. J. Kłoczowski, J. Sziling, K. Śmigiel,

---

2. Kazimierz Śmigiel, *Kościół katolicki w tzw. okręgu Warty 1939-1945* (Lublin, 1979) 19.

3. *Ibid.*, 96, 135.

4. A good example is Wiktor Jacewicz and Jan Woś (eds.), *Martyrologium polskiego duchowieństwa rzymskokatolickiego pod okupacją hitlerowską w latach 1939-1945*, 5 vols. (Warsaw, 1977-1978), including biographies of thousands of spiritual 'martyrs'.

5. Adam Chruszczewski, Krystyna Dębowski, Jerzy Kłoczowski, *et al.* (eds.), *Żeńskie zgromadzenia zakonne w Polsce w 1939-1947*, 15 vols. (Lublin, 1982-2001).

6. Marian Koszewski, *Kościół katolicki na Ziemi Kościańskiej 1939-1945* (Kościan, 1999) 4.

Z. Zieliński and others). Moreover, several overviews have been written or compiled in Polish and in other languages.[7]

In all, various aspects of Church history during the war years in Poland have been investigated in detail, including subjects such as the German policy towards the churches, the extermination of the clergy, the devastation of Catholic buildings and properties, the involvement of priests in the resistance, and the help offered to the Jews by Catholic clergymen. However, other aspects are discussed only marginally. On possible collaboration or the accommodation policies of local and higher clergymen, most studies are silent. What is more, leading historians explicitly state that there was no collaboration at all in Poland. Jerzy Kłoczowski, Professor at the Catholic University of Lublin, wrote that "Poland, unlike other occupied countries, did not know collaboration with the aggressor. From the campaign of 1939 on, national solidarity was the rule."[8] And also Norman Davies, the most important Western specialist in Polish history, declared that "For the Poles, there was no question of collaboration. There was never any Polish Quisling, for the simple reason that in Poland the Nazis never really tried to recruit one."[9] Of course, it is true that no political or social groups in Poland collaborated with the Germans because they wanted them to win. On the other hand, there were certainly Poles who collaborated with the Germans for pragmatic, opportunistic, or even worse reasons.

This is illustrated by recent research on Polish-Jewish relations in the war period. In 2000, the American scholar Jan T. Gross published a book entitled *Neighbors* about the murder of 1600 Jews in July 1941 in Jedwabne, a small village near Łomża, in the north-east of Poland, which had been occupied by the Soviets from September 1939 till June 1941. Gross shows that the pogrom was not initiated or led by the German occupiers, who had moved into the region a month earlier, but that

---

7. The most important Polish monograph giving an overview, is Zenon Fijałkowski, *Kościół katolicki na ziemiach polskich w latach okupacji hitlerowskiej* (Warsaw, 1983); a rich compilation is Zygmunt Zieliński (ed.), *Życie religijne w Polsce pod okupacją hitlerowską 1939-1945* (Warsaw, 1983). Five years earlier, dozens of Polish historians participated in a Western language conference in Warsaw on Christian Churches in Nazi Europe, so that the *acta* are a good introduction of the Polish research. *Miscellanea historiae ecclesiasticae. IX. Congrès de Varsovie 25 juin – 1er juillet 1978. Section IV: Les églises chrétiennes dans l'Europe dominée par le IIIe Reich* (Wrocław/Brussels, 1984). A shorter overview is Kłoczowski and Müllerowa, "La guerre."

8. Kłoczowski and Müllerowa, "La guerre," 483: "La Pologne, contrairement aux autres pays occupés, ne connut pas de collaboration avec l'agresseur. Dès la campagne de 1939, la solidarité nationale fut la règle."

9. Davies, *God's Playground*, II, 464.

it was initiated and executed by the local Polish population. After two years of Soviet occupation, the Poles welcomed the Nazis with great enthusiasm and spontaneously took revenge on their Jewish neighbours, who were accused – falsely according to Gross – of collaboration with the Russians. The publication of Gross's book provoked a real shock among the Poles. For the first time, they were confronted with a book that represented them as collaborators and murderers instead of the victims and heroes of their popular self-image.[10] Although several historians and commentators continue to refute Gross' conclusions, Poland's intellectuals have acknowledged them and started to debate them in articles, essays, editorials, reviews and television and radio programs. A new monument in honour of the Jedwabne victims has been erected, which was unveiled on July 10, 2001, the 60th anniversary of the massacre. Public apologies have been given by the President, the Prime Minister and by about one hundred bishops, led by the Polish Primate Józef Glemp: "We want, as pastors of the Church in Poland, to stand in truth before God and the people, but mainly before our Jewish brothers and sisters, referring with regret and repentance to the crime that in July 1941 took place in Jedwabne and in other places."[11]

This engagement of the episcopate should be seen as a counter to the fundamentalist Catholic organizations who still negate Polish

---

10. The massive reception of Gross's book is new; his ideas however are not totally. Already in the 1980s, Jewish publications referred to Polish anti-Semitism and even pogroms (e.g. the pogrom in Warsaw in February 1940); see: Nechama Tec, "Polish Anti-Semitism and the Rescuing of Jews," *East European Quarterly* 20 (1986) 303; on the anti-Semitic sermons of "a long list" of Catholic clergymen, see: Shmuel Krakowski, "The Polish Catholic Church and the Holocaust: Some Comments on Prof. Zieliński's Paper," *Judaism and Christianity under the Impact of National Socialism*, ed. Otto Dov Kulka and Paul R. Mendes-Flohr (Jerusalem, 1987) 395. But on the other hand, an article by Andrzej Żbikowski of the Jewish Historical Institute in Warsaw, dating from 1993 and containing a lot of references to other literature, shows how Poles still thought about the pogroms at that time. Żbikowski charges especially the Ukranians with anti-Semitic actions. About the Radziłów pogrom (by Poles, see below), he wrote that there are a lot of doubts about the testimony and that it was initiated by the Germans. About the Jedwabne pogrom, he stated that the information is little exact. See: Andrzej Żbikowski, "Lokalne pogromy Żydów w czerwcu i lipcu 1941 roku na wschodnich rubieżach II Rzeczypospolitej," *Biuletyn Żydowskiego Instytutu Historycznego w Polsce* 43, nos. 2-3/162-163 (1992) 3-18, especially 15-16.

11. Gross, *Neighbors*. The book was published in Polish in 2000 and has been translated in several Western languages. A good example of the discussions that have been provoked by the book, are the texts of the plenary session on the Jedwabne Massacre in *The Polish Review* 46, no. 4 (2001). The quotation by bishop Stanisław Gadecki was found in the daily report on Central and Eastern Europe of Radio Free Europe/Radio Liberty of May 29, 2001 (http://www.rferl.org/newsline/search/).

participation in the Jedwabne crime, rather than as an apology for the involvement of clergymen or Catholic militants in the pogroms. Indeed, Gross does not mention any complicity of the local clergy of Jedwabne, on the contrary he awarded them a conciliatory role. The pogroms and murders of individual Jews that were committed immediately after the arrival of the Germans, were stopped by a local priest on June 26, 1941 – but unfortunately, his influence proved to be only temporary.[12] But, Gross also gives an extensive account by a Jewish survivor of a pogrom that took place in Radziłów on July 7, 1941, killing 800 Jews, only a few days before and only a few kilometres away from the one in Jedwabne. According to this eye-witness, the priest of Radziłów, Aleksander Dogolewski, was asked to prevail upon his worshippers to take no part in the persecution of the Jews, but he answered that all Jews were Communists and that he had no interest in defending them.[13]

It is clear that the history of the Polish Catholic Church in the Second World War has not yet been written completely. Moreover, these few examples show that it is a Pandora's box that will open up to provoke blasphemous accusations or semi-official denunciations. On the one hand, the Radziłów pogrom proves that current historical research is one-sided and withholds or even falsifies some aspects of the war record of the Polish Church. But, on the other hand, one can not ignore the extreme damage the Nazis caused to the Polish Church: thousands of priests were killed during the war because of their faith and their function. So, each imputation of individual collaboration will be answered with examples of collective persecution.

This contribution does not aspire to take up a definitive standpoint in this debate (if this is possible at all). For that, new in-depth study of the original sources would be needed, and this is not the place for detailed arguments. So, only an overview will be given based on secondary literature of the most important facts and the main interpretations. This will be done critically, paying special attention to the blank pages in historiography and by comparing Poland with other European countries. Most attention will be given to the territories that were occupied by Germany from 1939 onwards; space is lacking for the territories that were conquered by the Soviet Union in 1939 and by the Nazis in

---

12. Gross, *Neighbors*, 17. Also in the 1930s, the Roman Catholic clergy could calm down anti-Semitic agitation (see *ibid.*, 40), and survivors of the Jedwabne massacre could find a safe shelter at the bishop's house of Łomża (see *ibid.*, 71).
13. *Ibid.*, 62-63.

June 1941.[14] For the same reason, only the Church as an institution (and the clergy) will be discussed, not Catholicism as a whole (i.e. not Catholic parties or movements).

II. Background: the Polish Church and the German Occupation

Inter war Poland was a very different country to the post war Poland we know now. It had completely different boundaries: its territory stretched about 200 kilometres further to the east, and included cities such as Wilno (Vilnius, the current capital of Lithuania) and Lwów (Lviv, now in Ukraine), but excluded regions such as Pomerania, East-Prussia (respectively west and east of Gdańsk) and most of Silesia. Its population was much more heterogeneous. According to official statistics, of the 32 million inhabitants of Poland in 1931, only 68.9% were Poles, against 13.9% Ukraines, 8.6% Jews, 3.1% Belorussians and 2.3% Germans.[15] This ethnic diversity was also reflected in the religious divisions: 64.8% of the Polish population was Roman Catholic, 11,8% Orthodox, 10.4% Greek Catholic (i.e. Uniat), 9.8% Jewish and 2.6% Evangelical.[16]

Despite this heterogeneity, the Catholic Church was the dominant faith in Polish society. Even before 1918, Catholicism was deeply rooted

14. The research on these regions is more recent and dates largely from the 1990s – the fact that the Soviet Union occupied the territories until 1941 certainly has to do with that. Important titles are for instance: Tadeusz Krahel, "Z dziejów archidiecezji wileńskiej w czasie okupacji hitlerowskiej (1941-1944)," *Wiadomości Kościelne Archidiecezji w Białymstoku* 15, no. 3 (1989) 112-139; Jerzy Sidorowicz, "Życie kościelne w Białymstoku w latach 1939-1944," *Białostocczyzna* 9, no. 3 (1994) 55-63; Wojciech Wysocki, "Straty Kościoła katolickiego w południowo-zachodniej części archidiecezji wileńskiej, 1939-1944," *Nasza Przeszłość* 81 (1994) 315-348; Zygmunt Zieliński, "Kościoły chrześcijańskie w Polsce w polityce okupantów," *Acta Universitatis Wratislaviensis 1943: Studia nad faszyzmem i zbrodniami hitlerowskimi* 20 (1997) 223-238 and Zygmunt Zieliński, *Życie religijne w Polsce pod okupacją 1939-1945: Metropolie wileńska i lwowska* (Katowice, 1992).
15. Henryk Zieliński, *Historia Polski 1914-1939* (Wrocław a.o., 1985) 125.
16. *Ibid.*, 126. Consequently, one must be aware of the fact that this contribution is limited to only one religion, and does not analyze all the churches in Poland during World War II. The fate of the Jews is commonly known. About the Uniat and the Orthodox Churches, who collaborated with the Germans, see a.o.: Kłoczowski and Müllerowa, "La guerre," 463 ff. and 481 ff.; Jan Sziling, *Kościoły chrześcijańskie w polityce niemieckich władz okupacyjnych w Generalnym Gubernatorstwie (1939-1945)* (Toruń, 1988); and the articles by R. Torzecki, W. Gastpary, M. Getter and others in *Miscellanea historiae ecclesiasticae IX*. About the Jews in Poland, whole libraries have been written. A short introduction to their extermination is: Beata Kosmala, "Ungleiche Opfer in extremer Situation: Die Schwierigkeiten der Solidarität im okkupierten Polen," *Solidarität und Hilfe für Juden während der NS-Zeit: Regionalstudien 1*, ed. Wolfgang Benz and Juliane Wetzel (Berlin, 1996) 21-32.

in the traditions of the Polish population and it became an essential element of the Polish 'national réveil'. Already in the Ancien Régime, victories were attributed to divine interference, such as by the Black Madonna of Częstochowa during the attack by the Swedes in the 1650s (the 'Potop' or Deluge). In the age of Romanticism, the national bard of Poland, Adam Mickiewicz, seized on this optimistic faith and combined it with his Messianistic ideas that Poland was the Christ among the nations, who had to suffer for all nations but would finally be resurrected. In daily life in 19th century Poland, religion and nationalism were also interwoven. Both the Russian as well as the German occupier had to fight not only the Polish nation, but also the Catholic Church (e.g. in the *Kulturkampf*) and, as it is often the case, they achieved the opposite result.

After Polish independence, the Catholic Church actively tried to infiltrate various fields of daily life. This was not only inspired by the spirit of the time (e.g. Catholic Action), but also motivated by the need to respond to the anticlerical attitude of Socialists, Liberals and even the Agrarian party. So, the Catholic Church became involved in education and youth movements, in charity and workers' social movements, in the cultural sectors and the press. However, in the field of politics the clergy was less active. Firstly, there was not a Catholic party in Poland. Christian Democracy only developed in the former German territories and the peasants were connected to the Radical-Popular movement. Secondly, a far-reaching separation of Church and State was prescribed in the Concordat of 1925. Thirdly, the new Polish Primate August Hlond, who was Archbishop of Gniezno and Poznań between 1926 and 1948, defended the new political stance of the Vatican, forbidding the direct interference of the Church in the political affairs. Consequently, the relationship between the Catholic Church and the Polish Sanacja-regime, as the dictatorship of Marshal Józef Piłsudski was called, was quite friendly. The State wanted to collaborate without involving the Church in governmental affairs, and the Church looked for a certain harmony with and even protection from the State, by putting stress on activities and religious forms that could amplify its link with the Polish nation (such as pilgrimages to Częstochowa). However, this does not mean that everything passed off smoothly. On the contrary, certainly after the death of Piłsudski in 1935 and the following radicalization of the Sanacja-regime, more and more tensions rose. Some clergymen were accused of cooperating with the opposition, both with the right-wing National Democracy as well as with the more left-wing Christian

8 IDESBALD GODDEERIS

Democracy.[17] With the German invasion in September 1939 however, State and Church were again put together on one line.

During the first weeks after the German conquest of Poland, a new administrative division was introduced. The north and the west of Poland were joined to the 'Third Reich'. Some of these regions were added to existing provinces, such as Upper-Silesia and Eastern Prussia; some other ones were the base of two new administrative units, namely the *Reichsgau* Danzig-Westpreussen in the north and the *Reichsgau*

Diocesan and administrative structures of Poland in the Second World War

17. A general introduction to the Church history in the interwar period in Poland: Ryszard Bender, "La première guerre mondiale et la Pologne indépendante (1914-1939)," *Histoire religieuse de la Pologne*, ed. Jerzy Kłoczowski (Paris, 1987) 429-461. Details about the Concordat in Zieliński, *Historia*, 158-160.

Wartheland in the west (including cities as Poznań and Łódź). The rest of Poland under German occupation was restructured in a *Generalgouvernement*, led by Hans Frank from the former Kings' Palace on the Wawel hill in Cracow. Initially, the *Generalgouvernement* consisted of four districts (Cracow, Lublin, Radom and Warsaw); after the German attack on the Soviet Union and the conquest of the rest of Poland, the fifth district of Galicia was founded. The rest of the captured areas were restructured in the *Reichskommissariat* Ost and the *Reichskommissariat* Ukraine (the region of Białystok was incorporated in the *Dritte Reich*). These new administrative zones formed separate territories, between which contact was difficult. For the Church, this was problematic, as the new administrative frontiers did not accord with the diocesan ones. Many dioceses were divided up and many parishes were torn away from their bishops.

The new administrative division had still greater consequences: it also determined the policy of the Nazis, which differed in each territory. In theory, the Nazis had only one ambition concerning Poland: to remove the Polish people and replace them with Germans. In practice however, their attempts to realize this aim proceeded by means of different methods and with varying success. This was the same for the Church as well. In theory, Catholicism and National Socialism were uncompromising, not only for philosophical and ideological reasons, but, in Poland, also for national ones. The Church was considered as a very important carrier of the Polish national identity, a guardian of Polish independence and a centre of anti-Nazi resistance. Governor-general Hans Frank understood in March 1943 that "Die Kirche ist der im Stillen fortleuchtende Zentralsammelpunkt des polnischen Gemütes und hat so etwa die Funktion eines ewigen Lichtes. Wenn alle Lichter für Polen erlöschen, dann war immer doch die Heilige von Tschenstochau und die Kirche da. Die polnische Kirche hat es daher auch nich nötig, aktiv zu sein; denn der Katholizismus ist in diesem Lande keine Konfession, sondern eine Lebensbedingung."[18] In practice however, the Nazis at several occasions looked for a *modus vivendi* with the Church, certainly for the time of the war. The concrete interpretations of their policy were different in each of the new administrative units. Consequently, in any discussion of the situation of the Church in Poland under German occupation, one needs to make clear distinctions between the territories.

---

18. Quoted in Jan Sziling, "Die Kirchen im Generalgouvernement," *Miscellanea historiae ecclesiasticae IX*, 279.

III. The Incorporated Provinces:
Wartheland, Danzig-Westpreussen, Kattowitz

It is generally understood that the Polish Church was most damaged by the war in the provinces that were incorporated in the *Dritte Reich*, where the Nazis were already aiming for total Germanization during the war. This was certainly the case in the province of Wartheland. The Germans tried to reshape it into a homogeneous German region not only by Germanizing, but also by eliminating its Polish population (by far the largest ethnic group)[19] after having used them as cheap labour. To do this, an impermeable division between Poles and Germans was set up: Germans were not allowed to have any contact with Poles except professionally. Consequently, the religious life of the two Catholic ethnic groups developed separately. The only light in the darkness for the Poles was the fact that the Polishness of their Church was not contested. In contrast to their compatriots in the other incorporated provinces, the Polish Catholics in Wartheland could still use their own Polish language and prayer-books.[20]

However, this was little consolation, as even if Polishness was tolerated the very existence of the Polish Catholic Church was under attack. Soon after German installation, almost all the bishops of Polish ethnicity residing in Wartheland left or were removed. Two bishops fled the country when the Germans arrived, including the Polish Primate, Cardinal August Hlond, who left his seat in Poznań on September 4. The suffragan Bishop of Włocławek was arrested in November 1939 and deported to Dachau, where he died in 1943. Three other

---

19. I did not find numbers of the ethnic composition of Wartheland in 1939, but in August 1942, so already after the deportation of many Poles, the region was inhabited by 4,517,000 men, among them 788,000 Germans (17%) and 3,516,000 Poles (78%). Although not mentioned, one may accept that the Jewish population is included in the Polish one. Fijałkowski, *Kościół*, 262.

20. The most important studies on the Catholic Church in Wartheland (and the other incorporated territories) are Jan Sziling, *Polityka okupanta hitlerowskiego wobec kościoła katolickiego 1939-1945: Tzw. okręgi Rzeszy Gdańsk-Prusy Zachodnie, Kraj Warty i Regencja Katowicka* (Poznań, 1970) and Śmigiel, *Kościół*. Although both monographs were written in the 1970s, their authors are nowadays still considered as the specialists on that subject, as can be derived from their participation in the recent study. Antoni Galiński and Piotr Budziarek (eds.), *Akcje okupanta hitlerowskiego wobec Kościoła katolickiego w kraju Warty* (Łódź, 1997). Both Sziling as Śmigiel wrote some contributions in Western languages too (e.g. in *Miscellanea historiae ecclesiasticae IX*; the book of Śmigiel was published in German too [Düsseldorf, 1984]). Another detailed overview about the Polish Catholics in Wartheland, can be found in Fijałkowski, *Kościół*, 217-271.

Bishops were imprisoned, two of them outside Wartheland. Consequently, the Polish Catholic Church in Wartheland was virtually decapitated.[21] The following months, the curias were dismantled too (definitely in May 1941).

The lower clergy also fell victim to the Nazis. Between September 1939 and November 1941, several waves of arrests took place in which many clergymen (and other members of the intelligentsia) were deprived of their freedom. These acts were well prepared: all politically active clergymen were arrested in 1939; others were dealt with later. Initially, they were all confined in confiscated monasteries, but from 1940 they were either sent to concentration camps (the young clergymen), or banished to the *Generalgouvernement* (the old and sick). The Nazi repression of the Polish clergy in Wartheland was devastating. Of the approximately 2100 secular clergymen in Poland in 1939, 133 were executed immediately and 1523 were arrested. Of the last group, 1092 were sent to concentration camps (where 682 lost their lives) and about 400 were exiled. The regular clergy was also subject to the repression of the Nazis, but quantitative surveys on this aspect are lacking. All together, 72% of the clergy in Wartheland were imprisoned in prisons or camps, of which 52% were sent to concentration camps, and 38% perished.[22] From October 1941 on, only 73 Polish priests (i.e. 3% of the pre-war numbers) were allowed to minister to parishes, with a maximum of two priests per district.[23]

This decimation of the clergy went hand in hand with drastic institutional measures (most important: the Thirteen points, issued in July 1941). All the Churches in Wartheland, including the Evangelic ones, were reduced to religious associations (*Religionsgesellschaften*), with the status of an artificial body in private (instead of public) law. Only adults who had made a written declaration could become members of these associations, and only priests who were born in the Warthegau could be active in it. These religious associations were deprived of fundamental rights: they could for instance not possess buildings or land, and were forbidden to be involved in teaching or charity activities. By September 1941, four religious associations were officially recognized: three Evangelic ones and the 'Römisch-katholische Kirche Deutscher Nationalität

---

21. The details (and names) of the bishops in Fijałkowski, *Kościół*, 219-221. See also Śmigiel, *Kościół*, 74 ff. and 85 ff. and Sziling, *Polityka*, 68-69.
22. Śmigiel, *Kościół*, 105-117.
23. Sziling, *Polityka*, 261 and Śmigiel, *Kościół*, 201.

im Reichsgau Wartheland'.[24] The Polish Church was thus even not officially acknowledged as a legal association.

The Thirteen points also stipulated that religious associations could only accumulate funds through contributions from their members, and that clergymen should also have a secular job. Indeed, the material situation of the Catholic Church was curtailed in every way. Several measures in 1940 and again in 1941, allowed the new state authorities to confiscate all the Catholic Church's property. Some churches were merely closed down but others were converted into painters' studios, hospitals for German soldiers, arms depots or granaries. The Cathedral of Gniezno, the heart of the Polish Church, was used as a concert hall. At least one hundred churches and chapels in Wartheland were destroyed;[25] only a small number were reserved for the Polish Catholics: in rule only one per district, and two or three in big cities.[26] The priests who were joined to these churches were obliged to submit detailed reports of their receipts and expenditure and were hindered in acquiring funds – collecting money during celebrations was for instance gradually forbidden. The Germans also had a huge interest in gold and silver crucifixes, art, religious objects (all were taken), candles and linen (of which respectively 20 and 6 tons were collected between October 1941 and February 1942), and bell metal, which was melted down and used in the arms industry. According to K. Śmigiel, 97% of all sacral objects were confiscated.[27] From 1941 on, the Polish Catholic Church was even deprived of its cemeteries. Old graves were violated and the Polish dead were to be buried at other locations without any religious signs and well away from German graves.

This last example is only one illustration of the way the Germans tried to regulate the religious life of the Poles in Wartheland. Numerous other restrictions were applied. The length of the Mass celebration was limited because the Germans feared that they could turn into political

---

24. Besides, this German Catholic Church in Wartheland was also the victim of repressive measures by the Nazis, far more than other provinces. The main reason for this exception was the fact that the German Catholics in Wartheland were mainly *Volksdeutsche* who settled down in Wartheland very recently (e.g. deported from Galicia in the south-east of Poland), and that the Nazis thought they could Germanize them more quickly if they would loose their contacts with the Church. See e.g. Fijałkowski, *Kościół*, 264-269.

25. Śmigiel, *Kościół*, 153. Sziling, *Polityka*, 221 even counts 200 destroyed churches and is followed here by Fijałkowski, *Kościół*, 251.

26. Details in Sziling, *Polityka*, 182.

27. Śmigiel, "Die christlichen Kirchen," 313.

meetings and because they wanted to prevent large gatherings of people (e.g. at funerals). Therefore, churches were opened only during specific hours, mostly two or three hours on Sundays and one hour, or not at all, on weekdays. Only five Christian festivals on weekdays were recognized; the others were to be observed on the following Sunday. Baptismal celebrations, marriages and funerals could only be attended by the close family. Corteges were initially admitted, but without crosses or other religious signs; by the end of the war, these were forbidden too, just like all other processions and pilgrimages. Churchgoers were also often intimidated by the Germans, and more than once, the German police raided a church during a celebration, rounding young men up for forced labour in Germany. All these measures had just one goal: to diminish the religiosity and the patriotism of the Polish population in Wartheland.

In the other incorporated provinces, Danzig-Westpreussen (or Pomerania) to the north of Wartheland and Kattowitz to the south, the Nazis attacked Polish patriotism as well, but they made use of a different strategy. They wanted to Germanize the population, not the area: Poles were to be Germanized, not eliminated. This approach is related to several factors: the different opinions of the *Gauleiters* Arthur Greiser (Wartheland) and Albert Forster (Danzig-Westpreussen); the different ethnic structures of the regions; the economic crisis in Wartheland and the possibilities for new German 'Junkers' to colonize this rather agrarian region; the historical experiences in Wartheland (the heir of the 19th-century Grand Duchy of Poznań, which Bismarck had not been able to Germanize) and Germany's conviction that Upper-Silesia and West-Prussia were formerly German areas that had been Polonized after 1918. This different strategy had consequences for the Church too. Contrary to Wartheland, where Polish Catholicism was to be destroyed together with the Polish population, the Catholic Church in the other incorporated provinces was to be part of the Germanization of the region. Consequently, the Catholic Church's situation in the other incorporated provinces differed fundamentally from its position in Wartheland.

In the incorporated provinces the Polish and German Catholic Churches were not separated, as this would isolate the Polish population and impede its Germanization. Instead, the Nazis tried to transform the Polish Church into a German institution and to suppress everything that evoked Polish Catholicism. The use of the Polish language was generally forbidden for ceremonies, praying, singing and even confessing.

All objects, inscriptions and images that could remind people of Poland were removed. Moreover, there were far less restrictions on religious practices than in Wartheland, as the Church and the religiosity were considered as instruments in Germanizing the Polish population. It seems, the measures in Wartheland concerning for instance the duration of celebrations or the festivals were not applied in West-Prussia or Upper-Silesia. Only processions were sometimes prohibited, and age limitations were put on marriages between Poles. It is true that most Church buildings, grounds and valuables were confiscated, especially in West-Prussia, but churches were soon rendered accessible again for celebrations albeit Germanized. Even the status of the (Germanized) Church as an artificial body in public law was conserved, and German priests received a pension from the authorities.

The situation described above applies to both Upper-Silesia and West-Prussia. However, these two regions were treated differently in relation to certain specific interests. Upper-Silesia was an economically important region so it was in the German's interest to maintain harmony. In contrast, the incorporated provinces in the north had to be Germanized more quickly for several reasons. West-Prussia was an important corridor between East-Prussia (around Königsberg) and the '*Heimat*', and the West-Prussian city of Danzig symbolized the German roots of the whole Baltic southern coast. Danzig and other West-Prussian cities indeed were largely German before 1945, but the countryside was populated by a Polish majority.

As a consequence, the Germanization of Danzig and West-Prussia was more extreme than that of Upper-Silesia. This is especially visible in German attitudes towards the local Polish clergy. Because Polish priests were seen as barriers to Germanization, they were simply eliminated – often even physically – and replaced by German clergymen. In Danzig, for instance, only two of the twelve Polish priests escaped arrest on September 1, 1939, but only because they were not in the city on that day. Two of the ten detainees were released after a short stay in prison, seven were killed and the last one survived for six years in concentration camps.[28] In West-Prussia, the Polish clergy were often arrested and they often died. In the diocese of Chełmno (with its seat in Pelplin), more than two thirds of all the priests (i.e. 450 or, according to some historians 550) were

---

28. Fijałkowski, *Kościół*, 301. There were 98 Roman Catholic priests in Danzig in August 1939. So, the number of Polish priests also gives an idea of the ethnic proportions in the city.

arrested in the first weeks of the occupation.[29] After the war, it appeared that about half of the priests of the diocese had been killed by the Nazis.[30] This number is one of the highest death tolls of all the Polish dioceses, even exceeding the most dioceses in Wartheland. According to Kłoczowski, 46.5% of the Polish clergy in the diocese of Chełmno died, versus 50.2% in Włocławek, 38.0% in Łódź, 36.5% in Gniezno, 35.4% in Poznań and 30.4% in Płock – one case excepted, all other Polish dioceses lost less than 20%, and often even less than 15% of their priests.[31] The eliminated Polish priests were partially replaced by a few dozen German clergymen, some of whom were moved from the *Altreich*.[32] Moreover, sixteen *Bischöfliche Komissare* (a newly created function that had no basis in canon law) were installed in the *Reichsgau* Danzig-Westpreussen. They represented the apostolic administrator in the field, controlled the local clergy and often collaborated with the NSDAP and the Gestapo.[33] These German initiatives, however, proved useless. In contrast to other Polish regions, religiosity in West-Prussia fell significantly and the Nazis were unable to use the Church as an instrument in their policy of Germanization.[34]

For the Silesian Poles, the situation turned out differently than for their compatriots in the other incorporated provinces. Silesia was divided at the beginning of the 1920s following insurrections and

29. Compare Sziling, *Polityka*, 243 (550 arrested priests) with Fijałkowski, *Kościół*, 301.

30. Numbers differ, but are all in the same order: 311 of the 668 priests (i.e. 46.56%) according to Kłoczowski and Müllerowa, "La guerre," 478; 323 of the 701 (i.e. 46.07%) according to Fijałkowski, *Kościół*, 302; 311 of the 600 (i.e. 51.83%) according to Lidia Müller, "L'église de Pologne en 1939-1945: Géographie et statistiques," *Miscellanea historiae ecclesiasticae. IX*, 275.

31. Kłoczowski and Müllerowa, "La guerre," 478. The death rate in the diocese of Płock, the greatest part of the Polish territory that was incorporated in East-Prussia, is an illustration of the fact that the policy in East-Prussia was very similar to the one in Danzig and West-Prussia.

32. About their number, see: Zofia Waszkiewicz, "Kościół katolicki na Pomorzu w latach II wojny światowej," *Universitas Gedanensis* 3 (1989) 81.

33. Sziling, *Polityka*, 75 and Fijałkowski, *Kościół*, 195.

34. For some specific case-studies of the Catholic Church in Danzig-Westpreussen (parishes or districts), see: Koszewski, *Kościół katolicki na Ziemi Kościańskiej*; Zygmunt Milczewski, "Kościół powiatu morskiego w latach okupacji hitlerowskiej," *Studia Pelplińskie* 20 (1989) 97-99; Jan Walkusz, "Kościół katolicki w Kartuskiem (1939-1945)," *Nasza Przeszłość* 70 (1988) 149-224 and Jan Walkusz, *W cieniu połamanego krzyża: Studia i szkice z dziejów Kościoła katolickiego na Pomorzu Nadwiślańskim w latach 1939-1945* (Tczew-Pelplin, 1999). On the Catholics in Western Pomerania, the region between West-Prussia and the Oder that became Polish only in 1945, see: Bogdan Frankiwicz, "Duchowieństwo katolickie Pomorza i pogranicza pod uciskiem hitlerowskim," *Przegląd zachodniopomorski* 11, no. 4 (1996) 107-127.

plebiscites. The greater part of the territory remained German, but the east of Upper-Silesia, including Katowice, was assigned to the new Polish state. In 1939, this region (somewhat extended to the east) was returned to the German Empire as the *Regierungsbezirk* Kattowitz. It included the whole diocese of Katowice and parts of the dioceses of Częstochowa, Cracow and Kielce. The situation in these two dioceses differed somewhat. Here, I will only concentrate on the most interesting one, i.e. the diocese of Katowice.[35] Like West-Prussia, it was populated by Germans and Poles, though it is almost impossible to give an exact idea of the ethnic proportions.[36]

The Katowice area was industrialized, which was the main reason for a far more moderate policy towards the Polish inhabitants and their Catholic Church. The first concern was to keep the steel and mining industries going, and therefore, the many skilled workers – mostly Poles – were not to be deported or given any reason to put up resistance. In order to conserve their loyalty, Germanization was toned down. Measures such as banning the Polish language or reducing the number of Polish clergymen were carried out but not as harshly as in West-Prussia. The Katowice Bishop Stanisław Adamski was banished to the *Generalgouvernement* but not until February 1941 and he had not been deprived of the right to exercise his function until that time. The brutal elimination of the clergy seen in Wartheland and Danzig-Westpreussen did not occur in Upper-Silesia. In all, 'only' about one hundred (of the nearly five hundred) Polish priests from the Katowice diocese – most of whom were known as patriots of the Silesian insurrections – were sent to concentration camps. As 'only' 61 of them perished, the death toll was much lower than in the other incorporated provinces.[37] Most other Polish priests could stay in their parishes although they did have to join the *Deutsche Volksliste* and they sometimes were forced into physical labour. As a rule, each parish was manned by at least one German priest, but in practice, local initiatives introduced a temporary segregation between

---

35. The German policy in the other dioceses was more moderate and resembled the policy in the *Generalgouvernement*. The clergy was hardly hindered, but new Polish priests could not settle down.

36. According to a Polish source of 1931, the province was inhabited by 90,600 Germans and 1,195,600 Poles. In a German census at the end of 1939 however, only 50,005 people declared to be Pole, versus 998,568 German (concerning the mother tongue, 818,076 declared to speak German, 125,133 Polish and 105,655 Silesian or *Wasserpolnisch*, as this Slavic dialect, close to Polish, is called in German). See: Sziling, *Polityka*, 20 ff.

37. Sziling, *Polityka*, 261; Kłoczowski and Müllerowa, "La guerre," 478.

the Polish and German Churches (that was never officialized by the higher authorities). So, the position of the Church in Silesia more resembled that of the *Generalgouvernement*.

IV. The *Generalgouvernement*

German Church policy in the *Generalgouvernement* was far more moderate than in the incorporated provinces Wartheland and Danzig-Westpreussen. The Germans had other intentions for this region, and the important cities of Warsaw, Cracow, Lublin and – important from ecclesiastical perspective – Częstochowa. In the long term, the *Generalgouvernement* was to be transformed into a new area for German colonization (*Lebensraum*). Preparations were taken already during the war. Under German direction, the area was made a *Generalgouvernement* and not a satellite state such as, for instance, Slovakia, which illustrates that from the beginning, the Germans did not see any advantages in cooperating with the Poles. Moreover, ethnic differences were encouraged and emphasised in order to break up Polish predominance (in 1940, the *Generalgouvernement* was populated by almost 12 million people, of whom about 80% were Poles, 13% Jews, only 1% Germans and 6% Ukrainians; the Ukrainian part in the population grew with the annexation of Galicia in 1941).[38] For example, mountain 'tribes' such as the Łemkos were profiled by the Nazis as a distinct people,[39] the Ukrainians were supported in their struggle for independence or autonomy (consequently, the Uniat or Greek Catholic Church was much less persecuted), and German colonies were founded around Lublin and the Bug and San rivers. The (largely realized) *Endlösung* of the Jewish minority is commonly known.

In the short term, however, for the duration of the war, the objectives were less ambitious. On the one hand, the Nazis used the *Generalgouvernement* as a pool of cheap labour for the German economy and the war machine. On the other hand, they were mainly interested in the

---

38. Sziling, *Kościoły*, 12. Fijałkowski, *Kościół*, 61-62 gives other, but similar data. Both monographs are considered the most important studies on the Church in the *Generalgouvernement*. More recent research has been done only on the local field and does not undermine the most important visions and conclusions of Sziling and Fijałkowski. A good example is: Edward Jarmoch, "Duchowni podlascy w czasie II wojny światowej," *Podlasie w czasie II wojny światowej*, ed. Władysław Ważniewski (Siedlce, 1997) 109-124.

39. Just like other uplanders, the Łemko's speak a Polish dialect very similar to Ukrainian. The distinct people were called *Gorallenvolk*, from the Polish word for mountaineer, *górale*.

passiveness, or at least political quiet, of the region. These short-term objectives determined Church policy too. For one thing, they inspired the Germans to a certain level of repression, with the intention to unlink the Church from the Polish state, nation and certainly the Polish resistance. On the other hand, however, they behaved also with certain moderation towards the Church, because it had the task of pacifying Polish society. Moreover, the Germans tried to involve the Church in their policy and to convince clergymen to cooperate, for example in the recruitment of Polish candidates for labour in Germany. Priests had to remind the worshippers during the Sunday Mass of their 'obligations' towards the occupier, and were forced to take seat, together with other influential persons as doctors and teachers, in committees founded by the Germans to urge the population to leave voluntarily to Germany. After the initial assault on the Soviet Union in June 1941, and certainly after being repelled by the Soviets in 1942, the Germans tried to use the Church in the propaganda campaign against the Communists.

The difference between the policy in the *Generalgouvernement* and the incorporated provinces is seen in the German attitudes towards the clergy. In the *Generalgouvernement*, only two bishops were arrested (an ordinary bishop who survived the war in detainment and the suffragan Bishop of Lublin who died in a concentration camp). Although from European perspective, this might seem repressive – bishops in most other countries were not arrested or detained by the Nazis –, this was exceptionally moderate for Poland. The lower clergy too, on the whole, were left in peace (although their situation was also determined by local authorities and could differ from one region to another). Only in the beginning were priests subject to collective arrests in big cities as Cracow, Warsaw and Lublin, but these arrests were above all intimidation measures and most of the clergymen were released after a short time. Once the German occupier had settled, arrests decreased and were limited to priests who engaged in resistance or in illegal patriotic activities through charity or education. During the Warsaw Rising of August-September 1944, repression intensified again, as clergy often gave shelter to insurgents. But, all in all, the death toll of the clergy in the *Generalgouvernement* was relatively low. In the diocese of Warsaw, 11.5% of the priests died, in Lublin 10.9%, but in the dioceses of Cracow, Tarnów, Sandomierz and Siedlce, the death rates of the diocesan clergy were respectively 'only' 4.2%, 4.3%, 5.6% and 6.8%.[40] In fact, the number of

---

40. Kłoczowski and Müllerowa, "La guerre," 478.

priests in the *Generalgouvernement* even rose because of the influx of exiled clergymen from the incorporated provinces. On the other hand however, in the long term their existence was threatened because of measures obstructing the training of priests. Not only were all minor seminars and all theological faculties closed (such as all universities *tout court*), but also no new candidates were allowed to enter the major seminaries. Nevertheless, these measures could be circumvented by private lessons – for example, one of the war pupils of the Cracovian Archbishop Adam Sapieha was Karol Wojtyła.

In the *Generalgouvernement*, churches, like the priests, were less affected than in the incorporated provinces. A large number of churches and other buildings were confiscated, but only at the beginning of the war and most were returned after a few weeks. Of course, some Polish sanctuaries in the *Generalgouvernement* were plundered or destroyed. For example, the famous altar of Veit Stoss (or Wit Stwosz) in the Maria church in Cracow was removed, but it was recovered in Nürnberg after the war. Six hundred church bells were taken, and 13 churches were demolished in the diocese of Warsaw before the summer of 1944. Only one of these was in the city of Warsaw but, of course, this number increased during the Rising of Warsaw.[41] Nevertheless, the greater tolerance towards the church is illustrated by the fact that there were no restrictions on the religious activities in the basilica of Częstochowa (even though they were under surveillance). The other national sanctuary of Poland, the Wawel Cathedral, was closed as the whole Wawel hill was the central seat of governor-general Hans Frank.

In the light of the high number of priests and churches, it is not surprising that the religious life of Polish Catholics could continue during the war. Indeed, the only limitations the Germans imposed concerned patriotic aspects of religiosity. Some nationalist songs were forbidden and commemorative plaques and historical paintings reminding of the Polish nation were removed. Processions and pilgrimages were mostly prohibited, some expressions were deleted from prayers, religious education in schools was restrained to one hour a week, Jews were not allowed to be baptized as Christians, and most Catholic publishing houses were closed down. It is clear that the Nazis wanted to disconnect the Catholic Church from Polish nationalism and the resistance. Sometimes, they even checked sermons for possible nationalist content, and there are cases of arrests and death in concentration camps in relation to such an

---

41. Fijałkowski, *Kościół*, 99, 94.

offence. However, for the duration of the war, the Nazis did not aspire to attack the Church as such. On the contrary, they wanted to involve clergymen in their policy and to encourage them to collaborate. However, they did not succeed in this project. All Polish historians stress the rise of religiosity and community spirit, and the central role of the Church as an essential carrier of the nation. Collaboration by clergymen or even the searching of a certain *modus vivendi* with the occupier are called exceptions, if they are recognized and discussed at all. However, this does not mean that there are no nuances at either a historical or historiographical level. This is what will be discussed now with respect to both the episcopacy and the lower clergy.

V. The Attitude of the Polish Episcopacy

In Polish historiography, more polemics have focussed on the attitude of the Polish episcopacy than on the Church policy of the Nazis. There were indeed some controversial Bishops, such as Carl Maria Splett in Gdańsk, Stanisław Adamski in Katowice and the Polish Primate, August Hlond, who left Poland in September 1939. But on the other hand, these debates should not be overestimated. There is almost no discussion about the wartime role of Archbishop Adam Sapieha, the Cracovian spiritual leader of the Polish Church. In addition, there has been no further research on the accommodation policy of some other Polish bishops mentioned in studies from the 1980s.

The Polish episcopacy was judicially decapitated by the departure of August Hlond in September 1939. Hlond left his seat in Poznań on September 4 and fled via Warsaw and Romania to Rome, where he arrived on September 19, 1939. After the Italians joined the war in June 1940, he escaped to Lourdes, but two years later, he was forced to move to a Benedictine monastery in Savoie, where he was arrested in February 1944 (he was released by the Americans in Wiedenbrück (Westfalen) in April 1945). Hlond's flight was greatly criticized by Polish historians, not just because he appeared to have neglected his moral authority and pastoral tasks, but also because he refused to compromise with the Communists after the war (contrary to his successor, Stefan Wyszyński, the Polish Primate between 1948 and 1981). However, there has been a gradual shift in opinion and over the last decades, more attention has been paid to understanding the reasons he ran away. His decision to flee was taken gradually and in consultation with the Polish government (according to some publicists even under "resolute pressure"). Moreover, Hlond already tried to return to Poland at the end of September 1939 (which was forbidden by the Germans), and in exile, he continued to devote himself to his fatherland, for instance by giving moral support through radio broadcast or by informing the outside world about the situation in Poland. Moreover, in judging the Polish Primate's escape, one should not forget that his Archbishopric of Gniezno and Poznań was incorporated into Germany and was subject to a high degree of repression. The question remains open about the role Hlond could have played if he had stayed in Poland.[42]

The departure of Hlond created a vacuum at the top of the Polish episcopacy, that was filled in – though never officially – by the nestor of the Polish bishops, the Cracovian Archbishop Sapieha (who was already 72 years old in 1939).[43] Sapieha is represented in the literature not only as the moral leader of the Catholic Church, but also as a pivotal force in Polish social life during the war and as a leading figure of the suffering, resisting Polish nation. It is true that he asked his priests to minister to their parishes as normally as possible, but at the same time, he continued to labour for the fate of his compatriots. Most historians stress that Sapieha had contacts with the Holy See, with the Polish government in exile, with some leaders of the Polish political and military underground and even with the German Catholic resistance movement *Kreisauer Kreis*, although the intensity of these relations is not always clear. Equally, Sapieha was involved – both actively as morally – in several charitable and social organizations. Moreover, he wrote some letters to Hans Frank, in which he initially raised only religious affairs, but later on also touched on other things, such as the collective responsibility of the Poles, street raids, forced labour, concentration camps, the extermination of the Jews, the closing of higher education facilities, and the restrictions on Polish charity. Sapieha also participated in some conferences that were organized by the Germans and where possible he would introduce these issues into the debate. However, he did not meet with Hans Frank in person until April 1944. Sapieha had declined an earlier

42. On Hlond see for instance: Tadeusz Wyrwa, "Prymas Hlond we Francji 1940-1941," *Zeszyty Historyczne* 87 (1989) 17-30; Kazimierz Orzechowski, "Naród, Polska i Kościół w nauczaniu Augusta Hlonda w latach II wojny światowej," *Chrześcijanin a Współczesność* 7, no. 3 (1989) 23-30 (quotation on p. 24: "zdecydowany nacisk") and Śmigiel, *Kościół*, 75-79.

43. His most important 'competitor' was the Vicar Capitular of Warsaw, Archbishop Stanisław Gall, who received more support from the Vatican, but had less authority among his compatriots and colleagues. Sapieha was able to organize some Episcopal conferences in Kraków, the first one in November 1940.

invitation in April 20, 1940, because he did not want to be photographed with the governor-general on the Führer's birthday.

With all these lobbying activities, Sapieha achieved little to no results. The Germans demanded his official condemnation of the Polish resistance, which he refused. Also, Sapieha was not ready to cooperate with the Germans concerning anti-Communist propaganda. To such an appeal, he answered, "the clergy has been propagating this since a long time. To do that today ex professo would not have the desired effect; on the contrary, viewing the present existence of the people, it would only call up irritation. A far more efficient opposition is the deepening of the Catholic principles, related with charity. However, charity has been limited the last time precisely by the authorities."[44] For this attitude, and in spite of the lack of results of his policy, Sapieha was generally praised by contemporaries and historians. His most detailed biographer, Jerzy Wolny, wrote in a somewhat hagiographic, but also characteristic style that, "Sapieha's brave pronouncement irritated the Germans and informed them that there was somebody in this subjugated country, who got up the courage to put their heavy crimes simply under their eyes."[45] Sapieha is also given credit for negotiating with the Red Army and in that way preventing Cracow from being destroyed. In other words, Sapieha has never been the target of criticism. Only recently was his name mentioned in the debate on the silence of Pius XII about the Holocaust. According to some scholars, the pope cannot be accused of doing nothing, as some sources reveal that he did write an anti-Hitler encyclical, but this was burnt by Sapieha for fear of reprisals against the Polish Church.[46]

These criticisms are, however, in no way comparable to the negative views of Carl Maria Splett, the Bishop of Gdańsk found in Polish

---

44. Quoted from a letter from March 17, 1943, in: Sziling, *Kościoły*, 36: "Duchowieństwo od dawna głosiło takie nauki. Dziś zaś głoszenie ich ex professo nie wywarłoby spodziewanego skutku, a wobec dzisiejszego bytowania ludności mogłoby tylko wywołać rozdrażnienie. Daleko skuteczniejszym przeciwdziałaniem jest pogłębienie zasad katolickich, połączone z akcją miłosierdzia. Ta ostatnia zaś w ostatnich czasach spotkała się ze znacznym ograniczeniem ze strony właśnie wład."

45. Jerzy Wolny, "Abp Adam Sapieha w obronie Narodu i Kościoła polskiego podczas II wojny światowej," *Księga Sapieżyńska*, ed. Jerzy Wolny and Roman Zawadzki (Kraków, 1986) 203-472 (quotation on p. 281: "odważne wystąpienie Sapiehy zdenerwowało Niemców, uświadomiło im, że w tym podbitym kraju jest ktoś, kto zdobył się na odwagę wytknąć im prosto w oczy ich ciężkie zbrodnie"). A recent biographical study on Sapieha's war years is: Stanisław Dobrzanowski, "Archidiecezja krakowska podczas okupacji niemieckiej 1939-1945," *Książę niezłomny: Kardynał Adam Stefan Sapieha*, ed. Roman Bogacz (Kraków, 2001) 124-155.

46. Margherita Marchione, "Pope Pius XII's Presumed 'Silence'," *Homiletic & Pastoral Review* (March 2001) 48-51.

historiography. Splett has been reproached for continually breaking canon law and the concordat. For instance, he accepted the position of apostolic administrator of the diocese of Chełmno while the legal Bishop, who was in exile in Rome and later in Madrid, had not yet renounced his function. Equally, he usurped some rights, such as the changing of the official language or the creation of *Bischöfliche Komissare*. Splett has also been held responsible for the rigorous measures in the *Reichsgau*. He put his signature on numerous decrees and celebrated a mass of thanks after the German conquest of Gdańsk. After the war, Splett was condemned to eight years' imprisonment, and in 1956, he moved to the German Federation. Shortly after his death in 1964, he was rehabilitated by some German historians and publicists, who called him a friend who had helped the Poles as much as he could. It is true that Splett appealed to the Holy See and to the German episcopacy for financial support for the Polish clergy and that he strove to authorize confession in Polish as well as to help a number of Polish monks. Nevertheless, Polish historians fiercely repudiate his rehabilitation. Only Tadeusz Bolduan is willing to see things in a different perspective. Bolduan stresses that although Splett was a German, he spoke Polish too and that because Splett defended the interests of the Germans in his diocese (in Gdańsk about 90% of the population) this does not mean he is responsible for Nazi policy as a whole. Moreover, although it is true that Splett confirmed the edicts of *Gauleiter* Forster, he actually did nothing else than what the nuncio in Berlin or the pope himself did whereas they were in a far safer position to criticize.[47]

Another controversial Bishop is Stanisław Adamski, the ordinary Bishop of the diocese of Katowice. From the very beginning of the war, Adamski was of the opinion that it was useless to defend the Polishness of the Church in Upper-Silesia, and that subjection to the occupier was the only way to ensure the survival of the Church. On September 13, 1939, he wrote a pastoral letter, which was signed by a few dozen priests, in which he called on his diocesans to cooperate with and trust the German authorities. When the Germans introduced the so-called *Volksliste* in December 1939, he encouraged the Polish clergy to register as Germans, in order to be allowed to stay in their parishes (himself, he registered as a Pole). A month later, he replaced his Vicar-General, the Pole

---

47. Tadeusz Bolduan, "Biskup Carl Maria Splett – od mitów ku prawdzie," *Studia Pelplińskie* 20 (1989) 79-95. One can find typical Polish appreciations, in Waszkiewicz, "Kościół," 75 ff.; Sziling, *Polityka*, 71 ff. and 106 ff.; and Fijałkowski, *Kościół*, 273 ff. German publicists who are particularly attacked, are F. J. Wothe and Franz Manthey.

Juliusz Bieniek, with the German Franz Strzyz. When the Germans closed the Silesian seminary in Cracow, Adamski sent the 46 seminarists to Germany, instead of to seminaries in the *Generalgouvernement*. All these measures, though some of them very understandable in a certain sense, have been heavily criticized both by contemporaries and by historians. Remarkably, in the 1990s, Adamski was defended and, indeed, in recent publications, the focus is not on the above-mentioned measures, but on the goal of Adamski's lesser evil policy and on its results. After all, Catholicism was not compromised in Upper-Silesia. Adamski was also engaged in charitable work, and made it even more efficient by decentralizing the main organization. He showed himself as being concerned about the Polish soldiers in the *Wehrmacht*, and made several interventions for the Polish Church in Silesia and the other incorporated provinces. Moreover, his own fate was not that favourable. From mid-November 1939 on, he was under house arrest and he was restricted in receiving visitors, and in February 1941, he was banished to the *Generalgouvernement*. Adamski moved to Warsaw, and remained active there. He is known to have participated in at least 33 conferences and in August 1944, he was a witness to, and maybe even a participant in, the Warsaw Rising.[48]

Stanisław Adamski is the clearest example of a Polish Bishop seeking for a certain *modus vivendi* with the Nazis, but he is certainly not the only one. Especially in the first months of the occupation, some bishops in the *Generalgouvernement* pursued a similar policy. In May 1940, the Bishop of Kielce, Czesław Kaczmarek, called on his people to obey the Germans in everything if it did not clash with the Catholic conscience. One of the only things he got in exchange for this loyalty was his own diocesan printer. Jan Kanty Lorek, the Bishop of Sandomierz, asked unemployed men in an open letter to report voluntarily for forced labour in Germany in order to relieve their parishes and to save their compatriots. Mid-September 1939, in the chaos of the Polish withdrawal and the German take-over, Bishop Teodor Kubina of Częstochowa even gave a survey of all the Catholic organizations and their militants in his diocese to the *Einsatzgruppe*, i.e. the security forces installed to intimidate the population. In May 1940, Kaczmarek, Lorek and Kubina had also a

---

48. Compare the earlier representation of Adamski in Fijałkowski, *Kościół*, 357-368 with some recent views as Jerzy Myszor, "Posługa pasterska biskupa S. Adamskiego w okresie okupacji hitlerowskiej 1939-1945," *Biskup Stanisław Adamski: Duszpasterz czsu wojny i okupacji 1939-1945*, ed. Jerzy Myszor (Katowice, 1994); and Władysław Jewsiewicki, "Ks. bp. Stanisław Adamski – duszpasterz powstania warszawskiego," *Przegląd Powszechny* 110, nos. 7-8 (1993) 146-153.

meeting with the governor-general, Hans Frank, whom they presented with a set of demands. These were not honoured. Maybe therefore, the bishops were less inclined to collaborate with the Germans after that meeting. The only exception is perhaps Bishop Czesław Sokołowski of Siedlce, who in 1941 and 1942 cooperated in collecting bells, called on the people to join the labour forces, accommodated the German secret police in his palace and chastised a priest for his membership of the underground army AK. He is represented in the literature as an opportunist. Only from 1943 on did some bishops sympathize with the anti-Communist propaganda of the Nazis, although they were all very conscious of the German threat too. A good example is Józef Kruszyński, the Rector of the Catholic University in Lublin who was granted authority by his arrested Bishop, was known as an enemy of Communism, and was charged for that after the war.

It can be concluded that the Polish episcopacy did not collaborate much with the German occupier. Indeed, the bishops discussed above are the only cases that were found in the literature, so one can assume that other bishops – and the above-mentioned bishops at other times – did not cooperate with the Nazis (although further research on this matter would be useful). Although collaboration was rare and accommodation was minimal, any evidence of it happening is generally underplayed in post 1989 Polish historiography. In fact, these cases were only revealed to by Zenon Fijałkowski in 1983 (although they were already known earlier in Germany).[49] This illustrates just how sensitive this subject is in Poland.

VI. The Attitude of the Lower Clergy

The historical treatment of possible collaboration or accommodation by the lower clergy is similar to that of the episcopacy. The subject has only been researched by Fijałkowski, who analyzed the opinions of the resistance and the exiles in London. Among these sources, he would have found several examples of individual collaboration. When the Germans

---

49. Fijałkowski, *Kościół*, 114-131, 159, referred to in only a few other Polish studies, such as Kłoczowski, *Histoire*, 486. In Franciszek Stopniak, "Duchowieństwo katolickie i Żydzi w latach II wojny światowej," *Acta Universitatis Wratislaviensis 815: Studia nad faszyzmem i zbrodniami hitlerowskimi* 11 (1987) 202, all these bishops are put in a favourable daylight. For the German historiography, see for instance Hans-Jürgen Karp, "Die katholische Kirche im Generalgouvernement 1939-1944," *Miscellanea historiae ecclesiasticae IX*, 294, quoting colleagues as Ch. Klessmann (1970) and H. Stehle (1963 and 1968)

arrested about 50 men, mainly 'democratic' agitators, in July 1942 in villages around Siedlce, the clergy openly approved and even declared that there should be more of these acts. At the end of 1943, a local priest was sentenced to death by the underground for having helped the German police in arresting 25 men who were all subsequently executed. The resistance also had to deal with priests who demanded exorbitant goods in kind for religious services such as baptisms or funerals. Such incidents lessened from the spring of 1943, but half a year later, clergymen began to be involved in anti-Communist actions, although these cases were local and rare. In September 1943, a priest was chastised by the 'Gwardia Ludowa' (the Communist resistance) of Radom (diocese of Sandomierz), because he had helped in the pacification of his village and the arrest of Communist militants. The *Kreishauptman* of Tarnów would have been very successful when he invited the local clergy to a conference in the spring of 1944 on the possibilities for anti-Communist actions.[50]

Other historians recorded collaboration as a marginal phenomenon in Polish society in which the clergy did not participate, but counteracted.[51] This does not mean that these historians collectively falsified history; they stated the truth in that collaboration was rare in Poland, equally among the lower clergy. Governor-general Hans Frank for instance wrote in 1943 that "The Polish clergy and the Polish educational establishments are – precisely because I have to tolerate them viewing the general policy – my main enemies. I know that Polish parish-priests and teachers keep this country systematically in trouble."[52] On the other hand, one cannot deny that Polish historiography treats the attitude of the local clergy one-sidedly. There has been a lot of

---

50. These and some other cases in: Fijałkowski, *Kościół*, 162-172.

51. A good example is E. Jarmoch, who wrote: "The long years of occupation favoured the moral laxity. Religious indifference and theft expanded a lot, not only in the cities, but also on the countryside. Also drunkenness spread, as it was promoted by the policy of the occupiers. Equally, one could observe certain signs of insensibilization of the human suffering and misery. There were cases of collaboration, spying and betrayal. Clergymen tried to counteract these pathological phenomena as much as possible," Jarmoch, "Duchowni," 115: "Długie lata okupacji sprzyjały rozluźnieniu moralnemu. Obojętność religijna, kradzieże, bardzo się rozszerzyły nie tylko w miastach, ale i na wsi. Szerzyło się też pijaństwo, ponieważ sprzyjała temu polityka okupanta. Zaobserwowano również pewne oznaki znieczulenia na ludzkie cierpienie i nędzę. Były też wypadki kolaboracji, donosicielstwa i zdrady. Tym zjawiskom patologicznym starano się przeciwdziałać w miarę możliwości duszpasterskich."

52. A quotation from his diary in: Fijałkowski, *Kościół*, 72: "Polski kler i polskie organa szkolne są – właśnie dlatego, że muszę je tolerować ze względu ogólnej polityki – moimi głównymi wrogami. Wiem, że polscy proboszczowie i nauczyciele utrzymują ten kraj systematycznie w niepokoju" (translation from German by S. Piotrowski).

research done on specific issues, especially those that place Poland and Catholicism in a favourable light. This has been done at the expense of other aspects such as collaboration or anti-Semitism which, as Fijałkowski and the case-study of Gross illustrate, also existed among the Polish clergy. Further research is required in order to determine the frequency, the level and motives for collaboration.

Here, only the main topics on which research has been done can been given. One of them is charity. Priests were, for instance, involved at all levels of the RGO ('Rada Główna Opiekuńcza', the successor of the interwar ministry of Labour and Social Protection, and the only legal Polish charity institution under German occupation). Hundreds of local priests engaged themselves in this organization (about 550 in 1942), some of them on the executive committee. Archbishop Sapieha gave moral support but was also active lobbying and collecting money.[53] Outside the RGO, the Church worked for charity too, but of course, this is less easy to quantify.

A specific example of charitable assistance was the help priests offered the Jews. Certainly from the spring of 1942 on, when the liquidation of the ghettos began and the plans of the Nazis became clear, a lot of Poles offered help to Jews and tried to save them from the Shoah. Encouraged by the government in exile, a committee called Żegota, was founded in September 1942 to help the Jews. Some clergymen were involved. A lot of other ones offered help on an individual basis. Some of them appealed for help in their sermons; others forged birth or baptism certificates so that people could get a *Kennkarte*. Catholic congregations saved Jews by hiding them in their monasteries and convents, or by giving them new names and admitting them to their schools, orphanages and hospitals. Especially children – mainly girls because of the easily identified circumcision of boys– were saved from being killed in this way. But adults also – mostly upper-class, assimilated Jews of non-Jewish appearance – were given shelter or supplied with food if they had taken refuge in the woods. All these deeds were extremely dangerous, as in Poland the death penalty was imposed for helping a Jew. This death penalty applied not only to the individual rescuer, but all the members of their community, monastery, convent (the Salesians from Praga in Warsaw for instance were all executed for this reason) or even school. The exact number of Jews who were saved by the Polish Catholic clergy cannot be given, but there are statistical data about specific cases. Of the

---

53. Fijałowski, *Kościół*, 175-195.

2500 Jewish children that were helped out of the Warsaw ghetto, about 500 were sheltered in Catholic monasteries and convents. During the whole of the war period, the Franciscan Sisters of the Family of Mary saved more than 500 children and about 250 adults in their five convents and orphanages in Warsaw. If we assume that almost every congregation participated to some degree in saving Jewish lives, we can infer that in total, thousands of Jews must have been rescued by Polish Catholic clergymen, most of them in the *Generalgouvernement*.[54]

Nevertheless, the rescue of Jews is a subject of frequent and heated debate between Polish and Jewish historians. The latter blame the former for their homogeneous and one-sided arguments and stress the diversity of the Church's attitude, revealing cases of Polish priests or Catholics with less noble opinions on the 'Jewish question'.[55] Moreover, they dispute the unselfish nature of some of the rescues, claiming it was more about proselytism and denationalization. Polish historians refute this. They state that, apart from young orphans and foundlings, children were only baptized at their own or their parents' request. The high number of baptisms must be attributed to the fact that baptism increased the chance of survival. In fact, these debates are only one aspect of the whole issue of dealing with the war experiences for the Poles and Jews. Contemporary Jews keep wondering how it was possible

---

54. All important historians of the Church in World War II have published on the rescue of Jews; see e.g. Zygmunt Zieliński, "Activities of Catholic Orders on Behalf of Jews in Nazi-Occupied Poland," *Judaism and Christianity under the Impact of National Socialism*, ed. Otto Dov Kulka and Paul R. Mendes-Flohr (Jerusalem, 1987) 231-394; and Jerzy Kłoczowski, "The Religious Orders and the Jews in Nazi-occupied Poland," *Polin* 3 (1988) 238-243. In 1992, a Ph.D. on the saving of Jewish children by Polish nuns was published: Ewa Kurek-Lesik, *Gdy klasztor znaczył życie: Udział żeńskich zgromadzeń zakonnych w akcji ratowania dzieci żydowskich w Polsce w latach 1939-1945* (Kraków, 1992). The most quantitative study, however, is still by Stopniak, "Duchowieństwo," who estimates that 769 clergymen in 389 institutions or in 273 cities and villages, saved Jews. Some local studies or examples are: Zofia Grzegrzółka, "Zakonnice warszawskie z pomocą Żydom," *Chrześcijanin w Świecie* 25, no. 1 (1995) 69-74 (quoted number on p. 70); Franciszek Stopniak, "Duchowieństwo katolickie z pomocą żydom w II wojnie światowej," *Saeculum Christianum* 2, no. 1 (1995) 89-99; Franciszek Stopniak, "Uwagi o efektach pomocy duchownych dla Żydów w okresie II wojny światowej," *Acta Universitatis Wratislaviensis 1169: Studia nad faszyzmem i zbrodniami hitlerowskimi* 14 (1991) 253-265. A German study is: Kosmala, "Ungleiche Opfer" (pp. 53 and 91ff. about the numbers of rescued Jews).

55. See for instance Krakowski, "The Polish," 396, quoting a report by the Polish underground to the Polish government in exile as follows: "As far as the Jewish question is concerned, it must be seen as a singular dispensation of Divine Providence that the Germans have already made a good start, quite irrespective of all the wrongs they have done and continue to our country. They have shown that the liberation of Polish society from the Jewish plague is possible."

that a whole Jewish population of more than three million people could be eliminated within a few years. Poles argue that their impotence was precisely related to the unthinkable dimension of exterminations, terror and danger, and are not afraid to accuse the Jews of passivity – "it is easier to help people who are defending themselves, who are fighting or who are escaping."[56] Furthermore, Jews blame the highest Polish Church authorities of having done nothing to guard congregants from the influence of local anti-Semites and Nazi propaganda. Poles reply to this charge with examples of the pro-Jewish activities of their Archbishops. Sapieha, for instance, would have understood after a few interventions that it was hopeless to lobby for the Jews, while Hlond published a report in the underground magazine *Témoignage Chrétien* in 1943 that played a major role in spreading the news of the Holocaust in the West. It is clear that the discussion is not yet resolved and perhaps it never will be.

Another aspect of the attitude of the lower clergy that has already been analyzed thoroughly by Polish historians, is their participation in the underground resistance against the Nazis. A number of priests rendered assistance or shelter to couriers, refugees and partisans, or ensured that prohibited education did continue (religious and general, primary, secondary and higher education). Some clergymen were even active in the resistance army, where they performed several functions, both pastoral (saving of souls, organizing field masses, administration of oaths, care of wounded soldiers...) as non-pastoral (organizational and even executive – though mostly local) functions. In the Warsaw Rising, a lot of churches and monasteries opened their doors for shelter and support. An Ursuline community e.g. prepared 1500 lunches and 900 breakfasts and diners each day. But, above all, the Church lent moral support, and organized big commemorative events during the insurrections: the 'Miracle at the Vistula' (August 15), the Blessed Virgin Mary of Częstochowa (August 27) and the German attack in 1939 (September 1).[57]

56. Kurek-Lesik, *Gdy klasztor*, 35: "łatwiej jest pomagać ludziom, którzy się bronią, którzy walczą, uciekają."
57. Some local case-studies are: Konrad Ciechanowski, "Duszpasterstwo Armii 'Pomorze' w 1939 r. oraz udział księży w ruchu oporu na Pomorzu w latach okupacji hitlerowskiej," *Univ. Gedanensis* 4 (1990) 35-57 and A. Marczyński, "Udział duchowieństwa w walce z okupantem w Gorcach i Beskidach w latach 1939 do 1945," *Nasza Przeszłość* 67 (1987) 197-236. On the resistance in Wartheland, see: Śmigiel, *Kościół*, 117-123. About the Warsaw Rising: Piotr Matusak (ed.), *Służba duszpasterska Armii Krajowej w powstaniu warszawskim* (Siedlce, 1996) (about the Ursuline monastery, see p. 21 of the introduction) and *Kościół a Powstanie Warszawskie. Dokumenty, relacje, poezja* (Warsaw, 1994).

Two general remarks must be made on the participation of clergymen in the Polish resistance. On the one hand, several historians stress that the level of participation was low, certainly at the beginning of the war and certainly among the lower clergy. Fijałkowski estimates the number of priests in the Home Army (AK) at 700, and only one hundred priests would have participated actively in the Warsaw Rising.[58] On the other hand, the resistance was inspired by and made use of Catholicism to a huge extent, as this religion was an essential part of Polish nationalism. The resistance was perhaps not borne by clergymen, but Catholic militants, both politicians (e.g. from the Christian Democratic SP) and social activists (e.g. youth organizations) played an active role in it. Even the Communist army that was founded in 1943 in the Soviet Union was inspired by Catholicism and had some priests among its ranks for the ministration of its soldiers.[59] Although this was primarily motivated by propaganda, it remains characteristic for Poland and perhaps unique in Central and Eastern Europe.

VII. The War Heritage of the Polish Catholic Church: The First Years of Communism

The Polish Communists who accompanied the Russians on their expedition through Poland, presented a manifesto in Lublin on July 22, 1944 – Poland's Constitution Day in Communist times – and claimed sole legal power. In December 1944, they set up a provisional government, which was recognized by the Soviet Union only. When some of the political leaders returned from exile to Poland in the summer of 1945 and made a Government of National Unity, the Western allies recognized the new authorities in Poland. Initially, Communists shared power with the Peasants' Party of Stanisław Mikołajczyk and the Christian Democrats of Karol Popiel. Officially, they took complete power only gradually and in a so-called democratic way: after a show referendum in June 1946, falsified elections in January 1947 and a new, temporary constitution in February 1947. In fact, Communists were pulling the strings in Poland from the very beginning, and already in

---

58. Fijałkowski, *Kościół*, 213 and 131 ff.; and Matusak, *Służba*, 3. Also Bogacz (*Książę*, 128) admits that the clergy rarely played an instigating role, but stresses that priests were accused by the Nazis of having such a great influence on the masses.

59. Dariusz Chodynecki, "Duszpasterstwo w ludowym wojsku polskim w czasie II wojny światowej," *Saeculum Christianum* 2, no. 1 (1995) 193-210.

June 1945, exhibition trials against sixteen Polish opposition leaders took place in Moscow. However, they needed several years to 'pacify' society and defeat the armed resistance, such as the AK and Ukrainian nationalist groups.

Precisely because of the fact that their position was not consolidated from the beginning, the Communists had an ambiguous policy towards the Church. In order to define this policy, historians have launched several terms. Jan Żaryń has called it a 'policy of reciprocal passing by' and stresses that the authorities left the Church alone. They did not help or favour the Church, but did also not sabotage or oppose it, and were mainly concerned about strengthening their own position. Ryszard Gryz goes even further and calls the Communist attitude during the first years a 'policy of open doors'. He stresses that the Church was invited to cooperate with the new regime that wanted to legitimize its position. Antoni Dudek, however, uses another image to define the Communist Church policy immediately after the war: the 'salami strategy'.[60] According to him, the Polish authorities wanted to counteract the Church in little steps, like a salami which is gradually sliced and consumed. This image seems to contradict the views of Żaryń and Gryz. However, the difference is only a matter of perspective. Initially, the Church generally (though certainly not completely) was left alone, and gradually, in steps like slicing a salami, its activities were counteracted by the Communist regime. These three images seem contradictory, but in fact, one can find examples of all these policies in the first years after the war.

The 'policy of reciprocal passing by' can be illustrated in numerous ways: the Church was not hindered in the restoration of its administrative, social and cultural structures. Archbishop Hlond could return from exile and fill the vacant bishop's chairs and priestly offices. Churches could be rebuilt – in total, 252 churches were rebuilt between 1945 and 1952, from which about 100 from the very foundations. Already in August 1944, the Catholic University of Lublin was re-established – it would remain the only free university in the Eastern Bloc until 1989. Charity organizations were tolerated, and Caritas for instance had branches in almost 6,000 parishes and almost 800,000 members all over the country. Monastic orders could continue their

---

60. Jan Żaryń, *Dzieje kościoła katoliciego w Polsce (1945-1989)* (Warsaw, 2003); Ryszard Gryz, *Państwo a Kościół w Polsce 1945-1956 na przykładzie województwa kieleckiego* (Kraków, 1999) 74; Antoni Dudek, *Państwo i kościół 1945-1970* (Kraków, 1995) 7.

education, catechetical or benevolent activities. Religious education in schools was hardly restricted. The Catholic press could flourish, and in 1947-1948, about 80 different titles appeared in Poland. One of them, *Tygodnik Powszechny* (General Weekly), would develop into one of the main opposition papers during Communism, and still exists today. It was founded in March 1945 as an organ of the Cracovian curia and stood under the protection of the Cracovian Archbishop Sapieha, but was meant for secular Catholics and was edited by Jerzy Turowicz. After destalinization in 1956, it gave birth to the Catholic opposition group 'Znak' (Sign) with for instance Tadeusz Mazowiecki).[61]

So, the situation of the Polish Church immediately after the war was far from bad. The Communist policy can even be described as a 'policy of open doors', as indeed, it was mainly the state that took the initiative for the good relations. The new regime gave the German and mainly protestant church buildings in the Western provinces of the new Polish state to the Polish Church that, of course, turned them into Catholic sanctuaries. The Communists also supported the reconstruction of the destroyed churches financially and even paid for liturgical equipment, such as chasubles, surplices and albs. Moreover, the good relations between the Church and the authorities were stressed in the Communist press. It was, for instance, underlined that party leaders participated in Church manifestations and masses, that national events were celebrated by the ringing of church bells and that Catholic symbols and priests were present at Communist celebrations such as the festivities on the first of May and so on. So, the Communists clearly did not remain totally faithful to their principles: the Communist leader Bolesław Bierut celebrated the Eucharist, and white-yellow flags (of the Vatican State) and ecclesiastical emblems decorated Częstochowa during a mass pilgrimage in September 1946 attended by Hlond and Sapieha. Of course, the Communists also had a hidden agenda. For instance, they also organized an industrial and agricultural exhibition during the pilgrimage in Częstochowa, and pilgrims who visited the exhibition were given huge reductions in the price of their return ticket.[62]

61. Żaryń, *Dzieje kościoła*, 64-69, 75-87; see even more details in Jan Żaryn, *Kościół a władza w Polsce (1945-1950)* (Warsaw, 1997); Andrzej Micewski, *Współrządzić czy nie kłamać? Pax i Znak w Polsce 1945-1976* (Kraków, 1981); Marian Jasiukiewicz, *Kościół katolicki w polskim życiu politycznym 1945-1989: Podstawowe uwarunkowania* (Wrocław, 1993) 96 ff.
62. Żaryń, *Dzieje kościoła*, 65, 75; Gryz, *Państwo a Kościół*, 72, 77-8, 91-93, 98, 103.

Indeed, the relationship between the Church and the Communist regime was certainly not problem free. On the contrary, attempts to build up a good understanding went together with acts of laicization and repression. It is true that this did not happen on a large scale during the first years, as the image of the salami illustrates, but nevertheless, it remains a fact that in nearly all the above mentioned areas, official 'tolerance' went along with other, restrictive measures. The charity organization Caritas, for instance, was tolerated but obstructed at the same time: the authorities did not pass on all the financial donations the Americans sent them. *Tygodnik Powszechny* was tolerated, but the Communists focussed on another paper, *Dziś i Jutro*, that claimed to unify the Catholic and Socialist worldviews. Religious education in primary schools was authorized, but for the first time, parents could also excuse their children from the courses. Life was made difficult for convent schools and many of them soon closed down. Anti-Church measures did not even end there. At a local level, tensions could mount after accusations and calumny or even after house of church searches and arrests. Between 1945 and 1947, several dozen priests were killed by the new authorities. It is obvious that the 'policy of the open doors' went together with measures of a very different nature.[63]

This was even seen at a national level. Early on, the Communists took measures that revealed their true objective: monopolization of the power and laicization of the state. In June 1945, they introduced civil marriages and deprived the Church of the control of the registration of births, deaths and marriages. It is clear that these were the first steps into the complete separation of Church and State. In the summer of 1945, they refused to recognize the five ecclesiastical administrators that were appointed by the Polish Primate for the administration of the newly conquered areas in the West of Poland, because the Vatican did not recognize the new regime in Poland and continued to collaborate with the Polish government in exile in London. A few months later, in September 1945, they even cancelled the Concordat with the Vatican that was concluded in 1925. Officially it was said that this was because the Vatican had not observed regulations by appointing bishops during the war while the legal bishops, who were in exile, had not yet renounced their functions. In 1947, the Polish government tried to restore relations by sending an *envoyé*, Ksawery Pruszyński, to

---

63. Gryz, *Państwo a Kościół*, 89-90; Jasiukiewicz, *Kościół katolicki*, 114 ff.; Żaryń, *Dzieje kościoła*, 66-67, 79.

the Vatican, but this was just a tactical ploy. A new Concordat was only concluded in the 1990s. All the Polish bishops that had been appointed by the Pope were not officially recognized by the Communist regime.[64]

It is obvious that the Church policy of the Polish Communists immediately after the war was two-faced. They generally left the Church in peace and even tried to gain its sympathy with some favourable measures, but their real objective was to legitimize and to consolidate their own position. The Communists tolerated Catholicism, but mainly because they wanted to neutralize the Church in their struggle with the main enemy of that moment, the Peasants' Party of Mikołajczyk. The Communists favoured the freedom of thought and religion in the Lublin manifesto, but that was only to get the support of the Polish people – 90% of whom were Catholic. The Communists assisted Catholic priests in the newly conquered Western provinces, but that was only because the ethnic cleansing and the Polonization of these areas and integration with the rest of Poland was easier to perform with the help of the Church than without it. Probably the Communists did not hinder the Church because their repression machinery was not yet up to strength in the first years after the war and they were not ready for open confrontation. That would soon change: repression increased after the puppet elections of 1947 and came to a climax at the beginning of the 1950s. The Polish Primate Stefan Wyszyński, who had succeeded Hlond in 1948, was confined from 1953 till 1956. After 1956, the Church policy liberalized. The charisma of the Church would only increase until the fall of Communism in 1989.

The attitude of the Polish Church towards this policy was ambiguous. On the one hand, the episcopacy searched a dialogue with the Communists and tried to find a *modus vivendi*, even when the Vatican opposed it. At the same time, however, it clearly criticized the new regime, which in its eyes was forced upon Polish society – a famous pronouncement is for instance "One can not serve two lords." The bishops not only condemned the materialist ideology of the Communists, but sometimes even took position in political themes. About the time of the referendum in June 1946, for instance, the episcopacy

64. Henryk Dominiczak, *Organy bezpieczeństwa PRL w walce z kościołem katolickim 1944-1990: W świetle dokumentów MSW* (Warsaw, 2000) 29-31; Zygmunt Zieliński and Marian Pereta (eds.), *Aparat ucisku na Lubelszczyźnie w latach 1944-1956 wobec duchowieństwa katolickiego* (Lublin, 2000) 26-27; Barbara Fijałkowska, *Partia wobec religii i kościoła w PRL. Tom I. 1944-1955* (Olsztyn, 1999) 38-50.

declared that Catholics were not obliged to participate. In general, however, the Polish Church was not really a political opponent but was more concerned with offering moral resistance and playing a stabilizing role. Of course, in this way, they were *de facto* in political opposition. This position was exceptional within the Eastern Bloc. In other countries, the Church was far more persecuted. In Hungary for instance, Archbishop Mindszenty was already arrested in December 1946 and condemned to life imprisonment in 1949.

The war heritage is one of the main explanations of this difference between Poland and the rest of the former Eastern Bloc. Indeed, the Second World War mainly strengthened the position of the Catholic Church in Poland. The Church had shared in the cruelties, had been one of the main victims of German barbarities and could, therefore, even claim martyrdom. It had participated in the resistance, and consequently came out of the war as the carrier of the Polish nation, as the axis of its struggle against totalitarianism. The main Polish Church leaders, in particular the Cracovian Archbishop Adam Sapieha, had shown courage and political understanding during the war and had never compromised themselves, which meant that they enjoyed a huge moral authority and were considered the real leaders in the Polish struggle for freedom. Of course, their popularity was also increased by the growing religiosity during the war. It is ironic that the Polish Catholic Church in effect profited from the genocides, territorial changes and ethnic cleansing during and immediately after the war. While before the war, less than two third of the Polish population was Catholic, after the war Poland had become far more homogeneous and 90% of the inhabitants were Catholics. The stereotype of 'Polak-Katolik' that originated during 19th-century Romanticism had almost become a reality.

The new regime in Warsaw was forced to take this social force into consideration. Sometimes, they tried to compromise the Church by means of the war heritage. Józef Cyrankiewicz, the Polish Prime Minister from 1947 until 1952, for instance tried to sow dissension among the Polish clergy. In June 1946, just after the referendum, he said: "We note that in a range of places, priests made use of the dignity of their soutanes, to convince their worshippers to vote three times 'no', and that happened precisely in the areas where during the occupation, bishops – both Lorek's as no Lorek's – had proclaimed that the Polish people should leave for Germany. We know from the occupation period, that not all Polish priests and not all Polish bishops had such an attitude and such a courage as cardinal Sapieha and the priests who died in Dachau."[65] A few days later, the Communists accused the clergy of participating in the pogrom of Kielce on July 4, 1946, in which 42 Jews where killed. This was a lie: local priests had actually tried to stop the anti-Semitists and the episcopacy openly condemned the events. Catholics have always stated that the pogrom was started by Communist security agents in order to destabilize Polish society and to divert attention from the disputable referendum, but recent research has shown that there was no conspiracy, and that the pogrom erupted spontaneously in a society that was totally disorientated after the war.[66] The Communists regularly tried to compromise the Church in other ways too. They denounced the attitude of the Vatican towards Germany, more precisely the fact that the Pope refused to recognize the new geopolitical situation and to adopt the diocesan circumscriptions to the new Oder-Neisse border (it would only do that in 1968). The new regime could also refer to Carl Maria Splett, the Gdańsk Bishop who was held responsible for the rigorous measures in Danzig-Westpreussen and therefore was condemned to eight years' imprisonment.

In other words, there were certainly attempts by the Communists to compromise the Catholic Church in the light of its attitude during the war; they tried to associate the Church with conservatism, reaction, resistance and consequently fascism and anti-Semitism. But in general, they could not achieve these goals. In consequence, one can state that the war heritage of the Polish Church was almost completely positive. Thanks to the Second World War, the Catholic Church gained a position that it would not lose until after the fall of the next totalitarian regime in 1989.

VIII. Conclusions: Some Comparisons

From comparative perspective, the position of the Polish Church during the Second World War was exceptional. On the one hand, it fell victim to Nazi policy to an extreme extent. The Polish Church was attacked not only because of its religiosity (which was in principle incongruous to the Nazi ideology), but also because of its strong ties

65. Hanna Konopka, *Religia w szkołach Polski Ludowej: Sprawa nauczania religii w polityce państwa (1944-1961)* (Białystok, 1997) 27.
66. Gryz, *Państwo a Kościół*, 147; Jan Śledzianowski, *Pytania nad pogromem kieleckim* (Kielce, 1998).

with the Polish nation, which was to be eliminated in the medium term. This was certainly the case in the *Reichsgau* Danzig-Westpreussen, which was the corridor between East-Prussia and the *Heimat* and therefore had to be Germanized completely as soon as possible, and Wartheland, which already during the war served as a test-case for the Church policy the Nazis wanted to pursue after the war in all the occupied regions. In both incorporated provinces, the Church was outlawed, religious life was subject to numerous restrictions and the clergy was decimated. Death rates among clergymen were extremely high (exceeding in some dioceses half of the pre-war number). In other European regions, such as in Slovenian Steiermark and Oberkrain, the number of clergymen drastically diminished too but priests were generally banished and not systematically physically eliminated. In the rest of German-occupied Poland (Silesia, the *Generalgouvernement* and the east of Poland that was conquered in 1941), the Church policy was softened for pragmatic reasons, such as industrial mobilization, political peace or anti-Communist propaganda. Nevertheless, in these areas also, Church policy was very restrictive from European perspective. Poland was one of the only countries occupied by Nazi-Germany, where bishops were arrested and even killed in concentration camps.

However, Poland does not only owe its exceptional position to Nazi Church policy. The attitude of the Polish episcopacy was remarkable too. This refers to Adam Sapieha, the Cracovian Archbishop who became the moral Church leader after the flight of the Polish Primate August Hlond to Rome and France. Contrary to other Primates in occupied Europe, such as Stepinac in Croatia, the behavior of Sapieha has not given cause for accusations of collaboration. On the contrary, Sapieha repeatedly protested against aspects of the Nazi policy, both openly and privately in personal letters to governor-general Hans Frank and his collaborators. So, accusations that Sapieha did not do enough against the Holocaust in his diocese lack nuance and do not take into account other aspects, such as the difficult position of the Polish Church and the permanent threat of reprisals. On the whole, the rest of the Polish episcopacy followed Sapieha's example. Only a few cases are known of bishops collaborating with the Nazis, and only in 1953, at the height of Stalinism, was Bishop Kaczmarek of Kielce charged for spreading anti-Communist propaganda during the war.[67] But these are rather

---

67. Karp, "Die katholische Kirche," 294. Jan Siedlarz, *Kirche und Staat im kommunistischen Polen 1945-1989* (Paderborn, 1996) 48 ff., 68 ff.

exceptions to the general conclusion that the Polish Church hardly compromised itself during the Nazi occupation.

Selective Bibliography

Adam Chruszczewski, Krystyna Dębowski, Jerzy Kłoczowski, *et al.* (eds.), *Żeńskie zgromadzenia zakonne w Polsce w 1939-1947*. 15 vols. (Lublin, 1982-2001).
Norman Davies, *God's Playground: A History of Poland*. 2 vols. (New York/London, 1980).
Antoni Dudek, *Państwo i kościół 1945-1970* (Kraków, 1995).
Zenon Fijałkowski, *Kościół katolicki na ziemiach polskich w latach okupacji hitlerowskiej* (Warsaw, 1983).
Jan T. Gross, *Neighbors: The Destruction of the Jewish Community in Jedwabne, Poland* (Princeton, NJ/Oxford, 2001).
Ryszard Gryz, *Państwo a Kościół w Polsce 1945-1956 na przykładzie województwa kieleckiego* (Kraków, 1999).
Jerzy Kłoczowski (ed.), *Histoire religieuse de la Pologne* (Paris, 1987).
Miscellanea historiae ecclesiasticae. IX. Congrès de Varsovie 25 juin – 1er juillet 1978. Section IV: Les églises chrétiennes dans l'Europe dominée par le IIIe Reich (Wrocław/Bruxelles, 1984).
Kazimierz Śmigiel, *Kościół katolicki w tzw. okręgu Warty 1939-1945* (Lublin, 1979).
Jan Sziling, *Polityka okupanta hitlerowskiego wobec kościoła katolickiego 1939-1945. Tzw. okręgi Rzeszy Gdańsk-Prusy Zachodnie, Kraj Warty i Regencja Katowicka* (Poznań, 1970).
Jan Żaryń, *Dzieje kościoła katoliciego w Polsce (1945-1989)* (Warsaw, 2003).
Zygmunt Zieliński (ed.), *Życie religijne w Polsce pod okupacją hitlerowską 1939-1945* (Warsaw, 1983).

The Catholic Church in Croatia and Bosnia-Herzegovina in the Face of Totalitarian Ideologies and Regimes

Jure Krišto

I. The Contours of a Misunderstanding

The position of the Catholic Church during the World War II and in the Independent State of Croatia (Nezavisna Država Hrvatska – NDH) is probably one of the most intriguing issues of the relationship between state and religion. Certainly, it is one of the most misrepresented issues in the painful history of the war, at least in reference to Croatia.[1] There are at least two important reasons for that misrepresentation. One is the fact that the Communists, who took the control of Yugoslavia at the end of the war, had their own political and ideological (anti-religious) reasons for misrepresenting the role of the Catholic Church not only in Croatia, but in general. The second reason stems from the intriguing relationship among the nations that constituted Yugoslavia from 1918, when they first decided to cast their lot with each other. Serbs never renounced the idea that Croatia is just part of Great Serbia.

The misrepresentation of the Church began as a political decision that eventually flooded into historiography.[2] The resulting historiography did not stop at the Yugoslav borders, but influenced the writing of many historians abroad, a situation that has not changed even now.[3]

---

1. For a study of the misrepresentation in historiography of former Yugoslavia see Stan Granic, "Representations of the Other: The Ustaše and the Demonization of the Croats," *Journal of Croatian Studies* 34 (1998) 3-56.

2. For a study of political influence on historiography, especially with regard to the representation of the Catholic Church in Croatia, see Jure Krišto, *Katolička crkva i Nezavisna Država Hrvatska* (Zagreb: Hrvatski institut za povijest, 1998) 17-42; id., "Stare i nove paradigme hrvatske historiografije," *Društvena istraživanja* 10, nos. 1-2 (51-52) (2001) 165-189.

3. I only mention some of the more recent works that reflect that negative influence of the Yugoslav politics on historiography: Holm Sundhaussen, "Der Ustascha-Staat: Anatomie eines Herrschaftssystem," *Österreichische Osthefte* 37, no. 2 (1995) 497-533; Michael Phayer, *The Catholic Church and the Holocaust, 1930-1965* (Bloomington, IN/Indianapolis, IN: Indiana University Press, 2000) 31-40; John Cornwell, *Hitler's Pope: The Secret History of Pius XII* (London: Viking, 1999). For a thorough critique of Cornwell's book see: Ronald J. Rychlak, *Hitler, the War, and the Pope* (Columbus, MS:

Jonathan Steinberg has written that the Ustaše, the holders of power in Croatia during the war, "combined Catholic piety, Croatian nationalism and extreme violence."[4] Yeshayahu Jelinek also has insisted that the Ustaša movement was "devoutly Catholic." Martin Broszat has become recognized by the thesis that Ustašism was "the Croat Catholic brand of fascism" and that "Catholic religiosity" could not be divorced from Ustaša ideology.[5] In Serbian nationalist historiography, the Ustaše are often seen as Catholic crusaders, whose policies can be understood only in association with militant Catholicism.[6] Some authors tend to look at Croatia during the war as if only Ustaše had existed then so that even Germans could not control and suppress their violence (the Nazi would be seen temporarily as the good guys). Other actors – Italians, Chetniks, Communist Partisans, Muslim nationalists, German minority, and Serbian Orthodox Church and other churches – are absent from the considerations of these authors or are mentioned only as accidental players.[7]

Genesis Press, 2000) 281-308, the Epilogue to the book. See further Menachem Shelah, "The Catholic Church in Croatia, the Vatican and the Murder of the Croatian Jews," *Holocaust and Genocide Studies* 4, no. 3 (1989) 323-339; id., "Genocide in Satellite Croatia during the Second World War," *A Mosaic of Victims: Non-Jews Persecuted and Murdered by the Nazis*, ed. Michael Berenbaum (New York/London: New York University Press, 1990) 74-79; id., "Croatia," *Encyclopedia of the Holocaust*, ed. Israel Gutman (New York: Macmillan Publishing Company, 1990) vol. I, 323-329; id., "Jasenovac," *ibid.*, vol. II, 739-740. (For an explanation of Shelah's – in fact Croatian Jew Raul Špicer's – motivations see: Frano Glavina, "Čovjek koji je krivotvorio povijest i prezirao domovinu," *Nedjeljna Dalmacija*, September 1, 1995, 36).

4. Jonathan Steinberg, "Types of Genocide? Croatians, Serbs and Jews, 1941-5," *The Final Solution: Origins and Implementation*, ed. David Cesarani (London/New York, 1994) 176-177.

5. Yeshayahu Jelinek, "Clergy and Fascism: The Hlinka Party in Slovakia and the Croatian Ustaša Movement," *Who Were the Fascists: Social Roots of European Fascism*, ed. Stein Ugelvik Larsen, *et al.* (Bergen/Oslo/Tromso: Universitetsforlaget, 1980) 370; Martin Broszat and Ladislaus Hory, *Der kroatische Ustascha-Staat: 1941-1945* (Stuttgart: Deutsche Verlags-Anstalt, 1965) 72.

6. Mark Biondich, "Religion and Nation in Wartime Croatia: Reflections on the Ustaša Policy of Forced Religious Conversions, 1941-1942," *The Slavonic and East European Review* 83, no. 1 (2005) 71-116. Among Serb authors, it would be hard to find exceptions, but among the most blatant cases are Vladimir Dedijer, *Vatikan i Jasenovac: Dokumenti* (Beograd: "Rad," 1987) *Jasenovac – das jugoslavische Auschwitz und der Vatikan* (Freiburg: Ahriman-Verlag, 1992); *The Yugoslav Auschwitz and the Vatican: The Croatian Massacre of the Serbs during World War II*, trans. Harvey L. Kendall (Buffalo, NY: Prometheus Books, 1992)]; Milan Bulajić, *Ustaški zločini genocida i suđenje Andriji Artukoviću 1986. godine*, 4 vols. (Beograd: "Slobodan Jović," 1988); Dragoljub R. Živojinović and Dejan V. Lučić, *Varvarstvo u ime Hristovo: prilozi za Magnum Crimen* (Beograd: Nova knjiga, 1988); Dragoljub R. Živojinović, *Vatikan, Katolička crkva i jugoslovenska vlast 1941-1958* (Beograd, 1994).

7. In addition to the already mentioned Serb authors, see Jonathan E. Gumz, "*Wehrmacht* Perceptions of Mass Violence in Croatia, 1941-1942," *The Historical Journal* 44, no. 4 (2001) 1015-1038.

It is not possible to respond to all those misrepresentations in an article, but I intend to show at least that Ustašism and Catholicism have nothing in common and that Ustašism was an aberration in Croatian history. That will become clear once the layers of prejudice and propaganda are removed under the pressure of fresh reading of already known and new documents[8] and once the political and military context is taken fully into account. I will address the position of the Catholic Church in Croatia in three distinct periods of European history: before World War II, during the war, and immediately after the war.

II. Croats and the Catholic Church in the Kingdom of Yugoslavia

The life of most Croats in the State that was created during the turmoil of the World War I was marked by the oppressive dominance of the Serbs in the multinational State, which, for Croats, meant a situation of exploitation, persecutions, the imprisonment of political leaders and innumerable other citizens, the murder of its parliamentarians even those in the Parliament in Belgrade, as well as the murder of many Croatian peasants, political leaders, and intellectuals.[9] At times, the representatives of the Catholic Church were involved in defending not only the religious but also the national rights of the Croats. The Catholic Church itself was under threat. The Serbian Orthodox Church was favoured, even though it was not considered a state religion, and the Catholic Church faced innumerable obstructions in its pastoral and educational missions.

1. Ethnic and Political Spectrum

The situation was more complicated by the fact that the new State was a multinational and multicultural State with long ingrained civilization differences (Table 1).

---

8. Actually, some decisive documents were published long ago. See: Richard Pattee, *The Case of Cardinal Aloysius Stepinac* (Milwaukee, WI: Bruce Publishing Company, 1953); Fiorello Cavalli, *El proceso de monsenor Stepinac* (Madrid: Ediciones Acción Católica Española, 1947); *Actes et documents du Saint Siège relatifs à la seconde guerre mondiale*, 11 vols., ed. Pierre Blet *et al.* (Vatican City: Libreria Editrice Vaticana, 1965-1981).

9. "Einstein accuses Yugoslavian Rulers in Savant's Murder," *The New York Times* (May 6, 1932) 1 and 3; James J. Sadkovich, "Terrorism in Croatia, 1929-1934," *East European Quarterly* 22 (1988); id., "The Use of Political Trials to Repress Croatian Dissent 1929-1934," *Journal of Croatian Studies* 28-29 (1987-88) 103-140; Bosiljka Janjatović, "Hrvatska 1929-1934. godine: vrijeme organiziranih političkih ubojstava," *Povijesni prilozi* 13 (1994) 219-244; id., "Represija spram hrvatskih seljaka 1918.-1921.," *Časopis za suvremenu povijest* 25, no. 1 (1993) 25-43.

Table 1. Yugoslavia's national structure, 1918[10]

	Number	Percent
Serbs	4,665,851	38.83
Croats	2,856,551	23.77
Slovenes	1,024,761	8.53
Bosnian Muslims	727,650	6.05
Macedonians or Bulgars	585,558	4.87
Other Slavic	174,466	1.45
Germans	513,472	4.27
Hungarians	472,409	3.93
Albanians	441,740	3.68
Romanians, Vlachs, and Cincars	229,398	1.91
Turks	168,404	1.40
Jews	64,159	0.53
Italians	12,825	0.11
Others	80,079	0.67
Total	12,017.323	100.00

Croats made up less than 24% of the population, but Catholics – the majority of Croats considered themselves, at least nominally, to be Catholics – show greater percentages, since the majority of Slovenes and Italians and a substantial number of Germans and Hungarians was Catholic. In Croatia proper, however, there lived a substantial number of the Orthodox population, who ethnically identified themselves as Serbs.

The politics were even more complicated.[11] The Croat political elite and intellectuals before the war in the Austro-Hungarian Empire promulgated the ideology of Yugoslavism, and by the time of entering a new State they were committed to Yugoslav unitarism. However, the Croat masses did not share that ideology. Stjepan Radić (1871-1928) articulated their dispositions and attracted them by appealing to the Republican form of government, the confederate status of Croatia in the new state, demands for the socialization of land and factories, and similar propositions. Radić, the head of the minor Hrvatska pučka seljača stranka (HPSS, Croat People's Peasant Party), soon became an undisputed leader

10. The census was taken in 1921. The table is borrowed from Ivo Banac, *The National Question in Yugoslavia: Origins, History, Politics* (Ithaca, NJ/London: Cornell University Press, 1984) 58.
11. Banac, *The National Question in Yugoslavia*; Jozo Tomasevich, *War and Revolution in Yugoslavia, 1941-1945*. Vol. 1: *The Chetniks* (Stanford, CA: Stanford University Press, 1975) 3-53.

not just of a strong political party (he changed its name to Croat Republican Peasant Party to reflect his republicanism), but of a Croat *movement*. Radić's party which could count on almost half a million voters became the third largest party in the country. Radić refused to acknowledge the centralized Vidovdan's constitution of 1921 and to participate in the Belgrade Parliament. However, during one of his many imprisonments, and after failing to find an audience in the international arena, Radić in 1925 made a fateful political turnaround and accepted conditions set by the unitarist forces. Three years later a Serb deputy, by the name of Puniša Račić, wounded Radić in that Parliament, and few months later he died.

While Radić had a supreme control of the countryside, he failed to attract a following in the cities, especially among the Croat intelligentsia. The Frankists, the followers of Josip Frank, occupied that niche.[12] As soon as the Croatian *Sabor* (Parliament) annulled all ties with Austria-Hungary and proclaimed the State of Slovenes, Croats, and Serbs (not to be confused with the Kingdom of Serbs, Croats, and Slovenes, created two months later), the Parliament club of the Pure Party of the Right believed their political program accomplished and announced the dissolution of the party. The events associated with the unification of the newly created State with the kingdoms of Serbia and Montenegro (which led to the creation of the Kingdom of Serbs, Croats, and Slovenes) forced them, however, to issue on December 2, 1918 an anti-unification manifesto, charging that the Croatian *Sabor* was not consulted about it.[13] On February 27, 1919 the Frankists proclaimed a new program of the party, freshly renamed

---

12. Josip Frank (1844-1911) native of the city of Osijek, born of Jewish parents, who arrived from Hungary, mostly spoke German at home, so that he never mastered Croatian. He studied law in Vienna and received his doctorate in 1868. He returned to Croatia in 1872, where he opened his own attorney's office in Zagreb. With his brother, Frank soon began publishing the newspapers *Agramer Presse* and *Kroatische Post*. He apparently married a Jewish woman in Vienna, but since their marriage was not recognized in Croatia, he remarried in Zagreb. That was probably the occasion when he converted to Catholicism. In his newspaper, Frank criticized the policy of *ban* (Viceroy) Ivan Mažuranić (1814-1891). He was therefore considered to be a liberal and a reformist. In the late 1880s, Frank defended some prominent members of the Croatian Party of (State) Rights (Hrvatska stranka prava – HSP), a party that defended Croatia's right to be a sovereign and independent state, based on the legalistic tradition of state rights – and in 1890 he joined the party himself. He quickly made a career in the party. When in 1895 the party split, Frank became the president of the Pure Party of Rights (Čista stranka prava – ČSP) and Ante Starčević (1823-1896), the founder and ideologue of the party, sided with him.

13. Banac, *The National Question in Yugoslavia*, 262.

Hrvatska stranka prava (HSP, Croatian Party of Rights), which called for a legal struggle for an independent Croat state.[14] The regime persecuted the party leaders – one of them was a Catholic priest Josip Pazman – and the party began to rely on Frankists émigrés, Josip Frank's son Ivica, Lieutenant Colonel Stjepan Duić, and former Austro-Hungarian commanding officer in Bosnia-Herzegovina Baron Stjepan Sarkotić, among them. The émigrés founded in Graz in 1919 the Hrvatske komite (Croat Committee) and in 1920 the Croat Legion.[15] Although the Frankist emigration was not united, through alliances with individuals and countries hostile to Yugoslavia and through its own propaganda it managed to portray itself as a great threat to Yugoslavia.

The party's rating was boosted in 1929 after King Aleksandar I Karadjordjević abolished the Parliament and imposed a dictatorship, following the assassination of two Croatian representatives and the wounding of Stjepan Radić in the Belgrade Parliament in 1928. Ante Pavelić (1889-1959), one of the leading men of the HSP, emigrated to Italy, determined to radicalize the Croatian struggle for freedom in which terrorism would not be excluded. He founded a revolutionary group Ustaša (Insurgent). They established training camps in Hungarian towns bordering Yugoslavia to promote revolutionary activity and, when they could no longer operate in Hungary, they moved to Italy. The Ustaše,[16] in collaboration with Macedonian nationalists, were behind the assassination of King Aleksandar in Marseilles in October 1934 (succeeded by the Governorship, headed by Duke Pavle, which governed instead of the King's younger son Petar).

The third political party Hrvatska pučka stranka (HPS, Croat People's Party), founded in 1919, claimed a Catholic tag. It grew out of the Croat Catholic Movement (begun by Bishop of Krk Antun Mahnić in 1903) and was influenced by the Slovenska Ljudska Stranka (SLS, Slovene People's Party). Driven by a sort of Catholic Yugoslavism, its leaders – among them the Greek Catholic priest Janko Šimrak and in Catholic areas of Bosnia and Herzegovina and Dalmatia, Franciscan friars – believed in a melting-pot effect on national and confessional differences in Yugoslavia. They also proposed to organize the State to maintain equilibrium between the

14. Rudolf Horvat, *Hrvatska na mučilištu* (Zagreb: Kulturno-historijsko društvo "Hrvatski rodoljub," 1942) 50-51.
15. Banac, *The National Question in Yugoslavia*, 264-266.
16. Plural of Ustaša.

Catholic and Orthodox provinces.[17] The leadership of the 'Catholic' party was opposed to Radić's party, accusing it of a lack of clear cultural, economic, social, and political principles. Given Radić's popularity, the critique of the 'clericalists' brought about their own downfall; in the elections of 1927, the party performed very badly, and it never revived after King Aleksandar banned it, together with other Croatian organizations, in 1929.[18]

Croatian historiography failed to notice that the existence of the Croat People's Party caused a division in the ranks of Catholic organizations. Many Catholics could not go along with the pro-Yugoslav ideology of the HPS and voted for Radić's H(R)SS, even though it was critical, often excessively so, of 'clericalism'. They organized themselves in the Croatian Eagle's Union (after 1929, Crusader's Brotherhood) and adhered to the principles of the Catholic Action, introduced in the Church as an official form of apostolate of the laypersons in 1922. True, the ideological differences between those two branches of the Catholic Movement diminished after King Aleksandar abolished all Croat organizations in 1929, but they never managed to unite their mutual organizations.[19]

Finally, an important role in Croatian politics between the two wars was played by the party of Croat Serbs, Demokratska stranka (DS, Democratic Party) and its leader Svetozar Pribićević (1875-1936). Driven by unitarist Yugoslavism, Pribićević and his followers – some of them were Croats – had great faith in a centralized state, determined to be achieved even at the price of annihilating the opponents. The opponents, of course, were Radić and other Croats, actually anyone or anything that showed Croat 'separatist' features,[20] and centralism meant furthering of Serbian predomi-

---

17. Zlatko Matijević, *Slom politike katoličkog jugoslavenstva: Hrvatska pučka stranka u političkom životu Kraljevine SHS* (Zagreb: Hrvatski institut za povijest/Dom i svijet, 1998).

18. *Ibid.*

19. Zlatko Matijević, "Katolici i politika: Spor između stranačkoga Hrvatskog katoličkog pokreta i izvanstranačke Katoličke akcije," *Časopis za suvremenu povijest* 29, no. 3 (1997) 437-456; id., "Hrvatski katolički Seniorata i politika (1912-1919)," *Croatica Christiana Periodica* 24, no. 46 (2000) 121-162; id., "Hrvatski katolički pokret i politika," *Croatica Christiana Periodica* 25, no. 47 (2001) 181-205; Jure Krišto, *Hrvatski katolički pokret 1903-1945* (Zagreb: Hrvatski institut za povijest/Glas koncila, 2004).

20. Banac, *The National Question in Yugoslavia*, 169-189; Hrvoje Matković, *Svetozar Pribićević i Samostalna demokratska stranka do šestojanuarske diktature* (Zagreb: Sveučilište u Zagrebu/Institut za hrvatsku povijest, 1972); Ljubo Boban, *Svetozar*

nance. The results of such trends are visible in the distribution of ministerial positions (Table 2).

Table 2. Yugoslavia's cabinets from 1918 to 1938[21]

Ministers	Ministries Total	Big[22]	Economic	Small
Serbians	399	208	133	58
Serbs from outside Serbia	53	23	19	11
Croats of National Parties	26	2	19	5
Croats by descent[23]	111	14	56	41
Slovenes	49	5	58	6
Bosnian Muslims	18	0	14	4
Total	656	252	299	125

The Croats experienced the oppressive nature of Fascism from the moment it assumed power in Italy. Securing, in the secret portion of the London Agreement of 1915, the promise of the acquisition of Dalmatia for engaging in the First World War on the side of the Entente, Italy in 1918 occupied the most important Croatian islands, as well as the city of Zadar. Through the Rapall Agreement with the Kingdom of Yugoslavia in 1922, Italy annexed Istria, some islands, and the city of Zadar (see Map 1). This concession to Italy by the Yugoslav government is stored in Croatian collective memory as a bitter episode. However, the experience that ensued under Fascist rule is more deeply imprinted in that memory. From 1922 to 1929, in Croatian occupied territories the Fascists issued laws and regulations that imposed Italian language as the official language in public offices, Italianized Croatian toponyms and last names, mandated Italian as the language of instruction in schools and educational institutions, and the like. The Croat population was submitted to

---

Pribićević u opoziciji 1929-1936 (Zagreb: Sveučilište u Zagrebu/Institut za hrvatsku povijest, 1973).

21. Table provided by Rudolf Bićanić, *Ekonomska podloga hrvatskog pitanja* (Zagreb: Vladko Maček, ²1938) 63-67, cited by Banac, *The National Question in Yugoslavia*, 217.

22. Big ministries are: premiership, foreign affairs, interior, army, finances, justice, and education.

23. Unitarist Croats.

Map 1. Croatian territory annexed by Italy after the first World War

some of the most brutal treatments; the Fascist speciality was the forceful application on a number of them of castor oil that causes heavy diarrhea.[24]

The role of the Catholic clergy in preserving the Croatian language and culture appeared more evident in the Italian dominated

---

24. Darko Dukovski, "Politički, gospodarski i socijalni uzroci egzoduza istarskih Hrvata u vrijeme talijanske uprave 1918.-1943.," *Talijanska uprava na hrvatskom prostoru i egzodus Hrvata (1918.-1943.)* (Zagreb: Hrvatski institut za povijest/Društvo "Egzodus istarskih Hrvata," 2001) 99-141, and other articles in that volume of the Proceedings of the international conference on Italian rule in Croatian territories and the exodus of Croats.

than in other Croat areas. Hence, the Croat Catholic clergy also became the target of Fascist harassment. After the Lateran Agreement that Mussolini signed with the Church in 1929, the Fascists were more successful in replacing Croatian parish clergymen by Italian ones. In 1927, the Fascists issued the ordinance for Istria that the religious education should also be taught in Italian. Failure to comply with the ordinance risked terrorizing carried out by the 'black shirts'.[25]

2. Developments before the War

In the late 1930's, Yugoslav politics echoed the turbulence in the rest of Europe. After the Croatian Peasant Party (Vladko Maček took over the party after the death of S. Radić in 1928) demonstrated its strength in the parliamentarian election in December 1938 (winning almost 800,000 votes), Serbian politicians began to realize that the political situation in Yugoslavia could not be settled without conceding some type of independence to Croats. The fact that in October 1938 Hitler seized Sudetenland and that the threat of war loomed closer was an important consideration. France and Great Britain, which traditionally had great influence on Yugoslavia, urged the Serbs to make an agreement with Croats for the benefit of Yugoslavia's future.[26] Indeed, Maček began negotiations in 1938 and concluded them with the Prime Minister Dragiša Cvetković in June 1939.[27] The Banovina Hrvatska was granted to the Croats, an autonomous unit that encompassed traditional Croat territories, (except those under Italian occupation), including counties in Northern Bosnia and in Herzegovina (see Map 2). Banovina had its *Sabor* and its *Ban* (Viceroy) that passed legislation and organized the functioning of all aspects of life: internal affairs, justice system, education, health, social services, trade, industry, etc. Ivan Šubašić, a deputy in the Narodna skupština (National Assembly of Yugoslavia), became *Ban*. In the restructuring of the Yugoslav government, Maček became vice president.

25. Dukovski, "Politički, gospodarski i socijalni uzroci," 109.
26. Ivo Perić, *Povijest Hrvata* (Zagreb: Centar za transfer tehnologije, 1997) 228; Josip Jurčević, *Bleiburg. Jugoslavenski poratni zločini nad Hrvatima* (Zagreb: Dokumentacijsko informacijsko središte, 2005) 20-29.
27. For more information on the Agreement see Branko M. Pešelj, "Serbo-Croatian Agreement of 1939 and American Foreign Policy," *Journal of Croatian Studies*, nos. 11-12 (1970-1971) 3-82.

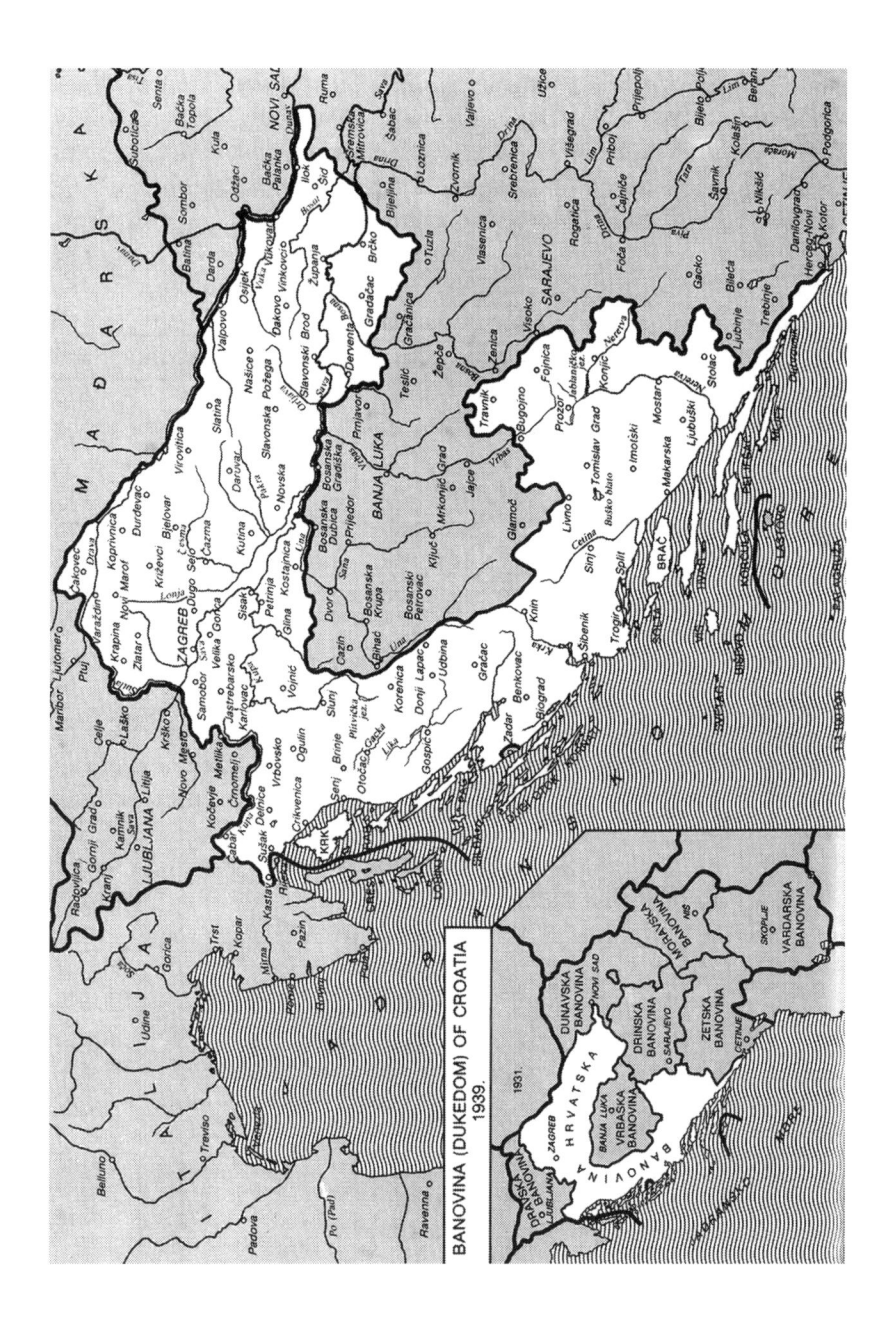

THE CATHOLIC CHURCH IN CROATIA AND BOSNIA-HERZEGOVINA 49

Map 2. Banovina of Croatia, 1939

Many were dissatisfied with that solution, however. Croatian nationalists suspected that Maček gave up the idea of an independent Croatia, while Serb nationalists thought that Banovina Hrvatska entailed the destruction of Yugoslavia and the betrayal of Serb interests (creation of Great Serbia). The latter initiated the movement Srbi na okup (Serbs assemble) and began an uprising against the Croatian banate.

The Archbishop of Zagreb, Alojzije Stepinac (read Stepinatz, 1898-1960), was one of the youngest prelates of the Church when in 1937 he succeeded Antun Bauer in the Zagreb archbishopric and became the primate of Croatia. He was inexperienced in political dealings, but he had a firm character and was a faithful follower of Church's moral and faith teachings. His archbishopric was huge and the most active part of the flock disunited. By the end of the 30's, however, both camps were drawn to Frankists (Ustaše) more than to Maček's HSS. Writers were attracted to new themes: Communism, Free Masonry, Jews, corporatism, and social encyclicals. Communism, Free Masonry, and Jews were put into the category of anti-Catholicism. Catholic intellectuals also agreed that the best state organization is based on principles of corporatism, even though they did not think that its concrete realizations in Italy, Germany, Austria, Portugal, and Poland were completely successful.[28] They argued that Christian corporatism differed from the Fascist form, which advocated the total control of corporate units by the state.[29] In fact, Croatian Catholics were explicit in their condemnation of Fascism and National Socialism as systems, especially their views on racism. The most unequivocal was Archbishop Stepinac. He warned of the godlessness of the National Socialist ideology in 1938.[30] He clearly assessed that National Socialism meant returning humanity to "paganism."[31] On March 12, 1940, while commenting on the general political situation, he noted "God protect us from the 'guardianship' of the National Socialist *Reich*. That would mean a definite end of European civilization, and especially of the Croatian people."[32] In a similar vein, he said to the leader of Croatian nationalists (Frankists or Ustaše)

---

28. J. Š. [Janko Šimrak], "Načela korporativnoga uređenja društva po enciklici 'Quadragesimo anno'," *Luč* 30, nos. 9-10 (1934-35) 7-8.

29. *Ibid.*; cf. Karlo Grimm, "Korporacijski uređeno društvo," *Život* 15, no. 8 (1934) 354-362; no. 9, 398-408; Tomo Habdija, "Problem korporativnog uređenja države," *Luč* 31, no. 1 (1935-36) 12.

30. See: *Novo doba* 21, no. 219 (1938) 2.

31. *Hrvatica* 2, no. 3 (1940) 3.

32. "Dnevnik Alojzija Stepinca," *Danas* (July 3, 1990) 66.

in Croatia, Mile Budak, "We [...] object to the evil idea of pagan nationalism as has appeared in Germany, because the Catholic Church cannot accept such a doctrine."[33]

III. World War II and the Proclamation of the Independent State of Croatia

1. Political and Military Situation

Following the German invasion of Poland on September 1, 1939, which brought about the beginning of World War II, the political leadership of the Kingdom of Yugoslavia tried to avoid giving Germany any pretext for drawing it into the war. The foreign minister Dragiša Cvetković on March 25, 1941 signed an agreement to join the alliance of Germany, Italy, and Japan. The Serbs, however, led by General Dušan T. Simović and the Serbian Orthodox Church, and instigated by British interests, conducted a *coup d'état* on March 27, 1941 (the seventeen-year old Petar II was placed on the throne).[34] In order to keep the peace, Simović's government assured the Croats that it would preserve the political and territorial autonomy granted to them earlier. Moreover, Vladko Maček was offered the position of deputy-prime minister in the government. Maček, with the urging of the American Consul to Zagreb, John James Meily,[35] accepted the offer and joined the government in Belgrade on the evening of April 3, 1941.[36]

On April 6, the Axis forces attacked Yugoslavia. King Petar II and the government fled Belgrade on April 7. Maček submitted his resignation

---

33. *Danas* (July 24, 1990) 67.
34. Tomislav Jonjić, *Hrvatska vanjska politika 1903-1945*. Vol. 3: *Hrvatska vanjska politika 1939-1942* (Zagreb: Libar, 2000) 213-250; Branko Petranović and Nikola Žutić, *27. mart 1941* (Beograd: Nikom, 1990); Tomasevich, *The Chetniks*, 34-47.
35. Gray to Hull, Belgrade, Telegram 315, April 3, 1941, 19h, *Records of the Department of State Relating to Internal Affairs of Yugoslavia 1930-1944* (Hereafter: *Records*), 860H.00/1268 (Washington, DC: National Archives Microfilm Publications) 1203, reel 16. Even though the State Department on April 21 expressed the opinion that the Zagreb Consulate should be closed, on the recommendation of consul Meiley it remained opened until June 22, when Mladen Lorković, the Minister of Foreign Affairs, following an identical step by Germany, asked the Consul to close the Consulate and to leave the country by July 15.
36. See: *Jugoslavenske vlade u izbjeglištvu 1941-1943. Dokumenti*, ed. Bogdan Krizman (Zagreb-Beograd: Globus/Arhiv Jugoslavije, 1981) 5-94; Jere Jareb, *Pola stoljeća hrvatske politike* (Zagreb: Hrvatski institut za povijest, 1995) 74-75; Jonjić, *Hrvatska vanjska politika*, 229-221.

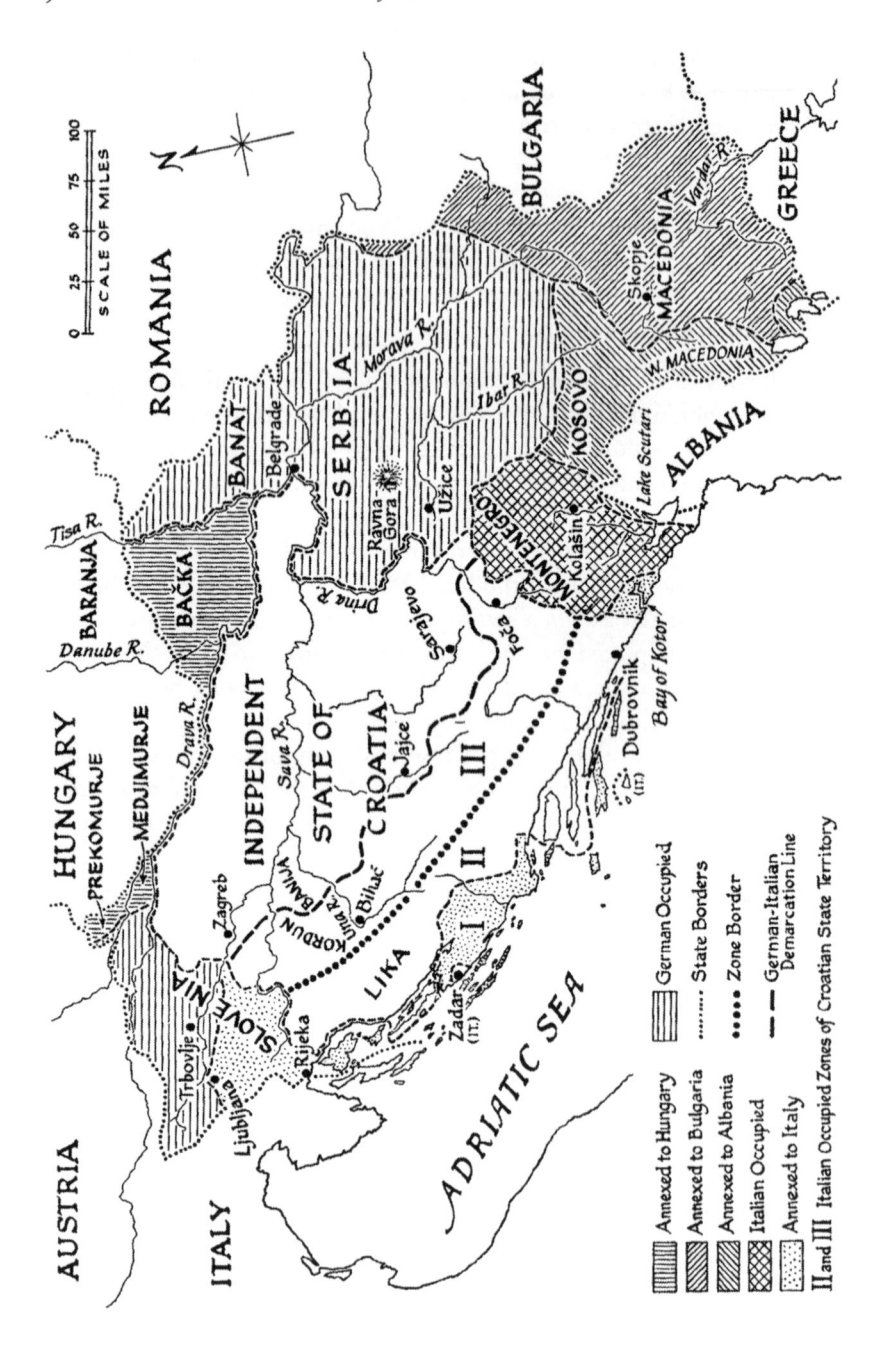

Map 3. The partition of the Independent State of Croatia, 1941

as deputy-prime minister and sent his deputy, Juraj Krnjević (1895-1988) to take his place in the government. He withdrew to his residence in Kupinec near Zagreb.[37] Croatian politicians of various ideologies and party affiliations (HSS, Ustaše, and independent members) took steps to proclaim Croatian independence.[38] They were helped by a spontaneous rebellion by the Croatian members of the Yugoslav Army and by the paramilitary units under HSS influence (*Građanska* and *Seljačka zaštita*), who began disarming Serbian officers and conscripts and proclaiming the independence of the Croatian state.[39] Vladko Maček, as the leader of the strongest Croatian political party, was offered by the Ustaše and urged by Germans to head the Croatian state, but he refused their offer. Slavko Kvaternik (1878-1947), the Ustaše leader and son-in-law of Josip Frank, took it upon himself to announce on the Croatian radio the establishment of the Independent State of Croatia (NDH) on April 10, 1941. The first German troops entered Zagreb as Kvaternik's radio message was being broadcast. On April 15, Ante Pavelić returned from Italy and assumed power in Zagreb as *Poglavnik* (Head).

In addition to the territories that Banovina Hrvatska encompassed, the Independent State of Croatia included eastern Srijem, which had been Croat territory before Croatia first entered Yugoslavia, and parts of Bosnia and Herzegovina that did not enter Banovina (see Map 3). The population of the state was around 6,000,000, of which close to 2 million were Serbs and almost 1 million Muslims. The Muslims lived predominantly in Bosnia and Herzegovina and a substantial number considered themselves Croats, so they did not have problems in siding with the NDH. That was not the case with the Serb population, which soon became subjected to the newly created state. Approximately 300,000 Croats remained under

---

37. Maček later asserted that the Germans forced him to withdraw to his property in Kupinec; see *Stepinac mu je ime*, ed. Vinko Nikolić, vol. 1, Knijžnica Hrvatska revija, 9 (München, 1978) 231-232. Cf. Zdenko Radelić, *Hrvatska seljačka stranka 1941-1950* (Zagreb: Hrvatski institut za povijest, 1996) 21-31; Jareb, *Pola stoljeća hrvatske politike*, 75-77; *Jugoslavenske vlade u izbjeglištvu*, 10.

38. Bogdan Krizman, *Pavelić i ustaše* (Zagreb: Globus, 1978) 362-363; Jere Jareb, "Svjedočanstvo Janka Tortića o Hrvatskoj seljačkoj stranci i o travanjskim događajima 1941," *Časopis za suvremenu povijest*, 28, no. 2 (1997) 325-367; Marko Sinovčić, *N.D.H. u svietlu dokumenata* (Zagreb: Vratna gora, ²1998) 95-98; Jonjić, *Hrvatska vanjska politika*, 283-285.

39. Ferdo Čulinović, *Dokumenti o Jugoslaviji* (Zagreb: Školska knjiga, 1968) 387-388; Vasa Kazimirović, *NDH u svetlu nemačkih dokumenata i dnevnika Gleza fon Horstenau 1941-1944* (Beograd: Nova knjiga/Narodna knjiga, 1987) 111; Fikreta Jelić-Butić, *Hrvatska seljačka stranka* (Zagreb: Globus, 1983) 47; id., *Ustaše i Nezavisna Država Hrvatska* (Zagreb: Sveučilišna naklada Liber/Školska knjiga, 1977) 77; Jareb, *Pola stoljeća hrvatske politike*, 82; Jonjić, *Hrvatska vanjska politika*, 266, 283-285.

Italian occupation. The cities of Rijeka and Istria were not included in the NDH, since they were under Italy, according to the provisions of the London Agreement of 1915. There was also a maximum of 35,000 Jews, including those that fled the Nazi persecutions in other parts of Europe. More than half of the Jewish population lived in Zagreb.

Most Croats were elated when they heard the proclamation of the NDH. The Catholic Church hierarchy and the lower clergy concurred with the people.[40] The reason for the joy was separation from Serbia and the establishment of a state of their own, with no attention to the circumstances. The elation did not last long, however. Before the new government was able to take full control of the administration of the country, it found itself engulfed in an upheaval that would prove to be the cause of its demise. The Germans and Italians defined their political and territorial interests within Croatia, thus dividing the country in half and placing the government of 'independent' Croatia under their control, especially regarding military and other security matters. The Italians, moreover, immediately annexed a good portion of the Adriatic littoral and most of islands, and later imposed their military rule over a major portion of 'their' part of the NDH (see Map 3).[41] These arrangements were agreed upon by the treaties signed in Rome on May 18, 1941.

In fact, Pavelić had little choice, even though he knew that those treaties were humiliating to Croats and a severe setback to Pavelić himself. As they had done earlier in Istria, the city of Zadar, and other annexed Croatian territories, the Italians applied cruel measures of subjugating the Croatian populace in the annexed parts, and in the part of the NDH controlled by them, in an attempt to eradicate the people's identity and traditions. They used the Serb population of the NDH to control, persecute, and expel Croats from areas where there was a substantial Serb population.[42] Italy organized several concentration camps for Croats, the biggest of which was on Molat Island.[43] The Germans, in 'their' part of the NDH, pressured the government on its policies towards the Jews (Italians

---

40. Jure Krišto, *Sukob simbola: Politika, vjere i ideologije u Nezavisnoj Državi Hrvatskoj* (Zagreb: Nakladni zavod Globus, 2001) 38-39.

41. Zdravko Dizdar, "Italian Policies toward Croatians in Occupied Territories during the Second World War," *Review of Croatian History* 1, no. 1 (2005) 179-210; Tomasevich, *The Chetniks*, 100; Frank P. Verna, "Notes on Italian Rule on Dalmatia under Bastianini, 1941-1943," *The International History Review* 12 (1990) 528-529; *Talijanska uprava na hrvatskom prostoru i egzodus Hrvata*.

42. Tomasevich, *The Chetniks*, 101-104; *Talijanska uprava na hrvatskom prostoru i egzodus Hrvata*.

43. Dizdar, "Italian Policies toward Croatians in Occupied Territories," 193-194.

applied far more lenient measures in the areas they dominated). Neither Italy nor Germany allowed Pavelić to develop any sizable armed forces.

The Orthodox Serbs mounted an armed revolt against the NDH and joined the Chetnik formations of Draža Mihailović to fight for the restitution of the Monarchy (actually for the creation of Great Serbia). They executed 246 Croatian civilians in eleven major massacres before the Croats responded in kind on April 27, 1941 by killing 176 Serbs near Bjelovar.[44] On June 22, 1941 the Croatian Communists began their uprising, and also fought against the NDH. They also wanted the renewal of Yugoslavia, but modelled after the communist Soviet Union. They were, therefore, interested in a Communist revolution that would be achieved in the entire territory of Yugoslavia. The Communist party had no significant strength in Yugoslavia before the war, even though they were well organized and their numbers increased in the late 1930's. Above all, they were prepared to obey the instructions of the Commintern. Hence, it is not surprising that they began their uprising on the day of Hitler's invasion of the Soviet Union. Their leader Josip Broz Tito, a Croat, soon after the founding of the NDH, moved to Belgrade, convinced that he would not have much success among the Croats, who obviously liked the idea of independence. In Serbia, Tito also had meagre success, because the leader of the Chetniks Draža Mihailović refused to join him in his resistance to Germany and Italy.

Finally, the Muslim population used the NDH to achieve their political and other goals. In the beginning, they used the Ustaše's inclination to settle old scores with the Serbian population in their villages, later, they sought Hitler's favour to achieve the independence of Bosnia, and finally they joined the Communists-led Partisans in massive numbers.[45] So the entire territory of NDH was engulfed in civil war, in which the fighting sides forged alliances and just as easily broke them. In addition to the presence of German and Italian military forces, both Communist-led Partisans and Chetniks fought the Croatian regular army, while at the same time Partisans and Chetniks tried to eliminate each other.

The Croatian government made the already difficult situation worse by introducing extremely bad policies in the areas and domains in which it was allowed to operate. The Serbs were excluded from practically all

---

44. Philip J. Cohen, *Serbia's Secret War: Propaganda and the Deceit of History*, East European Studies, 2 (College Station, TX: Texas A&M University Press, 1996); id., "Holocaust History Misappropriated," *Midstream: A Monthly Jewish Review* 38, no. 8 (November 1992) 18-20.

45. Enver Redžić, *Bosna i Hercegovina u Drugom svjetskom ratu* (Sarajevo: OKO, 1998).

government employment and from work in some professions, especially the mass media.[46] Pavelić reached an accord with Hitler in June 1941 that Croatia would receive any Slovenes Hitler expelled from Carinthia and other areas, and the same number of Serbs would be extradited to Serbia. At the end of June the government began organizing detention and work-camps and sending Serbs and other opponents of the regime to them. German data specify that 118,110 Serbs were transported to Serbia.[47] Many of them probably fled from their own choice. The program apparently ended when the Germans could no longer handle the influx of refugees in Serbia.

On April 30, 1941 racial laws were proclaimed, which were the foundation for the anti-Jewish measures that ensued. The Jews were ordered to wear yellow armbands, forbidden to sign business contracts, and their property was seized. Two weeks earlier, on April 14, 1941 the synagogue in Osijek had been burnt down, later the synagogue of Zagreb and other towns were destroyed. Surprisingly, the Jewish Religious Congregation was active during the entire duration of the NDH.[48] Many Jews and Gypsies were sent to the labour camps.[49]

It should be also noted that the Ustaša Government was an authoritarian regime that pretended to have some democratic features. Thus, Pavelić renewed the institution of the Croat *Sabor* made up of those members who had been in the session before 1918, and were designated 'important' persons from public life. The *Sabor* convened only three times during the four years of Pavelić's power and was under his control. Given the nature of the regime, Croats of the 'wrong' political and ideological viewpoints were not protected from persecution and imprisonment in labour camps. Communists and (leftist) members of the HSS were held to be under greatest suspicion. Even a Catholic priest was sentenced to death (later he received clemency) because he offended the *Poglavnik* (Pavelić).

2. *Church Opposition to Government and National Socialist Policies*

The organization of the Catholic Church did not change in the NDH (see Map 4). The Zagreb archdiocese encompassed most of the

46. Independent State of Croatia, Ministry of Justice and Religion, *Zbornik zakona i naredaba Nezavisne Države Hrvatske – 1941*; Tomasevich, *The Chetniks*, 106.
47. Cited by Tomasevich, *The Chetniks*, 106.
48. Harriet Pass Freidenreich, *The Jews in Yugoslavia: A Quest for Community* (Philadelphia, PA: The Jewish Publication Society of America, 1979) 191.
49. Narcisa Lengel Krizman, "Camps for Jews in the Independent State of Croatia," *Anti-Semitism, Holocaust, Anti-Fascism* (Zagreb: Zagreb Jewish Community, 1997) 89-101.

THE CATHOLIC CHURCH IN CROATIA AND BOSNIA-HERZEGOVINA

Map 4. Organization of the Catholic Church in Croatia

territory of Northern Croatia (Archbishop Stepinac), with the Djakovo diocese (Bishop Antun Akšamović) covering the east of the territories bordering with Vojvodina and Serbia. The archdiocese of Sarajevo (Vrhbosna – Archbishop Ivan Šarić) coincided with the territory of Bosnia and Herzegovina, with the dioceses of Mostar (Bishop Alojzije Mišić) and Banja Luka (Bishop Josip Garić). The diocese of Mostar was under Italian control, just as the dioceses along the Adriatic coast, Split (Bishop Kvirin Klement Bonefačić), Šibenik (Bishop Jeronim Mileta), and Senj (Bishop Viktor Burić). The dioceses of Istria with the city of Rijeka, the island of Krk, with some other islands, and Zadar were in the areas annexed by Italy.

As mentioned, most members of the Catholic higher hierarchy were pleased by the proclamation of Croatian independence and all of them undoubtedly considered the NDH a legitimate Croatian state. Catholic organizations in Croatia reacted similarly to the new state. The fraction of the Croatian Catholic Movement that organized the 'Catholic' Croat People's Party was dissolved, because its leadership was aware that the Ustaše, the core of the new government, disliked its pro-Yugoslav ideology. Nonetheless, some of their leading members were loyal to the new government, among them the literary critic Ljubomir Maraković, the writer Petar Grgec, the president of the Seniorate, Andrija Živković, and two clergymen: Janko Penić and Janko Šimrak. Others, however, went into the opposition, such as Vladimir Gortan, Milivoj Sironić, Mate Ujević, and Velimir Deželić, among others.[50] The other fraction, the Crusaders, embraced the new regime and some of their leading men and women took government positions, such as Ivan Oršanić, Felix Nedzielsky, Dušan Žanko, and Milivoj Cerovac. However, their president, Lav Znidarčić, kept the organization out of politics.[51]

The relations between the Church and the State began to change when, at the end of April 1941, the new authority began promulgating the racial policy of its Nazi ally. The Church hierarchy expressed its disagreement with such practice. The intensity of this disagreement increased with time, finally reaching the stage in 1942 and particularly in 1943 when some governmental bodies even considered physically liquidating the head of the Church and the most active Church prelate, Zagreb Archbishop Stepinac.[52]

50. Hrvatski Državni Arhiv (hereafter: HDA), Ministarstvo unutarnjih poslova Republike Hrvatske (hereafter: MUP RH), 001.4, 2. 9, 2.
51. Krišto, *Hrvatski katolički pokret*, 243-246.
52. Krišto, *Sukob simbola*, 79-80, 88-89.

Not all Church leaders reacted in the same way or with the same urgency. If one judges by the writing in the Sarajevo *Katolički tjednik* (Catholic Weekly), the leadership of the Vrhbosna Archdiocese of Sarajevo, headed by Archbishop Ivan Šarić, was the slowest to criticize the civil government. There are several reasons why some Catholic bishops were not in a hurry to criticize the new government and its policies. First, unlike previous political situations and regimes, Croats in general, and Catholics in particular, considered the new Croatian government, dominated by Ustaše as being eminently theirs. All previous governments had been foreign and oppressive, and now for the first time, the Croats had come into power. Second, many Catholics saw the writing of God's finger in allowing Croats to finally have their own state. It was part of the popular fantasy that the NDH was God's reward to Croats for their struggle for "the honoured cross and golden freedom" (Croats, like some other nations, claimed the title *antemurale Christianitatis*) and their past suffering.[53] The Catholics had an additional reason for their loyalty to the new government in the fact that Pavelić portrayed himself as a 'good Catholic' and promised to work on the introduction of 'Christian values' to the new Croatian society.[54] Indeed, the government paid considerable attention to public morality by issuing strict ordinances against prostitution, abortion, drunkenness, cursing, and similar public vices. The Ustaše often drastically punished their members for transgressions of public morality. Those policies of the government were often met with applause from the Church hierarchy.[55] Other policies, which definitely contradicted Christian morality, were looked upon as strictly government responsibility, while the Church should be preoccupied with the private moral domain.[56] The government itself advocated that view, often reminding Church leaders that their business was not to meddle in government policies. As mentioned, the bishops rejected such views with different speed and in different forms. The Government could count on some extra understanding by the Church leaders, because it had to deal with the rebellion against the country.

Nonetheless, after the initial enthusiasm had become deflated, even the most ardent supporters of Croatian statehood became critical of govern-

53. *Katolički list* (1941) nos. 21-22, 245.
54. "Za sistem ćudorednih reformi (Povodom mjera za zaštitu narodnog morala)," *Katolički tjednik* 17 (20), no. 21 (May 25, 1941) 1.
55. K, "U znaku žrtve (Uz povratak Hrvatskih Ustaša)," *Katolički tjednik* 17 (20), no. 17 (April, 27, 1941) 6.
56. "Pravni narod – pravna država," *Katolički tjednik* 17 (20), no 28 (July 13, 1941) 1; Č, "Dokument kulture i kršćanstva," *Katolički tjednik* 17 (20), no. 22 (June 1, 1941) 5-6.

ment policies. Since the government was repressive, the population reacted mostly through passive resistance and disobedience. Increasingly, people, especially in areas under Italian control joined active armed resistance.[57] The most eloquent critic among the Catholic elite, not only of the Ustaše government's policies, but of the National Socialist ideology and Fascist practices was the Zagreb Archbishop Stepinac. It is important to note that, due to the difficulties of communication caused by war operations, Catholic bishops delegated Stepinac, as the head of the Bishops Conference, to be their spokesman with the government, so that his activities in that regard may be considered the policy of the entire hierarchal body of the Church in the NDH. It should also be remembered that the bishops of the dioceses in the south and along the Adriatic coast, where Italians imposed their control, were preoccupied with a different sets of problems.

a. Public Protest in Sermons

Unfortunately, studies about the influences of parish priests' sermons on the behaviour of the faithful, and about multifarious forms of oblique meaning those sermons used to guide the faithful in inimical circumstances, have not been done for Croatia in the way that Vesna Drapac did for France, especially the city of Paris.[58] However, we have an abundance of public sermons by the Archbishop of Zagreb which illustrate how direct he was in criticizing both the National Socialist ideology and the Croatian government's policy. It was also common knowledge that even those who rarely attended church services made an effort to go to Stepinac's homilies.[59]

I will cite some portions of those sermons. For the feast of Christ the King, October 26, 1941, the Archbishop said: "During the last few decades, various Godless theories have succeeded in poisoning the world, so that the hatred seems to have become the motor of all human actions. The danger is that even those who pride themselves with a Catholic name, or should I say even with a spiritual vocation, become victims of the passion of hatred and forget the law that is the nicest characteristic of

---

57. See e.g. the position of Dr. Ins. Even though he presents a quasi-theological explanation of Jewish suffering as a consequence of their rejection of Christ as Messiah, he did not approve of political measures against the Jews, as he had done earlier; Dr. Ins, "Židovi," *Katolički tjednik* 17 (20), no. 31 (August 3, 1941) 3-4; "Kler," *Katolički tjednik* 17 (20), no. 29 (July 20, 1941) 1.

58. Vesna Drapac, *War and Religion: Catholics in the Churches of Occupied Paris* (Washington, DC: Catholic University of America Press, 1998).

59. Vladimir Žerjavić, of socialist leanings, told me about his and other people's visits to Zagreb Cathedral to hear the Archbishop.

Christianity, the law of love."[60] A year later, on a similar occasion, Stepinac addressed the issue of race on October 25, 1942. He emphasized the Christian belief that "all nations and all races come from God" and that "each nation and each race as they appear today on earth has the right to a life worthy of man and the right to treatment worthy of man. All of them without exception, be they members of the Gypsy race or some other, be they Blacks or refined Europeans, be they hated Jews or proud Aryans have the equal right to say: 'Our Father, who art in heaven! (Mt. 6,9).' And if God has given that right to all, no human authority may deny it." Stepinac further asserted that the Catholic Church adhered to those fundamental principles and that it, therefore, "condemned and it condemns today every injustice and violence perpetrated in the name of racial or national theories." Addressing the current political theory and practice, Stepinac specified that "it is not permissible to eradicate from the face of the earth the Gypsies or the Jews, because they are considered of an inferior race," because "no one has the right to kill or in any other way damage at will the members of other races or nationalities."[61]

The French ambassador in Zagreb translated that, and several of Stepinac's sermons, and sent them to his Government. In an accompanying letter dated November 6, 1942 he stated: "The Church […] once again condemned in Zagreb itself the excesses of the regime and its principles. Using the occasion of the feast of Christ the King, Msgr. Stepinac, Archbishop of Zagreb, from the top of the Chair of his cathedral chastised … the National Socialist doctrine concerning race and courageously reminded the congregation that "those before whom today tremble millions, tomorrow even their names will be forgotten."[62] Those were constant themes in Stepinac's public appearances, as the French ambassador communicated to his Government.[63]

---

60. *Katolički list* 92, no. 43 (October 31, 1941) 501-502.
61. *Službeni vjesnik Zagrebačke nadbiskupije* 33, nos. 2-3 (February 13, 1946) 15-16; Aleksa Benigar, *Alojzije Stepinac, Hrvatski kardinal* (Rome: Zajednica izdanja Ranjeni labud, 1974) 409-411.
62. *Archives diplomatiques des Affaires étrangères, Europe* (ADAE) 99, Vichy, 945, Serie Z, box 384, fasc. 1, Gueyraud to Laval, Zagreb, November 6, 1942: "L'Église cependant vient d'affirmer une fois de plus, à Zagreb même, sa condamnation des excès du régime et de ses principes. Saisissant l'occasion de la fête du Christ-Roi, Mgr Stepinac Archevêque de Zagreb, a du haut de la Chaire de sa cathédrale, flétri, … la doctrine nationale-socialiste en matière de race et rappelé avec courage que 'tels devant qui tremblent aujourd'hui des millions d'hommes, demain ils seront obliés jusqu'à leurs noms'…"
63. ADAE, Europe 15, Vichy, 945, Serie Z, box 384, fasc. 1, Gueyraud to Laval, Zagreb, March 20, 1943: "[L'Archevêque] n'a laissé passer aucune occasion de protester contre ces manquements du pouvoir civil à la morale chrétienne."

In 1943, Stepinac used the occasion of the commemoration of the Pope's coronation, on March 14, to address his faithful, which was an echo of the Pope's Christmas radio address. On that occasion the Archbishop said: "Indeed, one of the gravest errors of our times is undoubtedly that the dignity of the human person has come down to nothing... Every man, regardless of the race or the nation he belongs to, regardless of the fact that he has graduated from a university in a prominent European centre or he hunts in search for food in African jungles, each of them carries God's seal and has inalienable rights, which no human government has the right to snatch away or arbitrarily restrict."[64] At the conclusion of the penitential procession on October 31, 1943, Archbishop Stepinac again reacted in his homily to the inhuman treatment of different categories of people by the government: "Condemning all injustices, all killings of the innocent, all burning of peaceful villages, all destruction of the work of poor peasants [referring to Serbs], regretting problems and pains of all who unjustly suffer today, we say this: The Church is for that world order which is as old as the Ten Commandments... Our neighbour, whatever his name, is not a cog in the state machinery, be it coloured red or black, grey or green, but he is a free child of God, our brother in God. That is why we must recognize our neighbours right to life, property, honour... We must respect his family..."[65]

b. Interventions for the Jews

No issue of domestic or foreign politics illustrated better the partition of the country than the position of Jews. While in the southern portion of the NDH the rule "separate, but not eliminate" that the Italian government devised for the Jews was applied, in the northern portion, where the Germans set the rules, the Croatian government, as we have said, issued racial legislation and ran work camps, in which Jews, Croats of 'incorrect' political beliefs, and others were held. The largest and best-organized camp was in Jasenovac, a small town at the confluence of the Una and Sava rivers.[66] That was actually a group of

---

64. Benigar, *Alojzije Stepinac*, 405-407; cf. *Alojzije kardinal Stepinac nadbiskup zagrebački. Propovijedi, govori, poruke*, ed. Juraj Batelja and Celestin Tomić (Zagreb: AGM, 1996) 146-149.

65. Nadbiskupski duhovni stol u Zagrebu, no. 5997/46; *Stepinac mu je ime*, vol. 1, 45-50.

66. Vladimir Žerjavić, *Population Losses in Yugoslavia 1941-1945* (Zagreb: Dom i svijet/Hrvatski institut za povijest, 1997) 73-93; Mihael Sobolevski, "Jews in the Jasenovac Group of Concentration Camps," *Anti-Semitism, Holocaust, Anti-Fascism*, 102-116; Josip Jurčević, *Problem izučavanja žrtava Drugog svjetskog rata na području Hrvatske* (Master degree thesis Zagreb: Filozofski fakultet, Odsjek za povijest, 1996).

camps organized around various industries and enterprises, including a camp for women, where inmates were being taken from August 1941. There has been a great deal of manipulation about the number of persons that died in those camps, depending on political and/or propaganda effects that various groups or individuals wanted to achieve. The figures range from 21,000 to 1,2 million persons. Several counts of victims were ordered by Yugoslav government agencies, and some of them were favourably and falsely increased, because the numbers were too low in comparison to the ones the politicians stated,[67] even though the results were obtained after a proper and complete poll, similar to taking census. According to that poll, victims of *all* camps who were under control of the NDH government and who perished of various causes amounted to 74,835, and the number of victims in the Jasenovac camp was 49,874.[68] Surprisingly, even in the Republic of Croatia, the most widely accepted statistics are not those of the official poll, but of the Croat statistician Vladimir Žerjavić.[69] This is probably because Bogoljub Kočović, also a statistician, but a Serb, arrived at similar results as the Croat.[70] Žerjavić calculated that among the Jews living in Croatia there were a total of 26,000 victims (19,000 died on the territory of Croatia, Bosnia and Herzegovina and 7,000 abroad). Of that total 13,000 Jews died in the Jasenovac camp of various causes.[71]

There are many cases of Croat individuals and religious communities that were engaged in saving Jewish individuals and groups, many of whom have been acknowledged by Yad Vashem as "righteous among nations." Dragutin Jesih, a Catholic priest, was among these. He was shot by either the Ustaše of by the Germans because of protecting Jews as pastor of the parish in Šćitarjevo, near Zagreb. The Bishop of the Greek Catholic (Eastern rite) diocese of Križevci, Janko Šimrak, risked his life by hiding two Jewish youngsters in his seminary. He exposed himself and Archbishop Stepinac to an even greater danger when he

---

67. Mihael Sobolevski, "Prešućena istina – žrtve rata na području bivše Jugoslavije 1941.-1945. prema popisu iz 1964. godine," *Časopis za suvremenu povijest* 25, nos. 2-3 (1993) 87-114; Žerjavić, *Population Losses in Yugoslavia*, 53-103; Jurčević, *Problem izučavanja žrtava Drugog svjetskog rata*.

68. Sobolevski, "Prešućena istina," 96.

69. Vladimir Žerjavić, *Gubici stanovništva Jugoslavije u drugom svjetskom ratu* (Zagreb: Jugoslavensko viktimološko društvo, ³1989); Id., *Population Losses in Yugoslavia*, 53-103.

70. Bogoljub Kočović, *Žrtve drugog svetskog rata u Jugoslaviji* (London: Veritas Foundation Press, 1985).

71. Vladimir Žerjavić, "Demographic Indicators of the Jewish Ordeal in the Independent State of Croatia," *Anti-Semitism, Holocaust, Anti-Fascism*, 129-133.

transferred those boys to a safer place in Stepinac's automobile.[72] Bishops in areas under Italian control needed only be engaged in helping Jews materially, since their lives were not immediately threatened. Thus, Bishop of Split Klement Kvirin Bonefačić helped Jews who fled from Sarajevo, led by their great Rabbi V. Urbach.[73] The Italian authorities undertook measures to confine Jews and thereafter to place them in camps.[74] There they lived in private lodgings, had unrestricted movement, and paid a residency tax.[75] The Vatican has documented numerous interventions, mediations, petitions, and material assistance of the Holy See and its representatives in the NDH, Giuseppe Ramiro Marcone and his secretary Giuseppe Masucci.[76] As might be expected, most examples of helping Jews in various ways are connected to Archbishop Stepinac. He personally undertook private interventions with the Government in order to change legislation, to protect or save people or simply to voice his disagreement with various laws and practices.

As soon as Stepinac heard about the racial laws in Croatia, he wrote to Andrija Artuković, the Minister of the Interior, on April 23, 1941 that he should take into account the Jews who had become Christians.[77] Stepinac knew that there was pressure on the newly installed Croatian government to pass anti-racial laws. Indeed, in a letter to the Minister a month later, Stepinac shows that he was aware of those German pressures. It is for that reason that Stepinac called those laws "necessary." The government officials also gave Stepinac assurances that the laws they had to pass would not actually be enforced.[78] On May 22, 1941 the Archbishop wrote again to Minister Artuković, now reacting against the legal ordinance that Jews should wear a sign (a yellow star or an armband). Having reminded Artuković of his promise that racial laws would not be applied in practice and of the new laws which negated that promise, and while conceding that governments have an obligation to protect the common good, Stepinac continued: "But to take away all

---

72. Tomislav Vuković, "Križevački biskup Janko Šimrak i 'prekrštavanja' u NDH," *Glas koncila* (January 19, 1992) 13.

73. Mile Vidović, *Povijest Crkve u Hrvata* (Split: Crkva u svijetu, 1996) 400.

74. Jaša Romano, *Jevreji Jugoslavije 1941-1945: Žrtve genocida i učesnici NOR-a* (Beograd: Jewish Historical Museum, 1980); Dizdar, "Italian Policies toward Croatians in Occupied Territories," 197-198.

75. Dizdar, "Italian Policies toward Croatians in Occupied Territories," 198.

76. *Actes et documents du Saint Siège relatifs à la seconde guerre mondiale*, passim; Krišto, *Sukob simbola*, 265-322.

77. Pattee, *The Case*, doc. XXV, 299-300.

78. Nadbiskupski Ordinarijat, no. 117, May 22, 1941; Cavalli, *El proceso*, 163-164; Pattee, *The Case*, doc. no. XXVI, 300-302.

means of existence from members of other nations or races and to mark them with the stamp of infamy is a question of humanness and morals. Moral laws, however, apply not only to individuals, but to the state governance as well." Stepinac was quite clear that "members of another race" should not be treated as criminals if they had not committed any crimes, especially in light of the fact that the society had not branded as "infamous or criminal" convicted murderers after their rehabilitation, or notorious adulterers, or prostitutes. Stepinac also used the argument of the harmful consequences for the youth if those laws were promulgated and executed. He reminded Artuković that no human being is to be judged on the basis of race or nationality, and he proceeded by suggesting to the government how "the provision that the Jewish *insignia* must be worn ought to be fulfilled in such a way that generally they ought be suppressed." In the remainder of the letter Stepinac pleaded for the baptized Jews and warned Artuković that he would personally "be forced to tell the Jewish Catholics not to wear these *insignia* in order to avoid trouble and difficulties in the church" and that "the Holy See does not look with favour on these measures."[79] Further on he requested the Minister of the Interior "to give appropriate orders so that the Jewish laws and others similar to them (measures against Serbs, etc.) should be executed in such a way that for every man the personhood and human dignity be respected."[80] On May 30, 1941 Stepinac again wrote to Artuković and suggested how race criteria should not be applied to specific categories of people under repression, especially to baptized Jews.[81]

Throughout 1942, Stepinac was very closely involved in the saving of Jewish youngsters from Zagreb, most of whose parents were in camps. The Jewish Assembly in Zagreb wanted to transfer 200 youngsters to Italy, but the Italian Government was strongly against it. The Assembly then asked Stepinac to mediate with the Ministry of the Interior to

---

79. Nadbiskupski Ordinarijat, no. 117, May 22, 1941; *Stepinac mu je ime*, vol. 1, 54; *Fontes* 2 (1996) 159-161; Cavalli, *El proceso*, 163-164; Pattee, *The Case*, doc. XXVI, 300-302.

80. This request of Stepinac has been branded by some authors as scandalous (Ivo Goldstein, *Holokaust u Zagrebu* [Zagreb: Novi Liber/Židovska općina, 2001]). It seems, however, that such a conclusion is not warranted if the entire letter is taken into consideration. It seems that Stepinac appropriated sound moral standards from the very beginning of the new state, even if one takes into consideration that he, like other bishops, gave the new government a chance to recover from the disorder that had existed from its inception.

81. HAD, Ostavština Politeo, 328-330; Margareta Matijević, "Stepinčev 'Dossier'," *Croatica Christiana Periodica* 21, no. 40 (1997) 114-116; Pattee, *The Case*, doc. XXVI, 302-305.

allow the transfer of 50 young people to Turkey. Stepinac personally carried his petition to the Ministry, and 11 of them were allowed to depart in February 1943. Stepinac then asked that in addition to the remainder of the children from the group he petitioned, 50 more youngsters be allowed to leave for Turkey. The Secretary of State, Cardinal Maglione, mediated in securing their safe passage through Hungary, and the operation was successful. Among the youngsters saved from Zagreb was the son of the Zagreb Rabbi Miroslav Šalom Freiberger.[82] When news began to spread that the remaining Jews were being apprehended and taken to concentration camps, Stepinac on March 7, 1942 wrote once more to Artuković, asking that "all unjust treatment of citizens who have not committed any act for which they could be punished" must stop.[83] He was also aware, however, that the Government could not do much to help Jews.

c. The Catholic Church and the Orthodox Serbs

As already indicated, the Serbs showed determined opposition to having to live in a Croat state. The Ustaše responded in kind and, in fact, increased their terror tactics against the Orthodox community after June 22, 1941, the date of confluence of three important events: Hitler's invasion of Russia, the Communist rebellion in the NDH, and the decrease of German forces in the territory of former Yugoslavia because of war operations on the Eastern front.

Given past experience and the present political situation, it might be expected that Catholic Croats in general would be less prepared to assist the Serbs. Nonetheless, Catholic Bishops, and many faithful, applied the same principles to the endangered Serb Orthodox people as they did to the persecution of Jews. Catholic Bishops tried to put pressure on local government representatives to stop the persecution of innocent civilians or to alleviate their suffering.[84] In some areas, especially in Bosnia and Herzegovina, where Catholics were mixed with Muslims and the Orthodox population, the Bishops' influence was minimal or completely nonexistent. The new rulers in Croatia promoted the ideology that Muslims were the 'purest' section of the Croatian nation, which was one of the reasons why so many Muslims of Bosnia and Herzegovina joined the

---

82. See Krišto, *Katolička crkva*, 305-306; id., *Sukob simbola*, 284-289.
83. HAD, Ostavština Politeo, 120; Ivan Cvitković, *Ko je bio Alojzije Stepinac* (Sarajevo: "Oslobođenje" 1986) 199.
84. Krišto, *Sukob simbola*, 134-144.

Ustaše ranks. They were actually behind many persecutions and massacres of civilians there, because Muslims have had a long-standing grievance against the Serbs.[85] Those Muslims and others behind the massacres earned the name of 'wild Ustaše' or *nastashe*, a Croatian word indicating their *becoming* Ustaše for opportunistic reasons.[86]

The first known intervention of a Bishop in favour of the Serbs was already in April 1941, when Archbishop Stepinac mediated the release from prison of the Zagreb Orthodox Metropolitan Dositej.[87] Stepinac's strongest known written protest against the persecution of Serbs was the letter to Pavelić of May 14, 1941, after he learned about the killing of 260 Serbs in Glina, a town south-east of Zagreb. Stepinac was aware that the Serbs had committed grave crimes against the Croats during the preceding twenty years, but he was also convinced that "according to the Catholic morals, this is not permissible," and he, therefore, asked Pavelić "to take the most urgent measures, in the entire territory of the Independent State of Croatia, that no Serb be killed, if there is no proof that he committed a crime that deserves death."[88]

Other Croatian bishops also showed their concern. The Archbishop of Belgrade Josip Ujčić, a Croat, tried in different ways to intervene for Orthodox Serbs in the NDH. Informing Archbishop Stepinac on June 11, 1941 of protests by the Serb refugees from Croatia concerning their treatment, he asked Stepinac to convey his concerns to the Croatian government.[89] Ujčić's letter to Stepinac of July 9, 1941 was of the same intonation.[90] On December 29, 1941 Ujčić asked Stepinac to inquire about the fate of the Orthodox Bishop Sava Trlajić and to intervene for his release if he was in prison.[91] Each time Stepinac tried to do what he could; he responded to Ujčić that his inquiry about Bishop Trlajić was unsuccessful.[92]

---

85. Redžić, *Bosna i Hercegovina*, 125-126; Krišto, *Sukob simbola*, 325-335.
86. Mons. Josip Garić, the Catholic Bishop of Banja Luka, wrote an extensive letter to Marko Došen, the President of the Croatian Parliament, about the massacres of the Orthodox by Muslims. See Krišto, *Sukob simbola*, 331-333.
87. *Stepinac mu je ime*, vol. 1, 227. After the release from prison, he was sent to Serbia. Some Croatian communist authors have stated that the Metropolitan was murdered Ferdo Čulinović, *Okupatorska podela Jugoslavije* (Beograd, 1970) 345. Some Serbian authors write that he died of consequences of the torture by the Croatian government, Veljko Đ. Đurić, *Golgota Srpske pravoslavne crkve 1941-1945* (Beograd: By the author, ³1998) 139.
88. Krišto, *Sukob simbola*, 134-135.
89. "Stepinčev dnevnik," *Danas* (August 28, 1990) 67.
90. *Službeni vijesnik zagrebačke nadbiskupije* 32 (November 19, 1945); Benigar, *Alojzije Stepinac*, 374.
91. *Sluga Božji* 4 (1994) doc. no. 12.
92. *Sluga Božji* 4 (1994) doc. nos. 25 and 26.

Archbishop Ujčić also asked the Holy See to send a representative to Croatia to examine the allegations about the persecution of Serbs and to recommend moderation to the government.[93] From one of the Ujčić's letters to Stepinac we learn that the Bishop of Banja Luka Josip Garić intervened for the Orthodox Bishop Platon of the same city.[94] In two letters to Archbishop Stepinac Bishop of Mostar Alojzije Mišić, in spite of his advanced age, powerfully expressed his assessment of the people who grabbed and misused political power.[95] Early in 1942 the Bishop of Senj Viktor Burić sent a letter of concern to Archbishop Stepinac about the rumours that the churches of Orthodox Serbs might be destroyed. Stepinac sent a copy of that letter to minister Artuković, expressing the hope that no such thing would happen.[96]

As with the persecution of Jews, the Holy See was also involved in the alleviation of suffering of the Orthodox Serbs in the NDH. Responding to the letter of the Vatican's representative in Croatia, Ramiro Marcone, Cardinal Maglione, the Secretary of State, wrote on September 3, 1941 thanking Stepinac for his efforts to assist the Orthodox community and the Jews and encouraged him to continue such efforts.[97] The Holy See tried to assure the Yugoslav Ambassador that the Catholic Church in general, and especially in Croatia, was trying to do everything possible to alleviate the problems of the Orthodox population in the NDH.[98] The Yugoslav side was never satisfied with the efforts of the Catholic Church, and the Vatican diplomats were certain that there was much propaganda in the Serb interventions.

Archbishop Stepinac was also aware that the Serbs had a tendency to spread a great deal of anti-Catholic and anti-Croatian propaganda. That was the reason for his trip to Rome on May 30, 1943, when he carried the proof of what the Catholic Church in Croatia had done for the Orthodox (and Jewish) populace in the NDH.[99] In the enclosed letter

---

93. *Actes et documents*, vol. 5, doc. no. 20, 104-105.

94. *Ibid.* Đurić, *Golgota Srpske pravoslavne crkve*, note 383, implies that Bishop Garić had improper involvement in Platon's fate.

95. *Službeni vjesnik Zagrebačke nadbiskupije* 32 (November 19, 1945) 26.

96. *Ibid.*, 27.

97. Maglione to Marcone, Vatican, September 3, 1941, *Actes et documents*, vol. 8, doc. 139, 261-262; Krišto, *Sukob simbola*, 147-148.

98. Secretariat of the State to the Yugoslav Mission, Vatican, September 27, 1941, *Actes et documents*, vol. 8, doc. 162, 293; Krišto, *Sukob simbola*, 148-149.

99. The list of those documents are in the Notes of the Secretariat of the State, Vatican, May 31, 1943, *Actes et documents*, vol. 9, doc. 130, Annex III, 224-229; Jure Krišto, "Navodna istraga Sv. Stolice o postupcima hrvatskoga episkopata vezanima za vjerske prijelaze u Nezavisnoj Državi Hrvatskoj," *Croatica Christiana Periodica* 26, no. 49 (2002) 161-173.

for the Secretary of State, Stepinac was quite direct in asserting that the motivation and aim of the Orthodox propaganda was the hatred of the Catholic Church and the maligning of the regime in Croatia.[100] Stepinac addressed the issue of what the Catholic Church had done for the persecuted during the war in a sermon on October 31, 1943. He pointed out how he always urged all concerned that they should follow "the principles of God's eternal law," but that, on the other hand, the Church cannot force anyone to adhere to those principles.[101] Stepinac could be certain of his arguments because he received letters from the Orthodox Serbs themselves thanking him for interventions and assistance.[102]

The most controversial issue in regard to the Orthodox community in the NDH was that of religious conversions. The government had issued a statute, which facilitated the change of religious affiliation[103] and hoped that many Orthodox believers would ask for admission into the Catholic Church, thus eliminating one of the reasons for their opposition to Croatian statehood. The leadership of the Catholic Church tried from the very beginning to persuade the government of the exclusive right of the Church to deal with the issue of religious conversion. The clearest sign of this is the *Memorandum* that the Bishops Conference sent to Pavelić on November 20, 1941.[104] The government, on the other hand, wanted expediency and at least non-interference from the Church if it could not get support for this policy of conversion to Catholicism. This is the reason why the leadership of the Church engaged in an exchange of documents with the government, always trying to reserve the right of the Church to deal with the issue of what it considered to be "the matter of the soul" and for which some preceding steps had to be taken, primarily adequate instruction and free choice.[105]

The bishops knew, of course, that free choice was not always involved for those who petitioned for admission into the Church. The Church

---

100. Stepinac to Maglione, Zagreb, May 24, 1943, Nr. 150/Pr, *Actes et documents*, vol. 9, doc. 130, Annex II, 218-219; Krišto, *Sukob simbola*, 160-161.
101. Nadbiskupski duhovni stol u Zagrebu, 5997/46; *Stepinac mu je ime*, vol. 1, 45-50; Krišto, *Sukob simbola*, 163-166.
102. "Dnevnik Alojzija Stepinca," *Danas* (September 11, 1990) 66.
103. Zakonska odredba o prijelazu s jedne vjere u drugu, Zagreb, May 3, 1941, no. LV/87-Z.p.1941, *Narodne novine* (May 5, 1941); Stella Alexander, *Church and State in Yugoslavia since 1945* (Cambridge: Cambridge University Press, 1979) 26, incorrectly dates the document May 15.
104. Krišto, *Sukob simbola*, 194-202.
105. *Ibid.*, 172-244.

ordinarily tried to refuse admission in those cases,[106] but if it meant avoiding persecution, it allowed admission into the Church, with the reminder that after the war everything would return to its previous state.[107] Stepinac even issued a Clarification in that sense.[108] Occasionally Orthodox believers even threatened Catholic priests in order to obtain certificates stating they had become Catholics.[109] Here, as in other matters, complete unanimity of the bishops was absent. Thus, Viktor Burić, the Bishop of Senj, routinely approved all petitions, but he had instructed his parish priests (generally in remote mountain areas) beforehand, on how to proceed with the petitioners.[110] The Djakovo Bishop Antun Akšamović adopted a similar policy. The Bishop of Šibenik, Jeronim Mileta, on the other hand, adopted as strict a policy for the admission into the Church as Archbishop Stepinac.[111] Bishop Šimrak of the Greek Catholic diocese of Križevci (Uniate) was concerned with many petitioners for conversion who were once Greek Catholic and had become Orthodox believers under political or other types of pressure. Nonetheless, he instructed his priests to proceed strictly according to the Church ordinances regarding those matters, and that separate parishes should be organized for the newly converted, obviously expecting that after the war they would choose the side they wanted.[112]

All bishops had some problems with the defiance of some of the lower clergy in matters of conversions. Contrary to the clear instructions by the bishops that the matter of religious conversions are regulated by Church laws and pertain strictly to the Church hierarchy, the Government was able to find some local priests willing to 'witness' to the massive conversions (entire villages) conducted by government officials. But here, as in other matters, Communist propaganda exaggerated the involvement of priests and the number of 'converted'. While Yugoslav and Serb historiography talked about hundreds of thousands

106. Krišto, *Sukob simbola*, 189.
107. Giuseppe Masucci, *Misija u Hrvatskoj. Dnevnik od 1. kolovoza 1941. do 28. ožujka 1946*, ed. Marijan Mikac (Madrid: "Drina," 1967) 45.
108. Cited in Benigar, *Alojzije Stepinac*, 395.
109. Stepinac's statement at the trial October 3, 1946; Benigar, *Alojzije Stepinac*, 391. In a letter to his legal defender Ivo Politeo October 6, 1946, Stepinac explained that he would have been accused anyway for refusing at least formal admission of Orthodox believers into the Catholic Church in order to save lives, *Sluga Božji* 3, no. 3 (1996) 79.
110. Krišto, *Sukob simbola*, 214-216.
111. *Ibid.*, 203-214.
112. Apostolska administratura Križevačke biskupije, br. Prez. K. 587-1942.

conversions,[113] recent studies had to downgrade the number to a few ten thousands. Biondich calculated that 30,341 Orthodox Serbs changed religious affiliation in the NDH.[114] That figure should be corrected by the information from Church sources. S. Kožul calculated that in the diocese of Zagreb 35,602 Orthodox believers joined the Catholic Church.[115] In a study of the Djakovo diocese, Grgo Grbešić concluded that 6,147 people changed religious affiliation, including those who had returned to Catholicism, and the spouses in mixed marriages.[116] In a study of the diocese of Šibenik, I published a document which shows that in the city of Knin only 54 persons 'converted' to Catholicism, including those who rejoined the Catholic Church, and that there were fewer than a 100 cases in the entire diocese.[117] In a similar study of the diocese of Modruš-Senj, I found 487 converts to Catholicism.[118] It is not surprising that Biondich concluded that the government policy of the forced change of religion in the NDH was a failure. His conclusion that it was due to the indifference of local officials and the opposition of the policy by parish priests seems also quite plausible.[119]

Bishops urged their priests to stay out of politics, and most of them complied with the counsel. There were only a few exceptions. Zvonko Brekalo of the Sarajevo diocese was accused of offensive behaviour. Archbishop Stepinac referred the matter to the Military Vicar Vilim Cecelja, since Brekalo was a military chaplain, with the recommendation that he should be immediately suspended if accusations proved to be well founded.[120] Stepinac himself suspended Ivo Guberina of the diocese of Šibenik, who was a member of the Ustaša organization and accepted a Government position. The Archbishop judged that his

---

113. Veljko Đ. Đurić, *Prekrštavanje Srba u Nezavisnoj Državi Hrvatskoj: Prilozi za istoriju verskog genocida* (Beograd: By the author, 1991) 127-133, writes that 240,000 Orthodox Serbs converted to Catholicism in the NDH.
114. Biondich, "Religion and Nation," 92.
115. Stjepan Kožul, *Stradanja u zagrebačkoj nadbiskupija vrijeme Drugoga svjetskog rata i poraća* (Zagreb: "Tkalčić," 2004).
116. Grgo Grbešić, *La Questione dei "passagi" della Chiesa ortodossa serba alla Chiesa cattolica nella diocesi Đakovo e Srijem dal 1941 al 1945* (Roma, 1999).
117. Jure Krišto, "Vjerski prijelazi u Nezavisnoj Državi Hrvatskoj – primjer šibenske biskupije," *Časopis za suvremenu povijest* 25, no. 2 (1997) 235-248.
118. Jure Krišto, "Prijelazi na katolicizam u Senjsko-modruškoj biskupiji 1941.-1943.," *Prošlost obvezuje: Povijesni korijeni Gospićko-senjske biskupije, Zbornik biskupa Mile Bogovića* (Rijeka: Teologija u Rijeci/Riječki teološki časopis, 2004) 475-502.
119. Biondich, "Religion and Nation," 104.
120. Krišto, *Sukob simbola*, 98-99.

behaviour "was scandalous to the faithful," even though the exact reason for his suspension is not known.[121] Radoslav Glavaš, a Franciscan professor from the Herzegovina province, was also the head of the Office of Worship. He was opposed to the nomination of Petar Čule as Bishop of Mostar and Stepinac threatened him with suspension if he continued to oppose the decision of the Holy See.[122] Tomislav Filipović, a Franciscan of the Bosnian province, was expelled from the order in July 1942 because of the scandal he caused in 1941 by joining as military chaplain a unit that massacred the Serb population in three villages near Banja Luka.[123] Dionizije Juričev, a Franciscan from the Split province, met Pavelić in Italy and became his private chaplain among other things. He was then put in charge of the Religious Office of the State Administration of Renewal, where he remained until November 1941, and then became a military chaplain. Those are the only known 'problematic' priests in the NDH. The Yugoslav historiography, however, accused every military chaplain and many other prominent priests of collaboration, even of committing crimes.

d. Growing Antagonism between the Church Hierarchy and Governmental Authorities

The reactions and protests of Stepinac against the repressive policy of the Ustaše government seem to have been successful to a certain extent. A growing number of people became dissatisfied with the laws against Jews, and also of their persecution. The French ambassador in Zagreb was convinced that Stepinac's interventions were behind the relaxation of race laws in Croatia.[124] Even members of the Ustaše organization and State officials became involved in warning, hiding, saving, and indulging in other forms of protecting Jews.[125] The population was likewise dissatisfied with the treatment of Orthodox Serbs, and by the end of 1941 Pavelić realized that a change of policy was necessary. On April 3, 1942 he created a Croatian Orthodox Church.[126] An ever increasing

---

121. Pattee, *The Case*, 351.
122. ADAE, Europe 57, Vichy, 945, Serie Z, box 384. fasc. 2. Croatie, Questions religieuses.
123. Krišto, *Sukob simbola*, 100-104.
124. ADAE, Europe 94, Vichy, 945, Serie Z, box 384, fasc. 2, Gueyraud to Darlan, Zagreb, June 11, 1941.
125. Goldstein, *Holokaust u Zagrebu*, passim.
126. Veljko Đ. Đurić, *Ustaše i pravoslavlje. Hrvatska pravoslavna crkva* (Beograd: Beletra, 1989); Petar Požar, *Hrvatska pravoslavna crkva u prošlosti i budućnosti* (Zagreb:

number of people, especially from the areas dominated by Italians and Chetniks joined the Partisans, even though they were led by Communists. In spite of those political changes, the attitude of Archbishop Stepinac and other bishops led to growing tensions between the Church and the Government.

Frustrated by his inability to learn the fate of seven of Catholic priests from Slovenia, who were in service in his Archdiocese but had been removed to the Jasenovac concentration camp, Stepinac wrote to Pavelić on February 24, 1943: "This is a shameful stain and crime that cries to heaven for vengeance, just as the entire Jasenovac is a shame and stain for the Independent State of Croatia... The entire nation, particularly the close families of the murdered seek retribution, reparation, the bringing of the executioners before the court. They are the gravest misfortune of Croatia!"[127] When Heinrich Himmler, the chief of the German police, dissatisfied with Croatian ineffectiveness in the treatment of Jews, arrived in Zagreb in 1943, to personally conduct the round-up of the remainder of the Croatian Jews, on March, 6, 1943 Stepinac wrote to Pavelić that he ought to protect Jews since neither he nor several other members of his government had applied 'Aryan laws' on their own families.[128]

Stepinac's earlier mentioned offending homily of October 31, 1943 should be seen in this tense context. It caused a great stir in Ustaše circles and was responded by an open attack on the Archbishop by Dr. Julije Makanec, the Minister of Education, in the Ustaše paper *Hrvatski narod* of November 7, 1943. The article implied that Stepinac had not been called to conduct politics, and therefore, should leave it to those who had been called.[129] Moreover, the deterioration of relations culminated in plans to imprison and then to kill the Zagreb

---

Naklada Pavičić, 1996); Svetozar Lozo and Milenko Doder, "Hrvatska pravoslavna crkva agentura okupatora," *Vjesnik* (February 21, 1976); Ivan Mužić, *Pavelić i Stepinac* (Split: Crkva u svijetu, 1991); Miloš Obrknežević, "Razvoj pravoslavlja u Hrvatskoj i Hrvatska pravoslavna crkva," *Hrvatska Revija* 29, no. 2 (1979) 229-267; Krišto, *Sukob simbola*, 247-262.

127. *Službeni vjesnik zagrebačke nadbiskupije* 32, no. 6 (December 3, 1945) 35. Cf. *Stepinac mu je ime*, vol. 1, 56; *Fontes* 2 (1996) 141.

128. *Službeni vjesnik zagrebačke nadbiskupije* 32, no. 8 (December 31, 1945) 50-51; *Fontes* 2 (1996) 162-164. Pavelić's wife and the wives of his Ministers Slavko Kvaternik and Milovan Žanić were Jewish. Vilko Lehner, Robert Vinček, David Karlović, and David Sinčić had partly Jewish spouses. Ljubo Kremzir, Viktor Gutman, Ivo Korsky, and Vlado Singer, all high officials in NDH and members of the Ustaše, were Jewish.

129. *Stepinac mu je ime*, vol. 1, 51-53.

Archbishop: the entire city was talking about Stepinac's imminent arrest.[130] The Vatican's Secretary of State Cardinal Maglione was forced to warn Stepinac to moderate his rhetoric, even though he approved of his principled posture.[131]

IV. Doubtful Liberators

With regard to the issue of World War II, people in Croatia and Bosnia-Herzegovina continue to have serious disagreement about who was liberated, who were the liberators, and even who was the enemy. Of course, people do not have problems recognizing that the enemy was German National Socialism and Italian Fascism. Their problem was with the identity of the liberators and internal enemies. Communist-led Partisans presented themselves as liberators, while for many people the situation after liberation was worse than before. In addition, the forcefully imposed ideology was something that many rejected as horrifying.

The Catholic Church strongly denied the title of liberators to the Communists, which was undoubtedly the principal reason for its problems with Communists. That does not mean that the Catholic Church refused to acknowledge the Communist government as the *de facto* political authority. Indeed, Archbishop Stepinac explicitly acknowledged that the Communists became the political authority for the Church the moment they entered the Croatian capital on May 8, 1945.[132] The Catholic Church however, refused to accept the Communist interpretation of events during the war, and even less so their assessment of the post-war period. The root of this refusal is in the treatment of Catholics by the Communists during and after the war.

The assumption of the leading role of Communists in the resistance against the occupying Nazis and the Fascists was the result of political calculation and the fortunes of war. At the end of 1941, Tito left Serbia and moved to Bosnia. He was able to attract several categories of people (Serbs and Croats), which he organized in the Partisan units, later called People's Liberation Fighters and at the end of the war, the People's Liberation Army (Narodno-oslobodilačka vojska – NOV). They wisely

---

130. HDA, MUP RH, H. Helm, 3490/42, July 22, 1944, box 122; Krišto, *Sukob simbola*, 91-92; Vasa Kazimirović, *NDH u svetlu nemačkih dokumenata i dnevnika Gleza fon Horstenaua 1941-1944* (Beograd: Nova knjiga/Narodna knjiga, 1987) 280-281.
131. "Dnevnik Alojzija Stepinca," *Danas* (September 25, 1990) 66.
132. His address at the trial. Benigar, *Alojzije Stepinac*.

downplayed the Communist rhetoric and insisted on brotherhood and unity instead. After the capitulation of Italy in 1943, the Communist-led Partisans were assured of their victory, because they had captured all Italian weaponry. In ever increasing square kilometres of 'liberated territory', they not only established their 'people's power', but also increased their vengeance on a disloyal populace and potential ideological opponents, especially the Catholic clergy. Communists were even more assured of victory when early in 1944, at the instigation of the United States of America, the Allies switched their support from Draža Mihailović's Chetniks to Josip Broz Tito's Partisans.

The Catholic clergy was generally opposed to Communism even before war, primarily because of its inherent anti-religious positions and proclamations. Between the two world wars, the anti-religious position of the Communists in Yugoslavia assumed a form of anti-Catholicism. In May of 1940 Stepinac shared his insight about the Communist program: "[The Communists] will work with full force to sever the Croatian people from Christianity, particularly from Catholicism."[133] The position of Croat Catholics was based on the experience of the Orthodox Christians in the 'first land of socialism', the USSR. This was a primary reason that very few Croatian Catholic priests joined the Communist-led Partisans during World War II. The most prominent Catholic priest-partisan was Svetozar Rittig, although, given his political zigzagging in the past, he was not taken seriously. If Croat Catholics were opposed to Communism during the war, the Communists made every effort to strengthen their anti-Communist convictions in the transition period from war to peace. They instituted Military Courts, which condemned to death all ideological opponents, and Catholic priests ranked high on their list. With and, more frequently without, any court proceedings, by the end of the war in Europe, the Communists had killed or massacred almost 300 Catholic priests and seminarians as well as 30 nuns in the territories of the present-day Republic of Croatia and the Republic of Bosnia and Herzegovina (Table 3).[134]

---

133. "Dnevnik," *Danas* (July 17, 1990) 65.
134. Anto Baković, *Svećenici žrtve rata i poraća 1941-1945 i dalje* (Zagreb: By the author, 1994); Stjepan Kožul, *Spomenica žrtvama ljubavi Zagrebačke nadbiskupije* (Zagreb: AGM, 1992); Petar Bezina, *Franjevci provincije Presvetog otkupitelja žrtve rata 1942.-1948.* (Split: Zbornik "Kačić," 1995); Marijan Karaula, *Žrtve i mučenici. Stradanja bosanskih franjevaca u Drugom svjetskom ratu i komunizmu* (Sarajevo: Svjetlo riječi, 1999); "Prije pola stoljeća partizani su ubili šezdeset i šest hercegovačkih franjevaca," *Naša ognjišta* (March, 1995) 10-13.

Table 3. Perpetrators of priest killings during the war

Perpetrators	Number of killed
Communist-led Partisans	299
Serbian Chetniks	43
German Army	11
Italian Army	3
Allied Bombardments	27
Ustaše	2
Croatian Army – Domobrani (Home defenders)	1
Eastern Front	3
Typhus	6
Unknown	7
Total	412

Based on: A. Baković, *Svećenici žrtve rata i poraća*.

The pastors of Catholic parishes in areas of conflict, if they themselves were not forced to leave those areas, reported regularly to their bishops about the activities of various military units and about killings and destruction[135] which, in turn, confirmed for the Church hierarchy the attitudes of Communists toward Catholicism. The death sentence on Rev. Ivan Đanić, the pastor of Slavonska Orahovica, is unusual, but illustrative of the character of Communist Military courts. On June 29, 1943, the Military Court at the Headquarters of the Second Corpus of the People's Liberation Army (NOV) condemned Đanić to death by firing-squad because "he had divorced himself from the Catholic Church by breaking the sacred secrecy of confessional" and thus "has become a bandit." Presiding over that court was Josip Krajačić, a Croat, and two other members were Duško Brkić and Momo Kosanović, Croatian Serbs.[136] More often, the Communists did not even bother to include the courts in their killing of Catholic priests. The case of the Franciscan fathers of Herzegovina stands out, because Communist Partisans killed all professors and some of the students of their renowned High school in Široki Brijeg.

---

135. Following a decision of the Bishops' Conference, individual bishops asked in Spring 1943 their parish priests to collect information about material and life losses in each parish. The results for the diocese of Zagreb: see Stjepan Kožul, *Stradanja u zagrebačkoj nadbiskupiji*. See also Mile Bogović Slunjski, "Ratni zapisi iz 1942. godine," *Zvona*, no. 11 (1991) 5; id., "Svećenici s područja današnje Riječko-senjske nadbiskupije poginuli u Drugom svjetskom ratu," *Zvona*, no. 6 (1992) 5; Krišto, *Sukob simbola*, 364-375.

136. Hrvatski državni arhiv, MUP RH, Građa okupatora i kvislinga, I-5/189; Kožul, *Spomenica žrtvama ljubavi*, 21.

The nature of the conflict in World War II was such that many Catholic parishes were completely razed to the ground, and after the war they were never reestablished. There were 16 such parishes in the diocese of Banja Luka (Bosnia and Herzegovina), where 18,000 Catholics were a minority.[137] The churches in those towns were destroyed and many parish priests were massacred. Two cases stand out because of the cruelty sustained. Rev. Jure Gospodnetić (1910-1941) was a native of the island of Brač and when in 1939 he came to the Bosnian town of Grahovo as a young priest, where 980 Catholics were a minority among the Orthodox Serbs, he probably felt estranged. But he was well accepted and quickly gained friends in both religious communities. It is not clear whether he was killed by Chetnicks or Partisans, because contemporary observers tended to put both groups on the same level. What is clear is that Rev. Gospodnetić was baked alive, while his mother was forced to watch it.[138] Rev. Krešimir Barišić, the pastor of Krnjeuša, sustained similar torture, but at the end he was still alive and was thrown into his burning parish church.[139] Seven parishes in the diocese of Senj-Modruš also completely disappeared.[140] The place in the diocese of Zagreb that has shared such an unfortunate fate was Zrinj, which before the war had 753 Catholics.[141] It is important to keep in mind that most of these towns and villages were in areas with religiously mixed populaces or predominantly Orthodox believers, where the state institutions of the Independent State of Croatia were never really established or functioned.[142]

V. The Wrathful Vengeance at the End of World War II

It seemed that towards the end of war the angel of vengeance travelled with the advancing Partisans, now officially strengthened by many

---

137. The parishes that were leveled were: Bosansko Grahovo (before the war: 980 Catholics), Bosanska Kostajnica (920), Bosanski Petrovac (1,100), Bosanski Novi (1,480), Devetina (960), Gumjera (1,240), Kunova (1,520), Novi Martinac (3,750), Rakovac (1,964), Stara Dubrava (629), Šibovska (1,670), Krnjeuša (1,244) i Miljevac (630); Vidović, *Povijest Crkve u Hrvata*, 402.

138. *Vrhbosna*, nos. 4-5 (1943) 68-69.

139. *Ibid.*

140. Borićevac (before the war 2,000 Catholics), Bunić (350) Gračac (1,200), Kaluđerovac (900), Palanka (120), Rudopolje (550), and Udbina (1,600); Vidović, *Povijest Crkve u Hrvata*, 402.

141. *Ibid.*, 402-403.

142. The same area was in the centre of the "Krajina" that rebel Serbs created in the 1990's.

Chetniks. As the Partisan units advanced northwestwardly towards the Austrian borders, they eliminated not only enemy soldiers, but mostly ideological and potential political opponents. Among them was a substantial number of Catholics who before the war were members of Catholic organizations, and also some priests. The particularity of the war in Yugoslavia was that the Partisans, led by the Communists, eliminated most of their opponents *after* the enemy soldiers had surrendered and the war was officially over. This was done in several ways: by mass killings at the Yugoslav-Austrian border and in Slovenia, by forced marches, by summary executions, by the sentences of the Military Courts, through the Commission for War Crimes, through organized show trials, and finally through forced labour camps.

1. The Town of Bleiburg and 'The Way of the Cross'

Faced with imminent defeat, the NDH power-holders ordered a massive retreat of the military potential. Since hundreds of thousands of civilians had already swamped Zagreb in their flight for the Communists, most of them joined the military units to retreat towards the West in the hope of being welcomed by the Allies. The hordes of fleeing people were in great disorder and were met by British military units at the Austrian border. The centre of this assembly point was the town of Bleiburg. It is not clear whether the British military representatives in the area acted contrary to the instructions of their government, but certainly in contradiction to the Geneva Conventions they handed over to the furious Tito's partisans the disarmed soldiers and throngs of civilians.[143] Later, the British did the same with Croat prisoners-of-war, which implies a standing policy. The British military representatives lied that they would be transferred to other refugee camps, when they in fact directed trains back to Yugoslavia. Many of these refugees were killed by Communist Partisans in Carinthia and Slovenia, but Bleiburg has assumed within the collective consciousness of Croats a symbolic value of great suffering, destruction, and annihilation. The experience was so horrible that it evoked in survivors the biblical image of 'The Way of the Cross'. Some were able to march until they reached labour and concentration camps, and some marched as far as the south-eastern borders of Yugoslavia in South Serbia, but many were massacred by

---

143. Nikolai Tolstoy, "The Clagenfurt Conspiracy: War Crimes and Diplomatic Secrets," *Encounter* 60, no. 5 (1983); id., *The Minister and the Massacres* (London: Century Hutchinson Ltd., 1986).

Serbian peasants of the villages through which they were intentionally led. The experience of Bleiburg was for some the greatest tragedy of the Croatian people in modern history. Unfortunately, the victims have not yet been counted. Estimates range from no less than 50,000 to over 200,000 killed soldiers and civilians.[144]

2. Concentration Camps and Military Courts

Many ideological opponents, who were not eliminated in the weeks following the end of the war, were put in concentration camps, where they were supposed to be reeducated and made 'socially useful individuals'. The Communists have denied, even to this day, that they organized concentration camps, similar to those of the Nazis. The truth is that they organized many camps, and even the infamous Ustaše labour camp Jasenovac continued to serve the same purpose, but with inhabitants of the Croat 'nationalist' ideological strand.

The Military Courts that Communists used to practice 'revolutionary justice' were continued after the war. They represented a handy tool for a quick elimination of ideological and political opponents. In June, 1945, the Military Court of the Second Army District in Zagreb organized the trial of ten leading men of the NDH government. With the exception of three men who were sentenced to long terms of imprisonment, all of them were condemned to death for "war crimes and treason."[145] In October 1945, the Supreme Court in Belgrade tried 33 Croatian generals and higher officers: 17 were sentenced to death, 15 to long terms of imprisonment, and 1 was freed.[146]

Many Catholic priests were sentenced to death as well. The Franciscan friar, Radoslav Glavaš, was one of the condemned. As soon as the Communists entered Zagreb, they arrested him and sentenced him to death by firing squad. Rev. Kerubin Šegvić (1867-1946), already 79 years old, was sentenced in the same way because of his theory of the 'Gothic origin' of Croats. In June, 1945, the Supreme Court of the People's Republic of Croatia organized the trial of Erich Lisak and a group of Catholic priests, including Archbishop Stepinac's secretary Ivan Šalić. Šalić was targeted as a lure to get to Stepinac. After a long period of torture, he

---

144. *50 godina Bleiburga* (Zagreb: Hrvatski institut za povijest, 1995); *Spomenica povodom 50-te obljetnice Bleiburga i Križnog puta 1945.-1995.* (Zagreb: Hrvatski institut za povijest, 1995).
145. Nada Kisić-Kolanović, "Vrijeme političke represije: 'veliki sudski procesi' u Hrvatskoj 1945.-1948.," *Časopis za suvremenu povijest* 25, no. 1 (1993) 9.
146. *Ibid.*

broke down and agreed to sign whatever he was told to sign. Catholic intellectuals underwent the same sort of treatment, such as the prominent Catholic writer from Bosnia and Herzegovina Msgr. Čedomil Čekada (1896-1981), arrested on May 21, 1945 in Sarajevo and sentenced to 12 years of imprisonment with hard labour.[147]

Priests and high officials of other Churches and religious communities were also tried by the Military Court and executed. The most prominent among those was the elderly Metropolitan Germogen, because he was the head of the Croatian Orthodox Church, established during the NDH. Bishop Spiridon Mifka was executed because he belonged to the same Church. Among the executed was the Zagreb mufti Ismet Muftić, because he had collaborated with the Ustaše and had praised the Croatian State and its leadership.

3. Commission for War Crimes

The Communists were aware that the time for 'revolutionary justice' was running out and that they would have to arm themselves with more legal means. They resorted to legal justice, but of a kind that would also be of service to the revolution. One of the venues giving more credence to the imposition of totalitarian rule was the Commission of War Crimes, which was very active in the closing stages of the war and immediately after it. The International Commission for War Crimes was founded in London on October 20, 1943, and urged all allied countries to institute Commissions of their own. The Communist Antifascist Council of the People's Liberation of Yugoslavia (Antifašističko vijeće narodnog oslobođenja Jugoslavije – AVNOJ) instituted the State Commission for War Crimes (Zemaljska komisija za ratne zločine – ZKRZ) on November 30, 1943. Such commissions functioned not only in each federal unit, but every district, county, and commune had such organisations of their own. At the peak of their activities, there were 1,574 such bodies. Unfortunately, many people with some political influence used those commissions to exert revenge for any personal animosity or grievance against their neighbours. Indeed, in the Communiqués *(Saopćenja/Saopštenja)* of the State Commission, a book-length list of supposed criminal activities by individuals and groups, there are a great many innuendos, political charges, unfounded accusations, and ideological evaluations.

---

147. *Katolički tjednik*, no. 7 (February 16, 2003) 32-33.

The definition of a war crime in Communist quasi-legislation was very broad and imprecise, but the most punishable transgression was ideological opposition to the Communist Party. The sentencing to death of many writers, philosophers, journalists, and priests is a glaring example of that practice. In just a year (mid-1945 to mid-1946) 900,000 denunciations were gathered for war crimes. The Commissions issued 120,000 decisions, in which there were 65,000 war criminals, traitors, and 'enemies of the people'.[148] In addition, the State Commission requested the UN Commission for War Crimes to register 7,812 'war criminals' among those that the Communists were able to find, or that the Allies had not extradited (2,700 cases were accepted for registration).[149]

Within the structure of the Commissions for War Crimes there existed the Survey Commission, which was supposed to uncover "the intellectual originators of crimes, whom others later executed."[150] The sinister activity of this Commission began on June 6, 1945 and was completed a year later.[151] In addition to the one in Zagreb, there were 29 other such Commissions in so many districts. They investigated nearly all Croatian intellectuals who, during the war, had not participated within the ranks of the Partisans and branded them as criminals. Reading their publications was as well assumed as a crime. The criminal nature of a piece was determined by the fact that it was published in a particular newspaper or review.

Table 4. Victims of communists among priests, nuns and seminarians after the war

PRIESTS	NUMBER OF VICTIMS
Murdered immediately after war	177
Died in prison	27
Died as consequence of prison and torture	32
Murdered as conscripts of the Yugoslav Army	12
Nuns died as consequence of prison and torture	4
TOTAL	252

148. Josip Jurčević, *Nastanak jasenovačkog mita. Problemi proučavanja žrtava Drugog svjetskog rata na području Hrvatske* (Zagreb: Studia Croatica, 1998) 20.
149. Kisić-Kolanović, "Vrijeme političke represije," 3; Jurčević, *Nastanak jasenovačkog mita*, 21.
150. HDA Zemaljska komisija za ratne zločine (ZKRZ), box 685, doc. no. 18/45.
151. HDA ZKRZ, box 689, O. B/1946 (1-59), doc. no. 50/46.

The speciality of the Survey Commission was the Questionnaire-system (*Upitni arci*). Forms were sent to all cultural and educational institutions, including sanatoriums and institutions such as the Association of Widows, of which each employee or resident had to answer where she/he had been during the war, with whom he/she had had contact or associated with, and similar questions. The heads of those institutions were supposed to comment and/or pass judgments on each employee about their behaviour during the war and about their ideological positions. On the basis of those evaluations, many people were further examined and persecuted. All professors at the Faculty of Philosophy employed after April 10, 1941 (the day of proclamation of the NDH) were dismissed – there were 28 on the list.[152]

4. The Use of Propaganda

The aim of the Communist Party of Yugoslavia was to achieve quick and total control of all functions of the society. The fear produced by massive killings, expedient trials with death sentences, imprisonments, and concentration camps was just one form of that control. Other forms were the use of the media for propaganda purposes and the incitement of the people, especially the youth, to 'spontaneous reactions'. As soon as the Communist-led Partisans entered cities, they banned all Catholic organizations, reviews and newspapers and confiscated Catholic presses, while the non-Catholic papers and the radio were used for hostile incitements against the Catholic Church and their priests.[153] Among the victims of such spontaneous expressions of outrage was Archbishop Stepinac, who was several times assaulted by youngsters while he was trying to carry out his pastoral tasks.[154] The fate of Msgr. Josip Marija Carević (1883-1945), the Bishop of the Dubrovnik diocese, was much worse. Shortly after the war, a group of partisans arrested him in a small parish north-west of Zagreb where he had retired, tortured and killed him.[155]

---

152. HDA ZKRZ, box 686, doc. no.119/45.
153. Biljana Kašić, "Značajke partijske ideologije u Hrvatskoj (1945.–1948.).," *Časopis za suvremenu povijest* 23, nos. 1-3 (1991) 246; Katarina Spehnjak, "Uloga novina u oblikovanju javnog mnijenja u Hrvatskoj 1945.-1952.," *Časopis za suvremenu povijest* 25, nos. 2-3 (1993) 166; id., *Javnost i propaganda: Narodna fronta u politici i kulturi Hrvatske* (Zagreb: Hrvatski institut za povijest/Dom i svijet, 2002); Berislav Jandrić, "Tisak totalitarne komunističke vlasti u Hrvatskoj u pripremanju montiranog procesa zagrebačkom nadbiskupu Alojziju Stepincu (1946.)," *Croatica Christiana Periodica* 47 (2001).
154. Benigar, *Alojzije Stepinac*, 505-517.
155. Kožul, *Spomenica žrtvama ljubavi*, 29-33.

5. Elimination of Political Opposition

The Communist's aim to achieve complete control over Yugoslavian society implied as well the elimination of every form of political opposition. The propaganda and pressure against established political parties was so great that all of them dropped away from competition for the Constitutional Assembly. Even the minister of Foreign affairs, HSS member and formerly *Ban* of Croatia, Ivan Šubašić, resigned on September 7, 1945. At the elections for the Constitutional Assembly only the People's Front (Narodna fronta), dominated by the Communists, was represented. By the end of the trials, propaganda programs, and public executions, the Communists had secured total control of the society. They could now give further legal appearance to the continuation of that 'revolutionary justice'. They reintroduced the function of Public Prosecutor and promulgated appropriate legislation.

6. Organized Show Trials

The function of Public Prosecutor of the Democratic Federated Yugoslavia had been established on February 3, 1945 by the Presidency of the Antifascist Council of the People's Liberation of Yugoslavia.[156] It was decided at that time that each unit of the Federation should also appoint its own Public Prosecutor. On that basis and on the recommendation of the State Antifascist Council (Zemaljsko antifašističko vijeće narodnog oslobođenja Hrvatske) the Public Prosecutor of Federal Croatia was also instituted.[157] Already by mid-August 1945, Communist power-holders issued the Law of Criminal Activities against the State (Zakon o krivičnim djelima protiv države).[158] Further definitions of the office of Public Prosecutor were brought about by the Constitution of the Federated People's Republic of Yugoslavia of January 31, 1946.[159] In spite of the legal appearance, the incriminations through existing laws were often political in nature, and the practice disregarded all usual legal forms and practices.[160] In all subsequent changes and additions to that legislation,[161] its principal

---

156. *Službeni list* of Democratic Federated Yugoslavia, 4/45.
157. Privremena uputstva o organizaciji rada Javnog tužioca Federalne Hrvatske i njegovih organa.
158. *Narodne novine* (September 21, 1945).
159. *Službeni list* of the Federated People's Republic of Yugoslavia, 60/46, July 26, 1946.
160. Kisić-Kolanović, "Vrijeme političke represije," 6.
161. *Službeni list* of the Federated People's Republic of Yugoslavia, 51/54, December 8, 1954.

feature was that it gave large competences to the Public Prosecutor and that it bore serious imprecision on what was criminal activity, especially in the political domain.[162]

7. The Zagreb Archbishop Alojzije Stepinac's Trial in 1946

There is no doubt that among potential opponents to the totalitarian regime, the Communists considered the Catholic Church to be a special case. After they had achieved total control of society and eliminated any kind of opposition, they were afraid that the Catholic Church remained the strongest ideological opponent that might eventually represent a political threat to their authority, even though it had been decimated and, thus, held under control (Table 5). It was not under full control, however, and not under nearly as good control as had been exercised over the Serbian Orthodox Church or the Muslim religious community. The Party more or less succeeded in making the religious representatives of the two latter religious communities obedient executors of the will of the Party. It could not find a similar kind of cooperation among the leadership of the Catholic Church in Croatia and Bosnia-Herzegovina.

Table 5. Percentage of murdered priests in some dioceses and religious communities

Diocese/province	Percentage
Banjaluka	73,08%
Mostar-Duvno	69,57%
Sarajevo	56,45%
Franciscan Province of Herzegovina	43,30%
Franciscan Province of Bosnia	36,67%

Based on A. Baković, *Svećenici žrtve rata i poraća*.

Even during the war the Party leadership was already set on subjugating or even eliminating the Catholic Church in Croatia. Assured of an imminent victory, and in addition to killing many Catholic priests and nuns, the Communists began spreading the propaganda that the Church was most responsible for what had happened during the war. The Executive Council of the Bishops Conference on March 24, 1945 issued a Pastoral Letter, aimed at 'false witnesses', i. e. Communists. The Letter charged that Communists used lies as their *modus operandi*.[163]

162. Kisić-Kolanović, "Vrijeme političke represije," 2.
163. *Katolički list* 96, nos. 12-13 (March 29, 1945).

Soon after the Communists entered Zagreb, Archbishop Stepinac was placed under house arrest on May 17, 1945. It could not have been for reasons of his safety, as some Serbian authors argued,[164] because the Supreme Headquarters in Belgrade requested that he should be "interrogated" and "materials about his inimical activities" should be collected.[165] Moreover, the organs of the secret police (Odjeljenje za zaštitu naroda – OZNa, Section of People's Protection) from Zagreb responded that Stepinac "was today quietly *arrested*."[166] Stepinac's first interrogation session provided clues for future charges against him: contact and cooperation with Pavelić and other high Ustaše officials.[167]

Josip Broz Tito, the head of the Communist Party of Yugoslavia and leader of the Partisans, visited Zagreb on June 2, 1945 and met with the representatives of the Catholic clergy. Since Stepinac was under house arrest, the clergy was represented by Msgr. Franjo Salis-Seewis, the auxiliary Bishop. He expressed the hope that the relationship between the new power-holders and the Church would be correct and cooperative to the benefit of the people and that the Archbishop would soon be released, so that the government would have its counterpart for a dialogue (he was, indeed, released soon after that meeting).[168] In his speech, Tito criticized younger priests who were against the idea of Yugoslavia, and then expressed an idea that certainly surprised the listeners: he wanted the Church to be "more national" and "more suited to the people." More than a surprise, this idea was certainly perceived as a threat, because certain circles in Croatia had for decades propagated the idea of a "national Catholic Church," independent of Rome and more like the Serbian Orthodox Church, and Communists had obviously adopted the idea. Knowing the totalitarian nature of the Communists and remembering the many priests who had been eliminated, the Catholic clergy was undoubtedly afraid for the future of the Church.

Given the fact that the Communists did not stop at the killings of innocent people and with other oppressive measures, Archbishop Stepinac sent numerous letters to the highest Communist leaders and institutions protesting against government measures in various areas.

---

164. See: Radmila Radić, *Verom protiv vere. Država i verske zajednice u Srbiji 1945-1953* (Beograd: INIS, 1995) 221 with notes.
165. Ljubo Boban, "Na kraju feljtona," *Danas* (February 2, 1990) 67.
166. *Ibid*. Italics J.K.
167. *Ibid*.; Krišto, *Sukob simbola*, 408.
168. Nadbiskupski arhiv, Zagreb, Zapisnik posjeta klera kod maršala Jugoslavije Josipa Broza Tita, dne 2. lipnja 1945; Benigar, *Alojzije Stepinac*, 501-503.

The letter to Vladimir Bakarić, the head of the Party in Croatia, July 21, 1945 was especially detailed regarding the treatment of the Church and its priesthood by the Communists and represented one of the strongest protests against the summary killings of Croatian soldiers.[169]

Since Stepinac's letters to Tito, Bakarić and other men in power had no influence on the issue, Catholic bishops at the session of the Bishops' Conference September 17 to 22, 1945 issued a Pastoral Letter to the faithful, which enumerated all the grievances of the Church against the government, and listed the expectations of the bishops. The highest members of Party leadership reacted very strongly to the bishops' Pastoral Letter.[170] The internal Party documents testify that the Pastoral Letter was evaluated as the most explicit "inimical action," aimed at the mobilization of Catholics against the new Yugoslavia.[171] The police confiscated the Pastoral Letter, so that some pastors were unable to have it read in their parishes. At the same time, the attacks on the Church in the daily press were increasingly high-level. Early in November, the Archbishop was physically attacked by a mob as he tried to open a new parish in Zaprešić, near Zagreb.[172] The Church took those accusations and attacks quite seriously, and the Official Herald of the Zagreb Archdiocese (*Službeni vjesnik Zagrebačke nadbiskupije* – SVZN) on November 6, 1945 began publishing excerpts of official documents, which were supposed to demonstrate the opposite of the accusations by the Party.[173]

The Party leadership decided, however, to make a big move: to put Archbishop of Zagreb Alojzije Stepinac on trial. In January, 1946, the newspapers began to publish documents, which were supposed to demonstrate Stepinac's cooperation and collaboration with the Ustaše leading man Ante Pavelić. More sinister were the accusations that the Catholic clergy had participated in crimes and evil deeds. The Public Prosecutor's office was supposed to collect materials compromising Catholic priests and bishops, especially Archbishop Stepinac. By the end of December, 1945, the leading Communist of Croatia, V. Bakarić, wrote to the chief Party ideologue Edvard Kardelj of Slovenia, that enough materials had been collected to compromise the entire

---

169. Benigar, *Alojzije Stepinac*, 519-544.
170. *Vjesnik* (October 25, 1945).
171. Radić, *Verom protiv vere*, 228.
172. Vidović, *Povijest Crkve u Hrvata*, 416; Benigar, *Alojzije Stepinac*, 505-507.
173. "Dokumenti nedavne prošlosti," *Službeni vjesnik Zagrebačke nadbiskupije*, no. 6 (November 6, 1945) to no. 4 (February 20, 1946).

leadership of the Catholic Church.[174] The Party in Zagreb organized demonstrations against Archbishop Stepinac.[175] In August 1946, there was a renewed attack on the Church in the press, and high Party officials announced more drastic dealings with the leadership of the Church.[176] Only a week later, the trial of Lisak and a group of Catholic priests began in Zagreb.

After another bitter attack on the Church by Tito in speeches in Split and Korenica,[177] Stepinac was arrested September 18, 1946 at 5:30, just as he was preparing to celebrate his daily mass.[178] His trial began only 10 days after his arrest, and lasted just 12 days. The Public Prosecutor was Jakov Blažević, and the president of the court was dr. Žarko Vimpulšek, both Croats. The Spiritual Chair of the Archdiocese proposed two defence lawyers, Ivo Politeo and Radoslav Katičić, who were accepted. The charges were: collaboration with the occupiers and Pavelić, holding the office of military chaplain, supporting of organizations of the Crusaders and the Catholic Action, which cooperated with the Ustaše, the use of religious celebrations for political manifestations, glorification of Pavelić and the Ustaše, the forced conversions of the Orthodox to Catholicism, the inimical activity against the people and the state after the liberation. The official representative of the Holy See, Msgr. J. P. Hurley, attended all sessions of the trial, and he bowed to Archbishop Stepinac every time he passed by him.[179]

The Public Prosecutor read the charges, which task took no less than 48 hours, and Stepinac answered the charges for 38 minutes. That address of the Archbishop for his defence was never officially allowed publication during the entire rule of the Communists in former Yugoslavia,[180] and its clandestine distribution was treated as a criminal

174. Radić, *Verom protiv vere*, 227.
175. *Ibid.*, 228.
176. *Politika* (September 3, 1946) provides extracts from Andrija Hebrang's lecture in Zagreb and a week later extracts from Tito's interview to the French newspaper *Humanité*, Radić, *Verom protiv vere*, 228-229.
177. Radić, *Verom protiv vere*, 229.
178. Vidović, *Povijest Crkve u Hrvata*, 417.
179. The representative of Democratic Federal Yugoslavia with the Holy See, Nikola Moscatello, a Catholic priest of Yugoslavianist convictions, suggested to Pope Pius XII that the representative of the Holy See in Yugoslavia should be from a neutral or an allied country. The Holy See decided that its temporary representative would be Msgr. Joseph Patrick Hurley, the Bishop of Saint Augustine, Florida, USA; see Radić; *Verom protiv vere*, 223.
180. It did not appear in the voluminous book about the trial: *Suđenje Lisaku, Stepincu, Šaliću i družini, ustaško-križarskim zločincima i njihovim pomagačima*, ed. Milan Stanić (Zagreb: Milan Stanić, 1946).

activity, which required an appropriate sentence of imprisonment. The same fate awaited the expositions by his defence lawyers. On October 11, 1946, Stepinac was sentenced to 16 years imprisonment and forced labour and 5 years denial of any political and civic rights. Stepinac was sent to prison in Lepoglava.

VI. The Relationship between the Church and the Communist Government after the War

The Party leadership believed that an important chapter of its dealings with the Catholic Church was closed, and that the work on the creation of a 'national church' could begin. In December 5, 1946, Bakarić wrote again to E. Kardelj that the Party, specifically the secret police, which had now gone through a change of name (Uprava državne bezbednosti – UDBa, Direction of State Security), should work on establishing a 'national church' and that any opponents should be hit hard.[181] A pivotal role in that work was assigned to the specialized organization of the priests (Svećenička udruženja, Priest associations). Priests were offered monetary incentives, retirement benefits, and other material and political privileges if they supported the political program of the Communist Party and distanced themselves from the leadership of the Church.[182] The UDBa documents clearly show that this secret service was behind the creation of priests associations. Another attempt at controlling the Catholic Church was through the government's request that vacated bishoprics should be filled only by candidates having government approval.[183] The Church never agreed to that.[184] The pressure on the Church was also increased by complaints that the Vatican institutions had harboured war criminals and helped them to escape to South America.[185] The next step was the denial of state recognition of the

---

181. Radić, *Verom protiv vere*, 228.
182. Vidović, *Povijest Crkve u Hrvata*, 424-427; Radić, *Verom protiv vere*, 280-283.
183. Radić, *Verom protiv vere*, 231-232.
184. *Ibid.*, 232.
185. *Politika* (January 20, 1947) 4; (February 2, 1947) 1; Radić, *Verom protiv vere*, 232. The official representative of Yugoslavia with the Holy See, Msgr. Moscatello, resigned in protest of the trial and sentencing of Archbishop Stepinac. When today some authors sensationally announce that they have discovered new proofs about the harbouring of war criminals by the Vatican (Mark Arons and John Loftus, *Unholy Trinity: How the Vatican's Nazi Networks Betrayed Western Intelligence to the Soviets* [New York: St. Martin's Griffin, 1991]), they do not reveal that their sources are often those very accusations of the Communists from Yugoslavia and other countries under Communist dictatorship.

Catholic high schools for the education of future students of theology (seminarians) and the enforced closure of some of them. Under trumped-up charges theology faculties were closed in Rijeka (1955), Split (1956) and Djakovo (1960). When by the end of 1952, the Holy See named Archbishop Stepinac a Cardinal, the Yugoslav Party officials reacted by cutting off diplomatic relations with the Vatican. This occurred on the eve of Tito's visit to Great Britain.

The relations between the Holy See and Communist Yugoslavia were not reestablished until its international position changed and Stepinac died in 1960. From that moment on, the tensions lessened or in some cases intensified, depending on many factors, primarily on the feeling of the Party about its internal cohesion and strength. More 'normal' relations between the Church and State were not established until the Communists eventually lost power and Yugoslavia as a state disappeared.

VII. Conclusion

For over a century Croats have expended their energy to gain full sovereignty and independence. The struggle was far from easy, and generated a great deal of frustration, even anger, in addition to massive losses in population and economic resources. In the course of the twentieth century, they have sustained the brunt of three wars: two world wars and the war of 1991 to 1995. In the same century, Croats lived in four political systems (Austro-Hungarian Empire, monarchist Yugoslavia, NDH, and communist Yugoslavia), almost all of them unnatural associations in which they were forced to participate, before they gained full independence in 1990. In all of these, Croats were in a subordinate position.

Most of the frustrations Croats accumulated in the Kingdom of Serbs, Croats, and Slovenes/Kingdom of Yugoslavia. Part of the frustrations arose from the fact that the great expectations were not met, but the cause of most of them was the intention of the more populous Serbs to incorporate Croat lands into Great Serbia. That could not be accomplished without the use of various forms of force and oppression.

The next opportunity for independence and sovereignty for Croats turned up in an inopportune time of war and the clash in its territory of political, economic, and military interests of the big powers. Croats chose the wrong side in the hope of securing their independence. In addition, the political power fell in the hands of incapable, frustrated immigrants, who did not hesitate to punish the supposed instigators of their frustrations and bad fortune while themselves bending before those who installed them in power. The other half of Croats and many of the Croat ethnic Serbs chose to carry on the revolution for the benefit of another wrong side – the Communists. The end result was a civil war, accompanied by considerable bloodshed, mutual hatred, and loss of life.

At the end of the war, the Communists emerged as victors, acknowledged also by the Allies who had beaten Hitler's Nazi Germany. The Allies no longer cared that Communists only then began to put the finishing touches to their revolution. The core of the revolution was the elimination of former enemies and any potential political opponents: the Croatian regular army, members of the Croatian Peasant Party, the Catholic Church, intellectuals, rich farmers, industrialists, etc. The killing fields in that time of peace became larger than during the war, and prisons and concentration camps augmented the situation until the 'reeducation' of the 'bourgeois and anti-people's elements' was judged satisfactory.

In all those situations the Catholic Church tried to raise its voice, reminding the Church opponents and its faithful of moral principles. The Church leaders estimated their role differently in different political settings. During the period of the Austro-Hungarian Empire, the Church opposed 'liberalism' and its ideology. In monarchist Yugoslavia, while continuing to counter the liberal ideas then in a different garb, the Church often stood up in defence of oppressed Croat peasants and Croat rights in general. In the NDH, the Church tried to remind all sides of moral principles, criticizing on the one hand the Croatian Ustaše, Nazis, and Fascists and on the other hand the Communist ideology and policies. The Church leaders used public appearances, private correspondence, the prestige of the Holy See representatives and offices, and similar means to convey their opinion and judgment. Bishops' warnings had little effect, if anyone listened at all. The Church was most effective in works of charity, bringing about concrete help to the needy and the persecuted.

Under the Communist regime, the Church was denied even that. Silenced and deprived of the means for survival, the Church became the solace of those who lost family members at the hands of the Communists or were opponents of Communism. The Church never credited the Communists for freeing the country, thus becoming the refuge for the like-minded and, in the absence of political pluralism, a sole quasi opposition not only to the official ideology but to the government as well. That was the position forced upon the Church, a position it did not really know how to fill, nor enjoyed.

Selective Bibliography

Actes et documents du Saint Siège relatifs à la seconde guerre mondiale, ed. Pierre Blet, Angelo Martini, Burkhart Schneider and Robert Graham. 11 vols. (Vatican City: Libreria Editrice Vaticana, 1965-1981).
Stella Alexander, *Church and State in Yugoslavia since 1945* (Cambridge: Cambridge University Press, 1979).
Alojzije Stepinac. Propovijedi, govori, poruke (1941-1946), ed. Juraj Batelja and Celestin Tomić (Zagreb: AGM, 1996).
Anto Baković, *Svećenici žrtve rata i poraća 1941-1945 i dalje* (Zagreb: By the author, 1994).
Ivo Banac, *The National Question in Yugoslavia: Origins, History, Politics* (Ithaca, NJ/London: Cornell University Press, 1984).
Aleksa Benigar, *Alojzije Stepinac, Hrvatski kardinal* (Rome: Zajednica Izdanja Ranjeni Labud, 1974).
Fiorello Cavalli, *El proceso de monsenor Stepinac* (Madrid: Ediciones Acción Católica Española, 1947).
Philip J. Cohen, *Serbia's Secret War: Propaganda and the Deceit of History*, East European Studies, 2 (College Station, TX: Texas A&M University Press, 1996).
"Dnevnik Alojzija Stepinca." With foreword of Ljubo Boban. *Danas* (May 29 to October 2, 1990).
Veljko Đ. Đurić, *Ustaše i pravoslavije: Hrvatska pravoslavna crkva* (Beograd: Beletra, 1989).
Veljko Đ. Đurić, *Golgota Srpske pravoslavne crkve 1941-1945* (Beograd: By the author, ³1998).
Ivo Goldstein, *Holokaust u Zagrebu* (Zagreb: Novi Liber/Židovska općina, 2001).
Stan Granic, "Representations of the Other: The Ustaše and the Demonisation of the Croats," *Journal of Croatian Studies* 34 (1998) 3-56.
Jere Jareb, *Pola stoljeća hrvatske politike* (Zagreb: Hrvatski institut za povijest, 1995).
Tomislav Jonjić, *Hrvatska vanjska politika 1903-1945*. Vol. 3: *Hrvatska vanjska politika 1939-1942* (Zagreb: Libar, 2000).
Jugoslavenske vlade u izbjeglištvu 1941-1943. Dokumenti, ed. Bogdan Krizman (Zagreb/Beograd: Globus/Arhiv Jugoslavije, 1981).
Josip Jurčević, *Bleiburg: Jugoslavenski poratni zločini nad Hrvatima* (Zagreb: Dokumentacijsko informacijsko središte, 2005).
Nada Kisić-Kolanović, "Vrijeme političke represije: 'veliki sudski precesi' u Hrvatskoj 1945.-1948.," *Časopis za suvremenu povijest* 25, no. 1 (1993) 1-23.
Stjepan Kožul, *Stradanja u zagrebačkoj nadbiskupije za vrijeme Drugoga svjetskog rata i poraća* (Zagreb: "Tkalčić," 2004).
Stjepan Kožul, *Spomenica žrtvama ljubavi zagrebačke nadbiskupije* (Zagreb: AGM, 1992).
Jure Krišto, *Katolička crkva i Nezavisna Država Hrvatska* (Zagreb: Hrvatski institut za povijest, 1998).
Jure Krišto, *Sukob simbola: Politika, vjere i ideologije u Nezavisnoj Državi Hrvatskoj* (Zagreb: Nakladni zavod Globus, 2001).

Bogdan Krizman, *Pavelić i ustaše* (Zagreb: Globus, 1978).
Giuseppe Masucci, *Misija u Hrvatskoj Dnevnik od 1. kolovoza 1941. do 28. ožujka 1946*, ed. Marijan Mikac (Madrid: "Drina," 1967).
Margareta Matijević, "Stepinčev. 'Dossier'. Svetoj Stolici (31.05.1943)," *Croatica Christiana Periodica* 21, no. 40 (1997) 107-139.
Miloš Obrknežević, "Razvoj pravoslavlja u Hrvatskoj i Hrvatska pravoslavna crkva," *Hrvatska revija* 29, no. 2 (1979) 229-267.
Harriet Pass Freidenreich, *The Jews of Yugoslavia: A Quest for Community* (Philadelphia, PA: The Jewish Publication Society of America, 1979).
Richard Pattee, *The Case of Cardinal Aloysius Stepinac* (Milwaukee, WI: The Bruce Publishing Company, 1953).
Petar Požar, *Hrvatska pravoslavna crkva u prošlosti i budućnosti* (Zagreb: Naklada Pavičić, 1996).
Radmila Radić, *Verom protiv vere. Država i verske zajednice u Srbiji 1945-1953* (Beograd: INIS, 1995).
Ronald J. Rychlak, *Hitler, the War, and the Pope* (Columbus, MS: Genesis Press, 2000).
Marko Sinovčić, *N.D.H. u svietlu dokumenata* (Zagreb: Vrtna gora, ²1998 [Buenos Aires, ¹1950]).
Stepinac mu je ime: Zbornik uspomena, svjedočanstava i dokumenata, ed. Vinko Nikolić. 2 vols., Knjižnica Hrvatski revije, 9, 10 (München: Hrvatska revija, 1978-1980).
Nikolai Tolstoy, *The Minister and the Massacres* (London: Century Hutchinson Ltd., 1986).
Jozo Tomasevich, *War and Revolution in Yugoslavia, 1941-1945*. Vol. 1: *The Chetniks*. Vol. 2: *Occupation and Collaboration* (Stanford, CA: Stanford University Press, 1975, 2001).
Vladimir Žerjavić, *Population Losses in Yugoslavia 1941-1945* (Zagreb: Dom i svijet/Hrvatski institut za povijest, 1997).

Staat und Kirche in Slowenien 1941-1950

Tamara Griesser-Pečar

I. Slowenische Geschichtsschreibung – die Notwendigkeit einer Reform

Während in Westeuropa der 8. Mai 1945 als Tag des Sieges der Demokratie über das nationalsozialistische und das faschistische Terrorregime gefeiert werden konnte, war in Ostmitteleuropa die Freude über die Beendigung des Krieges getrübt. Dort wurde die nationalsozialistische Herrschaft mittelbar oder unmittelbar von einem System abgelöst, das eine neue, nämlich kommunistische, Diktatur begründete. Dies galt auch für Slowenien, das bis zum Zusammenbruch 1990/91 Teilrepublik Jugoslawiens gewesen war. In diesem Land, das erst am 25. Juni 1991 ein unabhängiger, demokratischer Staat wurde, herrscht heute eine heftige politische Kontroverse darüber, wie die Zeit des Zweiten Weltkrieges zu deuten sei. Diese Debatte setzt sich auch in den Reihen der Historiker fort. So stehen auf der einen Seite die Befürworter der nur wenig modifizierten alten Regime-Interpretation. In ihr wird – ganz in der Tradition der Propaganda vergangener Tage – der von den Kommunisten dominierte Volksbefreiungskampf verherrlicht und die Existenz eines Bürgerkriegs geleugnet. Auf der anderen Seite aber gibt es immer mehr Historiker, die eine ideologische Darstellung ablehnen und sich der Geschichtsschreibung als Wissenschaft verpflichtet fühlen.

Im Mittelpunkt dieser Auseinandersetzung steht auch die Darstellung der Rolle der Katholischen Kirche, die von der alten Regime-Geschichtsschreibung der Kollaboration mit dem nationalsozialistischen und dem faschistischen Okkupator bezichtigt wird. Viele Vertreter der Katholischen Kirche in Slowenien wurden nach dem Zweiten Weltkrieg von den kommunistischen Machthabern zu hohen Gefängnisstrafen verurteilt – einige auch zum Tode –, weil man ihnen vorwarf, in den Jahren 1941 bis 1945 mit den Besatzern kollaboriert und damit Verrat am slowenischen Volk begangen zu haben. Der Schlüsselprozess gegen die Katholische Kirche in Slowenien, die hier gewissermaßen als Gesamtorganisation am Pranger stand, war zweifellos der Prozess gegen den Bischof von Ljubljana, Dr. Gregorij Rožman, im August 1946. Die Revision seines in Abwesenheit des Angeklagten geführten Prozesses im August 1946 – er wurde zu 18 Jahren Gefängnis mit Zwangsarbeit verurteilt – scheiterte im neuen Slowenien bereits dreimal.[1]

Der Begriff "Kollaboration" wird von den Regime-Historikern völlig undifferenziert verwendet, im Sinne einer freiwilligen Zusammenarbeit mit dem Feind – was der Schweizer Historiker Werner Rings in seinem Standardwerk *Leben mit dem Feind* als "bedingungslose Kollaboration" bezeichnet. Diese "bedingungslose Kollaboration" bedeutet jedoch, auf die Tatmotive abgehoben, die absolute Solidarisierung mit dem Feind, die Teilung von Grundsätzen und Idealen sowie die Bereitschaft zu Opfern, sofern diese der gemeinsamen Sache dienen. Dass es auch andere (u.a. auch erzwungene) Formen der Zusammenarbeit gibt – Rings unterscheidet zwischen der "bedingungslosen," der "bedingten," der "taktischen" und der "neutralen" Kollaboration – wird von den Regime-Historikern ignoriert.[2]

Bei der heutigen Bewertung der damaligen Situation kann es natürlich nicht um Verfehlungen einzelner Priester und Ordensleute gehen, die es selbstverständlich gab, sondern um die Frage, ob und wie "die Kirche" hier gehandelt hat, das heißt also, ob und wie weit sich ihre wichtigen Entscheidungsträger und (oder) eine nennenswerte Anzahl von Kirchenleuten aufgrund einer bestimmten Richtlinienbefolgung auf eine rechts- und sittenwidrige Zusammenarbeit mit den Besatzungsmächten eingelassen hatten. Seit dem Anbruch der demokratischen Ära in Slowenien wird auch die Rolle geprüft, die Menschen in kirchlicher Verantwortung in jener Zeit tatsächlich wahrgenommen hatten, aber auch die Rolle, die die kommunistischen Machthaber nach dem Krieg spielten, als sie so viele – teilweise hochrangige – Kirchenvertreter zu schwersten Strafen verurteilten. Die Frage, ob es den kommunistischen Machthabern hier wirklich um die gerechte Bestrafung für angeblichen Verrat gegangen war oder vor allem darum, die Kirche als eine für ihre Ideologie gefährliche Organisation im neuen jugoslawischen Staat moralisch zu diskreditieren, muss jetzt in aller Klarheit gestellt und beantwortet werden, wenn die historische Wahrheit noch etwas bedeuten und mögliches Unrecht nicht weiterwalten soll.

---

1. Siehe mehr dazu: Tamara Griesser-Pečar, *Cerkev na zatožni klopi: Sodni procesi, administrativne kazni, posegi "ljudske oblasti" v Sloveniji od 1943 do 1960* (Ljubljana: Družina, 2005); Tamara Griesser-Pečar und France M. Dolinar, *Rožmanov proces* (Ljubljana: Družina, 1996).

2. Werner Rings, *Leben mit dem Feind: Anpassung und Widerstand in Hitlers Europa 1939-1945* (München: Kindler, 1979) 134-197.

Das besondere Problem bei der Durchleuchtung der "Kollaboration" in den Jahren 1941 bis 1945 in Slowenien liegt darin, dass es zu jener Zeit dort nicht nur einen (Widerstands-)Kampf der Unterdrückten gegen die Unterdrücker gegeben hat, sondern zugleich, diesen überlagernd, auch einen Kampf zwischen den Unterdrückten um die "richtige" Zielsetzung, die "richtige" Art von "Befreiung" also, um das Staats- und Gesellschaftssystem, unter welchem die Slowenen nach dem späteren Kriegsende leben sollten.

II. Die Slowenen und die Katholische Kirche im Königreich Jugoslawien

"Jugoslawien" – ein künstlicher Staat nach dem Ersten Weltkrieg, geschaffen von den Entente-Mächten, dem Königreich Serbien und dem Südslawischen Exilkomitee – wurde am 1. Dezember 1918 gegründet. Es hieß zunächst Königreich der Serben, Kroaten und Slowenen und wurde mit dem Dekret vom 3. Oktober 1929 in "Königreich Jugoslawien" umbenannt. Von Anfang an war der Staat geprägt und erschüttert von Auseinandersetzungen zwischen den Nationalitäten, wobei die Serben versuchten, den im Inneren sehr vielfältigen Staat immer zentralistischer zu gestalten. Die erste Verfassung – die 'St. Veits Verfassung' (28. Juni 1921) –, wurde wegen heftiger Auseinandersetzungen der Nationalitäten am 6. Januar 1929 von König Alexander I (1888-1934) außer Kraft gesetzt, die Parteien wurden aufgelöst, die demokratischen Freiheiten eingeschränkt. Im Oktober 1929 wurden dann die historischen Landschaften als Verwaltungsbezirke abgeschafft und statt 33 Regierungsbereichen neun Banschaften gebildet. Die Drau-Banschaft [Dravska banovina] umfasste nach der Korrektur im Jahre 1931, als der südöstliche Teil des slowenischen Gebietes, Bela Krajina [Weißkrain], dazu kam, in etwa das Gebiet, in welchem die Slowenen im neuen Staat lebten.

Eine neue Verfassung – die sogenannte Oktroyierte Verfassung – trat am 3. September 1932 in Kraft und behielt ihre Gültigkeit bis 1941. Auf dem Papier bekamen die Bürger eine Reihe von Grundrechten (die Gleichheit vor dem Gesetz, die Freiheit des Gewissens, die Unantastbarkeit der Wohnung, die Unabhängigkeit der Gerichte und die Gleichberechtigung der Konfessionen) zugebilligt, doch wurden diese Freiheiten in der Praxis durch das "Schutzgesetz" ausgehöhlt. Außerdem sah die Verfassung eine zentralistische und unitaristische Staatsordnung vor und stärkte die Rechte des Königs.

Zwei Tage nach dem unter massivem Druck der Deutschen vollzogenen Beitritt zum Dreierbund kam es am 27. März 1941 zum Putsch. Die Regierung wurde gestürzt und die Regentschaft für den minderjährigen König Peter II. (1923-1970) beendet. König Peter übernahm die Macht und ging nach dem deutschen Angriff auf Jugoslawien am 6. April 1941 mit seiner Regierung, in der auch zwei Slowenen saßen, ins Exil.

Die Katholische Kirche hatte im Königreich Jugoslawien nicht jene dominante Rolle wie zuvor in Österreich-Ungarn. Nach der Zählung von 1921 war sie die zweitgrößte Religionsgemeinschaft mit 4.708.673 Gläubigen, hinter der Serbisch-Orthodoxen Kirche mit 5.593.057 Gläubigen, zu welcher auch die königliche Familie und fast alle Mitglieder des Militärkommandos zählten. Es folgten die Muslime (1.345.271), die Evangelische Kirche (229.517), die Juden (64.746) und die Griechisch-Katholische Kirche (40.338). In Slowenien lebten nach dieser Zählung 1.054.919 Katholiken, 27.282 evangelische Christen, 6.622 Orthodoxe, 936 Juden, 649 Muslime, 531 Griechisch-Katholische.[3]

Kirchenrechtlich war das Gebiet, auf dem die Slowenen lebten, bis zum Zusammenbruch der Habsburger Monarchie in vier Kirchenprovinzen eingeteilt: Görz mit den Suffraganbistümern Laibach [Ljubljana] und Triest-Koper, Udine – die Slowenen lebten im Kanaltal und in den Tälern Natisone und Torre [Slavi Veneti] –, Salzburg mit den Suffraganen in Klagenfurt, Graz und Marburg [Maribor], schließlich Gram [Esztergom] mit dem Suffragan in Steinamanger [Szombately].[4] Die Friedensverträge von St. Germain, Trianon und Rapallo – sowie die Volksabstimmung 1920 in Kärnten – zerstörten die alten Strukturen. Ein Drittel der Slowenen blieb außerhalb der jugoslawischen Grenzen.

Das so genannte Küstenland, Venezia Giulia [Julisch Venetien] – das waren 350 Gemeinden mit 901.364 Einwohnern, davon 38 % Slowenen und Kroaten[5] – fiel 1920 an Italien und wurde seit der faschistischen Übernahme systematisch italianisiert. Ab 1923, nach der Bildungsreform, verschwand die slowenische Sprache aus den Schulprogrammen,

---

3. France M. Dolinar, "Die Katholische Kirche in Slowenien im 20. Jahrhundert," *Slovensko-avsrijski odnosi v 20. stoletju/Slowenisch-österreichische Beziehungen im 20. Jahrhundert*, ed. Dušan Nečak u.a. (Ljubljana: Historia, 2004) 434-435. Die evangelischen Christen waren am stärksten im Übermurgebiet, doch gab es auch je eine kleine Gemeinde in Marburg und Laibach, die Orthodoxen siedelten sich erst nach 1919 in Slowenien an, sie kamen zum großen Teil aus den Reihen der Soldaten und deren Familien. Die Juden lebten hauptsächlich in Prekmurje.
4. *Ibid.*, 429-432.
5. *Slovenska kronika XX. stoletja*, ed. Marjan Drnovšek und Drago Bajt, Bd. 1 (Ljubljana: Nova revija, 1995) 251.

1928 wurden alle slowenischen periodischen Druckerzeugnisse verboten, ebenso die Bildungs- und Kultureinrichtungen. Nach und nach verschwanden auch alle slowenischen Wirtschaftsinstitutionen. Dass die slowenische Sprache sich dennoch erhalten konnte, ist zu erheblichem Teil den Geistlichen zu verdanken. Insgeheim verbreiteten sie slowenische Bücher, Zeitungen sowie Lieder und stärkten, wo sie nur konnten, das slowenische Nationalbewusstsein. Die Kirche wurde zum Klassenzimmer – die Kinder hatten im Religionsunterricht auch ein slowenisches Lesebuch neben sich liegen.

Die Grenze zu Österreich wurde – gemäß dem Vertrag von St. Germain vom 10.9.1919 – nach der Kärntner Volksabstimmung vom 10.10.1920 festgelegt. Bei einer Wahlbeteiligung von 95,79% entschied sich die Bevölkerung in der Abstimmungszone A – in den Distrikten Völkermarkt, Ferlach, Rosegg und Bleiburg – zu 59,04% für Österreich und zu 40,06% für Jugoslawien. Die Abstimmung in der Zone B fand dann gar nicht mehr statt.[6]

Die Lage der Kärntner Slowenen und insbesondere slowenischer Priester war von Anfang an schwierig, obwohl sich das Kulturleben der Slowenen zunächst erfreulich entwickeln konnte – vor allem auch wegen des Einsatzes des slowenischen Klerus. Schon das katholische Österreich unter Kanzler Kurt v. Schuschnigg aber ließ in Kärnten die deutschnationalen Kreise gewähren, die vor allem im Kärntner Heimatdienst organisiert waren und deren Ziel es war, das Land zu germanisieren. Nach dem Anschluss Österreichs an das Deutsche Reich 1938 wurden die Germanisierungstendenzen wesentlich verschärft. Unmittelbar danach setzte auch die Verfolgung der slowenischen Priester ein, die, ähnlich wie im Küstengebiet, als Träger des Nationalgedankens und Pfleger der slowenischen Sprache den nationalsozialistischen Zielen im Wege standen. Die Geistlichen wurden in Gefängnisse geworfen, in Konzentrationslager geschickt, aus dem gesamten zweisprachigen Gebiet vertrieben usw. Während der Nazi-Herrschaft wurden in Kärnten rund 62 slowenische Priester vertrieben, verhaftet bzw. in Konzentrationslager eingewiesen, sieben von ihnen starben in den Konzentrationslagern oder an den Haft-Folgen nach ihrer Freilassung.[7]

Die neuen Staatsgrenzen Jugoslawiens teilten nicht nur die Bistümer, sondern auch, innerhalb dieser, die Pfarreien. So wurde ein Teil des von

---

6. Tamara Pečar, *Die Stellung der slowenischen Landesregierung zum Land Kärnten 1918-1920* (Diss. Wien, 1973).

7. Augustin Malle, "Koroški Slovenci in katoliška cerkev v času nacizma," *Volks- und staatsfeindlich: Die Vertreibung der Kärntner Slowenen 1942* (Klagenfurt: Hermagoras, 1942) 85-130.

den Slowenen bewohnten Kärnten Jugoslawien zugeteilt – Unterdrauburg, Mießtal, Seeland [Dravograd, Mežiška dolina, Jezersko]. Die Bistümer Görz und Triest kamen zu Italien, das Bistum Laibach verlor vier Dekanate. Die Slowenen im Übermurgebiet wurden der Verwaltung des Bischofs von Lavant [Maribor] unterstellt. Die Diözese Lavant wurde 1924 aus der Kirchenprovinz Salzburg ausgegliedert, die Diözese Laibach 1933 aus der Kirchenprovinz Görz. Beide wurden unmittelbar dem Heiligen Stuhl untergeordnet.

Heftige Auseinandersetzungen gab es im Königreich im Zusammenhang mit dem angestrebten Konkordat, welches Jugoslawien 1935 mit dem Vatikan schloss. Erst zwei Jahre später wurde dieser Vertrag der *Skupščina*, dem jugoslawischen Parlament, zur Ratifizierung vorgelegt und scheiterte vor allem an der serbischen Orthodoxie. Strittig waren vor allem die folgenden Passagen: Depolitisierung des katholischen Klerus (Widerstand der Kroaten), das Recht der Minderheiten, im Gottesdienst die Muttersprache zu verwenden, das Recht der Katholischen Kirche neue Bistümer zu gründen. Obwohl die überwiegende Mehrheit im jugoslawischen Parlament der Ratifizierung zustimmte, wagte es die Regierung unter Ministerpräsident Milan Stojadinović wegen der Drohungen der serbisch-orthodoxen Kirche und wegen der Demonstrationen in Belgrad nicht, das Ergebnis der Abstimmung dem Senat vorzulegen. Daher wurde es nicht rechtskräftig.[8]

Wegen der unterschiedlichen Rechtsnormen, die im neuen Staat aufeinandertrafen, gab es auch kirchenrechtlich in Slowenien erhebliche Probleme. So glaubte der König, dass er vom österreichischen Kaiser das Ernennungsrecht der katholischen Bischöfe geerbt hätte, doch räumte der Hl. Stuhl dem orthodoxen Monarchen dieses Recht nicht ein. Außerdem missachtete das Königreich Jugoslawien die Zweckbestimmung des Religionsfonds. Dies war das Vermögen, das entstanden war, nachdem Joseph II die Klöster und kirchlichen Vereinigungen aufgelöst hatte. Zwar wurde der Religionsfond staatlich verwaltet, doch standen dessen Erträge zur Gänze der Kirche zu. Nun aber bekam die Katholische Kirche im neuen Staat außer minimalen Zuschüssen, die den katholischen Priestern bezahlt wurden, nichts. Die aus dem Statut abgeleiteten Pflichten wurden nicht erfüllt, vor allem nicht bei den Erhaltungskosten der kirchlichen Gebäude. So wurden die Schulden des Staates gegenüber der Kirche immer größer, bis die Regierung nicht mehr in der Lage

---

8. Mehr dazu: Metod Mikuž, *Slovenci v stari Jugoslaviji* (Ljubljana: Mladinska knjiga, 1965) 453-455.

war, diese zu begleichen. So wurde 1939 die Verwaltung des Religionsfonds an die slowenische Katholische Kirche übertragen. Die Bedingung war, dass die angelaufenen Schulden des Staates gegenüber der Kirche damit gelöscht wurden.[9]

Es gab auch große Probleme in Erziehungs- und Schulfragen. Das neue Schulgesetz von 1929, das eindeutig die einheitliche "jugoslawische Nation" propagierte, erlaubte auch keine Neugründung von Privatschulen mehr. Die bestehenden mussten sich innerhalb vier Monate den neuen Vorschriften anpassen. Kirchliche Schulen hatten aber lange Tradition in Slowenien. Sie wurden – neben dem bischöflichen Gymnasium oberhalb von Laibach – hauptsächlich von den Ordensgemeinschaften der Ursulinen, Schulschwestern, Franziskaner und Salesianer geführt.

Die Auseinandersetzung um die Schule führte zu einem Hirtenbrief der jugoslawischen Bischöfe vom 5. Mai 1938, der den antiklerikalen und atheistischen Geist in den Schulen beklagte. Zur Verschärfung der Konflikte trug auch die Auflösung aller Turnvereine bei, die sich nicht in den neugegründeten allstaatlichen Verein Sokol des Königreiches Jugoslawien eingliedern wollten. Zu ihnen gehörte auch der katholische Turnverein Orel [Adler], der dann 1937 unter einem anderem Namen wiedergegründet wurde Der frühere Jugoslawische Sokolverein trat in den staatlichen Verein Sokol ein und genoss große Privilegien. Die katholischen Bischöfe kritisierten dessen antireligiöse Orientierung. Die Folge war, dass das Regime großen Druck auf die Priester ausübte.[10]

Das religiöse Leben in Slowenien war sehr rege. Es gab zahlreiche Kongregationen, Bruderschaften, Marianische Vereinigungen, den Dritten Orden des Hl. Franz von Assisi, Wallfahrten, feierliche Prozessionen und drei wichtige Kongresse in Laibach: 1930 den Internationalen Missionskongress der Akademiker, 1935 den Eucharistischen Kongress für Jugoslawien und 1939 den Internationalen Christ-Königs-Kongress.

Die letzten Parlamentswahlen in Jugoslawien fanden im Jahr 1938 statt. Stärkste Partei wurde die Jugoslawische Radikale Gemeinschaft [Jugoslavenska radikalna zajednica, JRZ], in welcher die bürgerlich-bäuerliche Slowenische Volkspartei [Slovenska ljudska stranka, SLS]

---

9. France M. Dolinar, "Verski sklad," *Ilustrirana zgodovina Slovencev* (Ljubljana: Mladinska knjiga, 1999) 196; Vinko Rajšp, "Verski sklad," *Gestrinov zbornik* (Ljubljana: ZRC SAZU, 1999) 217-227.
10. Dolinar, "Die katholische Kirche in Slowenien," 435-436; Tamara Griesser-Pečar, *Das zerrissene Volk: Slowenien 1941-1946. Okkupation, Kollaboration, Bürgerkrieg, Revolution*, Studien zur Politik und Wissenschaft, 86 (Wien/Köln/Graz: Böhlau, 2003) 11.

integriert war. Sie erhielt in Slowenien 78,64% der Stimmen. Die SLS fußte stark auf dem katholischen Glauben und war auf eine weitgehende slowenische Autonomie ausgerichtet sowie auf Gleichberechtigung der drei Völker. In ihr waren besonders viele katholische Geistliche aktiv. Lange Jahre bis zu seinem Tod im September 1940 wurde die Partei vom Geistlichen Anton Korošec angeführt, der jugoslawischer Innenminister war, danach Präsident des Senats in Belgrad und zum Schluss Unterrichtsminister.

Zweitstärkste Formation wurde mit den letzten Wahlen in Slowenien die Oppositionsliste mit dem Kroaten Vladimir Maček an der Spitze, in welche in Slowenien die Liberalen und die Sozialisten eingebunden waren. Sie erhielten 20,88% der Stimmen. Zwischen dem liberalen und katholischen Lager gab es besondere Spannungen, vor allem während der Alexander-Diktatur unter dem Ministerpräsidenten Petar Živković.

Die Kommunistische Partei Jugoslawiens war eine illegale Partei. Sie wurde per Beschluss des Ministerrats bereits Ende Dezember 1920 verboten – mit der Begründung, sie plane einen Staatsumsturz. Im August 1921 wurde jedwede kommunistische Tätigkeit untersagt und den kommunistischen Abgeordneten das Parlamentsmandat abgenommen.

Die slowenische Katholische Kirche war stark antikommunistisch geprägt. Sie stand fest hinter der Enzyklika *Divini Redemptoris* (Pius XI., 19.3.1937) sowie dem Hirtenbrief des jugoslawischen Episkopats vom 12.1.1937. In der Laibacher Diözese wurde dies auch mit den Beschlüssen der Diözesansynode vom 1940 bekräftigt.

In den dreißiger Jahren kam es innerhalb der katholischen Gruppierungen zu großen Spannungen und Konflikten. Vor allem in den Christlich-sozialen Gruppierungen wuchs die Polarisierung. Heftige Auseinandersetzungen gab es auch zwischen den verschiedenen akademischen Klubs. Auf der konservativen Seite stand neben der Katholischen Aktion der Studentenklub Straža [Die Wache].

III. Der Krieg

1. Die Politik der Besatzer

Nach dem Angriff Deutschlands auf Jugoslawien am 6. April 1941 wurde das 15.036 km² große slowenische Gebiet gleich von drei Mächten okkupiert: Deutschland, Italien und Ungarn. Den größten Teil besetzten die Deutschen – sie nahmen sich die Untersteiermark, das

Mießtal, Oberkrain, Zasavje –, während die Italiener Laibach, Innerkrain [Notranjska], Unterkrain [Dolenjska], Weißkrain okkupierten. Ein kleiner Teil war von den Ungarn besetzt: nämlich das Übermurgebiet im Nordosten – ausgenommen vier Gemeinden im westlicheren Teil, die an Deutschland fielen. Nach der italienischen Kapitulation am 8.9.1943 fiel auch das von den Italienern besetzte Gebiet unter deutsche Verwaltung.

Zum Zeitpunkt der Okkupation war die Drau-Banschaft kirchlich in zwei Diözesen organisiert: Lavant (Marburg a.d. Drau) und Laibach. Das Lavanter Bistum (später Bistum Marburg) wurde zur Gänze von den Deutschen besetzt. Damit übernahmen die Bistümer Seckau und Gurk ihre jeweiligen Pfarreien, die in Jugoslawien lagen und bis dahin vom Lavanter Bischof, Dr. Ivan Tomažič, als Apostolischem Administrator, verwaltet worden waren, wieder in ihre eigene Verwaltung. Die Apostolische Administration Murska krajina (Übermurgebiet), bestehend aus den Dekanaten Murska Sobota und Dolnja Lendava, die nach Anordnung des Lavanter Bischofs vom 24.4. bis zum 1.6.1941 von Generalvikar Ivan Jerič verwaltet worden waren, wurde zunächst vom Bischof von Szombathely, Josef Grösz, übernommen, dem 1944 Bischof Sandor Kovacs nachfolgte. Im April 1945 ging die kirchliche Verwaltung des Übermurgebietes dann wieder auf Dechant Jerič über – bis August 1946, als Jerič von den Kommunisten ins Gefängnis geworfen wurde und der Marburger Bischof Tomažič wieder die kirchliche Verwaltung und Jurisdiktion übernahm.[11]

Das Gebiet der Laibacher Diözese wurde infolge der deutschen und italienischen Besatzung in zwei Teile geteilt: 134 Pfarreien mit der Landeshauptstadt – die so genannte Provincia di Lubiana [Provinz Laibach] – fielen unter die italienische, der größere zweite Teil, Oberkrain und Zasavje mit 142 Pfarreien, unter die deutsche Besatzung. Die Verwaltung des deutsch-besetzten Teils kam in den Zuständigkeitsbereich des Kapitularvikars der Diözese Gurk (Klagenfurt), Andreas Rohracher.

Alle drei Besatzungsmächte strebten eine möglichst rasche Angliederung der jeweiligen Bereiche an ihr Staatsgebiet an. Die Italiener verabschiedeten am 3.5.1941 ein Autonomie-Statut für ihre besetzten Gebiete, die Ungarn vollzogen den formalrechtlichen Anschluss am 16.12.1941. Der Anschluss der deutsch-besetzten Gebiete an das Deutsche Reich sollte am 1.10.1941 erfolgen, doch wurde er zunächst verschoben, da erst die Einsetzung des neuen Gauleiters und Reichsstatt-

---

11. ŠAM, Medvojna in povojna leta I und Karthotek Jerič.

halters von Kärnten abgewartet werden sollte. Schließlich wurde der Anschluss bis auf weiteres fallengelassen – wegen der anhaltenden Partisanenkämpfe, mit welchen man zuerst fertig werden wollte, ehe das Land zum – auch formalrechtlich – ordentlichen Teil des Deutschen Reiches avancieren sollte. Nur das Mießtal wurde sogleich direkt dem Reichsgau Kärnten angegliedert.

Vieles spricht dafür, dass die deutschen, italienischen und ungarischen Besatzer das gleiche Ziel im Auge hatten, nämlich das slowenische Volk ethnisch zu vernichten. Dennoch unterschieden sich Vorgehensweise und Lebensbedingungen in den drei Zonen erheblich voneinander. Gemäß Hitlers Auftrag "Machen Sie mir die Untersteiermark wieder deutsch!" verboten die Deutschen alle slowenischen politischen und kulturellen Einrichtungen. So wurden zum Beispiel in Marburg a.d. Drau vom 25.9.1941 bis Ende 1942 451 Vereine und Organisationen aufgelassen bzw. liquidiert. 17 mussten den Namen ändern, 5 wurden neu gegründet. Bei den zwangsaufgelösten Einrichtungen handelte es sich vorwiegend um slowenische Kulturvereine, konfessionelle Organisationen, Stiftungen und gewerkschaftliche Gruppierungen.[12] Vor allem viele Geistliche setzten sich für die Erhaltung der nationalen und kulturellen Identität ein, weshalb sie den von radikalen Eindeutschungsplänen beseelten Nationalsozialisten besonders gefährlich erschienen. Diese Einschätzung wird unter anderem auch von einem Bericht bestätigt, der kurz vor dem deutschen Angriff vom Reichssicherheitshauptamt verfasst worden war. In ihm hieß es unter anderem: "Träger des deutschfeindlichen Gedankens sind der Klerus, der im Volke einen starken Einfluss hat, und die slowenische Intelligenz, insbesondere die Lehrerschaft und die Rechtsanwälte."[13] Doch eigentlich konnten sich die Slowenen ohnehin keinen Illusionen hingeben, die Berichte aus okkupierten Ländern Europas, vor allem über die Behandlung ihrer Landsleute unter dem Faschismus und dem Nationalsozialismus anderswo, sprachen eine deutliche Sprache.

Am 10.4.1941 wurden in Marburg im bischöflichen Ordinariat und in den benachbarten kirchlichen Gebäuden – im Domkapitelhaus und im Dompfarrhaus – Hausdurchsuchungen durchgeführt. Bald nach den ersten Durchsuchungen folgte die Beschlagnahme der ersten Gebäude in Kirchenbesitz, darunter auch des Sitzes des Domkapitels,

---

12. Stefan Karner, *Die deutschsprachige Volksgruppe in Slowenien* (Klagenfurt/Ljubljana/Wien: Styria, 1998) 90; Tone Ferenc, *Quellen zur nationalsozialistischen Entnationalisierungspolitik in Slowenien 1941-1945* (Maribor: Obzorja, 1980) 54, 73.

13. RHSA, Jugoslawien, 35.

des Priesterseminars usw. Aber auch Geld, Pretiosen, Sparkassenbücher, Wertpapiere, Mobiliar wurden mitgenommen.[14]

In der Karwoche, noch vor der Übernahme der Verwaltung durch die Deutschen, wurden die ersten Priester von Mitgliedern des Kulturbundes festgenommen. Nach der Übernahme der Verwaltung rollte am 15.4.1941 die erste große Verhaftungswelle an. Die Nazis kamen nach Marburg nämlich mit fertiggestellten Verzeichnissen von zu verhaftenden Personen. Dabei wurden von Sicherheitspolizei, SA und Wehrmacht 300 Personen festgenommen – vorwiegend Angehörige der slowenischen Intelligenz, Geistliche, Professoren und Lehrer. Die vorhandenen Gefängnisse konnten die Massen gar nicht aufnehmen, so dass an verschiedenen Punkten Sammelstellen eingerichtet wurden. Von dort wurden die Gefangenen in die Sammellager gebracht: nach Marburg a.d. Drau in die Kaserne Melling [Melje], die bereits nach einem Monat mit 1415 politischen Häftlingen, darunter auch 41 Frauen, gefüllt war,[15] nach Šmartno (bei Windischgrätz) ins Pfarrhaus, nach Cilli ins Gefängnis Stari pisker, aber auch in das Kapuzinerkloster und in die Kaserne sowie ins Schloss Borl bei Pettau. Zum Schluss wurde auch das Trapistenkloster in Reichenburg [Rajhenberg] zum Lager umfunktioniert.

Die Geistlichen wurden in den deutschen Gefängnissen besonders schlecht behandelt, sie wurden verhöhnt, verlacht, geschlagen, es wurde ihnen nicht gestattet, die Messe zu lesen. Besonders erniedrigend empfanden sie das sog. Pflicht-Turnen. Sie mußten Kniebeugen machen, sich auf dem Boden in den Schmutz werfen, dabei wurden sie geschlagen und mit Waffen bedroht. Mit bloßen Händen mußten sie die Senkgrube leeren und auf den Straßen den Abfall sammeln. In Marburg a.d. Drau wurden sie wie Vieh vor Waggone gespannt und mußten Lebensmittel für die Gefangenen transportieren. Außerdem wurden sie von den Nazis gezwungen, die serbisch-orthodoxe Kirche in Marburg abzureißen. Die Besatzer photographierten dies und nutzten es als Propagandamittel in Serbien.

Die erste Umsiedlungs-Welle begann mit dem ersten Transport am 7.6.1941 und endete mit dem 12. Transport, der Rajhenburg am 5.7.1941 verließ. Insgesamt wurden aus dem Lavanter Bistum 366 Priester verhaftet und nach Kroatien, teilweise Serbien ausgesiedelt.[16]

14. ŠAM, P8/VI, Aktennotizen von dr. Ivan Jožef Tomažič, 10.4.1941; Miloš Rybář, "Nacistični ukrepi zoper duhovščino Lavantinske škofije 1941-1945," *Zbornik ob 750-letnici Mariborske škofije 1228-1978* (Maribor: Škofijski ordinariat, 1978) 87.
15. Karner, *Die deutschsprachige Volksgruppe*, 90.
16. Tamara Griesser-Pečar, "Pomen, 'osvoboditve' za slovensko katoliško Cerkev," *Slovenija v letu 1945*, ed. Aleš Gabrič (Ljubljana: Zveza zgodovinskih društev Slovenije, 1996) 113. Rybář, "Nacistični ukrepi," 57.

Die Priester der Gurker Diözese in Slowenien wurden nach Klagenfurt überstellt und dann über das Lager in St.Veit oberhalb von Laibach ebenfalls ausgesiedelt. So gab es am 11.7.1941 einen größeren Transport mit 108 Priestern aus Oberkrain sowie 14 aus der Steiermark und dem Mießtal. Weil das Übermurgebiet zunächst von den Deutschen besetzt wurde, wurden auch dort Priester verhaftet. Generalvikar Jerič bat am 26.5.1941 die Nuntiatur um Intervention. Diese trat sofort an Kultusminister Dr. Hóman Bálint heran, der dann bei Bischof Grösz nachfragte, ob es irgendwelche Hindernisse gebe, die Priester aus dem Übermurgebiet zu repatriieren. Der Bischof verneinte dies und fügte eine Namensliste der bereits Zurückgekehrten bei.[17]

Auch in Oberkrain waren es vor allem Intellektuelle, in erster Linie katholische Priester und Ordensleute, die Opfer dieser ersten brutalen Maßnahmen wurden. So wie in der Untersteiermark war auch in den deutsch besetzten Teilen des Bistums Laibach die Religionsausübung schwer behindert. Die slowenische Sprache war in den Kirchen untersagt. Aus dem deutsch besetzten Bistum Laibach-Oberkrain, teilweise auch aus Unterkrain wurden im Laufe des Krieges 184 Weltpriester und 78 Ordensleute ausgesiedelt – die meisten nach Kroatien.

Einige Priester wurden in die Konzentrationslager geschickt, nach Dachau, Mauthausen und Jasenovac. In Dachau waren aus dem Bistum Laibach 3, aus Marburg 11, aus dem Küstengebiet 3 Diözesanpriester und insgesamt 9 Ordenspriester inhaftiert, 4 starben in Dachau. Ein Priester, der im illegalen Nachrichtendienst tätig gewesen war, starb in Mauthausen. 8 wurden im kroatischen Jasenovac umgebracht. Sie waren ausgesiedelt und dann auf Grund deutscher Anordnung von den Ustascha-Behörden verhaftet und nach Jasenovac gebracht worden. Außerdem erschossen die Deutschen 10 Geistliche – überwiegend als Geiseln –, die Italiener einen.

In der Untersteiermark gab es Ende 1941 nur noch 121 Priester – von 608 im April 1941 –, darunter waren 27 bereits pensioniert und acht nicht in der Seelsorge tätig. Bleiben durften nur jene, die bereits 1914 ihren Wohnsitz im Gebiet hatten. In Oberkrain und Zasavje war die Lage ähnlich. Von 260 Priestern wurden 205 vertrieben. Nahezu alle Ordensleute wurden vertrieben, nur die Barmherzigen Schwestern durften bleiben, weil sie in den Krankenhäusern beschäftigt waren. Viele slowenische Priester suchten sofort Zuflucht in der Provinz Laibach,

---

17. Ivan Jerič, *Moji spomini* (Murska Sobota: Zavod sv. Miklavža, 2000) 180-182. Insgesamt waren dies 54 slowenische Priester. Rybář, "Nacistični ukrepi," 84.

andere wiederum kamen später von Kroatien aus dahin, weil sich Bischof Gregorij Rožman bei den italienischen Besatzungsbehörden für sie massiv einsetzte. Dies hatte zur Folge, daß sich in der Provinz Laibach plötzlich 905 Geistliche für 134 Pfarreien befanden, was große Versorgungsprobleme auslöste.

In der Untersteiermark beschlagnahmten die Nazis Kirchen-, Pfründen- und Mensalgut zugunsten des Beauftragten des Reichskommissars für die Festigung des deutschen Volkstums. In deutschbesetzten Gebiet des Bistums Laibach (Oberkrain) wurde das gesamte kirchliche Vermögen, nicht nur der Pfründen- und Klosterbesitz, sondern auch Kirchen und Pfarrämter beschlagnahmt, eingezogen und teils dem Reichsgau Kärnten, teils den einzelnen politischen Gemeinden zugewiesen.[18]

In der Provinz Laibach war zwar die politische Betätigung der Slowenen verboten, doch konnten die slowenischen Kulturinstitutionen, Schulen, Zeitungen – trotz scharfer Zensur – weiterhin existieren. Auch durfte in den Kirchen weiterhin in slowenischer Sprache gepredigt werden. Überhaupt war das Verhältnis der italienischen Besatzer zur Kirche ein völlig anderes als das der Deutschen, deswegen konnte die Kirche auch weiter wirken und, wie später noch zu zeigen sein wird, vielen Menschen helfen.

Die ungarischen Militärbehörden im Übermurgebiet untersagten die Verwendung der slowenischen Sprache. Wie Ungarn überhaupt die Existenz des slowenischen Volkes leugnete. Die Slowenen im Übermurgebiet waren nämlich der ungarischen Interpretation zufolge keine Slowenen,

---

18. Als die Notseelsorge von der Diözese Gurk errichtet wurde, konnten die Kirchengebäude für einen geringfügigen Zins gemietet werden. Das Bistum Laibach verlor auch seinen Waldbesitz von insgesamt 24.758,1976 Hektar. Beschlagnahmt wurde jedoch auch das älteste slowenische Gymnasium in St. Veit [Šentvid], das Institut des Heiligen Stanislaus, das sich im Eigentum des Bistums Laibach befand. Lehrer, Erzieher und Zöglinge mussten die Schule innerhalb einer Stunde verlassen. Im italienisch besetzten Laibach konnte das Gymnasium dann allerdings fortgeführt werden, bis es von den Kommunisten 1945 aufgelöst wurde. In der Untersteiermark erließ der Chef der Zivilverwaltung, Gauleiter Siegfried Uiberreither, einige Vorschriften und Erlässe, die die Kirche in besonderer Weise berührten – so am 15.4.1941 über eine Verringerung der (kirchlichen) Feiertage in der Untersteiermark, am 16.4 über die Eheschließung, am 18.4. über Erleichterungen beim Austritt aus der Kirche (man erwartete eine Austrittswelle, die aber ausblieb), am 18.4 über die sog. Wahrung der Bekenntnisfreiheit (Verbot der Namensveröffentlichung jener, die aus der Kirche ausgetreten waren), am 27.7. über die staatliche Aufsicht für die kirchliche Finanzverwaltung, am 30.9 über Zivilheirat und Standesämter (kirchliche Standesregister wurden eingezogen). Am 14.4.1942 folgte das endgültige Verbot der Verwendung der slowenischen Sprache in der Kirche. NŠAL [Erzbischöfliches Archiv, Laibach], Schriften, Klerus. Griesser-Pečar, "Pomen, 'osvoboditve'," 113-114; Griesser-Pečar und Dolinar, *Rožmanov proces*, 45-46; Griesser-Pečar, *Das zerrissene Volk*, 20-22.

sondern "Wenden." So waren auch die ersten Bekanntmachungen in Wendisch verfasst, das in Wirklichkeit ein slowenischer Dialekt ist. Alle Ortstafeln und öffentlichen Anschriften wurden entfernt und durch ungarische ersetzt, die Familiennamen magyarisiert. Namen, die den Ungarn fremd klangen, wurden einfach geändert. Die Ämter, Bildungseinrichtungen und Schulen mussten ihre slowenischen Bücher abgeben, die dann verbrannt wurden. In Murska Sobota wurde eine ganze wissenschaftliche Bibliothek verbrannt. Alle slowenischen Vereine wurden aufgelöst. Slowenische Lehrer wurden entlassen, nur wenige einheimische Pädagogen durften bleiben.

Im Zuge der Besetzung wurden viele nationalbewusste Slowenen, vor allem zahlreiche Intellektuelle und Priester, verhaftet, nicht alteingesessene Slowenen (die nach dem ersten Weltkrieg von den jugoslawischen Behörden entlang der ungarischen Grenze bei Dolnja Lendava angesiedelt worden waren) in andere Gebiete Ungarns bzw. Lager verbannt. Auch Juden[19] wurden interniert.

Bischof Josef Grösz teilte den slowenischen Priestern mit, daß er die bedingungslose Loyalität dem ungarischen Staat gegenüber wünsche und die Verkündigung des Evangeliums in der Sprache verlange, die das Volk verstehe – seiner Meinung nach war dies im slowenischen Gebiet Wendisch. Mit Vorliebe versetzte der Bischof ungarische Kapläne in slowenische Pfarreien, obwohl eine genügende Anzahl an slowenischen Priestern vorhanden war. Er verbot auch das slowenische liturgische Buch. Die Ungarn unternahmen alles, um den Übermur-Dialekt möglichst der slowenischen Schriftsprache zu entfremden, etwa durch das Einflechten ungarischer Ausdrücke. Sie übten enormen Druck auf die Eltern aus, ihre Kinder in der Schule nicht zum Wendischen Unterricht anzumelden.

Trotz des enormen Drucks seitens der Kirchenoberen aber verlangten die slowenischen Priester im Übermurgebiet immer wieder die Verwendung der slowenischen Schriftsprache. Zum Anlaß des Bischofsbesuchs in Lendava am 13.7.1941 unterschrieben auf Initiative Ivan Jeričs 31 slowenische Priester die sogenannte "Resolution von Lendava." Später schlossen sich ihnen auch 11 Priester aus dem Dekanat Murska Sobota an. Sie verlangten die Respektierung der Minderheitenrechte, die im Jahre 1919 die ungarisch-königliche Regierung anderen Nationalitäten garantiert hatte.[20]

19. Von den 544 jüdischen Opfern in Slowenien starben 500 in deutschen Konzentrationslagern.
20. Jerič, *Moji spomini*, 202-208.

Der Einsatz für die slowenische Schriftsprache galt in Ungarn als Verrat an der Heimat, obwohl für eine solche Bewertung jede rechtliche Grundlage fehlte. Generalvikar Jerič selbst stand deshalb dreimal vor Gericht, unter anderem wegen Hochverrats – sein Prozeß wurde 1944 gestoppt. Viele Priester wurden aus dem slowenischen Gebiete des Übermurgebiets in rein ungarische Gemeinden versetzt.

2. Widerstand und Kollaboration

Da die Slowenen in der deutsch besetzten Steiermark und in Oberkrain gar keine Möglichkeit hatten, sich in irgendeiner Weise zu artikulieren, übernahm nun ganz natürlich die "Provincia di Lubiana" die Rolle des slowenischen Führungszentrums. Von hier gingen nun alle relevanten Bewegungen von Slowenen aus – bis schließlich nach der italienischen Kapitulation am 8. September 1943 die Deutschen auch dieses Gebiet besetzten. Doch anders als 1941 (die Untersteiermark, Oberkrain), wurde die Provinz Laibach – als Teil des Adriatischen Küstenlandes – 1943 nicht der massiven Germanisierung ausgesetzt.

In Slowenien sind zwei Ebenen des Geschehens zu beachten: die Ebene der Okkupation und des Widerstands dagegen, sowie die Ebene der Revolution und der Gegenrevolution. Man kann die beiden Ebenen voneinander nicht trennen. Die zahlenmäßig in Slowenien schwache (1280 Mitglieder), aber in der illegalen Arbeit erfahrene Kommunistische Partei sah in der Situation der Okkupation die einzige Chance, die Macht zu erlangen. Diese wurde ihr durch die Okkupation geboten. Das Mitglied des Politbüros des ZK KPJ Edvard Kardelj kündigte bereits im Oktober 1940 in Zagreb an, dass die Kommunisten den bewaffneten Widerstand gegen den Okkupator nur führen würden, wenn ihnen die Möglichkeit geboten werde, die Revolution durchzuführen.

Es entwickelten sich von Anfang an illegale Organisationen, sowohl in dem von den Kommunisten dominierten Lager als auch im Lager der Bürgerlichen und Königstreuen. Die KP organisierte so nach dem deutschen Überfall auf die Sowjetunion eine Art Dachorganisation des Widerstands, genannt "Befreiungsfront" [Osvobodilna fronta, OF], mittels welcher sie etliche linke Gruppierungen für sich gewinnen konnte und sie dann aufsog. Diese von der KP gelenkte "Befreiungsfront," die sich zunächst nur in dem italienisch besetzten Teil voll entfalten konnte, monopolisierte bereits am 16.9.1941 den Widerstand gegen den Okkupator – deswegen konnte es zu einer Vereinigung der kommunistischen und der bürgerlichen Illegalen nicht kommen – und erklärte jeden, der außerhalb der OF und den Partisaneneinheiten[21] gegen den Okkupator kämpfte, zum Verräter. Eine am selben Tag verabschiedete Schutzverordnung sah die Bestrafung der "Verräter" vor, durch irgendwelche obskure geheime Gerichte, die es in Wirklichkeit nicht gab.

Der kommunistische Sicherheitsdienst VOS [Varnostnoobveščevalna služba], der unter der ausschließlichen Kontrolle der KP stand, wurde mit der Aufgabe betraut, die Strafen, die die Schutzordnung vorsah, durchzuführen. Gnadenlos versuchte er, alle zu eliminieren, die hätten imstande sein können, die Organisation der Befreiungsfront und die von den Kommunisten geführte Volksbefreiungsbewegung zu gefährden oder auch nur ihr angemaßtes Monopol auf die Vertretung des Widerstands zu durchlöchern. Es begann in Laibach, wo die sogenannten Verräter – in aller Regel nationalbewusste katholische Slowenen, überzeugte Antikommunisten – auf der Straße und zuhause "hingerichtet" wurden.[22] Bis Ende 1941 brachte der VOS in Laibach allein 120 Personen um.[23]

In der ländlichen Region der Provinz eskalierte die Gewalt im Frühjahr 1942, kurz vor der italienischen Offensive (am 15. Juli). Dort litt die Bevölkerung nicht nur unter den Übergriffen der Italiener, sondern auch unter jenen der Partisanen. Slowenen, die sich nicht für die OF begeistern konnten, vielfach auch solche, die ganz unpolitisch waren und lediglich in relativer Ruhe leben wollten, waren somit von zwei Seiten schwer bedrängt: Einerseits kamen die Partisanen, requirierten Lebensmittel und Vieh, rächten sich an einzelnen Personen, teilweise aber auch an ganzen Familien, die sie als feindlich oder wenigstens als nicht oder zuwenig aktiv gegenüber der Besatzungsmacht einstuften, andererseits überzog der italienische Besatzer dieselben Dörfer und dieselben Familien mit seiner Gewalt, weil sie angeblich die Partisanen unterstützt oder diese zumindest nicht verraten hätten. Ganze Dörfer wurden abgebrannt, viele Menschen in Lager verbracht oder gleich ermordet, manchmal ganze Familien ausgerottet.

Nach Angaben des Instituts für neuere Geschichte, das mit der Zählung der Opfer des Zweiten Weltkriegs betraut war, fielen den Partisanen im Jahr 1942 2000 Menschen zum Opfer, der antikommunistischen

---

21. Auch diese wurden in Slowenien am 22. Juni 1941 vom slowenischen Zentralkomitee der KPS gegründet, am 27. Juni dann stellte das Zentralkomitee der KPJ sämtliche Partisanen-Aktivitäten Jugoslawiens unter einen kommunistischen Oberbefehl.

22. Ausführlich dazu: Griesser-Pečar, *Das zerrissene Volk*, 135-150, 383-410.

23. Boris Mlakar, "Krogi nasilja med Slovenci v vojnih letih 1941-1945," *Žrtve vojne in revolucije* (Ljubljana: Državni svet, 2005) 23

Seite 220. Im Jahr 1943 forderten die Partisanen 2500 Menschenleben, die Gegner 600, wobei die Zahl der getöteten Zivilisten in diesen beiden Jahren höher war als die der Bewaffneten.[24] Unter den Opfern der roten Gewalt in der Stadt und auf dem Land befanden sich in den Jahren 1942-1944 auch 35 Priester. Ein weiterer wurde im Zuge der Kampfhandlungen von den Partisanen tödlich verwundet.

Unter den oben genannten Opfern befand sich auch Universitätsprofessor Dr. Lambert Ehrlich, der am 26. Mai 1942 auf offener Straße zusammen mit einem zufälligen Begleiter von einem Mitglied des VOS erschossen wurde. Er war bei den Kommunisten besonders verhasst, weil er der geistige Führer des streng antikommunistischen akademischen Klubs Straža war., Nur wenige Wochen vor seiner Ermordung hatte Ehrlich eine Denkschrift verfasst, die eine scharfe Kritik an den willkürlichen Maßnahmen der italienischen Besatzungsmacht in der Provinz Laibach beinhaltete und auf die schwierige Situation der Bevölkerung verwies, die einerseits unter dem Druck der OF-Gewalt stand, andererseits den italienischen Repressalien ausgesetzt war. Er machte auch Vorschläge zur Verbesserung der Lage, wobei für ihn die Sicherheit der Bevölkerung die vordringlichste Aufgabe war. Er wollte eine slowenische Gendarmerie und Polizei unter der Führung früherer höherer slowenischer Polizeiorgane. Außerdem regte er auch einen autonomen Sicherheitsdienst an, die Verwaltung sollte stärker von den Slowenen mitbestimmt werden, die unschuldig Konfinierten und Internierten entlassen, die willkürlichen Brandstiftungen der Italiener eingestellt und die zerstörten Dörfer wiederaufgebaut werden. Das Schlagen und Foltern von Gefangenen sollte unterbunden werden. Er regte auch eine Reorganisation der Quästur und eine freiere Berichterstattung der Zeitungen an.[25]

Für die Vertreter der Kirche bedeutete die Tatsache, dass hier eine kommunistisch dominierte OF angetreten war, die eine Art Alleinvertretungsanspruch in Sachen Widerstand erhob, ein besonderes Dilemma. Einerseits verabscheute die Kirche die Menschenrechtsverletzungen und Unterdrückungsmaßnahmen wie überhaupt die brutale Diktatur der Besatzungsmächte, andererseits waren Marxismus und Bolschewismus mit der Lehre der christlichen Kirchen unvereinbar. Dazu kam noch, dass auch die Kommunisten, nicht nur die Besatzungsmächte, eine (nicht nur

---

24. Mlakar, "Krogi nasilja," 24-25.
25. Tamara Griesser-Pečar, "Umor Lamberta Ehrlicha," *Ehrlichov simpozij v Rimu* (Celje: Mohorjeva založba, 2002) 309-319; Griesser-Pečar, *Das zerrissene Volk*, 399-403.

notwehrhafte, verteidigungsgeprägte, sondern aggressive, machtorientierte) Gewalt ausübten, die die Kirche nicht gutheißen konnte.

Wegen der unerträglichen Lage der Bevölkerung wurden ab Frühjahr 1942 in verschiedenen Ortschaften spontan – und ausschließlich zum Zweck der Selbstverteidigung – Ortswehren gegründet. Diese sahen sich schließlich gezwungen, Waffen aus der Hand des italienischen Besatzers anzunehmen. Der kommunistische Terror gegenüber der ländlichen Bevölkerung wurde nämlich immer unerträglicher. Nach der Kapitulation Italiens im Herbst 1943 kam es zu einem der größten Verbrechen in Slowenien während des Krieges. Nach dem Fall von Grčarice (die Partisanen besiegten die Tschetniks) und Turjak (dort konzentrierten sich die Ortswehren) veranstaltete die "Volksmacht" in Gottschee den ersten politischen Schauprozess und sprach 16 Todesurteile aus. Hinter den Kulissen tötete sie aber etwa 600 Gegner, auch Verwundete. Dies geschah, obwohl damals Bemühungen im Gange waren, doch noch eine Einigung zwischen den beiden Lagern zu erzielen. Die Ortswehren, die sich auf dem Turjak konzentriert hatten, waren im Begriff, in die Illegale einzutreten – gegen den deutschen Okkupator. Als Antwort auf die Geschehnisse in und um Gottschee entstand dann aber die Slowenische Landeswehr, deren Ziel es war, den Bolschewismus zu bekämpfen – mit Hilfe der Deutschen.

Darüber hinaus aber gab es auf der bürgerlichen Seite illegale Organisationen, so verschiedene Legionen und – auch in Slowenien – die zahlenmäßig schwache Jugoslawische Armee (Tschetniks), deren Kommandant Draža Mihailović war, gleichzeitig auch Kriegsminister der jugoslawischen Exil-Regierung. Die Nachrichtendienste belieferten wenigstens bis Herbst 1944 die Exilregierung und die Alliierten mit Berichten aus dem okkupierten Land. Viele wurden deshalb verhaftet und nach Dachau verbracht.

Die slowenischen Vorkriegspolitiker versuchten dann ein nationales politisches Gremium aufzustellen. Nachdem der im April 1941 gegründete Nationalrat legal nicht mehr existieren und sich illegal nicht behaupten konnte, wurde 1942 der Slowenische Bund gegründet, schließlich, Ende 1944, der 'Nationalausschuss'. Immer deutlicher wurde den Beteiligten, dass sie in Richtung der westlichen Alliierten klare Zeichen setzen mussten. Eine am 29. Oktober 1944 datierte "Nationale Erklärung" sollte einige Weichen für die Nachkriegsordnung legen. Schließlich kam es am 3. Mai 1945 in Ljubljana zur Bildung einer slowenischen Regierung. Alle Einheiten, die auf der bürgerlichen Seite vorhanden waren, wurden in die slowenische Nationalarmee eingebunden.

Entgegen der Erwartung der bürgerlichen Seite landeten die westlichen Alliierten im Frühjahr 1945 nicht auf dem Balkan. Wegen des Vordringens der Partisanen zog sich die Nationalregierung und die slowenische Nationalarmee zum großen Teil in die britische Besatzungszone nach Kärnten zurück, wo sie im Lager Viktring untergebracht wurden. Viele Zivilisten begleiteten sie. Die Briten aber lieferten die Slowenische Landeswehr an die Tito-Truppen aus. Die meisten – mit jenen, die bereits auf der Flucht in Slowenien gefasst wurden, waren es 11.683[26] – wurden regelrecht abgeschlachtet und fanden ihr Grab in den Karsthöhlen Sloweniens. Der überwiegende Teil der Tschetniks allerdings ging nach Italien und überlebte.

3. Die kirchliche Situation

Die Situation in den beiden slowenischen Bistümern Laibach und Lavant war sehr unterschiedlich. Während in der deutsch besetzten Diözese Lavant sogleich nahezu alle Priester ausgesiedelt wurden und Bischof Dr. Ivan Tomažič in seinem bischöflichen Palais konfiniert wurde, also so gut wie nichts für seine Landsleute tun konnte, konnte sich der Klerus in dem von den Italienern besetzten Teil der Diözese Laibach frei bewegen und in slowenischer Sprache predigen. Im deutschbesetzten Teil des Bistums Laibach war die Lage ähnlich wie in der Untersteiermark. Nur von Laibach aus konnte man versuchen, für die deutschbesetzten Gebiete etwas zu tun. So bat der Laibacher Bischof Dr. Gregorij Rožman den Vatikan schon im Mai 1941, sich bei der italienischen Regierung dafür einzusetzen, dass diese bei der deutschen Regierung vorstellig werde wegen der Inhaftierung der slowenischen Priester in dem von den Deutschen besetzten Teil der Bistümer Laibach und Lavant. Tatsächlich intervenierte der vatikanische Staatssekretär bereits am 16.5.1941 beim italienischen Botschafter in dieser Sache. Eine Antwort bekam er aber erst am 20.10.1941. Darin teilte die italienische Botschaft dem Vatikan mit, dass die Intervention in Berlin keinen Erfolg gehabt habe.[27]

Da die Bevölkerung in den deutschbesetzten Gebieten ohne Seelsorger blieb und sich viele Oberkrainer Gläubige schriftlich und mündlich an den Kapitularvikar von Gurk, Dr. Andreas Rohracher, mit der Bitte wandten, ihnen Priester zu schicken,[28] errichtete dieser eine Notseels-

---

26. Tadeja Tominšek Rihtar und Mojca Šorn, "Žrtve druge svetovne vojne (april 1941-januar 1946)," *Žrtve vojne in revolucije* (Ljubljana: Državni svet, 2005) 19-21.
27. Griesser-Pečar und Dolinar, *Rožmanov proces*, 158-160.
28. DAG, Militaria 20, Bericht über die Seelsorge in den besetzten Gebieten Kärntens und Krains.

orge in Oberkrain und im Mießtal. Ähnlich auch der Bischof von Seckau, Ferdinand Pawlikowski, in der Untersteiermark. So wurden nach Oberkrain und Mießtal fünf Geistliche entsandt, die Jurisdiktion für 131 Pfarreien und ca. 200.000 Katholiken bekamen. An den kirchlichen Feiertagen kamen bis Ostern 1945 zusätzlich bis zu 20 Geistliche aus der Diözese Gurk in das Gebiet der Diözese Laibach, um die Bevölkerung mit Sakramenten zu versorgen. Der Bischof von Seckau bestimmte für die Seelsorge in der Untersteiermark zunächst zwölf Geistliche, doch schon Ende März waren dort 13 tätig und 49 weitere halfen alle zwei Wochen als Grenzpfarrer aus. Die Entsendungen erfolgten mit Genehmigung des Heiligen Stuhls und kraft Jurisdiktion der zuständigen Bischöfe. Die wenigen slowenischen Geistlichen, die nicht ausgewiesen wurden – in Oberkrain waren es 23, die bis auf zwei krank und gebrechlich waren – halfen auf eng begrenztem Gebiet.[29]

In Oberkrain blieben die meisten Pfarren bis Spätherbst 1941 ohne Gottesdienst und Sakramente, so dass sich in einigen Pfarren die Gläubigen selbst gegenseitig die heilige Kommunion spendeten. Aber auch danach konnte in den meisten Pfarreien nicht täglich Messe gelesen werden, in vielen gab es eine nur alle 14 Tage. Vor allem im gebirgigen Oberkrain, wo die Seelsorger große Strapazen auf sich nehmen mussten, war die Versorgung sehr schwierig. Nur zwei Geistliche verfügten über ein Motorrad, und auch diesen wurde kein Benzin zugewiesen. So legte z.B. Heinrich Beuke mit seinem Motorrad mehr als 90.000 km auf eigene Kosten zurück. Die anderen Seelsorger mussten weite Strecken, mitunter bis zu 30 km, mit unzulänglichen Verkehrmitteln und zu Fuß zurücklegen. Obwohl die deutsche Zivilverwaltung in Oberkrain und in der Steiermark bei der Erteilung der seelsorgerischen Genehmigung die Bedingung gestellt hatte, dass die deutschen Priester der slowenischen Sprache nicht mächtig sein durften und sie auch nachträglich nicht erlernen durften, hielten sich einige nicht an dieses Verbot. Man kann nicht sagen, dass sich die deutschsprachigen Seelsorger von den Nazis instrumentalisieren ließen.[30] Der Bischof von Laibach,

---

29. Peter G. Tropper, "Die Anfänge der 'Seelsorge im besetzten Gebiet'. Zu den bemühungen des Gurker Ordinariats um die Pastorierung in Oberkrain 1941," *Kirche in bewegter Zeit: Beiträge zur Geschichte der Kirche in der Zeit der Reformation und des 20. Jahrhunderts. Festschrift für Maximilian Liebmann zum 60. Geburtstag*, ed. Rudolf Zinnhobler u.a. (Graz: Styria, 1994) 369-387; Griesser-Pečar, *Cerkev na zatožni klopi*, 28-30; DAG, Militaria 20, Bericht über die Seelsorge in den besetzten Gebieten Kärntens und Krains.

30. Tamara Griesser-Pečar, "Slowenien, das zerrissene Volk: Die katholische Kirche während des Zweiten Weltkrieges," *Demokratie und Geschichte*, ed. Helmut Wohnout, Jahrbuch des Vogelsang-Instituts zur Erforschung der Geschichte der christlichen Demokratie in Österreich, 7/8 (2003-2004) (Wien/Graz/Weimar: Böhlau, 2005) 188-189.

Rožman, schickte seinerseits Freiwillige – verkleidete Priester – über die Grenze. Diese konnten wenigstens teilweise seelsorgliche Tätigkeiten in der slowenischen Muttersprache verrichten. Natürlich war dies gefährlich, da die deutsche Polizei intensiv nach diesen Priestern suchte.[31]

4. Bischof Rožman und Bischof Tomažič

Trotz der völlig unterschiedlichen Ausgangssituation unterschied sich die Einstellung des Laibacher Bischofs Rožman gegenüber den Besatzungbehörden nicht wesentlich von jener des Lavanter Bischofs Tomažič. Sie war streng legalistisch im Sinne von Paulus (Römerbrief 13:1-2). Dieselbe Stellung nahm die slowenische Katholische Kirche nach dem Krieg gegenüber der "Volksmacht" ein. Obwohl beide Bischöfe die Okkupation als aufgezwungenes Übel tragen mussten, trugen sie dennoch die Verantwortung für ihre Diözesen, für ihre Gläubigen. Jede Tat konnte die Situation des Bistums verändern, positiv oder negativ, und die Frage, die sich hier stellte, war, ob es sich ein Bischof erlauben konnte, durch seine Haltung die Situation der Bevölkerung noch zu verschlechtern.

Die ganze Verhaltensweise Rožmans gegenüber den Untaten der Besatzungsmächte belegt, dass der Bischof niemals ein Freund der Besatzer war, erst recht nicht der deutschen. Schon zur Zeit der Kärntner Volksabstimmung 1918-1920 hatte er sich, selbst gebürtiger Kärntner, als patriotischer Slowene so engagiert, dass er nach dem Ausgang der Abstimmung nicht mehr in Kärnten bleiben konnte. Und als die Berichte über die Gräueltaten der Nazis in Polen Slowenien erreichten, ließ er sie übersetzen und an die gesamte slowenisch-katholische Geistlichkeit verteilen. Nach der Okkupation drohten deutsche Kreise in Oberkrain damit, dass die Gestapo Rožman einsperren würde.[32]

Im Sinne der Kirchenvorschriften adressierte Bischof Tomažič am 16.4.1941 im eigenen Namen eine Loyalitätserklärung an Hitler sowie im

---

31. Henrik Goričan wurde auch tatsächlich im Jahre 1942 in Klagenfurt von der Gestapo verhaftet und später den Italienern übergeben. Nach seiner Freilassung im Mai 1943 nahm er sogleich seine illegale Tätigkeit wieder auf. Als Kurier ging er mindestens zwanzig Mal über die Grenze in das deutschbesetzte Gebiet der Untersteiermark und hielt auch Verbindung zwischen den beiden Bischöfen. So wurde er im Dezember 1944 erneut verhaftet und nach Dachau geschickt. Kaum aus Dachau zurück wurde er im "Weihnachtsprozess" 1945 zu 15 Jahren Haft mit Zwangsarbeit verurteilt – ein zweites Mal dann 1949 sogar zum Tode –, dann amnestiert. Er starb 1962 an den Folgen der Gefängnisbehandlung). *Palme mučeništva*, ed. Anton Pust, Zdravko Reven und Božidar Slapšak (Celje: Mohorjeva, 1995) 118-120; Griesser-Pečar, *Cerkev na zatožni klopi*, 29-30, 132-138.
32. Tamara Griesser-Pečar, *Stanislav Lenič. Življenjepis iz zapora* (Klagenfurt/Ljubljana/Wien: Hermagoras, 1997) 72-73.; NŠAL, Zapuščina msgr. Jagodic.

Namen der römisch-katholischen Bevölkerung und Geistlichkeit eine "Erklärung loyalen Gehorsams, wie ein solcher nach göttlichen Geboten und kirchlichen Vorschriften dem Souverän gebührt." Darin bat er, die staatlichen Behörden mögen "berechtigte Wünsche der katholischen Bevölkerung beider Nationalität" berücksichtigen und der katholischen Kirche die notwendigen Bedingungen für ihre Existenz sichern.[33]

Bischof Rožman adressierte seine Loyalitätserklärung an den Hohen Kommissar Emilio Grazioli – und dies erst dann, als Italien das Autonomiestatut (3.5.1941) verabschiedet hatte und die Italiener den Bischof hatten wissen lassen, dass sie eine solche Erklärung erwarteten. Rožmans Loyalitätserklärung beinhaltete nur das, was das Kirchengesetz verlangte. Das Autonomiestatut nahm Rožman "zur Kenntnis" eine aktive Zusammenarbeit bot er nicht an. Er sprach von "Ihren und unseren Bemühungen zum Wohle unseres Volkes."[34] Auf der Basis der Unterwerfung unter die Gewalt und die Anerkennung der Realität brachte der Bischof seine "volle Loyalität zum Ausdruck." Der Hohe Kommissar war mit der Erklärung des Bischofs unzufrieden. Doch wurde Rožman nun keineswegs die Abfassung eines neuen Textes aufgetragen. Vielmehr erledigte man alles für ihn. So konnte der Bischof schließlich in der Zeitung eine Erklärung lesen, die weder aus seiner Feder stammte noch irgendwann von ihm gebilligt oder gar unterschrieben worden war.

Die krassen Unterschiede zwischen beiden Texten sind unschwer zu erkennen. Schon der Adressat des Schreibens stimmt mit dem des Originals nicht überein: Rožman richtete seine Worte an den Hohen Kommissar. Nach der verfälschten Fassung sprach er direkt den Diktator Mussolini an, den Rožman in Wirklichkeit weder vor noch nach dieser Erklärung jemals kontaktiert, geschweige denn gesehen und gesprochen hatte. Offensichtlich sollte mit dieser gefälschten Anrede Rožmans an Mussolini eine besondere Begeisterung des Bischofs für den Duce vorgetäuscht werden. Nach der italienischen Version begrüßt der Bischof den Anschluss der slowenischen Gebiete "mit lebhaftem Jubel," spricht von "bedingungsloser Loyalität und Zusammenarbeit" und erbittet "den Segen Gottes für Ihre Werke, für das ganze große italienische Volk und für das slowenische Volk, das auf dem Boden des römischen Imperiums leben und gedeihen darf."[35] Diese Fälschung war

---

33. ŠAM [Bischöfliches Archiv Maribor], P 8/41, Aus der Unterredung mit R. Statth. Dr. Uiberreither 19.4.1941.
34. Griesser-Pečar und Dolinar, *Rožmanov proces*, 52-54.
35. *Ibid.*, 52-54.

so wirkungsvoll, dass sie sich bis heute aus Geschichtswerken und Schulbüchern nicht verbannen ließ.

Die beiden Bischöfe hatten im Interesse der Bevölkerung auch direkte Kontakte mit den Besatzern. Bischof Tomažič besuchte die deutschen Behörden, vor allem weil er die Freilassung der verhafteten Geistlichen erreichen wollte oder wenigstens deren bessere Behandlung. Am 19.4.1941 empfing ihn der Chef der Zivilverwaltung Siegfried Uiberreither. Schriftlich und mündlich äußerte Tomažič die Bitte, dass die Haftzeit der Priester verkürzt werde bzw., dass man sie verhören und anschließend freilassen möge.[36] Uiberreither wies seine Bitten schroff zurück: die verhafteten Priester hätten keine Seelsorge betrieben, sondern Politik. Sie seien als "Hetzpfarrer" unter der Leitung des verstorbenen "Hauptthetzers" Dr. Anton Korošec bekannt gewesen. Uiberreithers Motto war, "dass alles, was dem Deutschtum hinderlich sein kann, verschwinden muss – auch Priester." Er riet Tomažič, sich nach der Decke zu strecken und für die bisherigen Geistlichen Ersatz zu suchen, etwa beim Grazer Amtskollegen Pawlikowski. Er kündigte an, dass er keine nichtdeutschen Lehrer und Beamte dulden werde, auch in der Kirche müsste die deutsche Sprache eingeführt werden. Der Bischof wies darauf hin, dass die Kirche in den Städten, wo Deutsche lebten, so in Pettau, Marburg, Cilli, immer schon auch die deutsche Sprache benützt habe. Er schlug vor, wenigstens in der Übergangszeit Zweisprachigkeit zu erlauben. Nach Uibereithers Meinung jedoch war die Bevölkerung deutsch. "Das Deutsche Reich braucht nicht solche, die sich nicht als Deutsche fühlen. Solche wollen sich Platz suchen in Krain, Kroatien, Serbien u.s.w...."[37] Ähnlich zwecklos verliefen auch andere Gespräche – so mit dem Polizeibeauftragten Dr. Pfrimer, dem Bundesführer des Heimatbundes, Franz Steindl. und dem Referenten für Glaubensfragen, Dr. Hillinger, – wie auch die Bittschrift vom 21.6.1941 an Uibereither und eine Intervention des Bischofs Pawlikowski.[38]

Um slowenische Priester vor der Deportation zu retten und die Seelsorge zu sichern, empfahl Tomažič den Geistlichen den Eintritt in den Heimatdienst und reichte am 10.6.1941 sogar selber ein Ansuchen auf Aufnahme ein. Als "Schutzangehörige des Reiches" waren Priester nämlich rechtlos, als Mitglieder des Heimatdienstes hingegen wären sie Staatsangehörige gewesen, die im Land hätten bleiben können. Steindl aber belehrte Tomažič am 5.12.1941, daß Priester grundsätzlich nicht in den

---

36. ŠAM, P 8/41, 19.4.1941.
37. ŠAM, P 8/41. Rybář, 79-82.
38. *Ibid.*

Heimatdienst aufgenommen würden. Am 27.2.1942 erhielt der Bischof dann auch eine negative Antwort.[39]

Der Laibacher Bischof Gregorij Rožman zeigte zunächst keine Absicht, die Besatzer aufzusuchen, doch seine nähere Umgebung drängte ihn dazu. So besuchte er den Hohen Kommissar Emilio Grazioli schließlich in Begleitung am 20.4.1941. Grazioli erwiderte den Besuch Rožmans am nächsten Tag.[40]

Nun aber verhielten sich die italienischen Besatzer anfangs in der Tat ganz anders als die deutschen. Die Nationalsozialisten waren ausgesprochen kirchenfeindlich – die Kirchen-Mitgliedschaft war ungern gesehen, wer in der Partei etwas werden wollte, musste austreten. SS-Leute durften kirchlich nicht organisiert sein, während die Faschisten ihrer aktiven Elite keine Vorschriften solcher Art machten. Sie ließen Religion und Kirche gelten, führende Faschisten gingen oft sogar demonstrativ in die Kirche. Weshalb die Interventionen der Kirchenleute, vor allem des Bischofs, in der Anfangsphase der italienischen Besatzung auch einigen – wenigstens punktuellen – Erfolg hatten. Bald aber stellte sich für Rožman und andere Kirchenführer auch in der italienisch besetzten Provinz Laibach die Frage, ob neben all den Versuchen, durch Gespräche, Bitten und Interventionen bei der Besatzungsmacht etwas Praktisches für die leidgeprüfte Bevölkerung zu erreichen, nicht doch auch eine offene Anprangerung des Unrechts der Besatzer nötig war. Als jedoch Rožman im Mai 1942 bei Pius XII. vorsprach und ihm Überlegungen unterbreitete, den italienischen Okkupator wegen seiner harten Maßnahmen öffentlich zu kritisieren, riet ihm der Papst davon ab. Dann würde der Bischof verurteilt und interniert, meinte Pius XII., und er wäre nicht mehr in der Lage, jemandem zu helfen.[41] So verzichtete Rožman auf sein Vorhaben und konzentrierte sich darauf, durch Kontakte zu italienischen Entscheidungsträgern praktische Erleichterungen zu erreichen.

Freude und Zufriedenheit über die italienischen Besatzer gab es seitens der Kirche keineswegs. Aber Rožman war in erster Linie Seelsorger und sah seine Hauptaufgabe darin, den Menschen praktisch zu helfen, also zu versuchen, Inhaftierungen zu verhindern, Gefangene frei zu

---

39. Rybář, "Nacistični ukrepi," 69; Tamara Griesser-Pečar, "Duhovščina med nacizmom, fašizmom in komunizmom," *Cerkev na Slovenskem v XX. stoletju*, ed. Metod Benedik, Janez Juhant und Bogdan Kolar (Ljubljana: Družina, 2002) 288.

40. *Škofijski list*, 4-6 (31.7.1941); *Slovenec* (22.4.1941).

41. Griesser-Pečar und Dolinar, *Rožmanov proces*, 46, 156; Griesser-Pečar, "Duhovščina," 290.

bekommen, Geiseln vor dem Tod zu retten und so fort. Rožman intervenierte für nahezu alle, die an ihn herangetreten waren – an manchen Tagen hatte er rund 50 Bittsteller vor der Tür. Er setzte sich für Priester ebenso ein wie für Bauern, Intellektuelle und Offiziere, für Konservative ebenso wie für Liberale und Kommunisten, für Christen ebenso wie für Juden,[42] für Männer, Frauen und Kinder. Nach dem Krieg nahm die kommunistische Geheimpolizei Udba (Uprava državne bezbednosti – Verwaltung der Staatssicherheit) bei verschiedenen Hausdurchsuchungen im bischöflichen Palais eine Anzahl von Akten mit. Viele Dokumente wurden von der Udba beschlagnahmt und tauchten nie wieder auf. Inzwischen können aber wenigstens 144 Fälle einwandfrei Rožman zugeordnet werden.[43] Rožman setzte sich unter anderem für die Internierten auf der Insel Rab ein, wo eine sehr hohe Sterblichkeit verzeichnet wurde. Auf seine Bitte hin, so schrieb ihm am 26.4.1943 Gastone Gambarra, der Kommandant des italienischen XI. Armeekorps, wurden 122 Internierte freigelassen. Besondere Sorge bereiteten ihm auch die 1700 internierten Kinder. Unter anderem sprach er über sie mit dem italienischen Außenminister Graf Ciano. 200 Kinder im Alter von 8 bis 14 Jahren fanden mit Hilfe des Papstes Zuflucht in Collegio Illirico in Loretto (Ancona), 200 Mädchen bei den Ursulinen in Rom. Diese Zahlen beweisen, dass die Zahl seiner Interventionen wesentlich höher war als 144.[44] Freilich war nicht jede Intervention so erfolgreich.

In der späteren Phase der italienischen Besatzung nahm der Einfluss des Bischofs deutlich ab, weil die Italiener merkten, dass er bei den Menschen, für die er sich einsetzte, keine Auslese vornahm, sondern sich auch für Andersdenkende, mithin auch für Kommunisten verwendete. In einem Bericht des Hohen Kommissars an das Innenministerium in Rom vom 11.1.1943 stellte der Hohe Kommissar Grazioli fest, dass verschiedene Namenslisten, die Rožman ihm geschickt hatte, "Elemente" enthielten, "die in keinem Fall der Empfehlung des Bischofs würdig sind."[45] Er habe deshalb die Anweisung gegeben, dass Rožmans Interventionen künftig wie die eines Privatmannes behandelt werden müssten.

42. Viele kroatische Juden aus dem Unabhängigen Staat Kroatien suchten Zuflucht in der Provinz Lubiana. Da sie kein Aufenthaltsrecht hatten, bestand die Gefahr, daß sie von den Italienern zurückgeschickt werden. Rožman erreichte es, dass getaufte Juden nicht zurückgeschickt wurden, sondern in Italien konfiniert wurden.
43. Tamara Griesser-Pečar, "Rožmanova posredovanja pri okupatorju," *Rožmanov simpozij v Rimu* (Celje: Mohorjeva, 2001) 312.
44. Griesser-Pečar und Dolinar, *Rožmanov proces*, 165-166.
45. Ibid., 154.

Die Behauptung, Rožman habe die Besatzer niemals verurteilt, entspricht nicht den Tatsachen. Schon am 24.10.1941 schrieb er in seinem Hirtenbrief an die Priester: "Unter den gegenwärtigen Verhältnissen müssen wir auf unsere Gläubigen mit allen Kräften Einfluss nehmen, damit sie sich an Ruhe und Ordnung halten und nichts tun, was die Besatzer zwingen könnte, strenger und strenger aufzutreten ... Die Unternehmungen verschiedener Befreiungsbewegungen verantwortungsloser Leute nützen dem Volk unter unseren Verhältnissen nicht, sie schaden ihm sehr. Wer sein Volk wirklich liebt, wird nichts tun, was dem Volk tatsächlich schadet."[46] In diesem Hirtenbrief verurteilte er deutlich die deutschen Gewaltmaßnahmen gegen das slowenische Volk. Vor allem prangerte er die Tatsache an, dass 193 Seelsorger aus 148 Pfarreien sowie zahlreiche Ordensgeistliche und Nonnen aus 14 Klöstern und anderen kirchlichen Institutionen vertrieben worden seien. 200.000 Menschen müssten ohne geistlichen Beistand und ohne Sakramente leben, und nur selten könne ein Verstorbener kirchlich beigesetzt werden. Im Hinblick auf die gesamte Lage im Land sagte Rožman: "Im Laufe seiner 14 Jahrhunderte hat unser Volk ... nichts Schlimmeres erlebt. Und was wird noch Böses folgen? ... Wir haben nirgendwo auf der Welt eine Stütze, wir sind so vereinsamt, dass uns das Grauen überkommt. Nur Gott ist unseres Stütze, in ihn setzen wir unsere Hoffnung ... Domine Deus, ad te sunt oculi nostri, ne pereamus!"[47]

Zwar klagte Rožman den italienischen Okkupator niemals von der Kanzel herab an, doch wurde er am 26.9.1942 beim Hohen Kommissar vorstellig, überreichte ihm ein Memorandum und beschwerte sich mit offenen Worten über das unzulässige Handeln der Italiener – Erschießung von Geiseln, Brandstiftungen, Verhaftungen, Konfiskationen –, vor allem prangerte er aber die von den Italienern ausgeübte Kollektivbeschuldigung an – für Taten, die von den Kommunisten inszeniert worden waren. Er verlangte Gerechtigkeit und Legalität, basierend auf den Traditionen des Römischen Rechts, er bat den Hohen Kommissar, Ausnahmeregelungen, die die Militär- und Zivilbehörden seit dem 1.9.1941 eingeführt hatten, zu überprüfen und danach etliche aufzuheben oder zu mildern. Im Namen des slowenischen Volkes formulierte er einen 20 Punkte-Katalog an Forderungen. Zu ihnen zählte die Forderung, die Gesetze, die schon vor dem 6.4.1941 gegolten hatten, nicht in Frage zu stellen, soweit dies nicht durch die Kriegs- und Ausnahmesituation

---

46. Griesser-Pečar und Dolinar, *Rožmanov proces*, 86.
47. *Ibid.*, 44.

dringend geboten sei. Rožman kritisierte, dass die versprochene Autonomie der Provinz nie in die Tat umgesetzt wurde, dass das beratende Gremium Consulta, bestehend aus einflussreichen Slowenen, die Aufgaben, die ihm nach dem Statut vom 3.5.1941 zugedacht waren, nicht erfüllen konnte, weil es kein Recht auf Initiative und Mitverantwortung hatte, seine Ratschläge und Erläuterungen nicht berücksichtigt wurden und seine Funktion als Vermittler und Dolmetscher (zwischen Slowenen und italienischer Verwaltung) nicht richtig ausgeübt werden konnte, kritisierte die Einführung politischer Einrichtungen der Faschistischen Partei und sprach von Italianisierung. Der Hohe Kommissar reagierte sehr erregt und empört "und sagte offen, dass er die Vertreter der politischen Parteien hätte sofort einsperren lassen, wenn sie es gewagt hätten, persönlich vor ihm mit einer solchen Eingabe zu erscheinen."[48]

Das Bestreben des Bischofs und der kirchlichen Führung war es offensichtlich, der Bevölkerung so weit zu helfen, dass sie die Okkupation möglichst unbeschadet überstehen konnte. Rožman war überzeugt davon, dass ein bewaffneter Widerstand für ein so kleines Volk wie das slowenische sinnlos und aussichtslos war, dass die großen Opfer vergebens erbracht würden, jedenfalls in keinem Verhältnis zu einem hier und dort möglichen kleinen Teilerfolg stünden.[49] Tatsächlich änderten die verschiedenen gewaltsamen Widerstandshandlungen nichts an der Macht und Kraft der Besatzungsmächte, der spätere Abzug der Besatzer und deren Gesamtniederlage hatten mit jenen Handlungen im besetzten Gebiet nichts zu tun. Es war von vornherein völlig aussichtslos, hier etwas zur Schwächung der militärischen und politischen Machtposition der Besatzer zu erreichen. Allerdings ist der Wert eines bewaffneten Widerstands als "Signal" und Symbol der nationalen Selbstbehauptung sowie der Ablehnung des Unrechts nicht zu übersehen, doch konnte die Frage nicht ungestellt bleiben, in welchem Verhältnis diese positive Signalwirkung zu dem dadurch hervorgerufenen immensen Leid der Zivilbevölkerung stand, ob unter diesen aussichtslosen Umständen die vielen Menschenopfer, die dadurch provoziert wurden, vertretbar waren. War es – so fragte sich Rožman – verantwortbar, gewaltige Katastrophen für die slowenische Bevölkerung hinzunehmen, nur um ein – wenn auch wichtiges – Zeichen zu setzen, und war es vertretbar, der kommunistisch dominierten Befreiungsfront eine gute Startposition für die spätere Macht zu geben? Diese Frage stellte sich der Bischof und beantwortete sie mit einem klaren Nein.

48. Griesser-Pečar und Dolinar, *Rožmanov proces*, 47-48, 56.
49. Griesser-Pečar, *Lenič*, 84.

In den ersten Monaten nach der Gründung der kommunistisch beherrschten Befreiungsfront (OF) meldete sich der Bischof nicht zu Wort. Als dann aber die offene Gewalt auf der Straße ausbrach und viele – auch betont nationalbewusste – Slowenen sterben mussten, sehr oft als angebliche "Verräter" ermordet, verurteilte er diese Taten. Und je mehr sich die Gewalt steigerte, je mehr Morde der kommunistische Sicherheits- und Nachrichtendienst VOS verübte, desto deutlicher sprach sich Rožman gegen sie aus. Es wurde ihm nun immer klarer, dass die OF von den Kommunisten gelenkt war, die nach dem Krieg die Macht in Jugoslawien an sich zu reißen versuchten. Deshalb warnte er nun ausdrücklich vor dem "gottlosen Kommunismus," wie er dies auch schon vor dem Krieg getan hatte – auf dem Boden der Enzyklika *Divini Redemptoris*. Die "Liquidierungen" der VOS waren aus der Sicht der katholischen Moral gänzlich unhaltbar.

Rožman verurteilte den Terror des VOS mehrmals. Den Kommunismus lehnte er aber nicht aus politischen, sondern aus religiösen Gründen ab: "Niemand kann gleichzeitig Katholik und Kommunist sein ... Gottlosigkeit und Glaube an Gott sind unvereinbar wie Wasser und Feuer. Wer Kommunist ist, ist nicht mehr Christ ... Eine Zusammenarbeit mit dem gottlosen Kommunismus ist ohne Sünde unmöglich."[50] Später, in seiner Prozesserwiderung auf die Anklage, schrieb Bischof Rožman am 30.9.1946: "Die angenommene Zusammenarbeit (Kollaboration) bestand im offenen ideologischen Widerstand der Priester gegen den gottlosen Kommunismus. Auf der Grundlage der entschlossenen Gegnerschaft des gottlosen Kommunismus zum Christentum, die vom Wesen des Kommunismus ausgeht, kann kein katholischer Priester einen anderen Standpunkt haben. Das ist aber keine politische oder irgendeine andere Zusammenarbeit mit dem Okkupator."[51] Rožman hielt den Kommunismus – im ganzen gesehen – für gefährlicher als den Faschismus und wohl auch als den Nationalsozialismus. Denn vom Sieg der Alliierten war er überzeugt, die nationalistischen Diktaturen in Deutschland und in Italien hielt er – worin er ja auch recht bekam – für kurzlebige Erscheinungen. Dagegen fürchtete er, dass sich der Kommunismus, einmal ans Ruder gelangt, für eine lange, Generationen umgreifende Zeit an der Macht halten werde.

Die Strategie der kommunistisch beherrschten OF gegenüber Rožman bestand nicht nur darin, ihn direkt zu bekämpfen. Weil sie die tiefe

---

50. "Pastirsko pismo ljubljanskega škofa d. Gregorija Rožmana za advent 1943," *Škofijski list* (30.11.1943).
51. NŠAL, Rožmanov arhiv [Archiv Rožman], Mappe 5, Anmerkungen 20-21.

Verwurzelung der Slowenen in deren Glauben kannte, versuchte die OF gleichzeitig, auch den Bischof für sich zu mobilisieren. Viermal wandte sie sich direkt an Rožman, zum ersten Mal am 30.11.1941 mit dem Wunsch, persönliche Kontakte zu knüpfen. In einer längeren Denkschrift wurden ihm die Arbeit der OF und deren offizielle Ziele erklärt. Rožman aber lehnte jeden Kontakt ab.[52] Schließlich erhielt er einen am 20.9.1942 datierten unverblümten Drohbrief als "letzte Warnung," unterschrieben mit: "Politische Exekutive."[53] Genaueres über diesen Drohbrief ist bislang nicht bekannt.

Edvard Kardelj, der damalige Chefideologe der Kommunisten und spätere stellvertretende Ministerpräsident Jugoslawiens, hielt noch nach der Ermordung des Ex-Banus Natlačen durch den kommunistischen Sicherheitsdienst VOS am 13.10.1942 den Bischof für nicht endgültig festgelegt: "In der Tat vereinigen sich (jetzt) alle Fäden der Weißen Garde[54] in seinen [Rožmans] Händen, ziemlich gegen seinen Willen. Wir wissen, dass er immer noch schwankt, ob er diese Arbeit annehmen soll oder nicht."[55] Diese Äußerung steht freilich in Gegensatz zu der späteren kommunistischen Propaganda, die ihn schon 1941 als "Quisling," als unzweifelhaften Freund der Besatzungsmacht, bezeichnete.

Nun gab es nach der Ermordung des Ex-Banus[56] Dr. Marko Natlačen durch ein als Priester verkleidetes VOS-Mitglied im Oktober 1942 außer Rožman auf der katholischen Seite keine starke integrierende Persönlichkeit mehr, so dass ganz zwangsläufig viele beim Bischof Rat suchten – nicht nur die Vertreter der Volkspartei (SLS), sondern auch die Liberalen, die ihn immer wieder über verschiedene Ereignisse informierten. Deswegen wurde ihm später vorgeworfen, er habe die Politiker "gelenkt," er habe die Weißen Garden mitgegründet, habe mithin sein Amt für politische Zwecke missbraucht. Auch sei das bischöfliche Palais in gewissem Sinne eine politische Zentrale gewesen.

Es gab nachweislich zwei Sitzungen der Politiker im bischöflichen Palais, die während des Krieges ein illegales Netz ausbauten und vor allem die Exil-Regierung und die Engländer mit Informationen belieferten. Die

---

52. *Slovenski poročevalec*, Nr.13 (31.3.1942).
53. Griesser-Pečar und Dolinar, *Rožmanov proces*, 94.
54. Der Name "Weiße Garde," eine kommunistische Entlehnung aus dem russischen Bürgerkrieg, bezog sich nicht nur auf die Ortswehren und die Freiwillige Antikommunistische Miliz (MVAC), sondern wurde undifferenziert für alle gebraucht, die außerhalb der Befreiungsfront organisiert waren.
55. *Jesen 1942: Korespondenca Edvarda Kardelja in Borisa Kidriča* (Ljubljana: Inštitut za zgodovino delavskega gibanja, 1963) 125-126.
56. Banus = Chef der Drau-Banschaft.

erste Sitzung fand am 12.9.1942 auf massiven Druck der Italiener statt. Zuvor, im August 1942, hatten General Mario Roatta, Befehlshaber der II. Armee, und Mario Robotti, der kommandierende General des XI. Armeekorps, den Bischof aufgesucht. Der Schilderung des Bischofs zufolge betonte General Roatta zunächst, dass er im Auftrag Mussolinis gekommen sei, dann tat er kund, dass die italienische Obrigkeit auf dem Territorium der Provinz Laibach keine Widerstandsbewegung dulden werde. Jede dahingehende Bewegung werde radikal vernichtet, ihre Mitglieder würden ausgerottet. Es liege nun an den Slowenen, eine Lösung zu finden. Sollten diese nicht selbst dafür sorgen können, dass solche Angriffe von Partisanen und anderen unterblieben, stehe die italienische Armee bereit, dies zu tun, da sie über genügend Soldaten und technische Mittel verfüge, um dieses Problem – notfalls mit brachialer Gewalt – zu lösen. Der General drohte mit der Aussiedlung der ganzen Region.

Daraufhin rief Rožman die Vertreter der politischen Parteien zusammen, die im Verborgenen wirkten, so dass diese Zusammenkunft also nicht ohne Gefahr war. Er berichtete von seiner Zusammenkunft mit den Italienern und betonte, dass diese von ihm jetzt eine Antwort erwarteten. Bei den Beratungen, für welche Rožman nach Schilderung mehrerer Beteiligter nur die Räumlichkeiten zur Verfügung stellte, sich aber selbst politischer Äußerungen enthielt, traten die verschiedenen Standpunkte der Politiker klar zutage. Solche, die auf italienische Forderungen nicht eingehen wollten, weil nach der Haager Konvention die Italiener von den Slowenen zwar Loyalität, aber keinen eigenen Auftritt gegen die slowenischen Guerilla-Soldaten verlangen konnten, bis zu jenen, die sich für den Kampf gegen die Partisanenbewegung aussprachen. Die Konferenz ging unentschieden aus.

Nun aber musste den Italienern dennoch eine Antwort gegeben werden. Die Slowenen konnten es sich nicht leisten, die Antwort schuldig zu bleiben, die Besatzer hatten in den vorangegangenen Monaten zu deutlich gezeigt, wozu sie fähig waren. Die Denkschrift, die schließlich verfasst wurde, ist heute umstritten, da das Original verschollen und nur eine deutsche Übersetzung erhalten ist, die jedoch die Verfasser nicht nennt. Ob und inwieweit der Bischof an der Formulierung dieser Denkschrift beteiligt war, konnte bisher nicht festgestellt werden. Diese Denkschrift ist deshalb von Bedeutung, weil sie ganz klar eine slowenische Polizei anregt, die besser als die Besatzer imstande sein sollte, mit dem Terror fertig zu werden – schließlich kannte die einheimische Polizei die Verhältnisse ja weit besser als die italienische.

Die zweite Sitzung im bischöflichem Palais fand am 28.4.1945 statt, als der Nationalausschuss, ein illegales Gremium des konservativen Lagers, gebeten hatte, im bischöflichen Palais zusammenkommen zu dürfen, um mit dem Präsidenten der Provinzialverwaltung, Leon Rupnik, verhandeln zu können. Bischof Rožman war noch einmal um Vermittlung zwischen den unterschiedlichen Positionen im bürgerlichen Lager gebeten worden.

Rožman hatte mit der Gründung der Ortswehren und der Landeswehr nichts zu tun, doch angesichts der komplizierten Lage und des Terrors gegen die bürgerliche Seite und die Bauern stand er denen, die in diesen Truppen organisiert waren und die ja seine Gläubigen waren, sicherlich nahe. Dies hatte nichts mit den Besatzungsmächten zu tun. Tomažič war generell gegen die Gründung der Landeswehr in der Steiermark eingestellt, aber ebenso gegen die Befreiungsfront und gegen die Partisanen. Beide Bischöfe, Rožman und Tomažič, standen fest hinter der Enzyklika *Divini Redemptoris* (1937), das heißt, dass es nach ihrer übereinstimmenden Auffassung keine Zusammenarbeit mit dem gottlosen Kommunismus geben konnte, also auch nicht mit der Befreiungsfront, in der die führende Kraft die KP war. Aber die Stellung des Bischofs Tomažič war noch kompromissloser als die von Rožman. Rožman hielt zwar nichts von der Partisanenarmee, dennoch war er Metod Mikuž, dem Referenten für Glaubensfragen beim Generalstab der slowenischen Partisanen, behilflich, als sich dieser geheim an ihn wandte, um sich Utensilien für sein priesterliches Amt zu verschaffen – wissend, dass auch Partisanen oftmals geistlichen Beistand benötigten. Tomažič hingegen schickte bereits im Dezember 1941 allen Seelsorgern die Mahnung – diese wiederholte er im Januar 1945 –, dass sie sich jeder Handlung zu enthalten hätten, die in irgendeiner Weise in Zusammenhang mit dem bolschewistischen System zu bringen wäre. Ein katholischer Priester, der dabei mitwirke, stelle sich in Widerspruch zur kirchlichen Lehre, deswegen müsse ein guter Katholik jede Verbindung mit einer solchen Richtung zurückweisen.[57]

Zu den deutschen Besatzern hatte Rožman wenig Kontakt. Und er hatte schon wegen der Einstellung der Deutschen zur Kirche keinen Einfluss auf sie. Trotzdem versuchte er auch bei ihnen für Einzelne zu intervenieren, so z.B. für einige Franziskaner und den Prior des Kartäuser-Klosters Pleterje.

---

57. ŠAM, Osterbotschaft an die Geistlichen und Gläubigen der Diözese Lavant, 25.1.1945.

Oft wurde dem Laibacher Bischof seine Teilnahme an der Vereidigung der slowenischen Landeswehr am 20.4.1944 zum Vorwurf gemacht. Tatsächlich hielt er vor der Vereidigung – ohne Anwesenheit deutscher Soldaten – eine stille Messe, doch verließ er das Stadion, nachdem die Messe beendet war und alles, was er für sie benötigt hatte, wieder zusammengeräumt war. Bei der zweiten Vereidigung war er nicht anwesend – er hatte sich wegen Halsschmerzen entschuldigt, erschien dann aber beim Vorbeimarsch der Landeswehr vor der Ursulinenkirche. Diese unkluge Entscheidung des Bischofs, die er wohl gefällt hatte, um die Gläubigen unter den Soldaten nicht in Stich zu lassen, wirkte tatsächlich niederschmetternd in der Emigration und bei den Alliierten.[58]

5. Die Rolle der Militärgeistlichen

Auch den Militärgeistlichen, die während des Krieges auf der traditionellen Seite dienten – also nicht in der Partisanenarmee, sondern in der Slowenischen Legion, bei den Tschetniks, in der Slowenischen Landeswehr –, wurde der Stempel des Verrats aufgedrückt, wenn sie als Feldgeistliche tätig waren. Missachtet wurde dabei, dass die Militärseelsorge ein in fast allen Armeen der Welt praktizierter Dienst war und dass Soldaten in Zeiten der Not und der Lebensgefahr des geistlichen Beistands bedürfen.

Nicht von ungefähr hatte der Erzbischof von Zagreb und Vorsitzende der jugoslawischen Bischofskonferenz, Alojzij Stepinac, noch am 3.4.1941, drei Tage vor dem Kriegsausbruch in Jugoslawien, ein Rundschreiben erlassen, das Richtlinien für die Militär-Seelsorger aufzeigte. Der zuständige Bischof – im Falle von Laibach war dies Rožman – ernannte die zuständigen Geistlichen. In der Regel waren das in Slowenien Freiwillige. Nach Aussagen des Generalkurats Dr. Ignacij Lenček beim Kommando der XI. Corpo d'Armata waren auch alle Kurate während der italienischen Besatzungszeit von Bischof Rožman bestätigt worden.[59]

Auch auf der Seite der Partisanen gab es Geistliche. Metod Mikuž wurde am 12.1.1943 in der Partisanenarmee zum Referenten für Glaubensfragen ernannt, sicherlich nicht ohne die Absicht, damit eine propagandistische Wirkung zu erzielen. Denn OF, Partisanen und KP waren angesichts der Attraktivität des Katholizismus in Slowenien

---

58. Griesser-Pečar und Dolinar, *Rožmanov proces*, 131-139, 287-292.
59. Siehe mehr dazu: *ibid.*, 104-112, 270-280.

zunächst sehr darauf bedacht, den Eindruck zu erwecken, dass sie nicht grundsätzlich gegen Religion und Kirche eingestellt seien. Dass es sich in Wirklichkeit doch ganz anders verhielt, zeigte sich spätestens nach der kommunistischen Machtübernahme.

Bischof Rožman wünschte nicht, dass die Militärgeistlichen Waffen tragen, doch konnte er sich in dieser Frage nicht durchsetzen. Auch sie wurden von den Italienern bewaffnet. In einem Brief an Generalvikar Dr. Karel Čerin in Novo mesto [Rudolfswerth] schrieb Rožman – wahrscheinlich im Jahre 1944: "Priester, Hände weg von jeglichen Waffen, das ist Teufelswerk!"[60] Diesen Satz soll Rožman noch ausdrücklich unterstrichen haben.

Nun hatten die Militärgeistlichen auf der traditionellen Seite aber Angst vor möglichen Repressalien – und wie aus dem Brief Edvard Kardeljs an Ivan Maček-Matija vom 1.Oktober 1942 ersichtlich ist, nicht ohne Grund. Dort hieß es: "Vernichtet die Weiße Garde umbarmherzig! Zögert nicht und gebt nicht nach! Die Schläge sollen so sein, dass sie unsere Macht spüren werden... Die Priester in den Truppen – erschießt alle! Genauso Offiziere, Intellektuelle usw..."[61] Die Militärgeistlichen auf der Seite der Partisanen waren ebenfalls bewaffnet. Priester überschritten vereinzelt ihre Kompetenzen. Dabei verstießen sie gegen die ausdrückliche Anweisung des Bischofs. Rožman nahm die Verfehlungen nicht einfach hin, sondern versuchte die betreffenden Verstöße auch zu ahnden. Schwierig war die Lage insofern, als die Verbindung zum bischöflichen Ordinariat oftmals unterbrochen war und die Priester keine Möglichkeit hatten, in schwierigen Situationen die Vorgesetzten zu konsultieren.[62]

Auch bei der Slowenischen Landeswehr gab es Militärgeistliche – im Dezember 1943 sieben. Die Zahl wurde auf Rožmans Vorschlag im September 1944 auf 13 erhöht.[63] Folgende Begründung gab der Bischof an: "Die Landeswehr ist eine Armee der Freiwilligen, die sich vor allem aus ideologischen Gründen für den Kampf gegen den Kommunismus gemeldet haben. Wenn diese Ideen, die auch religiös-sittlichen Charakters sind, verblassen, fällt zwangsläufig der Kampfwille und die Begeisterung, die bei den Freiwilligen von wesentlicher Bedeutung sind, damit lockert sich aber auch die Disziplin. Deshalb ist es dringend nötig, das Bewusstsein von der Idee ununterbrochen in gleicher Stärke

---

60. Griesser-Pečar, *Lenič*, 164.
61. AS I, 1521, Edvard Kardelj, Material für das Buch *Jesen 1942*.
62. Griesser-Pečar und Dolinar, *Rožmanov proces*, 104-105.
63. *Ibid.*, 106-107.

und Klarheit zu erhalten, was vor allem die Arbeit der Kuraten ist."

Dass die Militärgeistlichen mit den Besatzungbehörden nicht sympathisierten, zeigt unter anderem der Tadel des SS-Obergruppenführers Erwin Rösener am 16.10.1944, als er die von Rožman aufgestellten neuen Feldgeistlichen zwar akzeptierte, aber darauf hinwies, "dass ein Teil der in der slowenischen Landeswehr tätigen Geistlichen sowie ein Teil der Neuzustellenden politisch mehr oder weniger anglophil eingestellt seien. Ich darf Sie, sehr geehrter Herr Bischof, deshalb bitten, Ihren Einfluss dahin geltend zu machen, dass diese Geistlichen ihre Tätigkeit innerhalb der slowenischen Landeswehr nur auf die seelsorgerische Betreuung abstellen und dadurch mithelfen, den Kampf gegen den Bolschewismus erfolgreich weiterzuführen." Kurat Franc Šeškar wurde nach Dachau transportiert, weil er in den Augen von Rösener "zersetzend" auf die Landeswehr gewirkt hatte.[64]

Außerdem gab es Auseinandersetzungen darüber, dass die Kurate immer wieder auch die Partisanen kirchlich bestatteten. Rösener verbot die Praxis, wonach jeder Tote auf dem Friedhof beerdigt werden musste. "Derartige Verbrecher," sollten "anderweitig verscharrt werden." Priester Leopold Čampa kam nach Mauthausen, weil er diese Anordnung nicht befolgte.[65]

IV. Die Nachkriegszeit 1945-1950

Da die Kirche sich also während des Krieges mehrheitlich nicht auf die Seite der von den Kommunisten geführten Befreiungsfront und den Partisanen stellte, aus Gründen, die bereits dargelegt wurden, sie aber einen großen Rückhalt innerhalb der Bevölkerung hatte, wurde sie schon während, besonders aber nach dem Krieg bekämpft.

Im Oktober 1943 fand in Gottschee der erste kommunistische Schauprozess in Slowenien statt gegen 21 ausgewählte Gefangene – darunter drei Priester –, der als Muster für ähnliche Prozesse nach dem Krieg dienen sollte. Mit Hilfe solcher Prozesse versuchte die sogenannte "Volksmacht," die ganze politische, intellektuelle und kirchliche Opposition auszuschalten. Die Verhandlung endete mit 16 Todesurteilen – darunter gegen zwei Priester – und vier Verurteilungen zur Zwangsarbeit – darunter gegen einen Priester. Der Prozess war eine grausame Schauveran-

---

64. NŠAL, Militärangelegenheiten. *Palme mučeništva*, 15.
65. NŠAL, Militärangelegenheiten, 24.9.1944; *Palme mučeništva*, 16.

Slowenien nach der Okkupation[66]

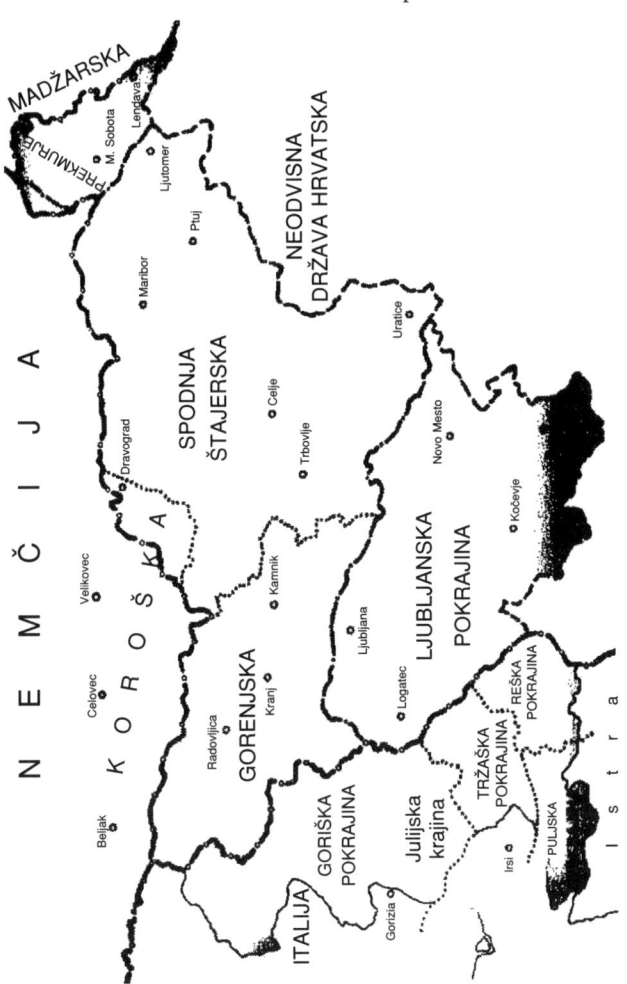

Nemčija = Deutschland
Koroška = Kärnten
Ljubljanska pokrajina = Provinz Ljubljana
Gorenjska = Oberkrain
Spodnja Štajerska = Untersteiermark
Prekmurje = Übermurgebiet
Madžarska = Ungarn
Italija = Italien

Goriška pokrajina = Provinz Görz
Julijska krajina = Julisch Venetien
Tržaška pokrajina = Provinz Triest
Reška pokrajina = Provinz Fiume
Neodvisna država Hrvatska = Unabhängiger Staat Kroatien
Beljak = Villach
Celovec = Klagenfurt
Velikovec = Völkermarkt

66. Miloš Mikeln, *Malo zgodovinsko berilo* (Ljubljana: Založništvo slovenske knjige, 1991) 23.

staltung, um der eigenen Bevölkerung und der Außenwelt zu demonstrieren, wie geordnet die Seite der "Volksmacht" angeblich agiere und wie gerecht sie die Feinde behandele. Doch gab es noch eine zweite Ebene des Geschehens in Gottschee und seiner Umgebung. Der Prozess sollte nämlich von dem schrecklichen Geschehen hinter den Kulissen ablenken. 21 Gefangene wurden spektakulär vor Gericht gestellt, damit die Beseitigung einiger Hundert, "unbemerkt" durchgeführt werden konnte.

Aus Angst vor schlimmen Repressalien verließen nach Ende des Krieges 275 weltliche Priester und Ordensleute Slowenien: 185 Diözesanpriester aus der Diözese Laibach, darunter Bischof Rožman, und 24 aus der Diözese Lavant sowie 66 Ordenspriester. Auch 62 Theologiestudenten wanderten ab. In Laibach blieben 75 Pfarrstellen unbesetzt, und in der Diözese Lavant kehrten die Geistlichen erst langsam zurück. Sie konnten aber ihren Dienst in den Gemeinden nicht sofort wieder aufnehmen, sondern mussten beim Ministerium für Inneres zuerst eine Genehmigung einholen.[67] Die meisten Priester gingen nach Österreich, wo sie in Lagern lebten und dort auch das kirchliche Leben in Form von ordentlichen Pfarreien organisierten. Nachdem sie das Lager Viktring verlassen konnten, wo das Leben noch nicht so organisiert gewesen war, lebten sie in den Lagern Pegez bei Linz, in Spittal a.d. Drau. Kellerberg, Fürnitz, St.Veit a.d. Glan und in Asten in Oberösterreich. Jedes Lager bildete eine Art Pfarre.[68] Nach und nach siedelten sich die Flüchtlinge in verschiedenen Staaten an, auch die Priester. Einige blieben in Europa, vor allem in Deutschland, Italien und Österreich, andere wiederum gingen nach Argentinien, in die Vereinigten Staaten und nach Australien.

Die Katholische Kirche in Slowenien war während des kommunistischen Regimes der Staatsfeind Nr. 1, weil sie die einzige noch organisierte Kraft außerhalb der Kommunistischen Partei geblieben war. Ähnlich wie die politische Opposition sollte nach dem Willen des neuen Regimes auch die Katholische Kirche vernichtet werden, doch erwies sich dieser Plan wegen der starken Verankerung des Glaubens in der Bevölkerung als undurchführbar. Eine große Rolle spielte auch die Tatsache, dass die Katholische Kirche international organisiert war und das Regime die Hierarchie nicht wirklich unter Kontrolle bekam. Einzelne Priester, auch durchaus solche mit einiger Verantwortung und Einfluss, wurden gebrochen und zur Zusammenarbeit gezwungen.

---

67. Griesser-Pečar, "Pomen 'osvoboditve'," 112.
68. NŠAL, Verlassenschaft Msgr. Jagodic.

Als das neue Regime erkannte, dass die Katholische Kirche nicht ohne weiteres vernichtet werden konnte, wurde ein dichtes System des Unterdrückungsapparates aufgebaut, in dem die Geheimpolizei ein umfangreiches Spitzel-Netzwerk unterhielt, auch in Kirchenreihen. Gleichzeitig versuchte man aber auch die Kirchenvertreter in den Augen der Bevölkerung moralisch zu desavouieren, mit dem Ziel, dass die Bevölkerung der Kirche den Rücken kehrt. Herausragende Vertreter der katholischen Kirche in Slowenien wurden daher nach dem Zweiten Weltkrieg von den kommunistischen Machthabern in Jugoslawien beschuldigt, in den Jahren 1941 bis 1945 mit den Besatzern kollaboriert und damit Verrat am slowenischen Volk begangen zu haben.

Die 'Kommission für Verbrechen des Okkupators und seiner Helfer' brandmarkte nach Kriegsende 47 Geistliche als "Kriegsverbrecher." Bereits im Mai 1945 begann die "Volksmacht" mit Massenverhaftungen von weltlichen Priestern und Ordensleuten. Von Mai 1945 bis März 1953 wurden in Slowenien 305 Priester verhaftet (bei rund 1000 Priestern).[69] Zahlreiche Priester und Ordensbrüder wanderten für viele Jahre in die Gefängnisse und Zuchthäuser. Auch die Todesstrafe wurde in nicht wenigen Fällen ausgesprochen, vollstreckt wurde sie viermal: einer wurde erhängt, drei weitere Geistliche wurden erschossen. Über diese "offenen" Hinrichtungen hinaus wurden jedoch viele Kirchentreue und Priester ermordet – so etwa 15 Militärgeistliche im Sommer 1945. Außerdem wurden auch harte Strafen auf Grund von Übertretungen administrativer Vorschriften verhängt, um der Kirche auch die noch verbliebenen finanziellen Mittel zu entreißen und die Arbeit der Kirche fast unerträglich zu erschweren. Zur Illustration: Von 1945 bis 1955 wurden auf diese Weise 1.033 Priester bestraft, davon wurden gegen 969 Geldstrafen ausgesprochen, gegen 64 Haftstrafen bis zu 30 Tagen.[70] Viele Strafmaßnahmen dienten einfach dazu, die Vertreter der Kirche einzuschüchtern.

Der Schlüsselprozess gegen "die Kirche" war, wie schon erwähnt, das spektakulär aufgezogene Strafverfahren gegen den Bischof Dr. Gregorij Rožman im August 1946. In Sammelverfahren wie dem Rožman-Rupnik-Prozess oder im sogenannten "Weihnachtsprozess" 1945, im Bitenc-Prozess und in vielen anderen Schau-Verhandlungen wurden Unschuldige, weniger stark Belastete und vermutlich Schuldige unter dieselbe Pauschal-Anklage gestellt – wie etwa Volksverrat, Kollaboration, Organisation der

---

69. AS I, AZ 1529 Boris Kraigher, Schachtel 12.
70. AS, KOVS 83, Jahresbericht 1955.

Weißen Garde und der Landeswehr, Kontakte zu Vertretern der Emigration, Fluchthilfe, feindliche Propaganda, Zusammenarbeit mit bewaffneten Einheiten jenseits der Grenze usw. Solche Pauschal-Anklagen waren absurd, da ja keine gemeinsame Tat zur Verhandlung stand. Doch der Plan war eben ganz offensichtlich der, dass der Schatten der Schuld eines wirklich Schuldigen, wie etwa des SS-Obergruppenführers Erwin Rösener, auch auf die anderen Angeklagten fallen sollte.

Von einem auch nur halbwegs rechtsstaatlichen Verfahren konnte keine Rede sein. Es gab kein Gleichgewicht zwischen Anklage und Verteidigung, und es wurde alles unternommen, um die Zeugen der Angeklagten gar nicht erst zu Wort kommen zu lassen oder die Vorlage entlastender Dokumente zu verhindern. Die Anklageschriften wurden sehr spät zugestellt, so dass die Verteidiger, sofern es sich dabei überhaupt um wirkliche Verteidiger im Interesse der Angeklagten handelte, oft keine Zeit hatten, sich mit den Angeklagten richtig zu besprechen. Die stundenlangen nächtlichen Verhöre zermürbten die Angeklagten dermaßen, dass sie sehr oft etwas unterschrieben, was sie so gar nicht gesagt und erst recht nicht gemeint hatten.

Es gab aber auch eine Reihe von spektakulären Priesterprozessen, in denen ganze Gruppen von Geistlichen und Ordensleuten auf den Anklagebänken saßen – so etwa den Prozess gegen den bischöflichen Sekretär Stanislav Lenič 1947, den Franziskaner-Prozess 1947, den Prozess gegen die Lazaristen 1948, den Jesuiten-Prozess 1949, den Tolmein-Prozess 1951 und viele andere. Oft wurden die Verhandlungen an Kirchenfeiertagen oder in ihrer zeitlichen Nähe abgehalten, so zum Beispiel der "Weihnachtsprozess" 1945.[71]

Der Generalvikar Ignacij Nadrah, der den abwesenden Bischof vertrat, veröffentlichte ein Rundschreiben, wonach der neuen Obrigkeit Respekt, Gehorsam und Loyalität zu zollen sei. Er fügte hinzu, dass nach der Heiligen Schrift nur dann Gehorsam verweigert werden könne, wenn etwas gegen den Willen Gottes verlangt würde (Apg 4,19). Diese Loyalitätserklärung wurde vom neuen Regime überhaupt nicht zur Kenntnis genommen, wie auch Nadrah von den neuen Machthabern wegen seiner Nähe zu Rožman nicht empfangen wurde. Nadrah wurde dann auch am 14. Juni 1945 verhaftet. Sein Nachfolger als Generalvikar wurde Anton Vovk. Am 11. Juli folgte dann der Besuch von 14

---

71. Tamara Griesser-Pečar, "Procesi proti duhovnikom in redovništvu po maju 1945," *Temna stran meseca: Kratka zgodovina totalitarizma v Sloveniji 1945-1990*, ed. Drago Jančar (Ljubljana: Nova revija, 1998) 113-125.

Kirchenvertretern beim slowenischen Ministerpräsidenten Boris Kidrič. Sie präsentierten ihm eine schriftliche Loyalitätserklärung, in der sie auch die Tätigkeit einiger Priester des Bistums Laibach während des Krieges verurteilten.[72]

Die Situation der Katholischen Kirche verschlechterte sich von Tag zu Tag. Daher beklagte die jugoslawische Bischofskonferenz am 20. September 1945 in einem Hirtenbrief die Verfolgung von Priestern und Ordensleuten sowie die Tatsache, dass 243 von ihnen ermordet und viele inhaftiert worden waren. Ferner verlangten die Bischöfe Pressefreiheit, Wiedereröffnung kirchlicher Schulen, ungehinderten Religionsunterricht, freie Betätigung karitativer Institutionen, Genehmigung zur Weiterführung kirchlicher Organisationen bzw. Vereine, Respektierung der kirchlichen Eheschließung – wie überhaupt die Wahrung der Menschenrechte. Auch forderten sie die Rückgabe des kirchlichen Vermögens.[73]

Die Folge dieser Demarche war eine weitere Verschärfung der Lage, besonders in Slowenien. Die Verabschiedung des 'Gesetzes über die rechtliche Stellung der Religionsgemeinschaften' am 27. Mai 1953 signalisierte nach außen hin eine Normalisierung der Lage. Formalrechtlich wurde die Kirche als Gesprächspartner anerkannt, doch kann man von einer gewissen Besserung der Lage in Slowenien erst in den sechziger Jahren sprechen. Allmählich veränderte sich die Form der Repression, sie war nicht mehr so grob, nach außen hin nicht so sichtbar, bestand aber bis zur Wende 1990 fort. Nach 1961 ließ der Druck auf die Priester etwas nach, dafür aber verstärkte sich der Druck auf die katholischen Laien. Gläubige hatten keine Chance, führende Positionen einzunehmen. Obwohl die Situation in den siebziger und achtziger Jahren allgemein besser wurde, blieben die Katholiken bis zur demokratischen Wende Menschen zweiter Klasse.

Die jugoslawische Verfassung beschloss am 21. Januar 1946 die Trennung von Staat und Kirche. Damit waren Priester und Ordensleute aus dem öffentlichen Leben endgültig ausgeschlossen. Ordensschwestern, die in vielen sozialen Einrichtungen tätig waren (in Krankenhäusern, Sanatorien, Pflegeheimen, Altersheimen, Waisenhäusern, Armenheimen usw.), wurden aus ideologischen Gründen aus diesen verdrängt, obwohl es zunächst keinen Ersatz für sie gab. Die kirchlichen Schulen wurden

---

72. Griesser-Pečar, "Pomen 'osvoboditve'," 119; France M. Dolinar, *Resnici na ljubo* (Ljubljana: Družina 1998) 12-21.
73. Griesser-Pečar, "Pomen 'osvoboditve'," 123-128; France M. Dolinar, "Katoliška Cerkev v Sloveniji po drugi svetovni vojni," *Temna stran meseca*, 224-225.

verstaatlicht (katholische und evangelische), Ordensschwestern und Priester durften nicht mehr unterrichten. Die Theologische Fakultät, die von Anfang an unter enormem Druck des Regimes stand, wurde 1952 aus der Universität ausgeschlossen.

In Slowenien (wie überhaupt in Jugoslawien) gab es keine wirkliche Religionsfreiheit. Die gesetzlich garantierte Freiheit des Glaubens beschränkte sich auf die Ausübung kirchlicher Zeremonien, wobei jedenfalls, vor allem in den ersten Jahren nach dem Krieg, von einer Freiheit der Predigt nicht die Rede sein konnte. Viele Interpretationen der Heiligen Schrift wurden als gegen den Staat gerichtet verstanden, Kritik an der antikirchlichen Propaganda wurde als staatsfeindlich eingestuft. Der Religionsunterricht wurde zunächst behindert, indem die notwendigen Genehmigungen für die Schulen nicht oder erst gegen Schuljahresende erteilt wurden – dann, 1952, wurde er in den Schulen überhaupt verboten. Dies wurde am 11. Mai 1953 noch in die gesetzliche Form gegossen – mit dem Gesetz über die rechtliche Stellung der Religionsgemeinschaften. Vor dem Verbot des Religionsunterrichts in Schulen war ein solcher Unterricht in der Kirche bestraft worden. Nach dem Verbot durfte der Religionsunterricht in der Kirche erteilt werden.

Viele Kirchen wurden total zweckentfremdet. So wurde zum Beispiel die Jesuitenkirche des Hl. Joseph in Laibach zum Filmstudio umfunktioniert und der Plečnik-Altar zugemauert. Die als Kunstdenkmal anerkannte Kreuzritter-Kirche in Laibach wurde kurzerhand, ohne Rücksprache mit der Katholischen Kirche, der in Laibach kaum vorhandenen Altkatholischen Kirche zugeteilt. An Wegabbiegungen und Straßenkreuzungen wurden viele Kreuze und Marterln niedergerissen und beschädigt – nie wurden die Täter entdeckt. Ähnlich geschah es auch mit vielen Kapellen. Die Kirche der Karmeliterinnen in Selo bei Laibach wurde unter fadenscheinigen Gründen niedergerissen, die Kirche der Heiligen Mutter Gottes auf Ptujska gora gegen den Willen der Kirchenvorsteher zum Museum erklärt.

Die Steuern, die die Kirche zu zahlen hatte, waren unverhältnismäßig hoch, obwohl auf der anderen Seite so gut wie kein Einkommen vorhanden war, da das Kirchenvermögen verstaatlicht war. Nach der Agrarreform 1945 wurden Güter der Kirche über 10 ha (in Ausnahmefällen 30 ha) ohne Entschädigung verstaatlicht. Spendensammlungen in Kirchen wurden zunächst nicht erlaubt. Ein besonderer Dorn im Auge der Behörden waren Spenden aus dem Ausland. Man wandte alle möglichen Tricks an, um legale Spenden unmöglich zu machen. Sachspenden wurden mit hohen Taxen belegt, so dass die Kirche sie nur schwer oder gar nicht zahlen konnte. Viele Bittschriften und Beschwerden an Ministerien und andere Behörden wurden nicht einmal beantwortet.

Die Behörden verhinderten Firmungen und andere sakramentale Handlungen. Bischof Vovk durfte die Grenzbezirke nicht besuchen, nicht einmal das Grab seiner Eltern. Es gab reihenweise körperliche Attacken auf Geistliche und aktive Laien. Den Höhepunkt bildete wohl der Anschlag auf Bischof Anton Vovk, der am 20. Januar 1952 in Rudolfswerth durch Brandattentat schwer verletzt wurde.

Mit der Gründung des Cyrill-Method-Vereins [Cirilmetodijsko društvo, CMD] durch die Geheimpolizei sowie mit der im Jahre 1944 im "befreiten Gebiet" in Črnomelj gegründeten Glaubenskommission und einigen mit den Kommunisten sympathisierenden Priestern versuchte das Regime, die Kirche zu spalten. Wie sehr die Geheimpolizei in die Belange dieses Vereins CMD verwoben war, zeigt zum Beispiel die Jahresversammlung von 1950. Von den 142 gewählten Kandidaten waren 75% informelle Mitarbeiter der Udba. Die Mitgliedschaft in CMD erreichte 1952 mit 526 Mitgliedern ihren Höhepunkt und sank danach kontinuierlich. Viele, vor allem ältere, Priester sahen sich gezwungen beizutreten, weil sie keine andere Möglichkeit des Überlebens sahen. Dagegen verhalf die Mitgliedschaft zu allerlei Privilegien und Vergünstigungen.

Die beiden Ordinarien nahmen von Anfang an eine negative Haltung gegenüber CMD ein. Das jugoslawische Episkopat verabschiedete am 18. Mai 1950 das *non expedit*, was so viel hieß wie dass es als unangebracht erachtet wurde, sich im CMD zu organisieren. Das kirchliche Verbot des Vereins, das in Zagreb 1952 erlassen wurde, wurde in Slowenien nie veröffentlicht. Drei Priester wurden jedoch wegen ihrer Mitgliedschaft vom Vatikan exkommuniziert. Aber der Druck des Regimes auf alle Geistlichen, dem Verein beizutreten, war sehr groß. Wer sich weigerte, wurde allen möglichen Repressalien ausgesetzt, viele wurden sogar aus ihren Ortschaften vertrieben.[74]

Kirchliche Druckereien wurden unter dem kommunistischen Regime beschlagnahmt, ebenso das gesamte religiöse Schriftgut, das sich in ihnen befand. Es war außergewöhnlich schwierig, irgend etwas zu drucken. So erschienen bis 1953 nur drei religiöse Bücher. Der Hermagoras-Verlag in Cilli durfte zwar Bücher veröffentlichen, aber nur solche mit neutralem Inhalt.

Selbstverständlich observierte die Udba nicht nur die Katholische Kirche, sondern auch andere Glaubensgemeinschaften, die bei weitem nicht

---

74. Griesser-Pečar, "Duhovščina," 296-297.

die Stärke der Katholischen Kirche hatten. Die Geheimpolizei rekrutierte überall informelle Mitarbeiter. Im Übermur-Seniorat der Evangelischen Kirche sammelte die Udba Material gegen den Senior Adam Luthar – er zeigte offenbar eine zu negative Einstellung gegenüber der "Volksmacht." Luthar kam in Untersuchungshaft, wurde dann aber wieder freigelassen, doch zwang ihn die Udba zum Rücktritt. Vor allem kreidete man ihm die Tatsache an, dass er den slowenischen Dialekt, das Wendische, gepflegt hatte. Auch andere wurden verhaftet und verurteilt, so etwa der heutige Pastor von Bodonci, Ludvik Jošar, dem "Propaganda gegen den Staat und die staatliche Ordnung in Jugoslawien" zur Last gelegt wurde.

V. Schlussfolgerung

Aus den Ergebnissen der obigen Untersuchung lässt sich unter anderem folgern:

1. Die wissenschaftliche Behandlung der Geschichte des Zweiten Weltkriegs in Slowenien muss sich von den zu einfachen Mustern der kommunistischen Regime-Geschichtsschreibung, die unter ideologischen Vorzeichen stand, verabschieden – was inzwischen auch zunehmend geschieht. Damit sind auch Stellung und Haltung der Katholischen Kirche zu jener Zeit in neuem Licht zu sehen.

2. Bei der Behandlung dieses Teils der slowenischen Geschichte, in welcher die Rolle der Katholischen Kirche von zentraler Bedeutung ist, müssen zwei Ebenen des Geschehens beachtet werden: zum einen das äußere Kriegsgeschehen mit der Besatzungslage und den verschiedenen Verhaltensweisen zu den Okkupationsmächten – von der Kollaboration bis zum Widerstand –, zum anderen die Entwicklung der kommunistisch-revolutionären Bewegungen, die sich die Situation für ihre Machtpläne zunutze machten, sowie der Gegenkräfte im traditionell-bürgerlichen Lager.

3. Die Katholische Kirche suchte während der Besatzungszeit im Interesse der Bevölkerung nach einem Weg des Überlebens-Arrangements mit den Besatzungsmächten, ohne mit diesen zu sympathisieren.

4. Nationalsozialisten und Faschisten verfolgten die Katholische Kirche – vor allem als Träger und Förderer der slowenischen Kultur.

5. Die Katholische Kirche stand wegen ihrer Ablehnung des "gottlosen Bolschewismus" und der vom kommunistischen Widerstand vielfach ausgehenden Gewalt gegen die slowenische Bevölkerung nicht auf der Seite des sogenannten "Volksbefreiungskampfes."

6. Nach dem Krieg wurde die Katholische Kirche in Slowenien als nach wie vor starke meinungsbildende sowie international verankerte Institution und als einzige intakte Organisation außerhalb der Kommunistischen Partei von den Machthabern des neuen Jugoslawien zum Volksfeind Nr.1 erklärt. Dies äußerte sich unter anderem in zahlreichen spektakulären Gerichtsverfahren gegen kirchliche Würdenträger, in Verbrechen an Kirchenangehörigen, in einer gewaltsamen Auflösung kirchlicher Einrichtungen und kirchlicher Finanzmittel sowie in einer allgemeinen Benachteiligung bekennender Christen im öffentlichen Leben. In veränderter Form wirkten diese staatlichen Gewaltakte, Schikanen und Benachteiligungen noch bis zur demokratischen Wende 1990/1991 fort.

Auswahlbibliographie

Stella Alexander, *Church and State in Yugoslavia since 1945* (Cambridge: University Press, 1979).
France Bučar, *Usodne odločitve* (Ljubljana: Časopis za kritiko znanosti, 1989).
Cerkev na Slovenskem v XX. stoletju. ed. Metod Benedik, Janez Juhant und Bogdan Kolar (Ljubljana: Družina, 2002).
Chiesa e società nel Goriziano fra guerra e movimento di liberazione (Gorizia: Istituto di storia sociale e religiosa, 1997).
France M. Dolinar, *Resnici na ljubo* (Ljubljana: Družina, 1998).
Tone Ferenc, *Quellen zur nationalsozialistischen Entnationalisierungspolitik in Slowenien 1941-1945* (Maribor: Obzorja, 1980).
Tamara Griesser-Pečar, *Cerkev na zatožni klopi: Sodni procesi, administrativne kazni, posegi "ljudske oblasti" v Sloveniji od 1943 do 1960* (Ljubljana: Družina, 2005).
Tamara Griesser-Pečar, "I sacerdoti nel ‚processo die Natale' in Lubiana," *Chiese di frontiera* (Gorizia: Istituto di storia sociale e religiosa, 2001) 179-186.
Tamara Griesser-Pečar, "Pomen 'osvoboditve' za slovensko katoliško Cerkev," *Slovenija v letu 1945*, ed. Aleš Gabrič (Ljubljana: Zveza zgodovinskih društev Slovenije, 1996) 111-137.
Tamara Griesser-Pečar, "Slowenien, das zerrissene Volk: Die katholische Kirche während des Zweiten Weltkriegs," *Demokratie und Geschichte*, ed. Helmut Wohnout, Jahrbuch des Karl von Vogelsang-Instituts zur Erforschung der Geschichte der christlichen Demokratie in Österreich, 7/8, 2003/2004 (Wien/Köln/Weimar: Böhlau, 2005) 183-204.
Tamara Griesser-Pečar, *Stanislav Lenič: Življenjepis iz zapora* (Klagenfurt/Ljubljana/Wien: Hermagoras, 1997).
Tamara Griesser-Pečar, *Das zerrissene Volk: Slowenien 1941-1946. Okkupation, Kollaboration, Bürgerkrieg, Revolution*, Studien zur Politik und Wissenschaft, 86 (Wien/Köln/Graz: Böhlau, 2003).
Tamara Griesser-Pečar und France Martin Dolinar, *Rožmanov proces* (Ljubljana: Družina, 1996).

Ilustrirana zgodovina Slovencev (Ljubljana: Mladinska knjiga, 1999).
Ivan Jerič, *Moji spomini* (Murska Sobota: Zavod sv. Miklavža, 2000).
Jesen 1942: Korespondenca Edvarda Kardelja in Borisa Kidriča (Ljubljana: Inštitut za zgodovino delavskega gibanja, 1963).
Stefan Karner, *Die deutschsprachige Volksgruppe in Slowenien* (Klagenfurt/Ljubljana/Wien: Styria, 1998).
Ljubljana v ilegali, 2 (Ljubljana: Ljudska pravica, 1961).
Tamara Pečar, *Die Stellung der slowenischen Landesregierung zum Land Kärnten 1918-1920* (Wien: Dissertation, 1973).
Anton Pust, Zdravko Reven und Božidar Slapšak (eds.), *Palme mučeništva* (Celje: Mohorjeva, 1995).
Werner Rings, *Leben mit dem Feind: Anpassung und Widerstand in Hitlers Europa 1939-1945* (München: Kindler, 1979).
Slovenci in leto 1941: Prispevki za novejšo zgodovino. ed. Zdenko Čepič, Damijan Guštin und Jurij Perovšed. Bd. 2 (Ljubljana: INZ, 2001).
Slovenci v XX. stoletju, ed. Drago Jančar und Peter Vodopivec (Ljubljana: Slovenska matica, 2001).
Slovenska kronika XX. stoletja, ed. Marjan Drnovšek und Drago Bajt. Bd. 1 (Ljubljana: Nova revija, 1995).
Temna stran meseca: Kratka zgodovina totalitarizma v Sloveniji 1945-1990, ed. Drago Jančar (Ljubljana: Nova revija, 1998).
Volks- und staatsfeindlich: Die Vertreibung der Kärntner Slowenen 1942 (Klagenfurt: Hermagoras, 1942).
Zbornik ob 750-letnici Mariborske škofije 1228-1978 (Maribor: Škofijski ordinariat, 1978).

Summary
Church and State in Slovenia during World War II

Slovenia was occupied by three powers: Germany, Italy and Hungary. The aspirations of the three occupiers were identical. They had the same goal: ethnic extermination of the Slovene nation. However the means they used, and the living conditions differed considerably in the three occupied zones. The situation of the Catholic Church in the three sectors differed completely. The Church in Slovenia respectively "Dravska banovina" [Drau-Banschaft] was organized into two dioceses: Lavant with the seat in Maribor and Ljubljana. The diocese Ljubljana was divided between two occupiers, Germany and Italy. Upper Carniola and Zasavje were German, while the rest, along with the Slovene capital Ljubljana was Italian, the so-called "Province of Ljubljana." The German part of the diocese was administrated by the Bishop of Klagenfurt. The diocese Maribor was completely under German rule. The administration of the so-called Apostolic Administration Murska krajina (Prekmurje) which covered the districts of Murska Sobota and Dolnja Lendava had been administered by the Bishop of Maribor until the war. After the Hungarian occupation it came under the administration of the Bishop of Szombathely.

According to Hitler's order to the newly appointed *Reichstatthalter* for Lower Austria Dr. Siegfried Uiberreither to "make Lower Styria German again" ["Machen Sie mir die Untersteiermark wieder deutsch!"] the Germans prohibited all Slovene political and cultural and religious institutions. The use of the Slovene language in religious services was forbidden. Because priests were supporters of the Slovene national ideas, they were a threat to the radical National socialist Germanization plans. The Germans deported almost all priests and members of religious orders from Styria and Upper Carniola to Croatia. Some of those deported fled to the Italy controlled "Province of Ljubljana," where the situation was better, because the Italians had a completely different attitude to the Catholic Church and its representatives. Church services were permitted to go on normally. Slovene was used in churches, schools, newspapers etc. The two bishops, Dr. Ivan Tomažič in Maribor and Dr. Gregorij Rožman in Ljubljana, were therefore confronted with a completely different situation. Tomažič was confined in house arrest and was therefore helpless, Rožman was able to intervene for numerous people: priests, children, Jews, arrested citizens, hostages, internees etc. He had less influence after the Italian capitulation in September 1943, because the Germans took over the province. But even then the situation in the province was much better than in the territory they took in 1941. They considered Styria and Upper Carniola as originally German territory, Ljubljana and Lower Carniola not. The situation in Murska krajina was somewhere in between. Bishop Jožef Grösz asked for unquestioning loyalty toward the Hungarian state and cooperation with the authorities as well as the use of a language that people understood – in his opinion that was not Slovene, it was "wendisch," a Slovene dialect. He liked to move Hungarian chaplains to Slovene parishes and prohibited the Slovene ritual-book.

But there was another problem in Slovenia. We have in Slovenia two levels of events: the occupation and the resistance, as well as revolution and counter-revolution. We cannot separate the two levels. The Communist party, in numbers rather weak but experienced in underground work – the KP was forbidden in Yugoslavia since 1920 – saw in the occupation the only chance of gaining power. They organized a sort of umbrella organisation of resistance named "Liberation front" and monopolized the resistance. Among the victims of the Red violence in towns and in the country were also 45 priests.

Die katholische Kirche in der Slowakei 1939-1945

Emilia Hrabovec

I. Außen- und innenpolitische Kräfteverhältnisse

Die am 14. März 1939 proklamierte Slowakische Republik entstand zwar in einer bewegten internationalpolitischen Situation und im Schatten der massiven machtpolitischen Präsenz des Deutschen Reiches in Mitteleuropa, doch von der überwiegenden Mehrzahl der slowakischen Bevölkerung wurde sie als Verwirklichung des Selbstbestimmungsrechtes und Schutz gegen die reale Gefahr einer Aufteilung zwischen Ungarn und Polen bzw. Deutschland begrüßt. Die außenpolitische Dominanz des Deutschen Reiches wurde durch die erzwungene Unterzeichnung des Schutzvertrages vom 18./23. März 1939, mit dem sich die Slowakei verpflichtete, ihre Außen- und Wirtschaftsbeziehungen im Einvernehmen mit dem Deutschen Reich zu gestalten, sofort sichtbar. Dennoch behielt die Republik innenpolitisch relativ große Freiräume, um deren christlich-katholische Ausgestaltung sich die dominante politische Elite bemühte.[1]

Diese politische Elite rekrutierte sich primär aus den Reihen der Slowakischen Volkspartei, einer 1905 entstandenen und im Dezember 1918, in der Geburtsstunde der Tschechoslowakei, erneuerten politischen

---

1. Zur Frage des Ausmaßes der deutschen Einflußnahme und der erkämpften und erstrittenen slowakischen Freiräume vgl. neuerdings Tatjana Tönsmeyer, *Das Dritte Reich und die Slowakei 1939-1945: Politischer Alltag zwischen Kooperation und Eigensinn* (Paderborn u.a.: Schöningh, 2003); zur Entstehung der Slowakischen Republik vgl. Stanislav J. Kirschbaum, "The First Slovak Republic (1939-1945): Some Thoughts on its Meaning in Slovak History," *Österreichische Osthefte* 41, nos. 3-4 (1999) 405-425; Milan S. Ďurica, *La Slovacchia e le sue relazioni politiche con la Germania 1938-1945*. I: *Dagli accordi di Monaco all'inizio della Seconda guerra mondiale (ottobre 1938-settembre 1939)* (Padova: Marsilio Editori, 1964); Jörg K. Hoensch, *Die Slowakei und Hitlers Ostpolitik: Hlinkas Slowakische Volkspartei zwischen Autonomie und Separation 1938-1939* (Köln/Graz: Böhlau, 1965); Dorothea H. El Mallakh, *The Slovak Autonomy Movement 1935-1939: A Study in Unrelenting Nationalism* (New York: Columbia University Press, 1979); vgl. auch die bibliographischen Aufsätze von Jozef M. Rydlo, "Prvá Slovenská republika (1939-1945) v domácej a zahraničnej historiografii: Výberová bibliografia," *Slovenská republika (1939-1945)*, ed. Ján Bobák (Martin: Matica slovenská, 2000) 222-270; sowie Ivan Kamenec, "Slovak Historiography on the Period 1938-1945," *Studia Historica Slovaca* 20 (1995) 113-119.

Partei, die das Programm der politischen Autonomie für die Slowakei und einer harmonischen Annäherung zwischen Kirche und Staat auf ihre Fahnen geschrieben hatte und mit einer kurzen Ausnahme bis zum Ende der Ersten Tschechoslowakischen Republik in der Opposition zu den unitaristisch und säkular gesinnten Prager Regierungen verharrt war. Sie war traditionell slowakisch-national gesinnt und bekannte sich zum konservativen, aber zugleich betont sozial orientierten katholischen Ideengut, welches auf den päpstlichen Sozialenzykliken *Rerum novarum* (1891) und noch deutlicher *Quadragesimo anno* (1931) fußte und nicht zuletzt aus den gesellschaftspolitischen Entwürfen der damals richtungsweisenden vor allem deutschen und österreichischen katholischen Theoretiker Inspiration schöpfte.

Die gesellschaftspolitischen Vorstellungen dieser traditionellen slowakischen katholischen Eliten gingen vom Grundsatz aus, wonach alle Macht und alles Recht von Gott ausgingen.[2] Der Staat dürfe daher kein Selbstzweck sein, da hinter ihm der göttliche Schöpfer stehe, der die Grenzen der staatlichen Macht und Kompetenz ziehe und dem Staat die Aufgabe gebe, das Gemeinwohl zu verwirklichen. Ein solches Gemeinwohl wurde weder liberal-individualistisch als Summe aller Partikularinteressen noch kollektivistisch als von diesen losgelöstes gesellschaftliches Interesse, sondern im christlichen Sinne als göttlich vorgegeben verstanden. Der Staat habe anzuerkennen, daß es außer ihm noch göttlich legitimierte naturrechtliche Individuen und Gemeinschaften mit eigenen ursprünglichen Rechten (menschliche Person, Familie, Stand, Nation) gebe, deren Rechte er zu beschützen und gegenseitig auszugleichen habe. Im Geiste des komunitären Personalismus wurde die menschliche Person zugleich in ihrer individuellen wie ihren sozialen Dimension angesehen, das heißt als Träger von gottgegebenen unveräußerbaren Rechten, die jedoch ihre volle Entfaltung lediglich in der Gemeinschaft finden könne. Als naturrechtliche Grundgemeinschaften und Fundament des Staates galten die Familie (für welche unter anderem der Familienlohn eingeführt wurde) und die Nation als gottgewollte Gemeinschaft, deren Respekt in den Bereich des vierten Gebotes inkludiert wurde, die allerdings nicht durch rassische, sondern durch kulturelle und moralische Kriterien definiert wurde. Die Freiheit aller naturrechtlichen Akteure sollte sich nicht als autonome Selbstüberhebung gegen die vom Staat zu schützenden göttlichen Ordnungen, sondern in anerkennendem Vollzug

---

2. Vgl. vor allem die Enzykliken von Leo XIII. "Diuturnum illud," *Acta Sanctae Sedis* (*ASS*) 14 (1881) 3-14 und "Immortale Dei," *ASS* 18 (1885) 162-175.

des Gemeinwohls realisieren, welches die Partikularinteressen nicht aufhebe, sondern in einer thomistisch aufgefaßten Synthese einschließe. Die Freiheit wurde also in diesem Ordnungsentwurf nicht im liberalen Sinne als Ausübung der individuellen Menschenrechte verstanden, sondern dem prinzipiellen Gemeinwohl- bzw. christlich definierten Wahrheitsvorbehalt unterworfen und durch diesen einerseits garantiert (z.B. durch das Postulat der Unveräußerlichkeit der Menschenwürde), andererseits limitiert.

Für die Anhänger dieser integralen Staats- und Gesellschaftsvorstellung galt das individualistische liberal-parlamentarische System, wie sie es aus den Zeiten der alten ungarischen Monarchie vor 1918 oder der Ersten Tschechoslowakischen Republik kannten und vor allem im Lichte der unerfüllten nationalen Forderungen, der sozialen Nöte und parteipolitischen Zerwürfnisse wahrnahmen und welches sie mit parteipolitischem Partikularismus, Gruppenegoismus und nach arithmetischen Stärken orientierter "mechanischer Demokratie"[3] identifizierten, als gescheitert und diskreditiert. Sie bemühten sich darum, sowohl die liberal-parlamentarische Demokratie als auch die verschiedenen ideologisch gefärbten kollektivistischen Systeme (Marxismus, Nationalsozialismus) mit deren heidnischer Vergötterung des Staates, der Partei oder der Rasse in einer neuen katholisch bzw. christlich fundierten und gesellschaftliche Konflikte ausgleichenden Synthese – in den dreißiger Jahren sprach man von einer "neuen Demokratie"[4] – zu überwinden, die implizit oder explizit als Alternative oder "dritter Weg" interpretiert wurde.[5] Im Geiste der sozialen Enzyklika *Quadragesimo anno*, die ihre Aussagen allerdings an kein konkretes politisches Modellsystem band und somit unterschiedliche Interpretationen ermöglichte, sah man den Weg zur Überwindung von sozialen und Klassenkonflikten im Korporativismus und in der Idee des Ständestaates. Das Ideal war also ein Staat, der nicht durch pluralistische gesellschaftliche Konflikte zerrissen, sondern die Einheit der ihn tragenden Gemeinschaft einrahmen und zum Instrument und Schauplatz der sozialen Umsetzung der göttlichen Ordnungen – und somit zum "christlichen Staat"[6] – werden sollte. Um die ihm zugedachten weitgehenden

---

3. Zum Begriff vgl. Karol Murín, *Spomienky a svedectvo* (Trenčín: Priatelia prezidenta Tisu, 1991) 20.

4. A. M. Višňovan, "Nová demokracia," *Kultúra* 7 (1935) 99-102.

5. So zum Beispiel in den Äußerungen des Mitbegründers und Chefs der katholischen Gewerkschaftsbewegung, Rudolf Čavojský, in *Slovenský robotník* (3. November 1938).

6. Bundesarchiv Berlin (BArch) R 70/112, Deutsche Pressebriefe in der Slowakei, Artikel aus *Slovenská Pravda* (14. März 1941); Murín, *Spomienky a svedectvo*, 37.

Aufgaben zu erfüllen, sollte der Staat kein liberaler "Nachtwächterstaat" sein, sondern reale Macht und Autorität besitzen, gegen deren Mißbrauch nicht so sehr liberaldemokratisch konzipierte Kontrollinstrumente "von unten," als vielmehr die moralische Inpflichtnahme und das Verantwortungsbewußtsein der politischen Akteure zu schützen hatten.[7]

Diese Ideen bildeten auch das theoretische Fundament der Verfassung der Slowakischen Republik vom 21. Juli 1939, die unter Einarbeitung einer Fülle von zum Teil recht heterogenen Quellen und Einflüssen wie die katholische Soziallehre, das Beispiel diverser autoritärer Systeme sowie überlieferte Einflüsse des demokratisch-parlamentarischen Systems ein autoritativ-ständestaatliches System begründete.[8]

In der Einleitung zum Verfassungsgesetz vom 21. Juli 1939 hieß es im Einklang mit den oben ausgeführten Grundsätzen:

> Die slowakische Nation, unter dem Schutz des Allmächtigen Gottes, hat sich seit Alters her auf dem ihr bestimmten Lebensraum erhalten, wo sie mit Hilfe dessen, von dem alle Macht und alles Recht ausgeht, sich ihren freien slowakischen Staat errichtet hat.
> Der slowakische Staat vereinigt gemäß dem Naturrecht alle sittlichen und wirtschaftlichen Kräfte der Nation in eine christliche und nationale Gemeinschaft, um in ihr die sozialen Gegensätze und die sich kreuzenden Interessen aller ständischen und Interessengruppen auszugleichen,

---

7. Zu den Staats- und Gesellschaftsvorstellungen der katholisch-konservativen Kreise, insbesondere von Jozef Tiso, dem Haupttheoretiker der Volkspartei, vgl. Štefan Polakovič, *Tisova náuka* (Bratislava: Nakladateľstvo HSĽS, 1941); Miroslav Fabricius und Ladislav Suško (eds.), *Jozef Tiso. Prejavy a články (1913-1938)* (Bratislava: Academic Electronic Press, 2002) 229-231, 300-309, 338-350, 351-354, 504-508; Lisa Guarda Nardini, *Tiso: una terza proposta* (Padova: CESEO/Liviana Editrice, 1977); Valerián Bystrický und Štefan Fano (eds.), *Pokus o politický a osobný profil Jozefa Tisu* (Bratislava: Slovak Academic Press, 1992); zu Tiso siehe weiter Milan S. Ďurica, *Jozef Tiso slovenský kňaz a štátnik. I. 1887-1939* (Abano Terme: Piovan Editore, 1989); Ivan Kamenec, *Dr. Jozef Tiso 1887-1947: Tragédia politika, kňaza a človeka* (Bratislava: Archa, 1998); vgl. auch Jozef Tiso, "Die Neuordnung der europäischen Mitte," *Europäische Revue* (April 1939) 327-332; Jozef Tiso, "Svetlo Betlehema," *Slovák* 21, no. 296 (1939) 1; zu ständestaatlichen Vorstellungen vgl. auch Karin Schmid, *Die Slowakische Republik 1939-1945: Eine staats- und völkerrechtliche Betrachtung*, vol. 1 (Berlin: Berlin Verlag, 1982) 354-355.

8. In ihrer ausführlichen Untersuchung der slowakischen Verfassung stellte die deutsche Rechtshistorikerin Karin Schmid fest, die Verfassung, welche "für die damalige Zeit in Mitteleuropa erstaunliche Kontrollmöglichkeiten gegenüber der slowakischen Regierung aufwies," habe ein Verfassungssystem begründet, welches sich "weder als ein totalitäres oder faschistisches noch als ein demokratisches," sondern "am ehesten als ein autoritäres System mit vergleichsweise erstaunlichen demokratischen Zügen" bezeichnen lasse. Vgl. Schmid, *Die Slowakische Republik 1939-1945*, 344-359, Zitate 353, 358, 359. Zur zeitgenössischen deutschen Sicht siehe Kurt O. Rabl, "Verfassungsrecht und Verfassungslehre in der neuen Slowakei," *Zeitschrift für ausländisches öffentliches Recht und Völkerrecht* 9 (1938-40) 821-880; 10 (1941-42) 127-167.

um als Vollstrecker der sozialen Gerechtigkeit und Hüter des Allgemeinwohls in harmonischer Einheit durch die sittliche und politische Entwicklung die höchste Stufe des Glücks für die Gesellschaft und die Einzelnen zu erreichen.[9]

Zu den Besonderheiten der slowakischen Verfassung zählten die im elften Hauptteil genannten speziellen Bestimmungen über die Kirchen. Darin wurde zuerst die "freie Erfüllung religiöser Pflichten," also die Bekenntnisfreiheit, gewährleistet, soweit diese nicht den gesetzlichen Bestimmungen, der öffentlichen Ordnung oder den christlichen Sitten entgegenstand.[10] In den weiteren zwei Bestimmungen wurden die Kirchen und anerkannten religiösen Gemeinschaften zu öffentlich-rechtlichen Körperschaften mit eigener Verwaltung und eigenem Vermögen und der von qualifizierten Kirchenangehörigen unter staatlicher Aufsicht zu erteilender Religionsunterricht in allen Volks- und Mittelschulen zur Pflicht erklärt.[11]

Das ambitiöse Programm der gesamtgesellschaftlichen Umgestaltung konnte in den gegebenen Umständen nicht verwirklicht werden. Die traditionellen slowakischen katholischen politischen Eliten, deren Vorstellungswelt die Verfassung entsprungen war, sahen sich bald einem doppelten Druck ausgesetzt: Dem Gleichschaltungsdruck des Deutschen Reiches, das in dem wenige Wochen später ausgebrochenen Krieg bald zur unbezwingbar erscheinenden Großmacht geworden war, einerseits, und der innerslowakischen Opposition andererseits. Die vorerst gefährlichste innenpolitische Opposition erwuchs den gemäßigten Konservativen in den Reihen der Radikalen um den Ministerpräsidenten Vojtech Tuka. Tuka, als Universitätsprofessor für die Philosophie des Rechtes und das Völkerrecht für die damaligen slowakischen Verhältnisse überdurchschnittlich hoch gebildet, war eine sehr schwierige und schwer durchschaubare Persönlichkeit, die bereits in den zwanziger Jahren, insbesondere im Zusammenhang mit dem 1929 gegen ihn angestrengten Hochverratsprozeß, für Kontroversen innerhalb wie außerhalb seiner Partei gesorgt hatte. Nachdem er im Herbst 1938, gesundheitlich angeschlagen und menschlich verbittert, aus der Internierung entlassen

---

9. *Slovenský zákonník* no. 185 (1939) vom 21. Juli 1939 (Übersetzung der Verfasserin).

10. Karin Schmid bemerkt dazu, daß die Schranke der "christlichen Sitten" auf antisemitische Tendenzen hindeuten könnte, fügt aber hinzu, es sei nicht festzustellen, daß aufgrund dieser Bestimmung Bürger mosaischen Bekenntnisses an der Ausübung ihrer religiösen Riten gehindert worden wären. Vgl. Schmid, *Die Slowakische Republik 1939-1945*, 350.

11. *Slovenský zákonník* no. 185 (1939), Hauptteil 11, §§ 88-90.

worden war, fand seine Rückkehr in die Politik in den maßgebenden Kreisen der Volkspartei nur wenig Begeisterung. Tuka und seine Anhänger, insbesondere der spätere Innenminister Alexander Mach, begannen bald einen "slowakischen Nationalsozialismus" zu predigen und sich um die Ausschaltung der Gemäßigten und die Machtübernahme im Land zu bemühen. Hinter ihrer zum Teil recht lauten Rhetorik, die sozialrevolutionär unterlegt war und verbal deutsche Vorbilder anrief, verbarg sich allerdings eine große inhaltliche Heterogenität und Orientierungslosigkeit. Sie widerspiegelte sich auch in der mit dem Nationalsozialismus völlig unvereinbaren, dennoch demonstrativ gezeigten katholischen Frömmigkeit vor allem Tukas, die aber zugleich durch dessen Taten sowie durch verschiedene Äußerungen einiger Vorkämpfer der Gruppierung, welche auf dem Höhepunkt des innenpolitischen Kampfes im Winter 1940/1941 unter anderem auf die Zurückdrängung der Kirche aus dem öffentlichen Leben hinausliefen, in Frage gestellt wurde.[12]

Die deutsche Führung unterstützte aus naheliegenden Gründen die Radikalen und hievte ihre Vertreter in einflußreiche staatliche Positionen. Das geschah vor allem bei der deutschen Intervention in die innerslowakischen Angelegenheiten in Salzburg am 28. Juli 1940, als auf deutschen Druck der um eine nach Möglichkeit eigenständige Außenpolitik bemühte Außenminister Ferdinand Ďurčanský entlassen werden mußte, während der germanophile Tuka das Außenressort und sein Gesinnungsgenosse Mach das Innenressort übernahmen.[13] Berlin war sich allerdings darüber im Klaren, daß die "Falken" eine kleine Gruppe ohne tragfähigen Anhang darstellten, während der traditionell-katholische Flügel und insbesondere einige seiner Persönlichkeiten, vor allem der Staatspräsident, der katholische Priester Jozef Tiso, in der Bevölkerung sehr populär waren und ihre brachiale Ausschaltung bzw. Märtyrisierung dem unmittelbar wichtigsten deutschen Interesse, der Beibehaltung von

---

12. BArch R 70/112 Bericht Nr. 1079/40 vom 14. November 1940; Leitartikel "Náboženstvo a Hlinkova Garda," *Gardista* (14. November 1940); vgl. auch BArch R 70/112, f. 57. Der ideologische Eklektizismus in den Äußerungen der Zeitung *Gardista* war sehr deutlich; vgl. z.B. die Behauptung, der Nationalsozialismus und die päpstlichen sozialen Enzykliken würden sich gegenseitig "nicht ausschalten, sondern ergänzen," *Gardista* (16. Mai 1941).

13. Der deutsche machtpolitische Eingriff in Salzburg darf freilich nicht nur in innerslowakischen Zusammenhängen gesehen, sondern sollte auch im breiteren Zusammenhang, als Bestandteil der Festigung der Macht des Deutschen Reiches und der Umsetzung seines Modells des "neuen Europa" auf dem Höhepunkt der deutschen Macht nach dem siegreichen Feldzug gegen Frankreich im Sommer 1940, interpretiert werden.

"Ruhe und Ordnung," kontraproduktiv gewesen wäre.[14] So wurden auch verschiedene Vorschläge des deutschen Gesandten Manfred von Killinger, Tiso durch die Ernennung zum Bischof und apostolischen Administrator von Trnava stillschweigend aus der Politik zu entfernen, fallengelassen.[15]

Gegen eine Demission Tisos, mit welcher sich der auch persönlich gedemütigt fühlende Präsident nach Salzburg beschäftigte, sprach sich, freilich aus anderen Gründen, als die Deutschen, auch sein Ordinarius, der Diözesanbischof von Nitra, Karol Kmeťko, aus, nicht zuletzt, weil er befürchtete, Tisos Rücktritt würde den Radikalen freies Feld eröffnen.[16] Bei einer 1942 abgehaltenen Bischofsversammlung in Banská Bystrica sollen die Bischöfe jedoch, einer Agentenmeldung zufolge, Tiso mit der Frage konfrontiert haben, "ob er aus der Slowakei eine römische oder germanische Provinz machen wolle," worauf er "sehr energisch" erwidert haben soll, "daß die Slowakei nur eine römische Provinz sein könne."[17]

Das entscheidende Ringen der beiden Flügel in der slowakischen Innenpolitik wurde im Winter 1940/1941 ausgetragen, nachdem Tuka in seiner berüchtigten Rede vor dem Nationaltheater in Bratislava eine "slowakische nationalsozialistische Revolution" angekündigt hatte. Der katholisch-konservative Flügel, auf den Parteiapparat, die Beamtenschaft und die Kirche abgestützt, bemühte sich dagegen, ein entschiedenes Bekenntnis zu "unserem überlieferten christlichem Erbe" zu manifestieren, jede "Nachahmung fremder Vorbilder" als unnötig zu verwerfen und dem Gegner mit der Behauptung den Wind aus den Segeln zu nehmen, auch das bisherige politische Programm sei national und im Sinne der päpstlichen Enzykliken sozial gewesen.[18] Doch während das Lager Tisos

---

14. Johann Kaiser, *Die Politik des Dritten Reiches gegenüber der Slowakei 1939-1945: Ein Beitrag zur Erforschung der nationalsozialistischen Satellitenpolitik in Südosteuropa* (Bochum 1969), 493-500; Tönsmeyer, *Das Dritte Reich und die Slowakei*, 97.

15. Der amtierende apostolische Administrator von Trnava, Bischof Pavol Jantausch, sollte dem schwer kranken Bischof von Banská Bystrica, Marián Blaha, als Weihbischof *cum iure successionis* beigegeben werden und zugleich eine Neubesetzung des Bischofsstuhls von Trnava ermöglichen. PA AA, U.St.S. Luther 32, Bericht vom 27. Oktober 1940 Nr. 371, Anlage; vgl. auch Milan S. Ďurica, "Jozef Tiso v hodnotení Hitlerových diplomatov a tajných agentov," *Pokus o politický a osobný profil Jozefa Tisu*, 182.

16. BArch R 70/180, Bericht des SD vom 10. Dezember 1940.

17. BArch R 70/112, Bericht vom 17. Juli 1944.

18. BArch R 70/112 Bericht Dr. Mühlberger vom 24. Oktober 1940; vgl. auch die Rede Tisos vom 20. Januar 1941 abgedruckt unter dem Titel "Generálov bez vojska sa nemáme čo obávať" [Generäle ohne Armee brauchen wir nicht zu fürchten], *Slovák* (21. Januar 1941) 1.

mit der Kritik an der "Nachahmung fremder Vorbilder" die Imitation des Nationalsozialismus verwarf, wollte der radikale Innenminister Mach mit der Kritik am "Mißbrauch der Religion" für fremde Ideologien im Gegenteil die Gegner seines nationalsozialistisch angehauchten "Sozialismus der Tat" treffen und die Kirchen von allem "reinigen," was "an die alte, vergangene Welt erinnert."[19] Tiso, während seines Theologiestudiums in Wien ein Schüler Martin Schindlers und Ignaz Seipels, deren christlich-soziales Programm für ihn eine bleibende Inspirationsquelle darstellte, versuchte, die in der Verfassung angekündigte, jedoch unter den gegebenen Umständen nicht verwirklichbare katholisch-ständestaatliche Konzeption zumindest auf der Ebene der Partei umzusetzen und die Bildung von berufsständischen Partei- und Gewerkschaftsgliederungen zu initiieren, was vom deutschen Sicherheitsdienst sofort als Versuch einer "Auferweckung des christlichsozialen Österreichs" unliebsam registriert wurde.[20] Das innenpolitische Ringen ging mit dem Sieg des gemäßigten konservativ-katholischen Flügels aus – deutsche Berichte sprachen vom "Sieg des Klerikalismus" und des "politischen Katholizismus,"[21] und manche deutschen Kommentatoren meinten gar, die Slowakei mit ihrem konfessionellen Schulwesen "versinkt wieder in mittelalterliche Zustände."[22] Dieser Sieg erfolgte allerdings um den Preis der Straffung der autoritären Führung innerhalb der regierenden Partei HSĽS, die Tiso und seinem konservativen Flügel als wirksamste politische Stütze im Konflikt mit dem radikalen Tuka-Flügel und die nationalsozialistische Infiltration diente und in der zu diesem Zweck "alle zersetzerischen Bemühungen von Einzelpersonen, die unser öffentliches Leben vergiften wollen," bekämpft werden sollten.[23] Vor allem jedoch erfolgte er um den Preis der Akzeptanz einer gewissen unvermeidbaren

19. BArch R 70/112, SA 531, Zeitungsschau des Deutschen Pressedienstes vom 3. Dezember 1940, Artikel in *Grenzbote* über Machs Besuch im Staatskrankenhaus in Humenné.

20. BArch R 70/45 SD Bericht VA 116/41 Lä./Ma vom 18. August 1941. Zu Versuchen das ständestaatliche System einzuführen vgl. BArch R 70/48 Bericht des deutschen Beraters Hans Pehm vom 14. Januar 1941; R 70/112 geheimer Bericht Mühlberger an das RSHA vom 16. Oktober 1940; zur deutschen Wahrnehmung vgl. auch Tönsmeyer, *Das Dritte Reich und die Slowakei*, 244-254.

21. BArch R 77/112 Agentenmeldung VII Za/K. vom 15. Mai 1940; R 70/45 Meldung der Stapo-Leitstelle Wien vom 25. November 1940; R 70/113, Bericht Nr. 62 von 119 vom 26. Februar 1941; R 70/112 Agentenmeldung SA 15 SA 18 II W./Pr. vom 28. Dezember 1943.

22. BArch R 77/112 Agentenbericht SA 261 vom 4. März 1943.

23. *Organizačné zvesti Hlinkovej slovenskej ľudovej strany* no. 1 (1941); vgl. auch Ivan Kamenec, "Jozef Tiso vo funkcii predsedu Hlinkovej slovenskej ľudovej strany v rokoch 1939-1945," *Pokus o politický a osobný profil Jozefa Tisu*, 161.

Kollaboration mit den Deutschen, also der Politik des "kleineren Übels," die dem Volk (freilich nicht der jüdischen Bevölkerung) ein Überleben in relativer Ruhe und Wohlstand ermöglichte, jedoch eine nachwirkende psychologische Belastung erzeugte, die aber nach 1945 auch bewußt politisch und ideologisch instrumentalisiert wurde, um den slowakischen Katholizismus unter Druck zu setzen und die religiösen oder nationalen Forderungen der Slowaken zurückzuweisen.

II. Kirche und Staat, Kirche und Gesellschaft: Ein schwieriger Weg zur neuen Selbstverortung

Obgleich der Slowakische Staat von seinen weltanschaulichen und nationalen Gegnern von Anfang an als "klerikal" perhorresziert wurde, bleibt eine eingehende Untersuchung des Verhältnisses der katholischen Kirche zum Staat und zur Gesellschaft bis dato ein Desiderat. Fest steht, daß der Staat, der sich in der Verfassung und in den programmatischen Äußerungen zu christlichen Grundsätzen bekannte, der katholischen Kirche Freiräume und Möglichkeiten gewährte, welche mit der steten Abwehrstellung in der säkularen, in einigen Phasen offen kulturkämpferischen Tschechoslowakei deutlich kontrastierten und alle wichtigen traditionellen katholischen Forderungen erfüllte. Der Staat anerkannte alle kirchlichen Feiertage und sanktionierte die Sonntagsruhe, der Unterrichtsminister initiierte eine Reform des Schulwesens und erließ bereits im Oktober 1939 eine neue Schulordnung, derzufolge "die Erziehung vom sittlich-religiösen und nationalen Geist durchdrungen"[24] sein sollte. Die Mehrzahl der Volksschulen wurde in konfessionelle Schulen umgewandelt, der Religionsunterricht in der jeweiligen Konfession der Schüler im Einklang mit den Bestimmungen der Verfassung[25] für obligatorisch erklärt. Der Staat öffnete die öffentlichen Institutionen und die Armee für die aktive Seelsorge und ermöglichte gar die Dienstfreistellung von Beamten wegen Teilnahme an Exerzitien.[26] Auch das kirchliche Vereinswesen erlebte eine Gründungswelle. Diese Tatsachen sowie das allgemein verbreitete Bekenntnis zur nationalen Staatlichkeit banden die Kirche an den Staat. Der wellenartig spürbare deutsche Gleichschaltungsdruck, die Versuche, mit Hilfe slowakischer Helfer und Exekutoren eine dem Katholizismus feindliche Ideologie in der Slowakei

---

24. "Pokrokárska škola navždy pochovaná," *Slovák* 21, no. 229 (5. Oktober 1939) 4.
25. *Slovenský zákonník* no. 185 (1939) § 90.
26. BArch R 70/112, Blatt 31, Bericht aus dem *Slovák* (10. Oktober 1940).

einzupflanzen und Bemühungen einiger mit den Radikalen verbundener staatlicher Stellen, den staatlichen Einfluß in der Gesellschaft auf Kosten der Kirche auszudehnen, motivierten allerdings die Kirche gleichzeitig dazu, eine Distanz zu konkreten staatlichen Organen und Anordnungen zu suchen. So bestand die Kirche darauf, eine eigenständige katholische Presseagentur zu gründen und die eigene katholische Jugendorganisation *Sdruženie katolíckej mládeže* (Vereinigung der katholischen Jugend) aufrechtzuerhalten, obgleich die staatliche Hlinka-Jugend, *Hlinkova mládež*, sich satzungsgemäß ebenfalls zu christlichen Grundsätzen bekannte und von den deutschen Geheimdiensten als Organisation verunglimpft wurde, die "eher einer Kongregation gleicht, als einer revolutionierenden Jugend."[27] Die Kirche bekämpfte schleichende Tendenzen, katholische Schulen wieder in staatliche Hand zu überführen[28] und belegte viele staatlich importierte deutsche Filme mit der kirchlichen Zensur.[29]

In der heftigen Auseinandersetzung mit dem radikalen Tuka-Kreis und der Hlinka-Garde steuerte die Kirche dem gemäßigten katholischen politischen Flügel, mit welchem sie über die priesterlichen Parteimitglieder auch personell verbunden war, eine massive Schützenhilfe bei. Episkopat und Klerus scheuten sich nicht, in entscheidenden weltanschaulichen Fragen offen ihre Position zu verkünden. Die Theologische Fakultät in Bratislava, die neugegründete Katholische Akademie, die Dominikaner und die Jesuiten veranstalteten öffentliche Vortragsreihen, bei denen von katholischen Positionen aus der Nationalsozialismus und die politischen Strömungen der Zeit einer Kritik unterzogen wurden.[30] Katholische Priester betonten in der Öffentlichkeit, daß das slowakische Doppelkreuz, welches an das Kreuz Christi erinnere, nicht mit dem Hakenkreuz zu verbinden sei[31] und kritisierten den Mißbrauch des Namens des verstorbenen Parteiführers Andrej Hlinka.[32] Die Kirche engagierte ihr gerade im Oktober 1940 erneuertes traditionsreiches katholisches Wochenblatt *Katolícke noviny* (Katholische Zeitung) in eine heftige Pressepolemik gegen den radikalen *Gardista*

---

27. BArch R 70/112 Bericht DP Ho/Fl. vom 17. Juli 1944.
28. Leitartikel der *Katolícke noviny* 9. Februar 1941, 1; BArch R 70/45, Gestapo-Bericht aus Wien an das RSHA vom 10. Februar 1941.
29. *Katolícke noviny* 22. Dezember 1940; BArch R 70/ 112 SA 181 II vom 17. Juli 1944.
30. BArch R 70/112, Blatt 41 und 108-113 (Berichte über Vorträge des Dominikanerpaters P. Inocent Müller) und Blatt 69 (Bericht über die Katholische Akademie).
31. BArch R 70/112 Nr. 1079/40 Bericht vom 25. Oktober 1940.
32. BArch R 70/45 VA 190/41 Meldung vom 30. Januar 1942.

(Der Gardist), in welcher die katholische Zeitung den Nationalsozialismus als heidnische Ideologie angriff und jede Zusammenarbeit mit ihm als Verrat am Katholizismus und somit zugleich "Verrat am eigenen Volkstum" brandmarkte,[33] was ihr in den Meldungen des deutschen Geheimdienstes und den Berichten der deutschen Gesandtschaft wiederholt Vorwürfe einbrachte, ein deutschfeindliches, dem "politischen Katholizismus" verpflichtetes "katholisches Hetzblatt" zu sein, hinter welchem "klerikale Kreise" stünden, die inneren Widerstand und passive Resistenz gegen den "neuen Geist" manifestierten und vor "versteckten Attacken" gegen den deutschen nationalen Sozialismus nicht zurückschrecken würden.[34] Im Spätfrühling 1941 flammte die Auseinandersetzung mit den Radikalen anläßlich des Jubiläums der päpstlichen Sozialenzykliken nochmals auf und mündete in eine Polemik über die Grundsätze der katholischen Soziallehre, welche kirchlicherseits dem "neuen Kurs" als Alternative entgegengesetzt wurde.[35] Der aus der ungarisch besetzten ostslowakischen Stadt Košice ausgewiesene Bischof Jozef Čársky verwies wiederum auf die Grenzen der staatlichen Macht, als er bei seiner Installationsfeier in Prešov mit deutlicher Anspielung auf das Dritte Reich meinte, auch König Nabuchodonozor habe "geglaubt, ein Gott zu sein."[36]

Die Suche nach einer neuen Selbstverortung der Kirche gegenüber Staat und Gesellschaft war freilich auch eine Konsequenz der veränderten Rahmenbedingungen nach 1938/1939, in welchen die Kirche sich nicht mehr einem sich betont säkular gebenden andersnationalen, sondern einem sich explizit als national und christlich deklarierenden Staat gegenübersah, der Aufbau dieses Staates aber zugleich eine – in anderen Staaten längst vollzogene – natürliche Laisierung des institutionalisierten öffentlichen Lebens beschleunigte. Dabei wurde gleichzeitig sichtbar, daß die idealisiert als homogen katholisch bzw. christlich wahrgenommene slowakische Sozietät von modernen Säkularisierungsprozessen ebenfalls nicht frei geblieben war, die direkte und unmittelbare Autorität der Priester insbesondere im urbanen Milieu nicht mehr in dem Ausmaße dominierte, wie dies für das bäuerliche Milieu charakteristisch war und der Einfluß liberaler oder sozialistischer Ideen insbesondere in die Reihen der Bildungsbürger und der Arbeiterschaft, wenngleich in der Regel in recht konfuser Form, Eingang gefunden

---

33. BArch R 70/112 Bericht Dr. Mühlberger vom 9. November 1940.
34. BArch R 70/112 Bericht Nr. 62 von 119 vom 26. Februar 1941.
35. BArch R 70/45 Meldung an das RSHA 300/41 VA 116/41 vom 28. Mai 1941.
36. BArch R/70 Bericht Nr. 799 vom 30. Dezember 1939.

hatte.[37] Die christliche Definition des Staatszwecks und die daraus fließende – in der Praxis freilich vielfach lediglich theoretische – Erhebung der katholischen resp. christlichen Moral zur allgemeinverbindenden Norm mußten daher in diesen Schichten zumindest latent auf Widerspruch stießen.

In der neuen Situation ging es der Kirche darum, das Ausmaß und die Art und Weise der kirchlichen Einflußnahme auf den öffentlichen Bereich zu bestimmen und jenen Raum abzustecken, innerhalb dessen die Autonomie des Temporären akzeptiert werden durfte und mußte, um die Autonomie der Kirche gegenüber dem Staat zu wahren, der Religion jedoch zugleich die öffentliche Präsenz zu sichern und mögliche Gefahren sowohl eines oberflächlichen "katholischen Konjunkturalismus" als auch des Hineinziehens in politische Verantwortung für mit dem göttlichen und natürlichen Recht unvereinbare Handlungen abzuwehren.

Damit war auch die Frage der Beteiligung der Priester am politischen Leben und der Neugestaltung des Verhältnisses zwischen Klerus und Laien sowie Kirche und Gesellschaft verbunden. Die Priesterschaft stellte in der bis weit in die Zwischenkriegszeit bäuerlich-patriarchalisch geprägten slowakischen Gesellschaft, in welcher eine eigene, an das Magyarentum assimilierte historische Oberschicht und lange Zeit auch ein selbstbewußtes nationales Bürgertum absentierten, das Christentum dagegen ein tragender Bestandteil der nationalen Identität war, eine unangefochtene moralische und soziale Autorität und zugleich eine Art Ersatzoberschicht dar, welche in entscheidender Weise die nationalpolitische Bewegung trug und ihre nationalen und religiösen Postulate vereinigte. Ein "Priesterrat" stand 1918 auch an der Wiege der autonomistischen katholischen Slowakischen Volkspartei,[38] in welcher erst ab der Mitte der zwanziger Jahre die Zahl der Priester-Abgeordneten begrenzt und in der Folge, mit dem Heranwachsen einer jungen Laien-Elite, reduziert wurde.[39] In der Slowakischen Republik war bereits die überwie-

---

37. Ferko Skyčák, "Laicizácia Slovenska," *Duchovný pastier* 23, no. 6 (1942) 483-486; ders., "O zbožnosť mestských rodín," *Kultúra* 14, nos. 8-9 (1942) 337-340; Bischof Kmeťko an den Präsidenten Tiso 15. November 1943, *Vatikán a Slovenská republika (1939-1945): Dokumenty*, ed. Ivan Kamenec, Vilém Prečan und Stanislav Škorvánek (Bratislava: Slovak Academic Press, 1992) 166-168.

38. Zum Priesterrat vgl. Emilia Hrabovec, *Der Heilige Stuhl und die Slowakei 1918-1922 im Kontext internationaler Beziehungen* (Frankfurt am Main u.a.: Peter Lang Verlag, 2002) 64-67.

39. Seit Mitte der zwanziger Jahre begann sich im slowakischen Bischofskollegium die Bemühung zu manifestieren, die Anzahl der politisch aktiven Priester zu reduzieren oder zumindest nicht über den Status quo hinauswachsen zu lassen. Nach Rücksprache einiger Bischöfe in Rom wurde schließlich der Standpunkt des Heiligen Stuhls angenommen,

gende Mehrzahl der politischen Repräsentanz in der Hand von Laien, dennoch befanden sich noch Priester im Parlament und Staatsrat und spielten vor allem im unteren Parteiapparat eine Rolle. Der Episkopat war sich der Gefahr einer gewissen "Klerikalisierung" des öffentlichen Raumes bzw. der möglichen Konsequenzen aus der Übernahme der politischen Verantwortung in schwierigen Zeiten durchaus im Klaren, war jedoch überzeugt, daß der Staat in der Stunde Null auf die Mitwirkung der Priester, die ein großes Vertrauen der Bevölkerung genossen, noch nicht verzichten könne. Dennoch bekundete er dem Heiligen Stuhl gegenüber die Entschlossenheit, politisch aktive Priester schrittweise durch Laien zu ersetzen, sobald diese verfügbar sein würden,[40] und verabschiedete bei der Konferenz in Žilina am 24. Oktober 1939 eine Deklaration an den Klerus, in welcher es hieß: "Dissuademus, ut Clerus immisceat se in res mere materiales."[41] Im Frühjahr 1943 forderten die Bischöfe ihre Priester auf, politische Funktionen und Abgeordnetenmandate abzulegen.[42] Der gleitende Abgang der Priester aus dem politischen Leben war freilich bei einigen verdienten nationalpolitischen Aktivisten mit dem bitteren Beigeschmack verbunden, nun, da die Hauptziele erkämpft seien, um die verdiente Anerkennung gebracht worden zu sein. Welche sozialen Erwartungen einige Priester mit dem neuen Staat verbanden, widerspiegelt die bei einer Priesterkonferenz vorgetragene, freilich von Tiso selbst sofort zurückgewiesene Anregung, der neue Staat möge den Priestern besondere Begünstigungen wie zum Beispiel Ermäßigungen auf Fahrkarten zuerkennen.[43]

Eine besondere Frage stellte die Tatsache dar, daß selbst an der Spitze des Staates ein katholischer Priester stand. Jozef Tiso gehörte zu den Gründungsmitgliedern der Slowakischen Volkspartei, die er als Abgeordneter im Prager Parlament und 1927-1929 als Gesundheitsminister in

---

wonach die Slowakische Volkspartei 1925 nur so viele Priester kandidieren durfte, mit wie vielen sie ursprünglich ins Parlament eingezogen war (sieben Abgeordnete und ein Senator). Vgl. Slovenský národný archív Bratislava (Slowakisches Nationalarchiv, SNA), fond Andrej Hlinka, Karton 4, Schreiben des Bischofs Ján Vojtaššák an Andrej Hlinka vom 16. Oktober 1925.

40. Schreiben von P. Vendelín Javorka, SJ an den Sekretär für außerordentliche kirchliche Angelegenheiten Domenico Tardini vom 16. November 1939, Kopie im Privatarchiv der Verfasserin.

41. Erklärung "Directis ad fidem" vom 24. Oktober 1939, zitiert nach Štefan Šmálik, "L'Église catholique en Slovaquie dans le années 1939-1944," *Les Églises chrétiennes dans l'Europe dominée par le IIIe Reich. Miscellanea Historiae Ecclesiasticae VI* (Warschau/Louvain-La-Neuve/Wroclaw/Bruxelles: Polska akademia nauk/Collège Érasme/Ossolineum/Éditions Nauwelaerts, 1984) 267.

42. BArch R 70/112 Aufzeichnung vom 7. April 1943.

43. Murín, *Spomienky a svedectvo*, 37.

der Regierung vertrat. Er galt als pragmatisch handelnder gemäßigter Politiker und zugleich als einer der wenigen Parteimitglieder, die fähig waren, die programmatischen Postulate der Partei theoretisch zu begründen und als ideologisches Gesamtgebilde darzustellen. Nach dem Tod des langjährigen Parteiführers Andrej Hlinka wurde er von den meisten Parteimitgliedern für dessen Nachfolger gehalten, zumal kein anderer Politiker zur Verfügung stand, der über eine vergleichbare Autorität in der Bevölkerung verfügte und imstande gewesen wäre, die unterschiedlichen Strömungen in der Partei zusammenzuhalten. Die Haltung des Heiligen Stuhls zur Kandidatur Tisos auf das höchste Amt konnte bis heute nicht voll geklärt werden, zumal in den staatlichen Archiven keine relevanten Dokumente vorliegen und die vatikanischen Archive noch nicht zugänglich sind. Der päpstliche Diplomat Raffaele Forni, der Mitte April 1939 von Berlin über Prag in die Slowakei reiste, um den Kardinalstaatssekretär Maglione über die Lage in diesem Land zu informieren, kam aufgrund persönlicher Gespräche mit den katholischen Bischöfen und mit Tiso selbst zur Überzeugung, daß Tiso "von den besten Absichten beseelt sei. Möglicherweise wird er das Land retten können, aber wenn er verliert, wie es Schuschnigg und Hácha ergangen ist, würde der Mißerfolg leider im selben Maße auf die Religion zurückschlagen, in dem der Katholizismus in der Slowakei verwurzelt ist." Forni meinte, "ein geschickt ins Werk gesetzter Amtsverzicht Tisos – ohne daß er die Slowakei verließe – könnte die beste Vorbeugungsmaßnahme sein, scheint aber heute noch verfrüht, auch deswegen, weil es niemanden gibt, der tatsächlich fähig wäre, ihn zu ersetzen, wenn man nicht den fanatischen Nazisten in die Hände fallen wird." Forni schloß seine Lagebeurteilung mit der Feststellung ab, die Bischöfe seien "ganz und gar einer Meinung mit dem Hl. Stuhl, was die Nichtteilnahme des Klerus an der Politik anlangt," unter den gegebenen außergewöhnlichen Verhältnissen jedoch "ihr Vertrauen bezüglich der Zukunft des Landes auf Tiso setzen."[44] Am 8. September 1939 empfing Papst Pius XII. in Castel Gandolfo den slowakischen Weihbischof Michal Buzalka in Audienz. Während der Unterredung kam auch diese Problematik zur Sprache. Der Papst soll nach Buzalkas späterer Aussage einige ernsthafte Bedenken geäußert haben: "Er fragte mich weiter, was ich darüber denke, daß an der Spitze der Slowakei nun ein Priester

---

44. Raffaele Forni an Kardinal Maglione vom 14. April 1939, Walter Brandmüller, *Holocaust in der Slowakei und katholische Kirche* (Neustadt an der Aisch: Verlag Ph.C.W. Schmidt, 2003) 116-124, Zitat 120-121 (italienisches Original) und 124-131, Zitat 128 (deutsche Übersetzung).

steht… Ich habe es damit erklärt, daß nach Hlinkas Tod niemand sonst für die Spitze der Volkspartei Hlinkas in Frage kommen konnte außer Dr. Jozef Tiso, da das Volk es so wollte und immer so dachte, daß nach Hlinka nur Tiso in dessen Fußstapfen treten kann… Der Papst wurde nachdenklich und sagte: "Und wird es eines Tages nicht schlecht für die Kirche, daß an der Spitze der Regierung jetzt ein Priester steht?" Ich habe geantwortet: "Vielleicht, doch das ist für die Person irgendwie schicksalhaft"… Pius XII. merkte dazu an: "Das ist es, daß die geheimen Kräfte, die gegen die Kirche arbeiten, in der Geschichte nicht selten die Tatsache eines Regimes gegen die Kirche verwenden, in dem ein Priester an der Spitze und an entscheidender Stelle stand."[45] Die eigentliche Entscheidung über die Annahme des Amtes scheint der Papst jedoch Tiso selbst überlassen zu haben. Nachdem schließlich am 26. Oktober 1939 die Wahl zum Staatspräsidenten erfolgt war und Tiso sie dem Oberhaupt der Kirche schriftlich mitgeteilt hatte, nahm sie Pius XII. zur Kenntnis, beglückwünschte den neuen Staatspräsidenten gemäß den diplomatischen Usanzen mit einem allerdings ziemlich reserviert formulierten Breve zu dessen Wahl und erteilte der slowakischen Nation seinen apostolischen Segen.[46]

Der schrittweise Rückzug des Klerus aus dem politischen Leben, die Akzeptanz der "gesunden Laizität des Staates," um ein späteres Wort Pius' XII. zu verwenden, und die Entlassung des gebildet und selbstbewußt gewordenen Laienstandes in die Eigenverantwortung waren langwierige und schmerzliche Prozesse, die sich in der slowakischen Gesellschaft seit den späten zwanziger Jahren angebahnt hatten und durch die Eigenstaatlichkeit beschleunigt, aber nicht abgeschlossen wurden.

III. Das Verhältnis der Slowakei zum Heiligen Stuhl und die Bemühungen um ein Konkordat

Der Heilige Stuhl anerkannte relativ rasch den neu entstandenen Slowakischen Staat, wenngleich nicht durch ein explizites Anerkennungsschreiben, sondern auf dem Wege der "stillen" völkerrechtlichen

---

45. Róbert Letz, "Biskup Michal Buzalka a politický život," *Biskup Michal Buzalka. Zborník príspevkov z vedeckej konferencie pri príležitosti 40. výročia úmrtia*, ed. Róbert Letz und Ivan A. Petranský, Libri Historiae Slovaciae, Scriptores III (Bratislava: Lúč, 2002) 94.

46. Das Faksimile des Schreibens ist abgedruckt bei Karol Sidor, *Šesť rokov pri Vatikáne* (Scranton, PA: Obrana Press, 1947) 63.

Anerkennung. Bereits im Juni 1939 reiste der slowakische Gesandte beim Heiligen Stuhl, Karol Sidor, an seinen Bestimmungsort ab, an dem er bis zum Kriegsende und dem Untergang des Staates verblieb. Schwieriger gestaltete sich die Konstituierung der apostolischen Nuntiatur in Bratislava. In die neue Hauptstadt wurde zwar gleichzeitig mit der Betrauung Sidors Nuntius Saverio Ritter entsandt, doch kam es zwischen ihm und der Regierung zu Spannungen, die zu seiner baldigen Abreise führten. Grund dafür waren nicht so sehr Ritters zweifellos vorhandene und aus seiner vorherigen Tätigkeit in Prag herrührende protschechoslowakische Sympathien, sondern vor allem die unklare Formulierung des Beglaubigungsschreibens, nach welchem Ritter, vorher Nuntius in Prag, "in der Erfüllung derselben Funktionen in der Slowakei fortfahren" sollte.[47] Diese Formulierung, die vom slowakischen Außenminister Ferdinand Ďurčanský als indirekte Umschreibung der Kontinuität mit der vorherigen Staatlichkeit zurückgewiesen wurde,[48] widerspiegelte die damalige Unsicherheit über die weitere völkerrechtliche Stellung der Slowakei, die nicht zuletzt mit der Unsicherheit über das weitere Vorgehen Hitlers und über die Lösung des deutsch-polnischen Konfliktes zusammenhing und erst nach Abschloß des Polenfeldzugs durch eine Stabilisierung der Lage abgelöst wurde.

Die slowakische Regierung und die katholische Kirche empfanden die Absenz eines Nuntius in Bratislava als sehr schmerzlich. Um so mehr, da die Notwendigkeit, mit dem Heiligen Stuhl über den Berliner Nuntius Orsenigo zu kommunizieren, indirekt die ungeliebte Dominanz Deutschlands unterstrich, während die aus Budapest vermehrt kommenden Berichte über die Slowakei in Anbetracht des tiefen Konfliktes der beiden Nachbarstaaten selbst im Vatikan als parteiisch angesehen wurden.[49] Im Juni 1940 wurde schließlich Giuseppe Burzio an die Nuntiatur in Bratislava entsandt, allerdings nur im Rang eines Chargé d'affaires, da die deutsche Regierung die für Nuntien vorgesehene Vorrangstellung des Doyens des diplomatischen Korps für ihren Gesandten reklamierte.[50]

---

47. Sidor, *Šesť rokov pri Vatikáne*, 5.
48. Aufzeichnung über das Gespräch zwischen Ďurčanský und Ritter am 20. Juni 1939 in: *Vatikán a Slovenská republika (1939-1945): Dokumenty*, 24.
49. Brandmüller, *Holocaust in der Slowakei und katholische Kirche*, 60.
50. Zu den Beziehungen zwischen der Slowakei und dem Heiligen Stuhl in den ersten Jahren nach der Entstehung der Republik vgl. Milan S. Ďurica, "Vzťahy medzi prvou Slovenskou republikou a Svätou stolicou v rokoch 1939-1940," *Historický zborník* 14, no. 1 (2004) 87-103; Róbert Letz, "Vzťahy Svätej stolice a Slovenska v rokoch 1938-

Die Regierung und die katholische Kirche bemühten sich sehr um freundschaftliche Beziehungen mit dem Heiligen Stuhl. In Anbetracht der schwierigen außenpolitischen Situation der Slowakei, die sich mitten auf dem Schachbrett widerstreitender (Groß)Mächteinteressen wiederfand, erblickten viele slowakische Politiker wie katholische Würdenträger und einfache Gläubige im Papsttum die potentiell einzige uneigennützige politische und moralische Stütze der slowakischen Interessen.[51] Diese auch emotional tief verwurzelte explizit proromische Einstellung war freilich auch historisch begründet: Während der Gedanke der nationalen Emanzipation in den umliegenden Völkern seit dem 19. Jahrhundert häufig eine antirömische Spitze besaß und nationalkirchliche Ambitionen motivierte, ging die slowakische nationalemanzipatorische Bewegung in Absenz jeglicher "nationalreformatorischen" Traditionen und in einer Situation, in der das überwiegend katholische Christentum die Säule der nationalen Identität bildete, einen anderen Weg. In ihren nationalen Selbstbehauptungsbestrebungen gegenüber der magyarisch gesinnten und der St. Stephansidee verpflichteten ungarischen Hierarchie, aber auch später gegenüber der Ideologie des Tschechoslowakismus, glaubte sie gerade in Rom den natürlichen und historisch bewährten Verbündeten ihrer nationalen Ambitionen zu erblicken. Die gezielt hervorgehobene Erinnerung an die Existenz der ersten selbständigen slowakischen Kirchenprovinz unter Erzbischof Method bereits im 9. Jahrhundert und die auf ihrem Gebiet verwendete slawische Liturgie, die man Rom verdankte, sowie der moralische Sieg im Streit zwischen dem ungarischen Bischof Párvy und dem national engagierten slowakischen Priester Andrej Hlinka, in welchem Rom sich im Jahre 1909 zugunsten des zu Unrecht abgesetzten Priesters aussprach, erfüllten die slowakischen Katholiken mit Stolz und Dankbarkeit gegenüber dem Oberhaupt der Kirche und wurden zu Ecksteinen ihres betont romtreuen historischen Bewußtseins,[52] das

---

2003," *Renovatio spiritualis: Jubilejný zborník k 70. narodeninám arcibiskupa Jána Sokola, prvého metropolitu Slovenska*, ed. Jozef M. Rydlo, Libri Historiae Slovaciae, Scriptores V (Bratislava: Lúč, 2004) 117-140.

51. So schrieb Bischof Kmeťko dem Präsidenten Tiso am 15. November 1943: "Wir wissen nicht, ob gerade der Heilige Stuhl nach dem Kriege nicht unsere einzige Rettung sein wird." Vgl. *Vatikán a Slovenská republika (1939-1945): Dokumenty*, 169.

52. Vgl. dazu Hrabovec, *Der Heilige Stuhl und die Slowakei*, 134; Emilia Hrabovec, "Zwischen Nation und Religion, Thron und Altar: Der slowakische Katholizismus in der Ära Bach," *Die Habsburgermonarchie und die Slowaken 1849-1867*, ed. Dušan Kováč, Arnold Suppan und Emilia Hrabovec (Bratislava: Academic Electronic Press, 2001) 92-93.

auch gegenüber Pius XII. immer wieder in Erinnerung gerufen wurde.[53]

Die slowakische Regierung erblickte eine ihrer wichtigsten kirchenpolitischen Aufgaben darin, das Verhältnis zur katholischen Kirche auf eine konkordatäre Basis zu stellen. Damit war nicht zuletzt die Hoffnung verbunden, den alten slowakischen Traum – eine selbständige slowakische Kirchenprovinz zu verwirklichen. Im Auftrag der Regierung arbeitete der Professor für kanonisches Recht an der Juridischen Fakultät der Slowakischen Universität, Ľudovít Knappek, einen Konkordatsentwurf, der allerdings gemäß dem Schutzvertrag der deutschen Seite vorgelegt werden mußte. Der Reichsaußenminister von Ribbentrop sowie Rechtsexperten des Reichskirchenministeriums äußerten vor allem ideologisch motivierte Bedenken. Sie kritisierten die weitgehenden Rechte, die der umfassende Entwurf der katholischen Kirche gewährte, vor allem die volle Freiheit der Ausübung der geistlichen Gewalt und der kirchlichen Jurisdiktion (Art. I), die uneingeschränkte Kommunikations- und Publikationsfreiheit der Kirche, die das Recht auf die freie Herausgabe von Hirtenbriefen einschloß (Art. II), die konkordatsrechtliche Verankerung der Militärseelsorge und die Überlassung der näheren Bestimmungen über die seelsorgliche Betreuung des Militärs dem Heiligen Stuhl (Art. VIII), die Verankerung des Rechtes der Kirche, einem Theologieprofessor an staatlichen Universitäten jederzeit die Lehrbefugnis zu entziehen und kirchliche Seminare ohne Staatsaufsicht zu führen (Art. XIX), den obligatorischen Religionsunterricht an allen Schulen mit Öffentlichkeitsrecht (Art. XX), die Gültigkeit der kirchlich geschlossenen Ehen auch für den staatlichen Bereich, welche "die Durchführung jeder Rassenpolitik ... unmöglich machen würde" (Art. XXII) und die Gewährung der vollen Freiheit für die Katholische Aktion und das katholische Vereinswesen (Art. XXXII).[54] Dem Ministerpräsidenten und Außenminister Tuka gelang es jedoch, vom Reichsaußenminister von Ribbentrop die grundsätzliche politische Entscheidung zu erreichen, wonach das Deutsche Reich dem Konkordatsabschluß keine Hindernisse in den Weg stellen würde, und im Dezember 1943 konnte der slowakische Gesandte beim Heiligen Stuhl, Karol Sidor, dem Staatssekretariat den offiziellen Konkordatsentwurf vorlegen. Für den Heiligen Stuhl kam es freilich nicht in Frage, mitten im Krieg und mit

---

53. So auch in der Antrittsrede Sidors am 7. Juli 1939, abgedruckt in Sidor, *Šesť rokov pri Vatikáne*, 36-38; vgl. auch *Litterae circulares ordinariatus Tyrnaviensis* no. 7 (1939) 48.
54. BArch R 5101/24044, RMKA an AA vom 25. Mai 1943 und vom 24. Juni 1943.

einem Partner, dessen völkerrechtlicher Fortbestand nach dem Krieg zu jenem Zeitpunkt bereits mehr als fraglich schien, einen Vertrag abzuschließen. Als Zeichen des Wohlwollens ernannte Pius XII. allerdings den allseits geschätzten Bischof von Nitra, Karol Kmeťko, zum Erzbischof *ad personam*.[55]

IV. Die katholische Kirche und die Verfolgung der jüdischen Bevölkerung

In eine schwierige Situation wurde die katholische Kirche durch die antijüdischen Maßnahmen des Slowakischen Staates gebracht, welche im krassen Widerspruch zu christlichen und naturrechtlichen Grundsätzen standen.

In allen Ländern Ostmitteleuropas, so auch in der Slowakei, waren verschiedene vor allem sozial und national motivierte, aber auch durch religiöse Argumente zusätzlich untermauerte Vorbehalte gegenüber den Juden vorhanden. Insbesondere in den damals sehr zahlreichen und von sozialen Problemen und Armut geplagten bäuerlichen Kreisen der ostmitteleuropäischen Region herrschte ein Unmut über den als übermäßig empfundenen wirtschaftlichen Einfluß einiger jüdischer Bevölkerungsteile und ihre dominante Rolle in einigen sozialen und beruflichen Schichten, vor allem im Handel und Finanzen und in den freien Berufen. So wurde die jüdische Bevölkerung, obgleich sie in ihrer sozialen Zusammensetzung bei weitem nicht homogen war, von außen primär als Bestandteil der dominanten sozialen Schichten wahrgenommen. Die soziale und professionelle Struktur der Juden, ihre traditionelle Loyalität gegenüber dem jeweiligen Staatsgebilde, in dem sie lebten, und die gleichzeitige Absenz jeder Form der Staatlichkeit oder auch nur politischen Autonomie der Slowakei im Rahmen der Staaten, deren Bestandteil sie historisch gebildet hatte, bewirkten, daß sich die überwiegende Mehrzahl der Juden nicht mit ihren bäuerlich geprägten und politisch und sozial bedrückten und marginalisierten unmittelbaren slowakischen Nachbarn, sondern mit den politisch und sozial dominanten Nationen

---

55. Vgl. die Erinnerungen Sidors, *Šesť rokov pri Vatikáne*, 205-215; Jozef M. Rydlo, "La Santa Sede e la prima Repubblica Slovaca negli anni 1939-1945," *Relazioni internazionali giuridiche bilaterali tra la Santa Sede e gli Stati: esperienze e prospettive*, ed. Marek Šmíd und Cyril Vasiľ (Città del Vaticano: Libreria Editrice Vaticana, 2003) 295-298. Der vollständige Text des Konkordatsentwurfes ist abgedruckt bei Jozef M. Rydlo, "Sedemnásť cirkevnoprávnych dokumentov z cirkevných dejín Slovenska," *Renovatio spiritualis*, 366-379.

bzw. der herrschenden Staatsmacht identifizierte, die aber infolge der harten Magyarisierung im alten Ungarn und später des unitaristischen staatsnationalen "Tschechoslowakismus" der ČSR von den Slowaken als Unterdrücker angesehen wurde. Diese Faktoren erleichterten in einigen Teilen der slowakischen Bevölkerung die mentale Bereitschaft, staatlichen Maßnahmen, die ab Herbst 1938 die Einschränkung des jüdischen Eigentums und die Ausschließung der Juden von einigen Berufen dekretierten,[56] zuzustimmen. Die Einleitung der offenen Verfolgungsmaßnahmen allerdings, in deren Vorfeld ein großer deutscher Druck, aber auch slowakische Initiative und Mitwirkung insbesondere von seiten der Radikalen um Tuka standen, und schließlich die Deportationen "zur Ansiedlung in den Osten" riefen in der Mehrzahl der slowakischen Bevölkerung Empörung hervor, die auch dem deutschen Gesandten in Bratislava, Hans Elard Ludin, nicht entgangen war,[57] und ließen die bei manchen Katholiken ursprünglich vorhandenen antijüdischen Vorbehalte mehrheitlich zugunsten einer christlich und menschlich geprägten Solidarität umschlagen.[58]

Die katholische Kirche reagierte bereits im Winter 1938/1939 – also noch vor der Entstehung der Slowakischen Republik – mit der Ablehnung von allen staatlichen Maßnahmen, die auf rassistischer Grundlage fußten und den christlichen und naturrechtlichen Grundsätzen widersprachen. Bereits im Februar 1939 initiierte zum Beispiel die theologische Fakultät in Bratislava eine öffentliche Vorlesungsreihe, welche mit einem Vortrag ihres Dekans, des Philosophieprofessors Alexander Spesz, eröffnet wurde, der vom kirchlichen Standpunkt aus jede Rassenlehre verurteilte.[59]

---

56. Zu diesen Maßnahmen vgl. die Dokumentensammlung *Holokaust na Slovensku: Dokumenty*. I: *Obdobia autonómie 6.10.1938-14.3.1939*. Bd. II: *Prezident, váda, Snem SR a Štátna rada o židovskej otázke (1939-1945)* (Bratislava: Nadácia Milana Šimečku, Židovská náboženská obec Bratislava, 2001-2003).

57. Vgl. Telegramm Ludins nach Berlin vom 26. Juni 1942, in Raul Hilberg, *Die Vernichtung der europäischen Juden II* (Frankfurt am Main, 1990) 784; Gabriel Hoffmann und Ladislav Hoffmann, *Katolícka cirkev a tragédia slovenských židov v dokumentoch* (Partizánske: G-print, 1994) 82.

58. Róbert Letz, "Pomoc prenasledovaným Židom na Slovensku v rokoch 1939-1945," *Viera a život* 9 (1999) 178-219; vgl. weiter Bischof Kmeťko an den Präsidenten Tiso vom 15. November 1943, *Vatikán a Slovenská republika (1939-1945): Dokumenty*, 165; *Actes et Documents du Saint Siège relatifs à la seconde Guerre Mondiale*, ed. Pierre Blet u.a. (Città del Vaticano: Libreria Editrice Vaticana, 1969-1981) (ADSS), vol. 8, Burzio an den Staatssekretär 31. März 1942, 486-489.

59. BArch R70/113 Blatt 6-8 Agentenmeldung mit der Übersetzung eines Artikels aus dem *Slovák* (16. Februar 1939).

Deutlichere Reaktionen wurden nötig, nachdem die antijüdischen Maßnahmen nach der deutschen Intervention in Salzburg unter dem deutschen Druck radikalere Züge anzunehmen begannen. Der umgebauten Regierung wurde SS-Hauptsturmführer Dieter Wisliceny als Berater zugeteilt, dessen Aufgabe es war, die "Judenfrage" im nationalsozialistischen Sinne zu "lösen."[60] Den ersten Höhepunkt der antijüdischen Maßnahmen stellte die ohne Mitwirkung des Parlaments und des Präsidenten aufgrund einer auf ein Jahr befristeten Ermächtigung erlassene Regierungsverordnung Nr. 198 vom September 1941 ("Judenkodex"), die im wesentlichen die Nürnberger Gesetze kopierte mit der Ausnahme, daß sie unter den Paragraphen 255 und 256 die Gewährung von vollen oder teilweisen Ausnahmen von ihren Bestimmungen vorsah.[61] Die katholischen Bischöfe reagierten auf die Regierungsverordnung mit dem Memorandum vom 7. Oktober 1941, welches an den Ministerpräsidenten Tuka gerichtet war und gegen die Weltanschauung des "sogenannten Rassismus" protestierte.[62] In diesem Memorandum konzentrierten sich die Bischöfe zwar mit Rücksicht auf den Adressaten meist auf Forderungen, die vor allem getaufte Juden betrafen, um dadurch der Gefahr zu entgehen, wegen Inkompetenz bzw. Einmischung in politische Angelegenheiten zurückgewiesen zu werden, doch ihre grundsätzlichen Äußerungen, die jeden Rassismus verwarfen und die Gleichheit aller Menschen vor Gott hervorhoben, stellten eine klare Aussage dar, welche die Diskriminierung aller Juden verurteilte. Als Ende Februar – Anfang März 1942 sich in der Slowakei die Kunde verbreitete, daß die jüdische Bevölkerung gemäß einem Abkommen mit dem Deutschen Reich zur "Umsiedlung in den Osten" deportiert werden sollte, richteten die katholischen Bischöfe am 12. März 1942 ein scharfes Protestschreiben an die Regierung. Innenminister Mach soll daraufhin, der Meldung eines deutschen Agenten zufolge, erklärt haben, er sollte alle Bischöfe verhaften lassen und würde es auch tun, wenn der Präsident des Staates nicht katholischer Priester wäre.[63] Die Bischöfe ließen es bei amtlichen Protesten nicht bewenden, sondern wagten eine in Ostmitteleuropa einmalige kollektive öffentliche Erklärung, die auf

---

60. Katarína Hradská, *Prípad Dieter Wisliceny. (Nacistickí poradcovia a židovská otázka na Slovensku)* (Bratislava: Academic Electronic Press, 1999); Tönsmeyer, *Das Dritte Reich und die Slowakei 1939-1945*, 139-154.
61. *Slovenský zákonník* no. 198 (9. September 1941).
62. Brandmüller, *Holocaust in der Slowakei und katholische Kirche*, 29-30, und Anhang no. 3, 137-154 (Text des Memorandums im Original und in der deutschen Übersetzung).
63. BArch R 70/112 Agentenmeldung an den SD-LA Wien vom 25. März 1942.

dem Titelblatt der *Katolícke noviny* abgedruckt wurde und in der die Geltung naturrechtlicher und staatlich-gesetzlicher Normen auch für den Umgang mit Juden gefordert wurde.[64] In der Kontinuität dieser Aussagen, aber mit steigender Deutlichkeit und Radikalität wurde schließlich der Hirtenbrief der slowakischen katholischen Bischöfe vom 8. März 1943 verfaßt, der am Palmsonntag in allen slowakischen Kirchen gelesen wurde. Die Bischöfe reagierten damit auf die Gerüchte über eine mögliche Wiederaufnahme der Transporte und brandmarkten darin die antijüdischen Verfolgungsmaßnahmen mit aller Klarheit als schweres Unrecht.[65]

Die katholische Kirche – einzelne Bischöfe, Priester, Pfarrämter, Ordenshäuser usw. – leitete im Frühjahr 1942 breitgefächerte aktive Hilfsmaßnahmen ein, die darauf abgezielt waren, bedrohte Menschen zu verstecken oder ihnen zur Gewährung einer Ausnahme oder zum Verlassen der Slowakei zu verhelfen. Später, als die Situation in der Slowakei stabiler und günstiger wurde, als in den umliegenden Ländern, wurden wiederum bedrohte Menschen in die Slowakei geschmuggelt. Es kam auch zu Rückdatierungen von Taufscheinen bzw. Änderungen in den Matrikeln, da Personen, die vor dem 14. März 1939 in einer christlichen Kirche getauft worden waren, den Deportationen nicht unterlagen und dadurch auch ihre Verwandten schützten.[66]

Auch der Heilige Stuhl entwickelte eine fieberhafte Aktivität und intervenierte wiederholt über seinen Chargé d'affaires in Bratislava, Burzio, sowie über den slowakischen Gesandten Sidor bei der slowakischen Regierung, um die Einstellung der Deportationen zu erreichen.[67]

Die Tatsache, daß die Deportationen – entgegen den Bemühungen Tukas und seiner Protektoren – im Oktober 1942 beendet und erst nach der militärischen Besetzung der Slowakei im Herbst 1944, als die slowakische Regierung keinen Einfluß mehr auf den Lauf der Dinge ausüben

---

64. Katolíckej verejnosti! [An die katholische Öffentlichkeit!] *Katolícke noviny* no. 17 (26. April 1942) 1; deutsche Übersetzung: Brandmüller, *Holocaust in der Slowakei und katholische Kirche*, Anhang no. 4, 159-163.

65. BArch R 70/112 Meldung an den SD-LA Wien vom 2. April 1943; vgl. auch Brandmüller, *Holocaust in der Slowakei und katholische Kirche*, 42-43 und Anhang no. 5, 164-174.

66. Vgl. Letz, "Pomoc prenasledovaným Židom," 178-219; Hoffmann und Hoffmann, *Katolícka cirkev a tragédia slovenských židov v dokumentoch*, 40-57; *Katolícke noviny* 61, no. 38 (22. September 1946) 4; Brandmüller, *Holocaust in der Slowakei und katholische Kirche*, 48-54.

67. Zur Tätigkeit der Diplomatie des Heiligen Stuhls vgl. Brandmüller, *Holocaust in der Slowakei und katholische Kirche*, 55-105; Pierre Blet, *Pio XII e la Seconda Guerra mondiale negli Archivi Vaticani* (Milano, 1999) 223-236.

konnte, in der Regie der deutschen SS- und Polizeistellen wieder aufgenommen wurden, war nicht zuletzt das Ergebnis des sehr entschiedenen Widerstandes der katholischen Kirche: Der vatikanischen Diplomatie des slowakischen Episkopats und Klerus sowie der einfachen Gläubigen, der Aktivität vieler katholischer Abgeordneter und auch der Tatsache, daß der Präsident und die Ministerien von ihrem im Gesetz Nr. 68/1942 unter §255 verankerten Recht, Ausnahmen zu erteilen, zahlreich Gebrauch machten.[68]

V. Die Kirche und der Krieg

Obgleich die Slowakei mitten im kriegszerrissenen Europa lag, blieb sie von den direkten Kriegsgeschehnissen lange Zeit verschont. Die Teilnahme am Polenfeldzug, zu der sie aufgrund des Schutzvertrages mit dem Deutschen Reich verpflichtet war, blieb symbolisch, das an die Ostfront entsandte Kontingent relativ klein und das Staatsgebiet kannte – von dem kurzen, aber schmerzlichen ungarischen Überfall ohne Kriegserklärung im März 1939 abgesehen – bis Sommer 1944 keine direkten Kriegshandlungen. Doch wie begrenzt die Miteinbeziehung in den Krieg auch war, in der Bevölkerung war sie äußerst unpopulär, und die Motivation der Soldaten, im fremden Interesse auf die slawische Bevölkerung im Osten, der gegenüber sie keine historische Feindschaft verspürten, zu schießen, gering. Tatsache ist, daß die slowakischen Soldaten die einzigen im Achsenlager waren, mit denen sich die weißrussischen und ukrainischen Bauern zu verständigen vermochten und mit denen sie eine ähnliche Mentalität verband. So entwickelten sich bald vielfache menschliche Kontakte, bei denen häufig eine Halskette mit dem Kreuz oder ein Rosenkranz Türen und Herzen öffneten. Für die jungen slowakischen Männer, die häufig zum ersten Mal fern der Heimat waren, bedeutete diese Lebenserfahrung auch die erste negative Begegnung mit dem kommunistischen System. "Ich weiß nicht, was das für ein scheußliches Regime ist, dieser Bolschewismus," schrieb ein junger Soldat nach Hause, "daß hier so endlose Weizenfelder sind und die Menschen dennoch so schrecklich hausen! Weizenfelder weit und breit, und die Menschen haben nichts!"[69]

---

68. Vgl. dazu Ladislav Lipscher, *Die Juden im Slowakischen Staat 1939-1945* (München/Wien: Oldenbourg Verlag, 1980) 791; Letz, *Pomoc prenasledovaným Židom na Slovensku*, 183, 197-198.

69. Martin Lacko, "Slováci vo vojne proti ZSSR," *Proglas* 13, no. 1 (2002) 28.

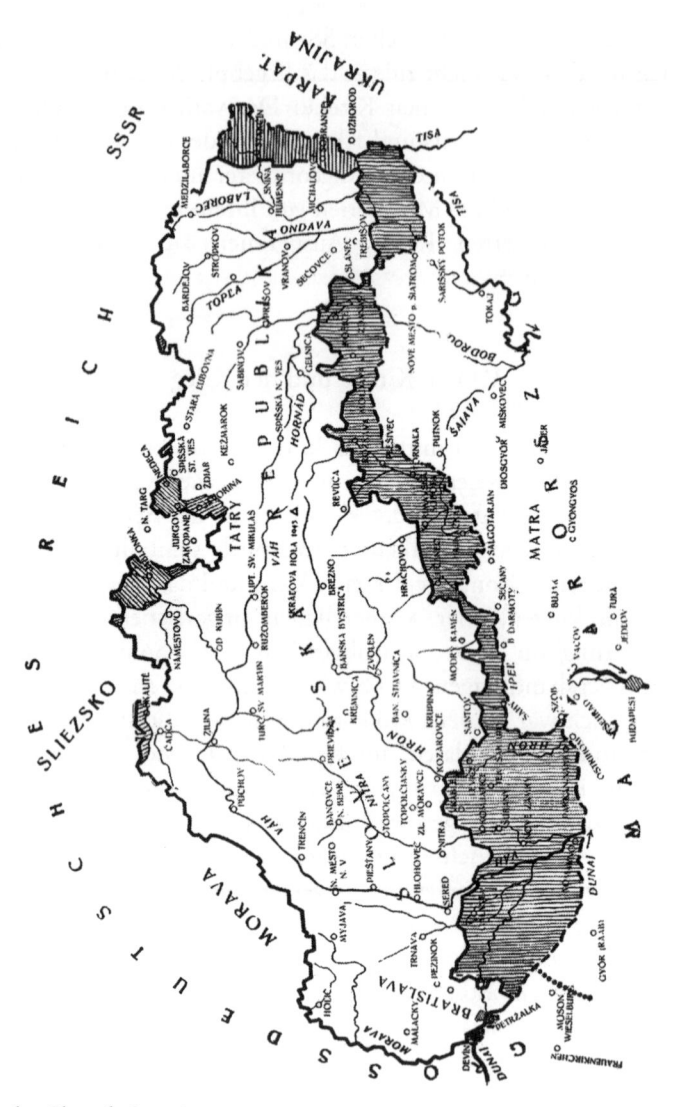

Karte der Slowakei 1918-1939

Rechtsschraffiert, linksschraffiert:	1920, 1924 und 1938 an Polen abgetreten und 1939 wiedererlangt
Vertikal schraffiert:	Nach dem Ersten Wiener Schiedsspruch vom 2. November 1938 an Ungarn abgetreten
Horizontal schraffiert:	Im Zuge des "Kleinen Krieges" im März 1939 von Ungarn okkupiert
Grau markiert:	Im Oktober 1938 vom Deutschen Reich besetzt

Im Jahre 1945 wurde der territoriale Status quo ante vom September 1938 wiederhergestellt.

Kurz nach der Selbständigkeitserklärung der Slowakei, also noch mehrere Monate vor dem Ausbruch des Krieges, ersuchte der Verteidigungsminister Ferdinand Čatloš die katholischen Bischöfe der Slowakei, eine Militärseelsorge zu konstituieren. Nach innerkirchlichen Verhandlungen, die über den Berliner Nuntius Cesare Orsenigo geführt wurden, wurde im Juni 1940 vom Heiligen Stuhl der Weihbischof Michal Buzalka, der einzige Bischof, der in der Hauptstadt residierte, zum Feldvikar der slowakischen Armee ernannt. Buzalka, der daneben auch der Katholischen Aktion vorstand und Rektor des Priesterseminars war, übte dieses Amt außerhalb des aktiven Militärdienstes aus, aus dem er altersbedingt bereits in der Zwischenkriegszeit entlassen worden war.[70] Die konkrete Ausübung der Militärseelsorge oblag den aktiven Feldkuraten, deren Tätigkeit von der Abteilung für den geistlichen Dienst des Verteidigungsministeriums geleitet wurde. Alle Soldaten hatten einen Eid zu leisten, der sich auf christliche und nationale Ideale des Volkes berief und eine betont religiöse Gestalt aufwies.[71] In diesem Geiste wurden auch Buzalkas Hirtenbriefe an katholische Soldaten verfaßt. So hieß es im Hirtenbrief vom November 1940, daß jeder Angehöriger des Militärs "nur dann ein guter, treuer Soldat und ein Verteidiger unserer Heimat sein [wird], wenn er sich dessen bewußt bleibt, daß er nie von seinem Gotte, von seinem Glauben entfernt werden darf. Die Uniform und die Waffe entbindet euch nicht von den zehn Geboten Gottes."[72] Bischof Buzalka initiierte auch die Herausgabe eines Gebetbuches, das aus den Mitteln des Verteidigungs- und des Außenressorts finanziert und an alle katholischen Soldaten verteilt wurde.[73]

Im Laufe des Jahres 1943 wurde es auch den slowakischen Katholiken klar, daß ihre Ausnahmesituation, mitten im wütenden Weltkrieg relativ unbehelligt zu leben, bald ein Ende finden werde. Die düstere Perspektive der herannahenden Front schien um so beklemmender, da sie mit der Aussicht nicht nur auf das Blutvergießen, sondern auch die nachfolgende Eingliederung in die sowjetische Machtzone, Etablierung des

---

70. František Duraj, "Michal Buzalka a ozbrojené zložky," *Biskup Michal Buzalka: Zborník príspevkov z vedeckej konferencie pri príležitosti 40. výročia úmrtia*, ed. Róbert Letz und Ivan A. Petranský, Libri Historiae Slovaciae. Scriptores III (Bratislava: Lúč, 2002) 124-127.
71. So begann er mit den Worten "Wir schwören auf den allmächtigen Gott" und endete mit: "So helfe uns Gott"; vgl. Albín Krasna, "Duchovná správa," *Kalendár Slovenského vojska* (Bratislava: Ministerstvo národnej obrany, 1942) 161.
72. BArch R 70/112, Deutsche Pressebriefe aus der Slowakei vom 7. November 1940.
73. *Verný priateľ – Modlitebná a poučná knižka pre slovenských katolíckych vojakov* (Bratislava: Ministerstvo národnej obrany, 1941).

kommunistischen Regimes und darüber hinaus den Verlust der Eigenstaatlichkeit verbunden war, zumal die Bemühungen verschiedener katholischer politischer Gruppierungen, auf dem Umweg über eine ostmitteleuropäische Föderation der kleinen katholischen Völker dieser doppelten Gefahr auszuweichen, sowie die ähnlich wie in Ungarn stark verbreitete Hoffnung auf einen angelsächsisch-deutschen Ausgleichsfrieden mit antisowjetischer Spitze, sich als völlig aussichtslos erwiesen.[74] Die allgemeine Unsicherheit und Zukunftsängste bewirkten, daß noch mehr als zuvor verschiedene Gebete für den Frieden Verbreitung fanden und alle Friedensappelle des Papstes mit großer Aufmerksamkeit verfolgt wurden. Von 6. bis 8. Dezember 1943 wurden in allen Pfarrkirchen der Slowakei Gottesdienste für den Frieden abgehalten und am letzten Tag dieses Triduums ein besonderer Friedenshirtenbrief der katholischen Bischöfe verlesen.[75]

Die Deutschen versuchten in dieser Situation, den bis dahin von ihnen als "klerikal" und "antideutsch" kritisierten slowakischen Katholizismus auf der Basis des Antikommunismus als Verbündeten zu gewinnen, allerdings mit ziemlichem Mißerfolg: Der lange Weihnachtshirtenbrief 1943, der Erklärung der Ursachen des Krieges gewidmet, sprach kein Wort von einem antikommunistischen Kreuzzug, sondern sah im Einklang mit den päpstlichen Äußerungen die Wurzeln des Krieges in der Sündhaftigkeit der Menschen und in unchristlichen Weltanschauungen. Seine kritischen Hinweise auf "Millionenorganisationen der Gottlosen," Rückkehr zum "lächerlichen Heidentum" und Verweigerung von Lebensmöglichkeiten für die Kirche, aber auch den zunehmenden Hedonismus und praktischen Unglauben trafen, ohne sie beim Namen zu nennen, genauso den Nationalsozialismus wie den Kommunismus oder den Liberalismus.[76]

Ein Jahr später, als nach den bewegten Ereignissen des Aufstandes die Slowakei bereits zum Kriegsschauplatz geworden war, beschränkten sich die Bischöfe, trotz ausdrücklicher Aufforderung der deutschen Militärstellen, explizit den Bolschewismus zu verurteilen, wiederum darauf, den Krieg aus katholisch-theologischer Perspektive zu deuten und die

---

74. Vgl. z.B. BArch R 70/112 Agentenbericht Nr. 2197 an den SD-LA Wien vom 6. September 1943; zu den ungarischen Ausgleichsbemühungen mit den Westmächten vgl. Lapo Lombardi, *La Santa Sede e i cattolici dell'Europa orientale agli arbori della guerra fredda* (Roma/Budapest: Editrice Pontificia Università Gregoriana/METEM, 1997) 10-12.

75. BArch R 70/112, Bericht Nr. 2197 an den SD-LA Wien vom 6. September 1943 und ebenda, Bericht SA 181 II Wa/Fk. vom 6. Dezember 1943.

76. BArch R 70/112 Agentenmeldung SA 181 II W/Fk vom 6. Dezember 1943 mit der deutschen Übersetzung des Hirtenbriefes.

Bevölkerung aufzurufen, für alle seine Opfer zu beten und der Kirche treu zu bleiben.[77] Weiter Teile vor allem der einfachen katholischen Gläubigen begann sich in der aussichtslos erscheinenden Situation eine abwartende, beinahe lethargische Stimmung zu bemächtigen, die zu einem pragmatischen Rückzug in das Familienleben führte.

Obgleich in der slowakischen katholischen Intelligenz seit den zwanziger Jahren ein ausgeprägter Antikommunismus gepflegt wurde, zum Teil auch im bewußten Gegensatz zur dominanten linksliberal-sozialistischen Staatsideologie der Tschechoslowakei, unterschied sich dieser von den verwandten weltanschaulichen Positionen im polnischen oder ungarischen Katholizismus durch die völlige Absenz jeglicher antirussischer Ressentiments und latente, nicht selten emotionalisierte slawische Sympathien, die sich zum Teil aus dem alten, naiv idealistischen Panslawismus der Vätergeneration, zum Teil dem katholischen Unionsgedanken nährten, waren doch gerade slowakische Jesuiten des östlichen Ritus ein tragendes Element des im Umkreis der Ostkirchenkongregation und des Kollegium *Russicum* gepflegten damaligen römischen Unionismus.[78] Ein äußeres Zeichen dieser Einstellung waren häufige "Gebete für Rußland," die die Missionszeitschrift *Hlasy* veröffentlichte,[79] oder seelsorgliche Bemühungen der slowakischen Feldkuraten unter der weißrussischen und ukrainischen Bevölkerung, die auch zahlreich an Feldmessen der slowakischen Armeeeinheiten teilnahm.

Die totalitären Ideologien und Diktaturen, aber auch der kämpferische Laizismus wurden im slowakischen Katholizismus häufig aus der Perspektive der Herrschaft des satanischen Elementes gedeutet.[80] In Teilen der slowakischen Geistlichkeit tauchte bereits Anfang der vierziger Jahre die Meinung auf, der jüngste Tag sei nicht mehr ferne, da der

---

77. Ein deutscher SD-Agent bezeichnete den Hirtenbrief als "Aufruf zum Defaitismus" und "alles in allem ein typisches Beispiel dafür, auf der einen Seite der deutschen Besatzungsmacht ihren Wunsch zu erfüllen, sich aber auf keinen Fall gegen die Feinde des Reiches und der jetzigen Slowakei festzulegen." BArch R 70/112 III Tgb. Nr. 1487/44 vom 23. Dezember 1944.

78. Zur hervorragenden Gestalt des ersten Rektors des Russicum, des slowakischen Jesuiten P. Vendelín Javorka S.J., vgl. Constantin Simon, S.J., *Russicum: Pioneers and Witnesses of the Struggle for Christian Unity in Eastern Europe*. I (Roma: Opere Religiose Russe, 2001) 43-135.

79. Vgl. die Gedichte "Gebet für Rußland" und "Gebet für verirrte Brüder," *Hlasy* (Oktober 1940); vgl. auch BArch R 70/112 Agentenmeldung vom 4. Oktober 1940.

80. Allgemein zu den religionsphilosophischen Antichrist-Deutungen im 20. Jahrhundert vgl. Vladimir Kantor, "Der Antichrist als Problem des totalitären Zivilisationsbruchs (am Beispiel der russischen Kultur des 20. Jahrhunderts)," *Das Christentum und die totalitären Herausforderungen des 20. Jahrhunderts: Rußland, Deutschland, Italien und Polen im Vergleich*, ed. Leonid Luks (Köln/Weimar/Wien: Böhlau Verlag, 2002) 13-30.

Antichrist – gemeint war Adolf Hitler – schon da sei.[81] Der Chef des slowakischen Katholischen Pressebüros Belo Hreblay apostrophierte wiederum das bolschewistische System als die "Satansgeißel."[82]

VI. Kulturelle und innerkirchliche Entwicklungen

Obgleich die Jahre 1939-1945 eine kurze Zeitspanne darstellten, hinterließen sie im slowakischen Katholizismus sehr tiefe geistige und intellektuelle Spuren. Die katholische Kultur und Bildung erlebten vorher ungekannte Entfaltungsmöglichkeiten, es wurden katholische Bildungsinstitutionen, Schulen, Akademien, Internate (am bekanntesten das *Svoradov*, eine Brutstätte der katholischen Intelligenz) und Vereine und eine Reihe neuer katholischer Zeitschriften gegründet, die Generation der katholischen Schriftsteller, die später als Katholische Moderne in die Literaturgeschichte eingehen sollte,[83] erreichte den Höhepunkt ihres Schaffens, es entstanden mehrere intellektuelle Zentren, unter welchen wohl jenes um den praktischen thomistischen Philosophen Ferko Skyčák und den Kulturphilosophen Ladislav Hanus in Spišská Kapitula am bekanntesten war.

Kulturelle und geistige Entfaltungsmöglichkeiten des Katholizismus und seine verstärkte Präsenz im öffentlichen Leben waren freilich nur eine Seite der Entwicklung der slowakischen Gesellschaft. Die andere, für manche unerwartete Seite war ein weiterer Laisierungsschub im öffentlichen Leben. Er wurde beschleunigt durch den Ausbau der staatlichen Institutionen und des Beamtenapparates des sich konstituierenden Staates sowie durch die Entfaltung des Bildungssektors, die bereits in der Zwischenkriegszeit initiiert worden war, deren Ergebnisse sich jedoch infolge der hohen Akademikerarbeitslosigkeit zuerst nicht ganz hatten auswirken können und die nach 1939 in Gestalt neuer Gründungsinitiativen und erweiterter Beschäftigungsmöglichkeiten zum Vorschein kam. Diese Laisierung wurde von der Kirche einerseits als natürlich und positiv quittiert, andererseits aber mit einem gewissen Mißtrauen beobachtet, zumal sie auch säkularisierende Wirkungen zeitigte. Der katholische Episkopat und Klerus waren sich, wenngleich mit unterschiedlicher Intensität und Klarheit, durchaus

---

81. BArch R 70/112 Stellung der Geistlichkeit in der gegenwärtigen Situation vom 25. Oktober 1940.
82. BArch R 79/45, 458/1 VA 11/41 Agentenbericht an das RSHA vom 8. Juli 1941.
83. Július Pašteka, *Tvár a tvorba slovenskej katolíckej moderny* (Bratislava: Lúč, 2002).

auch der Tatsache bewußt, daß das immer wieder angerufene Bild der tief religiösen slowakischen katholischen Bevölkerung nicht ganz der Realität entsprach, die Säkularisierung auch in die slowakische Gesellschaft Eingang gefunden hatte und die nach außen hin demonstrierte Volksreligiosität der Bevölkerung häufig mehr ein Ausdruck von Tradition, Gewohnheit und oberflächlicher Äußerlichkeit als der inneren Stärke und Überzeugung war, und sie befürchteten, daß sie nur solange unversehrt weiterbestehen könnte, solange die äußeren Lebensumstände erhalten blieben. Sie führten diese Phänomene primär auf die Einwirkungen der kirchenfeindlichen Ideologien, insbesondere des seit dem 19. Jahrhundert voll einsetzendem Liberalismus, und die geistigen Spuren der laizistischen tschechoslowakischen Schule zurück, doch rückten zunehmend auch innere Ursachen und Versäumnisse, die den Glauben geschwächt und die äußeren Einflußnahmen begünstigt hätten, ins Bewußtsein. Sie wurden in der unzulänglichen religiösen Bildung gesucht, die dem allgemeinen Bildungsstand der Menschen nicht angemessen sei, und von einigen kritischeren Geistern auch in Unterlassungen der katholischen Seelsorge, die entweder zu passiv, oder allzu sehr auf institutionalisierte Erfassung in Vereinen und Organisationen konzentriert gewesen sei, die Übermittlung der Inhalte, Formierung der praktischen moralischen Haltungen und Vertiefung der Spiritualität jedoch vernachlässigt habe.[84] Ferko Skyčák, der große Geist der slowakischen thomistischen Philosophie der dreißiger und vierziger Jahre und ein scharfer Analyst des Zeitgeistes, kritisierte auch einen allzu großen katholischen Traditionalismus, der nicht die positiven Traditionen weiter entfalte, sondern den überlebten Formen und Wegen nachhänge.[85]

Die Kirche reagierte auf diese Entwicklungen und Einsichten unterschiedlich: Mit der Intensivierung traditioneller Methoden der Mission und der Pastoration, aber auch mit dem Wagnis neuer spiritueller, seelsorglicher und Bildungswege und der Mobilisierung der

---

84. Überlegungen dieser Art gab es bereits in den dreißiger Jahren, vgl. Karol Körper, "Duchovný vývoj inteligenta-katolíka," *Kultúra* 7 (1935) 56-61; ders., "Úlohy katolíckych Slovákov," *Kultúra* 8 (1936) 24-33; vgl. auch Ferko Skyčák, "Laicizácia Slovenska," *Duchovný pastier* 23, no. 6 (1942) 483-486; ders., "O zbožnosť mestských rodín," *Kultúra* 14, nos. 8-9 (1942) 337-340; Bischof Kmeťko an den Präsidenten Tiso 15. November 1943, *Vatikán a Slovenská republika (1939-1945). Dokumenty*, 166-168; Ladislav Hanus, *Spomienky na Ferka Skyčáka* (Cambridge, Ont.: Slovenskí jezuiti, 1982) 47-48.

85. Ferko Skyčák, Výchova v spišskom kňazskom seminári," *Spišský kňazský seminár v minulosti a prítomnosti* (Spišská Kapitula, 1943) 18-25.

katholischen Laien. Obgleich die Masse der Gläubigen nach wie vor im traditionellen Volkskatholizismus verankert blieb, begann sich insbesondere in gebildeten Schichten auch eine neue Auffassung von Religiosität und Pastoration die Bahn zu brechen. Sie sah ihre Aufgabe darin, die überlieferte "ländliche Seelsorge," die auf der Existenz von ohnehin tief gläubigen und ergebenen Schäfchen baute, ausgetretene Pfade verteidigte und die der Kirche sich entfremdenden Schichten kaum zu erreichen vermochte, zu überwinden und mit der Bildung von Berufs- und Familiengruppen, Bildungskursen, der Förderung intellektuell anspruchsvoller Zeitschriften und Akademien, häufigen geistigen Übungen für Laien, neuartigen Pastoralmethoden im urbanen Raum usw. neue Wege der Seelsorge zu beschreiten. Sie begann damit, die Laien in mehr Selbständigkeit zu entlassen, konfrontierte sie aber zugleich mit der Notwendigkeit, ihren Katholizismus nicht passiv und oberflächlich, sondern im Geiste eines "neuen Ideals des Laien mit apostolischem Geist und mit apostolischer Initiative" zu leben,[86] ihre katholischen Prinzipien im öffentlichen Leben umzusetzen und zu gesellschaftlichen Erscheinungen, die mit diesen nicht im Einklang waren, offen Stellung zu beziehen. Im intellektuellen katholischen Ambiente begann sich auch die Erkenntnis durchzusetzen, daß den modernen kulturellen und ideologischen Zeitströmungen, von welcher Seite sie auch kamen, durch autoritäre Defensive, wie sie von Teilen des traditionell formierten Klerus gepflegt wurde, bzw. den Rückzug in ein katholisches Ghetto, wie geräumig dieses anfangs auch sein konnte, nicht mehr beizukommen war, wollte die Kirche langfristig nicht auf die Mitgestaltung der Welt verzichten.

Obgleich diese Prinzipien häufig nur ein Ideal blieben, im relativ überschaubaren slowakischen Ambiente neue Wege und Ansichten sich nicht ohne Hindernisse durchsetzten und lange Zeit durch persönliche Gruppenbindungen geprägt waren und die Zeit, die zur Verfügung stand, kurz war, konnte sich schrittweise eine neue, junge katholische Elite formieren, die in den späteren massiven Verfolgungen unter dem in der Tschechoslowakei besonders radikal antikirchlichen kommunistischen Regime den slowakischen Katholizismus und die slowakische katholische Kultur im nächsten halben Jahrhundert tragen sollte.

---

86. Ferko Skyčák, "Laicizácia Slovenska," *Duchovný pastier* 23, no. 6 (1942) 483-486; vgl. dazu auch Ferko Skyčák, "O zbožnosť mestských rodín," *Kultúra* 14, nos. 8-9 (1942) 337-340; Ferko Skyčák, "O katolícku líniu," *Kultúra* 13, nos. 10-11 (1941) 434-436.

Auswahlbibliographie

Actes et Documents du Saint Siège relatifs à la Seconde Guerre Mondiale, ed. Pierre Blet, Robert A. Graham, Angelo Martini und Burkhart Schneider. 11 Vols. (Città del Vaticano: Libreria Editrice Vaticana, 1970-1981).

Walter Brandmüller, *Holocaust in der Slowakei und katholische Kirche* (Neustadt an der Aisch: Verlag Ph.C.W. Schmidt, 2003).

John S. Conway, "The Churches, the Slovak State and the Jews 1939-1945," *Slavonic and Eastern Europe Review* 52 (1974) 85-112.

Milan S. Ďurica, "Beziehungen zwischen der Slowakischen Republik und dem Heiligen Stuhl," *Slowakei* 11/12 (1973/1974) 58-89.

Milan S. Ďurica, *Katolícka cirkev na Slovensku 1938-1945 v hodnotení nemeckých diplomatov a tajných agentov* (Trnava: Spolok sv. Vojtecha, 2001).

Jörg Hoensch, "Grundzüge und Phasen der deutschen Slowakei-Politik im Zweiten Weltkrieg," *Studia Slovaca: Studien zur Geschichte der Slowaken und der Slowakei*, ed. Hans Lemberg, Michaela Marek, Horst Förster, Franz Machilek und Ferdinand Seibt (München: Oldenbourg, 2000) 249-280.

Holokaust na Slovensku: Dokumenty. I: *Obdobia autonómie 6.10.1938-14.3.1939.* Bd. II: *Prezident, váda, Snem SR a Štátna rada o židovskej otázke (1939-1945)* (Bratislava: Nadácia Milana Šimečku, Židovská náboženská obec Bratislava, 2001-2003).

Yeshayahu Jelinek, *The Parish Republic: Hlinka's Slovak People's Party 1939-1945* (Boulder: East European Quarterly, 1976).

Róbert Letz, "Pomoc prenasledovaným Židom na Slovensku v rokoch 1939-1945," *Viera a život* 9 (1999) 178-219.

Jozef M. Rydlo, "La Santa Sede e la prima Repubblica Slovaca negli anni 1939-1945," *Relazioni internazionali giuridiche bilaterali tra la Santa Sede e gli Stati: esperienze e prospettive*, ed. Marek Šmíd und Cyril Vasil' (Città del Vaticano: Libreria Editrice Vaticana, 2003) 285-307.

Karin Schmid, *Die Slowakische Republik 1939-1945: Eine staats- und völkerrechtliche Betrachtung.* Vol. 1 (Berlin: Berlin Verlag, 1982).

Karol Sidor, *Šesť rokov pri Vatikáne* (Scranton, PA: Obrana Press Inc., 1947).

Štefan Šmálik, "L'Église catholique en Slovaquie dans le années 1939-1944," *Les Églises chrétiennes dans l'Europe dominée par le IIIe Reich: Miscellanea Historiae Ecclesiasticae VI* (Warschau/Louvain-La-Neuve/Wroclaw/Bruxelles: Polska akademia nauk/Collège Érasme/Ossolineum/Éditions Nauwelaerts, 1984) 259-270.

Tatjana Tönsmeyer, *Das Dritte Reich und die Slowakei 1939-1945: Politischer Alltag zwischen Kooperation und Eigensinn* (Paderborn u.a.: Schöningh, 2003).

Summary
The Catholic Church in Slovakia 1939-1945

The Slovak Republic, proclaimed in March 1939, came into being in a period when the international political situation was difficult and in the shadow of the powerful presence of the German *Reich* in Central Europe. Nevertheless, the predominant part of the Slovak population saw it as the realization of national self-determination and greeted the independence as a protection against the real threat of being divided between Hungary and Poland or Germany. In spite of the German predominance that obliged the Slovak government to sign the Treaty of Protection, according to which Slovakia had to align her foreign and defense policies with those of Germany, in domestic politics the State still retained an appreciable amount of self-expression.

The new power elite originated from the traditional Catholic Slovak People's Party and was familiar with the papal social encyclical *Quadragesimo anno* and the ideas of Christian Socialism. It attempted to fill domestic politics with ideas which were in line with Christian and national traditions, i.e. to create a Christian Corporate State which would be able to overcome social and class conflicts, group particularism attributed to liberal parliamentarism, as well as political systems based on collectivistic and atheistic ideologies like Marxism or National Socialism. However, the moderate Catholic politicians were challenged not only by the strong political and ideological pressure of German power, but also by the domestic Slovak opposition which launched an ideological offensive designed to establish a variant of "Slovak National Socialism." In the course of the decisive struggle between the two factions, in the winter of 1940/1941, the moderates, supported by the Catholic Church, repeatedly tried to demonstrate their dedication to "our traditional Christian heritage" and to reject any "imitation of foreign models." To weaken their opponents they argued that their political programme had always been "national," and, in the sense of the papal encyclicals, "social." The confrontation ended with the victory of the moderate Catholic wing, though at the cost of strengthening the authoritarian style of political life and the reduction of the possibilities to reject some inevitable collaboration with the German *Reich*.

The State which, in the Constitution and in programmatic political statements had declared its support of Christian principles, granted the Catholic Church spaces of freedom, which openly contrasted with her permanent defensive position in the former secular Czechoslovakia, and which secured her possibilities of cultural and educational development not known before. This fact, as well as the general support for the national statehood, linked the Church to the State. The German *Gleichschaltungsdruck* and its attempts, with the aid of Slovak helpers, to infiltrate Slovakia with an anti-Catholic ideology, simultaneously motivated the Church to distance itself from some contentious measures of the State. The most evident example of such a stand was the reaction of the Church to the State's anti-Jewish legislation, which was in blatant contradiction to Christian principles and the principles of Natural Law. The Catholic bishops reacted with several official protest letters and two public declarations, in which they rejected the "so-called racist world view," protested against the prepared deportations and denounced the anti-Jewish measures as a grave injustice.

The anti-Jewish measures of the Slovak government also aggravated the relations between Slovakia and the Holy See. Mutual diplomatic relations were established in the spring of 1939 and lasted until May 1945. Slovakia tried to consolidate and further these relations through the conclusion of a Concordat which would establish an independent Slovak Church province and in this way would also contribute to the strengthening of the State sovereignty. The Holy See rejected such a far-reaching change as being unsuitable in a wartime situation. As compensation for this unaccomplished contractual solution Pius XII elevated the bishop of Nitra to the rank of Archbishop *ad personam*.

In the course of 1943 it became clear to the Slovak Catholics that their exceptional situation, which allowed them to live in the middle of war-torn Europe relatively peacefully and untouched by the clashes and their consequences, would soon come to an end. The dark perspective of the approaching frontline seemed all the more tormenting, as it implied not only the prospect of incorporation into the Soviet zone of influence and of the establishment of a Communist regime, but also of the loss of their own State. All the more so, since the failure of the efforts of some Catholic political groups which sought to avoid this double danger through the establishment of a federation of small nations in Central Eastern Europe. Likewise their hopes of a separate peace between the Anglo-Saxon powers and Germany with the anti-Soviet spearhead that was still widespread in Slovakia as well as in Hungary, turned out to be completely unfounded.

On the basis of the common feeling of anticommunism, the Germans tried to win over the Slovak Catholics – who had until then been attacked as "clerical" and "anti-German" – as an ally, however, without any great success. Despite the existence of strong anticommunist feeling among the Slovak Catholics, the long Christmas pastoral letter of their bishops of December 1943, intended to explain the causes of the war, did not say anything about the war as being "an anticommunist crusade," but – following the line of papal pronouncements – it saw the roots of the conflict in the sinfulness of mankind and in the anti-Christian *Weltanschauung*. Its critical allusions were to the "army of millions of godless," to the "return to the paganism," and also to the increasing hedonism and practical atheism, aimed at National Socialism as well as Communism and, in a sense, at Liberalism.

The need to redefine the position of the Catholic Church towards the State and the society was also a consequence of the changed political conditions after 1938/1939. The Church was no longer faced with a secular foreign national State, but with a State that explicitly defined itself as national and Christian, the construction of which, however, speeded up the secularisation (*Laisierung*) of public life. At the same time it became evident that the Slovak society, in a somehow idealized way until then perceived as homogeneously Christian, had been exposed to the modern processes of secularisation, too. In the new situation the Church had the task to define the extent to which she could and should influence the public sphere, and to mark out the space in which the autonomy of the temporary must and could be accepted, in order to preserve the autonomy of the Church towards the State and to avoid the danger of a superficial "Catholic boom" as well as being dragged into political responsibility for acts which were not in line with the principles of the Divine and the Natural law. This involved the question of political participation of priests and the question of reordering the relation between the clergy and the laymen on the one side, and between the Church and the society on the other.

The retreat of the clergy from its traditional role as a substitute for the missing social elite and the leading element of the national movement, the acceptance of the "sound laicity of the State" and the discharge of the laity into more personal responsibility, were the long-term processes, which were initiated in the Slovak society in the twenties and were accelerated, but not yet concluded, by the State sovereignty. Nevertheless, in precisely this period new, autonomously acting Catholic lay elites were formed who, under the particularly radical anti-Church Communist regime in Czechoslovakia, were later able to carry the ideas of Slovak Catholicism for the next half of the century.

The Catholic Church in Lithuania under Two Occupying Regimes

Vilma Narkutė[1]

During World War II Lithuania underwent two successive forms of governance: from June 1940 until June 1941 it was under Soviet rule and from July 1941 until the Autumn of 1944 it was under Nazi rule. This study will start from the pre-war period, which will allow us to get acquainted with the situation of the Lithuanian Church and religion during the period of Lithuanian independence – the period from February 16, 1918, or the day when the Declaration of Lithuanian Independence was issued[2] – until June 15, 1940, when Lithuania was occupied by the Soviet Union for the first time. We will then examine the situation in Lithuania during the first Soviet occupation and during the Nazi occupation.

I. Church and Religion during the Period of Lithuanian Independence (1918-1940)

The Lithuanian Church province was founded in the first half of the 20th century. From its Christianisation in 1387 until 1926 the Catholic Church in Lithuania had no unifying centre. All three dioceses depended on the greater units, the centres of which belonged to the church provinces of the neighbouring countries and were located outside of Lithuania. The dioceses of Vilnius and Samogitia were subject to the archdiocese of Mohilev (in present Belarus), and the dio-

---

1. This article is mainly based on the research leading to the doctoral dissertation of Vilma Narkutė, *Catholicism versus Communism: The Confrontation between the Roman Catholic Church and the Soviet Regime in the Case of Lithuania (1940-1978)* (unpublished doctoral dissertation, Faculty of Theology, K.U.Leuven, Leuven, 2005).

2. During the First World War, in 1914-1915, Lithuania was the battleground of the Russian and German armies, and later it was occupied by the German army. See Pranas Dauknys, *The Resistance of the Catholic Church in Lithuania against Religious Persecution*, Dissertatio ad Lauream in Facultate S. Theologiae apud Pontificiam Universitatem S. Thomae de Urbe (Rome, 1984) 19.

cese of Seinai was part of the archdiocese of Warsaw (in Poland). The situation changed on April 4, 1926, when Pope Pius XI with his bull *Lituanorum gente* united all Catholic churches in the territory of Lithuania into a separate church province, putting it in charge of Archbishop-metropolitan, Juozapas Skvireckas[3] and making it dependent only on the Vatican.[4] Consequently, a new administrative division of Lithuania was accomplished: the country was divided into the Archdiocese of Kaunas and four dioceses – Telšiai, Panevėžys, Vilkaviškis and Kaišiadorys.[5] The foundation of the separate Church province made the Lithuanian Catholic Church independent of foreign supervision, provided the Lithuanian Church hierarchy with greater freedom in the selection of the bishops and all pastors and allowed the exchange of diplomatic representatives with the Vatican.[6] Lithuania's contact with the centre of Christianity had started earlier, in the 13th Century, when Grand Duke Mindaugas was Christianised and crowned by Pope Innocent IV (1243-1254). Although not yet having official relations with Lithuania, from the end of 1922 the Vatican recognised the independent Lithuanian state *de jure* and *de facto*. An official step in the relations between the Vatican and Lithuania took place with the signing of the concordat, on September 27, 1927.[7] The concordat also defined relations between the Lithuanian Catholic Church and the Lithuanian state.[8]

3. J. Skvireckas: b. September 18, 1873 (Pašilučiai, dioc. of Samogitia), ord. June 24, 1899, cons. July 13, 1919 (dioc. of Kaunas). See *Annuario Pontificio* (Rome, 1948) 217.

4. Text of the bull *Lituanorum gente: Constitutio Apostolica erectio provinciae ecclesiasticae et nova dioecesium ordinatio in republica Lituana*, in *Acta Apostolicae Sedis* (*AAS*) 18, no. 4 (April 6, 1926) 121-123.

5. For the dioceses in the Baltic states before the first Soviet occupation see Map 1. From the beginning of the 1920s until 1939 the capital Vilnius belonged to Poland.

6. Juozas Vaišnora, "Nepriklausomybės ir okupaciniais laikais [The Time of Independence and Occupation]," *Lietuvių enciklopedija* [The Lithuanian Encyclopedia] 15 (Vilnius, 1990) 146-148.

7. Text of the concordat *Concordat entre le Saint-Siège et le Gouvernement de Lithuanie*, in *AAS* 19, no. 13 (December 10, 1927) 425-433.

8. According to the concordat, the Vatican sent an internuntio to Lithuania, while the Lithuanian government sent its representative to the Vatican (Art. 3); military forces were to have their own chaplains (Art. 7); the Church was given the right to choose theology professors who were to be paid by the state (Art. 13); clergy was authorised to keep the registers of birth, marriage and death and to give copies to the state (Art. 14); the state gave full freedom to religious organisations, especially to Catholic Action (Art. 25), etc. See *Concordat*, 426-432.

THE CATHOLIC CHURCH IN LITHUANIA 175

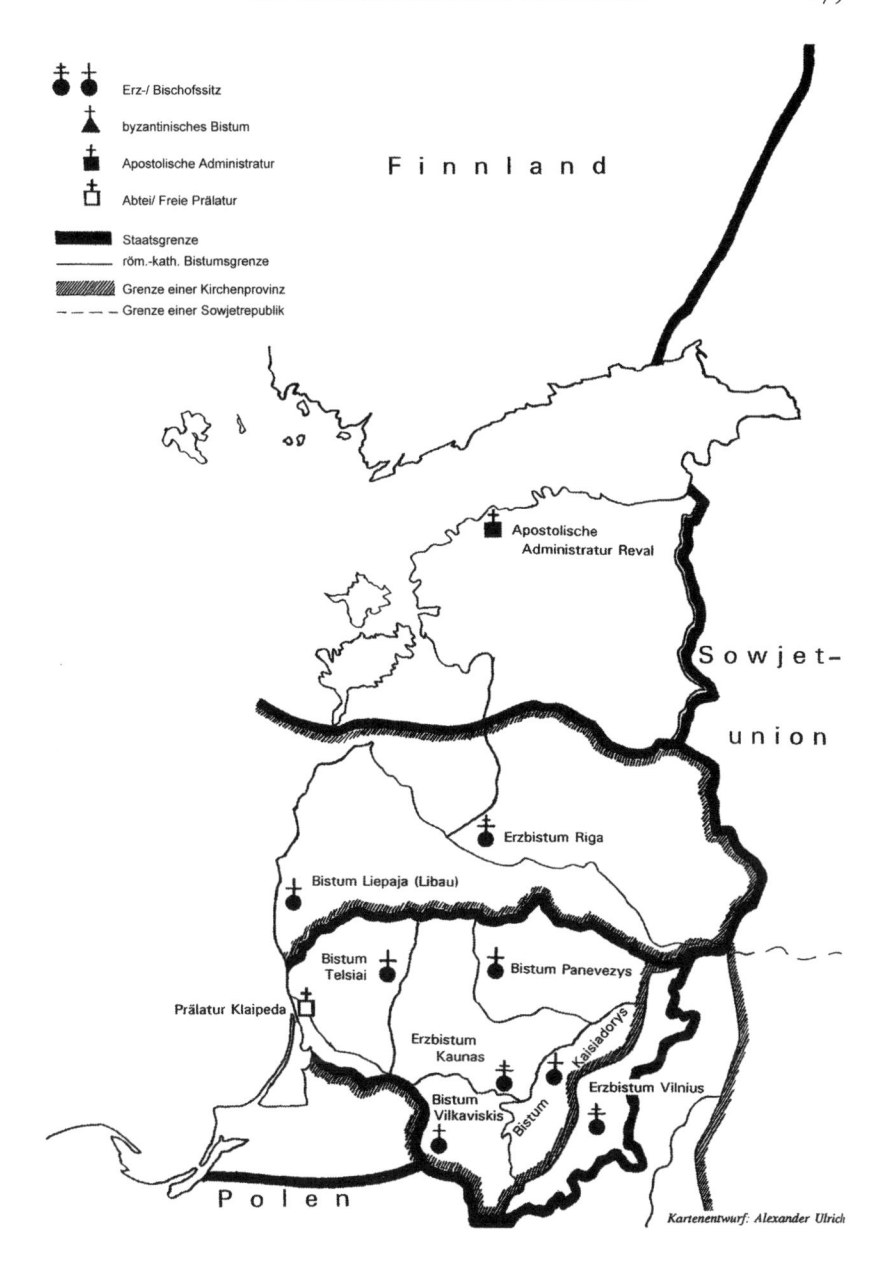

Map 1: The dioceses in the Baltic States before the first Soviet Occupation
Source: G. Adriányi, *Geschichte der Kirche Osteuropas im 20. Jahrhundert* (Paderborn/München/Wien/Zürich: Ferdinand Schöningh, 1992) 30.

According to the Lithuanian Constitution of 1922 and 1928, the state recognised all churches and similar religious organisations in Lithuania as long as they did not contradict morality and public order. Every church was considered to possess the rights of a legal person. The Constitution guaranteed the freedom to conduct religious services, to maintain places of worship, to administer theological schools and to propagate religion. The Constitution recognised the activity of religious orders, congregations and fraternities. All religious denominations were given a right to purchase real and movable property. Houses of religious worship and ecclesiastical establishments of all denominations were exempted from taxes. Moreover, national budget provisions were made to provide assistance for these institutions. The state paid the salaries of the clergy who were also exempted from military service.[9]

Concerning religious education, religion was a compulsory subject in primary and secondary state schools, except in special schools which were founded for children whose parents did not belong to any religious denomination. Religious instruction had to be that of the religion of the pupil. For this purpose, private denominational schools were organised.[10] Higher theological education was available at the University's Theology faculty and in three priestly seminaries of Kaunas, Telšiai and Vilkaviškis.

General education was greatly contributed to by the activity of regular clergy most of which worked in the fields of youth ministry, education and foster care, and were being trained in higher and specialised schools in Lithuania and abroad. The Capuchins, Franciscans, Marians, Sisters of St. Casimir and the Servants of the Sacred Heart of Jesus had opened secondary schools, boarding usually 50-600 pupils. The regular clergy also established about twenty craft-shops and courses. They participated in the work of orphanages, kindergartens, hospitals, and other pastoral activities. There were also three convents operating as charitable societies. During the period of national independence the number of orders and congregations tripled. From 1918 until 1940 the number of monastic houses increased from 7 to 96, many of which, however, were small, having only two to three members. By the Summer of 1940 there

---

9. K. Valančius, *Lietuvos Valstybės Konstitucijos* [Lithuanian State Constitutions] (Vilnius, 1989) 29-30, 53; Boris Iwanow (ed.), *Religion in the USSR*, Institute for the Study of the USSR, Series I, 59 (Munich, 1960) 103.

10. Dauknys, *The Resistance of the Catholic Church*, 22-23; Iwanow (ed.), *Religion in the USSR*, 103.

were fifteen orders and congregations: six for men (Jesuits, Capuchins, Salesians, Marians, Dominicans, Franciscans) and nine for women (Sisters of St. Benedict, Sisters of St. Francis, Sisters of St. Elisabeth, Salesian Sisters, Sisters of St. Catherine, Sisters of St. Casimir, Servants of the Sacred Heart of Jesus, Daughters of Mary – Help of Christians, Sisters of the Poor). In July 1940 there were 771 professed monks and nuns (281 men and 490 women), 137 novices (51 men and 86 women), and 132 candidates and postulants. An absolute majority of professed monks and nuns were younger than 40. Generally, monastic institutions provided a great moral influence in the country.[11]

An important and well developed sphere of religious activity was created by the religious press. Every Catholic organisation had its own publication, and in 1935 their total circulation was 7,030,200 copies. The Catholic press included three daily, seventeen weekly and seven monthly periodicals. The Catholic publishing houses issued 300-400 books yearly. The Marian Fathers, the Jesuits and the Franciscans had modern printing plants, book shops and distribution agencies.[12]

The activity of Catholics, the largest confession in the country, embracing more than 80% of the population, played an important role in the social life of Lithuania. About one-third of the whole population belonged to various lay Catholic societies, cultural and fraternal organisations, educational, charitable and other social institutions, many of which were subsidised by the Lithuanian government.[13] The activities of Catholic organisations were co-ordinated by the Catholic Action Centre which was governed by thirteen people, seven of whom were appointed by the Lithuanian episcopate. The Christian Democrat party had almost half of the seats in the Parliament, until the *coup d'état* of 1926 that brought the National Party to power, thus complicating the relations between the Catholic Church and the state. The government of the National Party, wanting to restrict the political activity of Christian Democrats, often identified it with the activity of Catholic organisations or of the Church itself that it attempted to restrict, thus provoking protests from the clergy and complaints about persecution of the Church. Nevertheless, even though the Lithuanian Catholics were no

---

11. Regina Laukaitytė, *Lietuvos vienuolijos XX amžiuje* [Lithuanian Monastic Orders in the 20th Century], Lietuvos Istorijos Institutas [Lithuanian Historical Institute] (2002). http://vienuolijos.iwebland.com (access June 25, 2004).
12. Iwanow (ed.), *Religion in the USSR,* 104; Dauknys, *The Resistance of the Catholic Church,* 19-25.
13. Iwanow (ed.), *Religion in the USSR,* 104.

longer in government through their party, they constituted a considerable political force until the end of the independence period.[14]

The talks about the persecution of the Church concerned not only the Lithuanian internal issue but also the reality in the Soviet Union (USSR) that had grown from three member-states (Russia, Belarus and Ukraine) in 1922, up to eleven members, in 1936.[15] The USSR majority religions were Russian Orthodoxy and Islam, while Roman Catholics represented a minority, found mostly in Belarus and Ukraine. In the late 1930s the death sentence was inflicted on a number of Catholic priests and the only Bishop, Alexander Frison.[16] Numerous churches were closed and demolished. By the mid-1939s there were only two Catholic churches left in the entire Soviet Union, both officially providing pastoral care to foreigners: St. Louis' church, attended by priest Leopold Brown, in Moscow, and the church of the Mother of God, attended by priest M. Florent, in Leningrad (now St. Petersburg).[17] Although the situation of Roman Catholicism in the Soviet Union had no direct impact on the currently independent Lithuania, we can say that the indirect conflict between the Lithuanian Catholic Church and the Soviet regime began before Lithuania's occupation. The Pope's reaction to the intensification of repression against believers in the USSR encouraged the Lithuanian bishops to raise their voice about the restriction of religious freedom in the Soviet state (it was, perhaps, Pius XI's letter, publicised in *L'Osservatore Romano,* in February 1930, where the Pope condemned the mass terror that the USSR had launched against religious organisations, and called for prayer for the persecuted). On March 10, 1930, Archbishop J. Skvireckas publicised a circular concerning the persecution of religious belief in Russia, encouraging Lithuanian believers to pray for the Catholics of the Soviet Union, and instructing the priests to pay more attention to the Church persecution in their homilies. In 1931-1932 Bishop Justinas Staugaitis[18]

---

14. Jean Chélini, *L'Église sous Pie XII: La tourmente (1939-1945)* (Paris: Fayard, 1983) 47-48, n. 6; Arūnas Streikus, *Sovietų valdžios antibažnytinė politika Lietuvoje (1944-1990)* [The Anti-Church Policy of the Soviet Government in Lithuania, 1944-1990] (Vilnius: Lietuvos gyventojų genocido ir rezistencijos tyrimo centras, 2002) 44-45.

15. On the eve of World War II the USSR was composed of Armenia, Azerbaijan, Belorus, Georgia, Kazakhstan, Kirghizia, Russia, Tajikistan, Turkmenistan, Ukraine, and Uzbekistan.

16. A. Frison: b. in 1875, (Baden, dioc. of Tiraspol), el. May 10, 1926, apostolic administrator of Odessa. See *Annuario Pontificio* (1933) 339.

17. Streikus, *Sovietų valdžios antibažnytinė politika*, 39-40.

18. J. Staugaitis: b. November 17, 1866 (Tupikai, dioc. of Seinai), el. April 5, 1926. See *Annuario Pontificio* (1940) 274.

published an article about the activity of the Union of Fighting Atheists (*Kovingųjų Bedievių Sąjunga – KBS*). At the end of 1937 there was an initiative to organise candle processions in solidarity with the believers persecuted by the USSR. However, the government did not permit the implementation of this idea.[19]

During the few months from the beginning of World War II until the Soviet occupation of Lithuania, the relationship between Lithuania and the Vatican moved a couple of steps forward. On October 18, 1939, the Lithuanian minister Stasys Girdvainis submitted his credentials to Pius XII and became the Lithuanian Minister of State at the Vatican. On February 19, 1940, Archbishop Luigi Centoz[20] was appointed nuncio of the Vatican for Lithuania.[21] Generally, we can say that in 1940, on the eve of the first Soviet occupation, the Catholic Church in Lithuania was a well-organised, strong and active body, and, therefore, very influential in the life of the republic.[22]

II. Lithuania during the First Soviet Occupation (1940-1941)

During World War II and during the first Soviet occupation Lithuania's situation was quite similar to the state of affairs in two other Baltic

---

19. Streikus, *Sovietų valdžios antibažnytinė politika*, 45-46.
20. L. Centoz: b. April 2, 1883 (San Pietro, dioc of Aosta), ord. June 9, 1906, el. January 28, 1932, cons. February 14, 1932. See *Annuario Pontificio* (1950) 479.
21. Vaišnora, "Nepriklausomybės ir okupaciniais laikais," 148.
22. Streikus, *Sovietų valdžios antibažnytinė politika*, 43. In 1940, before the first Soviet occupation took place, the population of Lithuania was comprised of 3,000,000 people. 85.70% were Roman Catholics, 3.80% Protestants, 2.34% Greek Orthodox, 0.5% other Christians and 7.6% Jews. The country was divided into two archdioceses, four dioceses, 680 parishes and it had 1,202 churches and public chapels. Concerning the number of the clergy, in 1940 there were 14 archbishops and bishops, 1,646 priests and 1,586 members of monastic orders. Religious orders ran 18 primary and 18 secondary schools. Theological education was available at four theological seminaries (in Kaunas, Vilnius (from 1939 on, when Vilnius was returned to Lithuania from its dependence on Poland), Telšiai and Vilkaviškis) and at the state universities in Kaunas and Vilnius (from 1939 on) where there were two faculties of philosophy and theology. In these institutions there were 470 theology students. The church did not have to pay any taxes but received state assistance of 1,383,278 Lt (Lt-*Litas*-Lithuanian currency). See Albert Kalme, *Total Terror* (New York: Appleton-Century, Inc., 1951) 182-183; Dauknys, *The Resistance of the Catholic Church*, 23. P. Dauknys presents different numbers of diocesan priests (1,494) and of monks and nuns (1,786).

states, namely, Latvia and Estonia. Therefore, we will look at Lithuania, as part of this greater unit.

1. *The Consequences of the Molotov-Ribbentrop Pact*

The scenario of occupation and later incorporation of all three Baltic states in the Soviet Union followed the same pattern. On August 23, 1939, one week before World War II started, the so-called Molotov-Ribbentrop pact was signed. The document outlined the policies of non-aggression between the German Reich and the Soviet Union. In the appended secret protocols both parties expressed their plans concerning the desired spheres of influence in Eastern Europe, which included not only the fate of Poland and Bessarabia, but also the division of Baltic states between Nazi Germany and the Soviet Union.[23] The border between the spheres of influence was to be the northern border of Lithuania. Thus, Estonia and Latvia were assigned to the Soviet Union, and Lithuania was assigned to Germany.[24] About one month later, on September 28, 1939, the secret protocol of the Hitler-Stalin Common Border and Friendship Treaty changed the decision of the Molotov-Ribbentrop non-aggression pact. It transferred Lithuania from the Nazi to the Soviet sphere of influence.[25] Shortly after the Nazis had invaded Poland, the Soviet Union launched efforts to take its part of the Baltic states in a seemingly more diplomatic but a nonetheless extortive way. The process of occupation of Estonia, Latvia and Lithuania started in September-October, 1939 (Estonia – September 28, Latvia – October 5, Lithuania – October 10), when the Soviet Union forced their respective governments to accept pacts called Defence and Mutual Assistance with the USSR. The pacts required compliance with the location of some Soviet garrisons and naval bases. As a result of the pacts, the troops of the Soviet army entered the Baltic states.[26]

---

23. As Romuald J. Misiunas and Rein Taagepera put it, Molotov defended the occupation of the region as a historical necessity for the development of the Russian state. According to him, the small nations would have to disappear, and the Soviet system would reign throughout the whole of Europe. R. J. Misiunas and R. Taagepera (eds.), *The Baltic States: Years of Dependence 1940-1980. Estonia, Latvia, Lithuania* (London: C. Hurst & Co., 1983) 25.

24. V. Kavaliauskas, *Suokalbis* [Plot] (Vilnius: Lituanus, 1989) 16.

25. For the Hitler-Stalin secret pacts of 1939 see Map 2.

26. The number of troops entering the Baltic States in 1939-1940 comprised 25.000 in Estonia, 30.000 in Latvia, and 20.000 in Lithuania. See Misiunas and Taagepera (eds.), *The Baltic States*, 15.

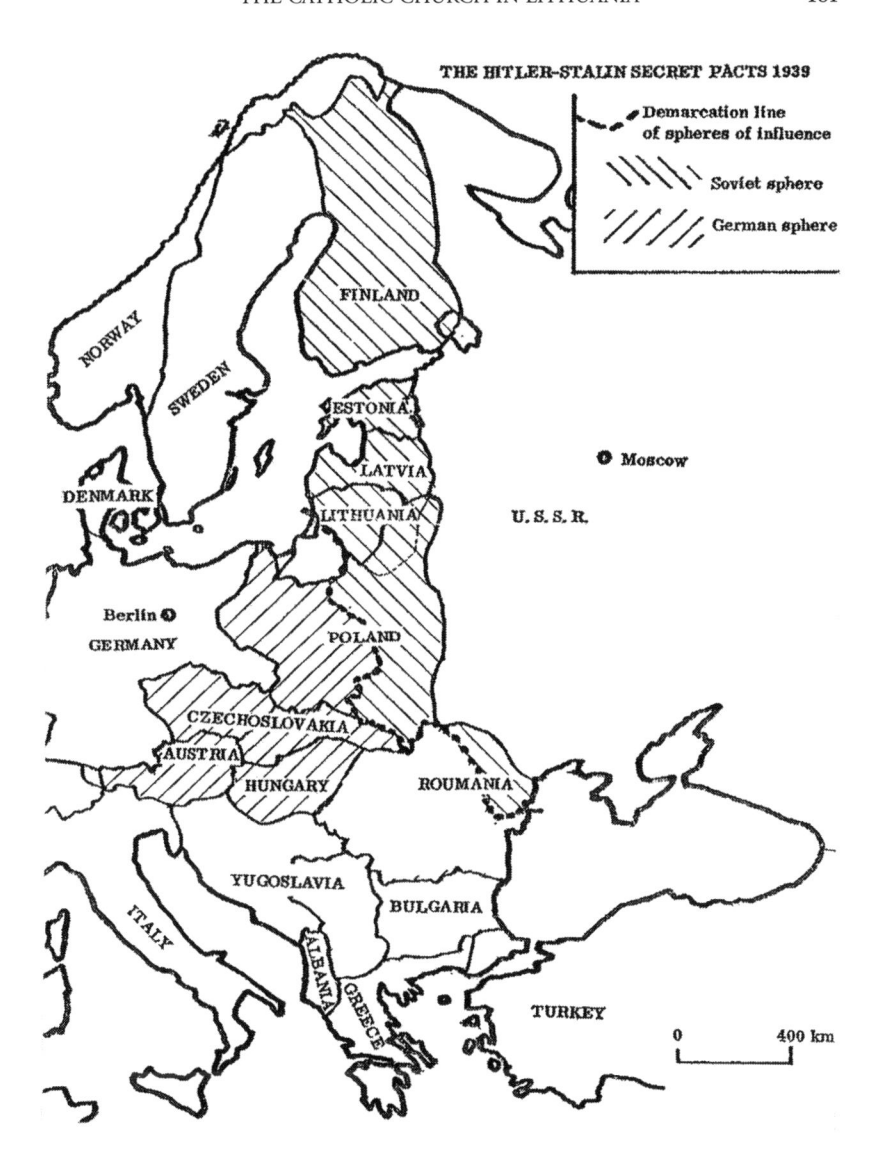

Map 2. The Hitler-Stalin Secret Pacts 1939
Source: Dauknys, *The Resistance of the Catholic Church*, 167

2. The Effects of the Soviet Occupation

June 15-18, 1940, when additional Soviet Army troops marched into the territories of Lithuania, Latvia and Estonia, marked the end of the process of their occupation, and introduced the period of the Soviet government's intensive and organised efforts to incorporate the three Baltic states into the Soviet Union. One of the means of implementing the Soviet regime was arrests and deportations introduced in July, 1940, and carried out very intensely. At the same time, the Soviet government sought to make the process of the incorporation look like an initiative and voluntary act of the Baltic peoples and governments. In July, 1940, after the first wave of arrests and deportations, the false elections of the so-called 'People's Assemblies' were organised and won by the 'Unions of Labour' due to massive vote fraud. Shortly after the elections, the new puppet parliaments of the Baltic republics petitioned for the incorporation of Estonia, Latvia and Lithuania into the USSR.[27] On August 3-6, 1940 the three states were incorporated into the Soviet Union, in addition to the other twelve Soviet republics.[28]

Incorporation into the Soviet Union brought with it immediate administrative changes to all the Baltic states: massive layoffs of leading officers, police commanders, district chairmen and school principals, and their replacement by Soviet officials; adoption of the Legal Code of Soviet Russia and acceptance of the Soviet Constitutions, which were formed according to the Soviet Constitution of the USSR of 1936. In the Baltic states, as in the entire Soviet Union, the Communist Party became the main body of power, led by the so-called First Secretaries: Karl Säre in Estonia, Jānis Kalnbērziņš in Latvia and

---

27. Iwanow (ed.), *Religion in the USSR*, 104-105.
28. Russia, Ukraine, Belorus, Uzbekistan, Kazakhstan, Georgia, Azerbaijan, Moldavia, Kirghizia, Tajikistan, Armenia and Turkmenistan. The governments of Germany and Sweden recognised the occupation of the Baltic States. Great Britain, Canada, France and Switzerland recognised it *de facto*. (During the war Britain signed a treaty with the USSR extending *de facto* recognition to the incorporation. Canada's government recognised that the Baltic states had *de facto* entered the USSR. France extended *de facto* recognition to the incorporation by closing the Baltic legations. The Federal Council of Switzerland did not recognise Estonian, Latvian and Lithuanian diplomatic and consular missions.) The Vatican, the USA, Ireland, Australia, Spain, Portugal and the Latin-American states refused to recognise the occupation of the Baltic States altogether. See Domas Krivickas, "The International Status of Lithuania," *Lituanus* 4, no. 4 (1958) 99-104; Misiunas and Taagepera (eds.), *The Baltic States*, 29.

Antanas Sniečkus in Lithuania. In addition to the administrative changes, other features of the newly imposed Soviet regime were introduced, such as Russification and destruction of the national culture.[29]

The Soviet Union tried to weave very rapidly all spheres of life of Lithuania, Latvia and Estonia into the Soviet system. One of these spheres, and a very important one, was religion. In a religious sense the three Baltic states were different from the other Soviet republics. Russian Orthodoxy and Islam were the most popular religions among the rest of the believers in the Soviet Union. The majority religion in Latvia and Estonia was Lutheran. Lithuania, on the other hand, was the only Soviet republic with a predominantly (more than 80%) Roman Catholic population. Besides being the majority in Lithuania, Catholic minorities did exist in Estonia, Latvia, Belarus, Ukraine, Armenia, Georgia and the German settlements (in Siberia and the Central Asian part of the USSR).[30] Latvia and Lithuania had their papal nuntios: nuncio L. Centoz resided in Lithuania and the nuncio of Latvia and Estonia, Antonino Arata,[31] resided in Latvia. When the Baltic states were being taken over by the Soviet army in June 1940, according to the words of H. Stehle, it was "the first time, a papal nuncio experienced with his own eyes a Communist seizure of power."[32] The Vatican continued to communicate with its representatives, by exchanging coded telegrams with nuncio L. Centoz in Kaunas and nuncio Antonino Arata in Rīga,

---

29. Misiunas and Taagepera (eds.), *The Baltic States*, 24, 29-30; Vytautas Tininis, *Sovietinė Lietuva ir jos veikėjai* [Soviet Lithuania and Its Statesmen] (Vilnius: Enciklopedija, 1994) 16-18.

30. Trevor Beeson, *Discretion and Valour: Religious Conditions in Russia and Eastern Europe*, Fontana Books, 27 (Glasgow: Collins, 1975) 114. For the religious traditions of the north-west of the USSR see Map 3. For the dioceses in the Baltic states before the Soviet occupation see Map 1. In Lithuania there were about two million Catholics. In Estonia there were about two thousand Catholics (six parishes and 14 priests) in 1940. (See Beeson, *Discretion and Valour*, 114). In Latvia there were 0.5 million Catholics in Latgalia, the south-east of the country. In 1940 there were 184 parishes, 187 priests, two weekly newspapers, four monthly religious publications. Walter Kolarz, *Religion in the Soviet Union* (London/New York: Macmillan/St. Martin's Press, 1961) 206; Kalme, *Total Terror*, 179; Chélini, *L'Église sous Pie XII*, 47-48.

31. A. Arata: b. October 28, 1883 (Piacenza), ord. June 9, 1906, el. July 11, 1935, cons. August 11, 1935, apostolic nuntio in Latvia and Estonia, nom. July 11-12, 1935. See *Annuario Pontificio* (1940) 468, 767, 768; (1945) 471.

32. "Capital and country are quiet, although immensely depressed," nuncio L. Centoz described from Kaunas, on June 17, 1940, the news about the Soviet invasion. Hans Jakob Stehle, *Eastern Politics of the Vatican, 1917-1979*, trans. Sandra Smith (Athens, OH/London: Ohio University Press, 1981) 200.

as well as making its final arrangements before the formal incorporation of the Baltic states into the Soviet Union.[33] Soon afterwards, on July 21, 1940, on a Soviet initiative the nuncios were ordered to leave Lithuania and Latvia.[34] After the start of the Soviet occupation of the Baltic States, the position of their believers changed noticeably for the worse. Besides revoking the nuncios, the common pattern of the Soviet anti-religious activity in Estonia, Latvia and Lithuania included the closing of most theological institutions; the exclusion of clergymen from the army, the educational system and the other governmental institutions; depriving them of their pensions and imposing on the clergy and their congregations extra taxes, rents and utility fees, as well as the abolition of church holidays. The anti-religious activity also disrupted church worship services and harassed the faithful.[35]

3. Soviet Policy towards Religion in Lithuania and the Reaction of the Church

Among the first anti-religious undertakings of the Soviet government in Lithuania was the cutting off of the Concordat and the introduction of the new Soviet Constitution. The decision on the Concordat was taken by the peoples' government, on June 26, 1940. On July 6, 1940, the Soviet government unilaterally denounced the Concordat[36] thus opening the door to the self-will of the Soviet regime: the juridical mechanism, guaranteeing the state's support of the Church and protecting religious communities against the government's groundless interference in the Church's internal affairs, was discontinued. The 96th article of the newly introduced Lithuanian Soviet Constitution separated church and state, and school from church. In addition, it acknowledged freedom for all citizens to perform religious rites or to spread atheistic propaganda. Nothing was said about the possibility of religious propaganda, thus, this Constitution acknowledged the spreading only of anti-religious convictions. The believers were given the right only to perform religious practices but not to propagate their belief.[37] However, even

---

33. Stehle, *Eastern Politics of the Vatican*, 201.
34. Chélini, *L'Église sous Pie XII*, 125; Bronis Kaslas, *La Lithuanie et la Seconde Guerre Mondiale: Recueil des documents* (Paris: G. P. Maisonneuve et Larose, 1981) 205.
35. Misiunas and Taagepera (eds.), *The Baltic States*, 37-38.
36. Streikus, *Sovietų valdžios antibažnytinė politika*, 47; Kaslas, *La Lithuanie et la Seconde Guerre Mondiale*, 205.
37. "Communism's Struggle with Religion in Lithuania," *Lituanus* 9 no. 1 (1963) 4; Chélini, *L'Église sous Pie XII*, 158.

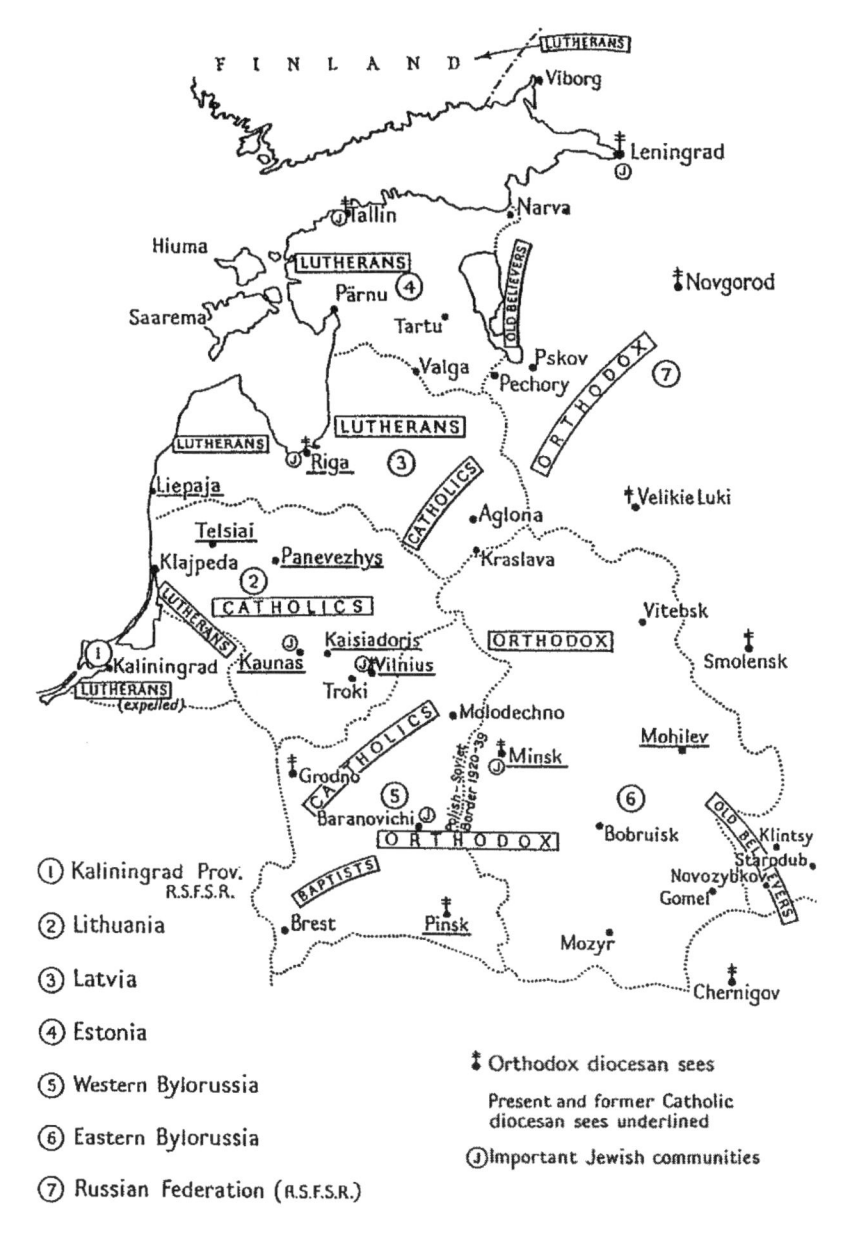

Map 3: Religious Traditions of the North-West of the USSR in 1940
Source: Kolarz, *Religion in the Soviet Union*, 206

these constitutional rights were not realised in practice. Instead, the active anti-religious activity and propaganda began.

The Soviet anti-religious undertakings directly affected the clergy and the hierarchy. All the bishops and a great number of priests were driven out of their residences, with no possibility of a decent settling elsewhere. The clergy's salaries were cut off and money in the banks was confiscated. Moreover, the priests were required to pay a three times higher rent for apartments, in comparison with other people (3 roubles instead of 1 rouble per square meter). Besides the economic restrictions, there was obstruction of their pastoral work, such as the removal of chaplains from schools, hospitals, prisons and the army, and forbidding the clergy to visit their parishioners and to give religious instruction. The priests were required to provide a signed promise not to teach religion to private individuals nor even in the churches. Moreover, according to the secret order[38] of Piotr Gladkov, Vice Commissar of Internal Affairs, given to the heads of the National Commissariat of the Internal Affairs (NKVD) on October 2, 1940, the activity of the Catholic Church in Lithuania was to be opposed, and all clergymen were to be placed under control. In other words, they had to be spied upon by agents who were to be enlisted by force even from among the regular and secular clergy itself. A file was then kept for each cleric.[39] These files were to be used in any case of indictment and trial. Already in the first half of the first Soviet occupation approximately 150 Catholic priests were arrested in Lithuania.[40]

The anti-religious policy also affected the immovable property of the church, religious media and education. The goods and the land of the parishes, monasteries and seminaries were confiscated.[41] The parishes were left with only 3 ha of land including the space under the church buildings and cemeteries. Church buildings and chapels were considered the property of the government. Therefore, some of them were taken over for army affairs, some were transformed into such objects as

---

38. Kaslas, *La Lithuanie et la Seconde Guerre Mondiale*, 151.

39. Besides the anti-government statements by each clergyman, these files were to contain information about his character, private life, family and other relatives.

40. Iwanow (ed.), *Religion in the USSR*, 107; Chélini, *L'Église sous Pie XII*, 158; Kaslas, *La Lithuanie et la Seconde Guerre Mondiale*, 208; see also Christopher Lawrence Zugger, *The Forgotten: Catholics of the Soviet Empire from Lenin through Stalin* (Syracuse, NY: Syracuse University Press, 2001) 334-335.

41. 17.614 ha of land was confiscated from the churches, 1,510 ha of land was confiscated from the monasteries. Vaišnora, "Nepriklausomybės ir okupaciniais laikais," 146-148.

museum of revolution, theatre, cinema or used for economic purposes. All Catholic organisations, associations and confraternities were closed, and their property was confiscated. The Catholic press was suppressed, the publishing of religious books and magazines interdicted, Catholic printing houses and book stores were nationalised. All religious books found in the nationalised bookshops or libraries were destroyed, even the best and the most rare. The teaching of the catechism and religion was prohibited, thus the theology-philosophy faculty at Kaunas' University and three out of four theological seminaries in Vilnius, Telšiai and Vilkaviškis were seized.[42]

Despite the Soviet anti-religious undertakings, neither the Catholic hierarchy nor the clergy or the laity ceased their activities. On July 2-3, 1940, the Bishops' Conference discussed the maintenance of the priestly seminaries and the encouragement of priests to serve their flock even if the ministry of the chaplains was abolished. The situation required fighting the spiritual and material poverty, reinforcing the apostolic and continuing the 'caritative' activity of the clergy. This included the provision of religious instruction in the churches before or after the mass, as well as at home, and the preparation of lay catechists for the assistance of priests. The bishops at the Conference also addressed Pope Pius XII, expressing their faithfulness to him and asking him to remember Lithuania during a period of hardship.[43] In response to the repressive actions of the Soviet government, including the surveillance of those attending public prayers, lay Catholics and the clergy actively protested and petitioned. Some members of religious organisations protested to the Council of Peoples Commissars against the suspension of the purely religious organisations that were accused of being dangerous to the security of the state. Parents asked to restore religious instruction in schools at their own expense. Archbishop J. Skvireckas addressed the president of the Lithuanian puppet government, Justas Paleckis and the First Secretary of the Lithuanian Communist Party (CPLi), Antanas Sniečkus, protesting against their repressive decrees and requesting freedom for

---

42. Iwanow (ed.), *Religion in the USSR*, 105-106; Chélini, *L'Église sous Pie XII*, 158; Kaslas, *La Lithuanie et la Seconde Guerre Mondiale*, 208.

43. Vincentas Brizgys, *Katalikų Bažnyčia Lietuvoje: Pirmoje rusų okupacijoje 1940-1941 M. Vokiečių okupacijoje 1941-1944 M.* [The Catholic Church in Lithuania. The First Russian Occupation 1940-1941. The German Occupation 1941-1944] (Chicago, IL: Draugo, 1977) 15-37; excerpts from the letter in "Selected Documentary Material on the Lithuanian Resistance Movement against Totalitarianism 1940-1960," *Lituanus* 8, nos. 1-2 (1962) 57-60.

political prisoners. However, these protests resulted in new anti-religious decrees.[44]

Despite the Soviet interference, the Vatican's attempt to keep in touch with the Lithuanian Church continued. Even before the formal incorporation of Lithuania into the USSR on August 3, 1940, the Vatican attempted to appoint and consecrate new bishops. Being aware that relations with the Lithuanian Church hierarchy could be cut off at any moment, and that the Archbishop of Vilnius, Romuald Jalbrzykovski,[45] was old and in failing health, the Vatican had asked the nuncio to find a Lithuanian candidate to assist and later to succeed the Archbishop. On July 9, 1940, the Vatican named Bishop Mečislovas Reinys[46] Archbishop and appointed him assistant and later successor to Archbishop R. Jalbrzykovski. On July 17 Cardinal L. Maglione told nuncio L. Centoz to try to remain in the country for as long as possible, and to consecrate priest Vincentas Padolskis[47] suffragan Bishop of Vilkaviškis, without waiting for the papal bull of appointment.[48] On July 22, 1940, the Lithuanian minister in the Vatican, S. Girdvainis, sent a letter to Cardinal L. Maglione, protesting against the occupation of Lithuania.[49] The reaction was positive: the Vatican was one of the states that refused to recognise the incorporation of Lithuania in the USSR either *de jure* or *de facto*. Instead, the Lithuanian legation in the Vatican was to continue its work and minister S. Girdvainis had to remain in his post.[50] The

44. Iwanow (ed.), *Religion in the USSR*, 106-107.
45. R. Jalbrzykovski: b. February, 7, 1876 (Letowo-Dab, dioc. of Seinai), ord. March 9, 1901, cons. November 30, 1918, ordinary and Vicar General in Lithuanian territory. See *Annuario Pontificio* (1948) 389.
46. M. Reinys: b. February 5, 1884 (Madagaskaras, dioc. of Samogitia), el. April 5, 1926, pr. July 18, 1940. *Annuario Pontificio* (1950) 462. M. Reinys studied in Vilnius, Rīga, St. Petersburg. After his studies in Belgium, at the Philosophy Institute of the Catholic University of Leuven, in 1909-1912, he obtained a Doctor's Degree in Philosophy. After some more studies in Leuven and Strasbourg, in 1913-1914, on the eve of World War I M. Reinys returned to Lithuania. In September 25, 1925 – April 21, 1926 M. Reinys worked as the Lithuanian Minister of Foreign Affairs. On April 5, 1926, Pius XI appointed him coadjutor of Vilkaviškis Bishop Antanas Karosas. In 1940 M. Reinys became Archbishop and worked in Vilnius till 1947. M. Reinys died in Vladimir prison, on November 8, 1953. See *Annuario Pontificio* (1948) 445; Aldona Vasiliauskienė, "Arkivyskupo Mečislovo Reinio kelio į altorių garbę fragmentai [Fragments of Archbishop Mečislovas Reinys' Path to the Altar of Honour]," *XXI amžius* [The 21st Century] (January 3, 2003) 6; Jonas Nemanis, "Prieš 50 metų užgeso arkivyskupo Mečislovo Reinio gyvybė [Archbishop Mečislovas Reinys died 50 years ago]," *Gimtinė* [Native Land] (November 1-30, 2003) 2.
47. V. Padolskis: b. April 21, 1904 (Virbalis, dioc. of Vilkaviškis), el. July 18, 1940. See *Annuario Pontificio* (1957) 650.
48. Stehle, *Eastern Politics of the Vatican*, 201.
49. Kaslas, *La Lithuanie et la Seconde Guerre Mondiale*, 133.
50. Vaišnora, *Nepriklausomybės ir okupaciniais laikais*, 148.

Soviet side wanted to cancel the contacts, however. After the formal incorporation of Lithuania, Latvia and Estonia into the USSR, on August 13, 1940, all diplomatic representatives in the Baltic capitals were asked to depart within two weeks. Nuncio L. Centoz left Lithuania on August 25, after exhorting the bishops to exercise great caution.[51]

The departure of the nuncio did not obstruct the communication between the Lithuanian Church hierarchy and the Vatican. On the Lithuanian side it was carried on mostly by Kaunas' suffragan Bishop Vincentas Brizgys,[52] who started sending the news to the nuncio via some confidential paths or via a detour through the Vatican's nunciature in Berlin.[53] Pius XII, on his part, tried to keep up to date with the situation in the country. Although the amount of news was not abundant, the Pope could become familiar with the circumstances of the seminaries, schools, monasteries, the hierarchy, clergy and lay people. In seeking to keep contact, Pius XII wrote *In Baltica Regione*, a letter of encouragement to all bishops of the Baltic states. Pius XII's fears seemed justified as the letter reached Lithuania only one year later, during the Nazi occupation.[54] One could see the Soviet regime's attempt to control information flowing from the USSR to Rome, to keep in check the Lithuanian Catholic Church contacts with the external world, and to manipulate the information in the interests of Soviet foreign policy. In the presence of the military conflict this attempt served the Soviet wish to ensure a positive or at least a neutral attitude of the Vatican which was considered as one of the centres of anti-Soviet activity.[55]

Due to the Soviet attempts to block contact between the Lithuanian and the external world, especially the Vatican, radio broadcasting appeared to be the most accessible way to transmit information thus

---

51. Stehle, *Eastern Politics of the Vatican*, 202.

52. V. Brizgys: b. November 10, 1903 (dioc. of Vilkaviškis), ord. June 5, 1927, cons. May 19, 1940, d. April 23, 1992, auxiliary of Kaunas, impeded. See "Brizgys, Vincentas," *Encyclopedia Lituanica* I (1970) 414.

53. Streikus, *Sovietų valdžios antibažnytinė politika*, 54. As for the situation in Latvia and Estonia, the Vatican was receiving their information from Rīga's Archbishop Antonius Springovics and from the apostolic administrator for Estonia, the Jesuit bishop Eduard Profittlich. Stehle, *Eastern Politics of the Vatican*, 202.

54. It seems that H. Stehle speaks about the same Latin letter (*Le Saint Siège et la guerre en Europe: Actes et documents du Saint Siège relatifs à la Seconde Guerre Mondiale* [*ADSS*], Città del Vaticano, Vols. I-IX, 1965-1975, Vol. 3, doc. no. 257 and 262), sent to the bishops of the Baltic Soviet republics, two weeks before Hitler's attack on the Soviet Union. Avoiding any political accent, the Pope addressed general consoling words and warnings against "laziness and avarice among the clergy," and advised preservation of the faith. Stehle, *Eastern Politics of the Vatican*, 206.

55. Streikus, *Sovietų valdžios antibažnytinė politika*, 54-55.

making the Lithuanian situation public. With the main initiative of Bishop Petras Būčys MIC,[56] minister S. Girdvainis presented the Vatican with an official request for permission to start transmitting Vatican radio programs in the Lithuanian language. The transmission started immediately after receiving the permission, on November 27, 1940, making the Lithuanian programme the eleventh-language-programme of the Vatican radio. The Lithuanian programme was edited by Bishop P. Būčys, and assisted by several Marian and Jesuit priests, and the Lithuanian minister in Italy, Stasys Lozoraitis.[57]

Besides the clergy's and hierarchy's persistence in keeping to their pastoral activity, protests, petitions and efforts to overcome the Soviet hindrances, we can notice their attempt to find a mutually acceptable solution. In the hope of preserving at least a minimum amount of Church activity and pastoral work, Catholic hierarchs and some clerics started looking for a compromise with the occupation regime. On October 7, 1940, the former chief of the Christian Democrat Party, priest Mykolas Krupavičius, prepared a memorandum about the co-operation of Catholics with communists, addressed to the members of the Presidium of the Lithuanian Supreme Council, the Council of Peoples' Commissars and to the Central Committee of the Communist Party. It seems that M. Krupavičius prepared the memorandum after consulting the Lithuanian bishops and the papal nuncio. Having admitted that believers and communists have different views to religion, the document stated that cooperation between the Church and the Soviet regime was possible, since they had a common aim: social justice. The fight between religion and communism was to be limited to the ideological sphere, with the opponents having equal possibilities. The memorandum raised a condition for possible cooperation – to renounce restrictions imposed on the Church activity. Following A. Streikus, in spite of some air of fawning to the Soviet regime, nothing in this memorandum contradicted the Church doctrine or expressed the Church's unconditional agreement with the regime. Therefore, the memorandum can not be considered as a sign of the Church's readiness to collaborate with the Soviet regime. This is also confirmed by the Soviet government's reaction to the document. The

56. P. Būčys: b. August 20, 1872 (Šilgaliai, dioc. of Seinai), ord. March 25, 1899, el. July 3, 1930, cons. July 6, 1930, bishop of Bizantine rite. See *Annuario Pontificio* (1950) 536.

57. Jolanta Kažemėkaitytė, "Lietuviškajam Vatikano radijui – 60 metų [The Lithuanian Vatican Radio at 60 Years Old]," *Ūkininko patarėjas* [Farmer's Guide], no. 140 (November 30, 2000) 5; "Vatikano radijo kelionė per dešimtmečius [Vatican Radio through Decades]," *Tėviškės žinios* [News of the Fatherland], no. 226, 20.

requested relaxation of the anti-religious policy was not implemented. Instead, at the beginning of 1941 there came new proposals for the destruction of the Church.[58]

In mid-1941, shortly before the end of the first Soviet occupation, there was a new outbreak of deportations and violence. Following the instruction of Ivan Serov, the Soviet Vice-Commissar of Public Security, an anti-Soviet contingent among the inhabitants of Estonia, Latvia and Lithuania, including approximately 700.000 Lithuanian inhabitants, almost all priests, directors and members of all Catholic organisations, as well as active lay Catholics, were to be deported to Siberia. The plan of arrests and deportations was carried out very intensely. Most of them took place in June, 1941: in just one week, from June 14 until 21, 1941, 34.620 people were deported from Lithuania. The execution of the entire scheme of arrests and deportations, as well as an approaching wave of persecution of believers planned by the Soviet occupation government was interrupted by the beginning of the Nazi-Soviet war on June 22, 1941, and the consequent Nazi occupation of Lithuania.[59] The Soviet troops, present in Lithuania, retreated hastily. While the clergy had been repressed during the entire period of the first Soviet occupation, the Soviet regime did not go so far as to openly persecute and kill its members. However, as the Soviet army left, there was a noticeable outbreak of violence against the Catholic clergy by the retreating troops. Such an outbreak of violence can be explained. According to W. Kolarz, the Soviet regime in the Baltic states did not feel strong enough to immediately embark upon the open persecution of the clergy because it would have antagonised the people. After the start of the war with the Nazi army, however, Soviet authorities became confused, no longer cared about popular reaction and revealed the real dimension of their hate of the Church. Thus, from June 22, 1941, until the last unit of the Soviet armed forces left Lithuania, fifteen priests were murdered and twelve priests were arrested and deported to the USSR.[60] Another expla-

58. Streikus, *Sovietų valdžios antibažnytinė politika*, 50-54; also Zugger, *The Forgotten*, 334.

59. Streikus, *Sovietų valdžios antibažnytinė politika*, 59-60; Vaišnora, "Nepriklausomybės ir okupaciniais laikais," 149; Iwanow (ed.), *Religion in the USSR*, 108; Edvardas Tuškenis, "Critical Dates and Events," *Lituanus* 32, no. 4 (1986) 6; Gediminas Rudis (ed.), *Lietuvos gyventojų trėmimai 1941,1945-1952 m.* [The Deportation of Lithuanian Inhabitants 1941, 1945-1952] (Vilnius: Mokslo ir enciklopedijų leidykla, 1994) 14-20; Chélini, *L'Église sous Pie XII*, 158.

60. See Kolarz, *Religion in the Soviet Union*, 206-207; Iwanow (ed.), *Religion in the USSR*, 108. A. Streikus mentions a different number, seventeen priests, murdered by the retreating armed Soviet activists. See Streikus, *Sovietų valdžios antibažnytinė politika*, 60.

nation for the outbreak of violence might possibly be the fact that priests seemed the most potential collaborators with the approaching enemy. After all, the single year of the first Soviet occupation ruined political, social, economical, cultural and religious life in Lithuania.[61]

Despite the short duration of the occupation, the losses inflicted on the three Baltic states were significant. The general estimates of population losses (from different causes: mobilisations, deportations, massacres, disappearances) during the first Soviet occupation was around 60,000 for Estonia (about 4% of its pre-war population), 35,000 for Latvia and 34,000 for Lithuania (about 1.5-2% of their populations).[62]

III. Lithuania During the Nazi Occupation (1941-1944)

Lithuania, Latvia and Estonia underwent quite a similar treatment not only by the government of the Soviet Union but also by the Nazi regime. Thus, let us first look at the broader context of Lithuania under Nazi occupation during World War II.

1. The Effects of the Nazi Occupation

The Nazi march eastwards in June 1941, forced the Soviet army to retreat from the occupied Baltic States, leaving behind the unfulfilled plan of arrests and deportations and breaking off the general accomplishments of the Soviet regime in the Baltic. The Nazi attack on the USSR took place on June 22, 1941, during the period of massive arrests and deportations taking place in Estonia, Latvia and Lithuania. The Baltic peoples considered it a chance to escape from the Soviet occupation and in June-July rose in revolt against the Soviet army presence and against the Soviet administration. As a result of the revolt, all three countries created national governments. The insurrection of the Lithuanian resistance (*Lietuvos Aktyvistų Frontas – LAF* – Front of Lithuanian Activists) arose immediately after the Nazi attack on the Soviet Union, on June 23-24, 1941, aiming at the restoration of Lithuanian independence. The insurrection was successful, and the insurgents entrusted the Provisional Premiership of Lithuania to Professor Juozas Ambrazevičius, a popular Catholic leader and a member

---

61. Kaslas, *La Lithuanie et la Seconde Guerre Mondiale*, 206; Chélini, *L'Église sous Pie XII*, 158.
62. Misiunas and Taagepera (eds.), *The Baltic States*, 41.

of the Lithuanian Academy of Science.⁶³ The period of conditional respite lasted only for a short time, however: soon after overrunning the Baltic states, the Nazi occupation force suppressed the national provisional governments and instituted a Nazi German civil administration. On July 17, 1941, Alfred Rosenberg, a Baltic German was appointed as Reich Minister for the Nazis' occupied Eastern territory. The Nazis began to consider Estonia, Latvia, Lithuania and neighbouring Belarus (which was also occupied by the Nazis), as one unit. It was given the name *Ostland*, with a seat in the Latvian capital Rīga and its own Reich Commissioner Hinrich Lohse, one of the deputies of the Reich Minister.⁶⁴

What was the goal of the Nazis in taking over the Baltic states? The long-range goal, or the so-called *Ostplan*,⁶⁵ was the colonisation of the Baltic region, annexing it to the Reich, expelling two-thirds of the population, and assimilating the remainder gradually with German immigrants.⁶⁶ Since the immediate goal was to win the war, the major wave of deportations, immigration and denationalisation was to be started only after victory. Meanwhile, they wanted to use the Baltic area economically for the general pursuit of the war effort. The occupation administration directed its policy towards the accomplishment of this socio-economic plan, which reflected their attitude towards the Baltic peoples as providers of agricultural products and labour. The first attempts were made as early as the middle of July, 1941, with invitations for voluntary work in East Prussia. Later, this organisation of workers lost its voluntary character, becoming more extensive and more coercive. In December, 1941, the decree about general work obligation was issued for everybody aged between 18 and 45. Because the inhabitants of the Baltic states resisted this decree, the methods of labour mobilisation became forceful. In total about 125,000 Baltic workers were sent to Germany (approximately 75,000 Lithuanians, 35,000 Latvians and 15,000 Estonians) during the exaction of the labour force, which continued during the whole Nazi occupation. Besides the German aim to recruit extra labour, the Nazis organised the mobilisation also of military and

---

63. Tininis, *Sovietinė Lietuva ir jos veikėjai*, 21; Dauknys, *The Resistance of the Catholic Church*, 37.
64. Misiunas and Taagepera (eds.), *The Baltic States*, 44, 46-48; Dauknys, *The Resistance of the Catholic Church*, 37-38.
65. There were several different plans proposed, but they agreed on one broad outline. See Misiunas and Taagepera (eds.), *The Baltic States*, 47.
66. Misiunas and Taagepera (eds.), *The Baltic States*, 47; Tininis, *Sovietinė Lietuva ir jos veikėjai*, 25.

paramilitary units, or the so-called 'Defence Battalions' and 'Waffen-SS National Legions'. Facing a similar lack of volunteers, they used coercion to get the necessary recruits for the military and paramilitary units as well.[67] On top of their efforts to use the Baltic states economically and militarily, the Nazis continued their anti-Semitic policy against the Jewish citizens, who were present in differing numbers in all three countries. In order to exterminate the Jews, the Nazis charged around 1.000 men with this task and even established some concentration camps in the Baltic region.[68] The Nazis also used those camps for the ethnic Lithuanian, Latvian and Estonian professors, students, leaders and intellectuals in general. Approximately 25,000 of them were exterminated in the local concentration camps and about 10,000 were transferred to concentration camps in Germany.[69]

The coercive Nazi policy provoked opposition in all three Baltic states. Anti-Nazi resistance, although generally strong, was expressed mainly not in armed conflict but by the activity of political organisations and sabotage of occupation demands.[70] In addition to the opposition to the repression, another way to react towards the regime was

67. Misiunas and Taagepera (eds.), *The Baltic States*, 53-58.
68. The most notorious concentration camps were at Salaspils, near Rīga; at Klooga, near Tallin; the so called Ninth Fort, near Kaunas, and in Aukštieji Paneriai, outside of Vilnius. See Misiunas and Taagepera (eds.), *The Baltic States*, 59.
69. After the Soviet retreat in Estonia there were about 1.000 Jews, in Latvia about 70,000 Jews (Misiunas and Taagepera [eds.], *The Baltic States*, 58-62) and in Lithuania about 240,000 Jews (Solomonas Atamukas, *Lietuvos Žydų kelias: Nuo XIV amžiaus iki XX a. pabaigos* [The Journey of Lithuanian Jews from the 14th until the 20th centuries] [Vilnius: Alma Littera, 1998] 234-235). The reaction of the Baltic peoples towards Nazi anti-Semitic policy revealed discord between the majority, who did no harm to Jewish citizens, and supported them – some individual citizens, families and priests helped them by risking their own lives – and the minority, who organised the massacres of the Jews even before the systematic killing by the Nazis, or who assisted (either under compulsion or of their own free will) the Nazis in the extermination of the Jews. R. J. Misiunas and R. Taagepera try to explain the main motivations for the appearance of anti-Semitism in the Baltic states during the Nazi occupation. First, anti-Semitism was inherited from the Tsarist period when Jewish urban population was disproportionately represented in the professional and middle class; the second and more important reason was the deflection of anticommunist hostility towards the Jews, because, while small in actual membership Lithuanian and Latvian communist parties were disproportionately represented by Jews. (In early 1941 Jews comprised only about 7% of the population in Lithuania, but about 15% of the members of Lithuanian Communist Party. See Misiunas and Taagepera [eds.], *The Baltic States*, 60.) Besides that, there were numerous newly installed non-party officials of Jewish heritage. That led towards the identification of 'Soviet' with 'Jewish' by some Balts. Of course, these explanations are nothing more than trying to find the possible motives, which, however, do not condone the indiscriminate murder of Jews. See Misiunas and Taagepera (eds.), *The Baltic States*, 60-61.
70. Misiunas and Taagepera (eds.), *The Baltic States*, 66-67.

flight out of the country in order to escape the Nazi occupation. In this way, people were not only avoiding the present, Nazi occupation, but a possible second Soviet invasion as well.[71]

As we know, in Estonia, Latvia and Lithuania the Nazis installed their own political administration to use the countries both economically and militarily. They also strictly supervised religious affairs. However, as R. J. Misiunas and R. Taagepera put it, "the Nazis, unlike the Soviets, did not act on a perceived need to infuse them immediately with a particular ideological aura." The Nazi authorities' anti-religious repression was mostly their reaction towards the involvement of the people in national resistance and anti-Nazi activity.[72]

2. Nazi Policy towards Religion in Lithuania and the Reaction of the Church

After the end of the first Soviet occupation, the new provisional government had a chance to abrogate the laws and decisions of the Soviet government, and the Church was able to begin on the restoration of its activity. The seminaries as well as the faculty of theology at Kaunas University were reopened, religious instruction in schools was renewed, chaplains were again appointed to hospitals and prisons, and monks returned to their monasteries.[73] No wonder that, as A. Streikus puts it, Lithuanians and their neighbouring peoples perceived Nazis as liberators from the Bolshevics, or at least as a lesser evil than the Soviet regime. The leaders of the Lithuanian Catholic Church had a similar perception of the Nazi army's mission. For example, the government of the Kaunas archdiocese publicly expressed its sympathy to the German army for having liberated the land from the Soviet terror. On July 4, 1941, Kaunas' daily newspaper *Į laisvę* [To Freedom] contained a statement, signed by Archbishop J. Skvireckas, Bishop V. Brizgys and the prelate Kazimieras Šaulys, condemning the Bolshevist crimes, thanking the German army for liberating Lithuania, expressing the hope that freedom of faith would be respected and that the inhabitants of Lithuania would be invited to

---

71. In 1944, about 60,000 Lithuanians moved to the West. Among those people there were three bishops: J. Skvireckas, Vincentas Brizgys and Vincentas Padolskis, and 250 priests. See J. Savasis, *The War Against God in Lithuania* (New York: Manyland Books, 1966) 23; Vaišnora, "Nepriklausomybės ir okupaciniais laikais," 149.

72. Misiunas and Taagepera (eds.), *The Baltic States*, 52-53; See also Chélini, *L'Église sous Pie XII*, 158.

73. See A. Bružas, "Karo Metai [The War Years]," *Katalikų Pasaulis* [The Catholic World] 24 (1991) 18; Vaišnora, "Nepriklausomybės ir okupaciniais laikais," 149.

unite together to rebuild the Bolshevic-destroyed land. On the following day, in Kaunas' cathedral a *requiem* was celebrated for Lithuanian insurgents and for German soldiers, killed during the first days of war in Lithuania. Despite their anti-Christian and anti-Catholic ideology, the Nazis tried to use this mood of the people and of the Church for the Nazi propaganda during the war. As later disagreements between the Lithuanian Catholic Church and the Nazi occupying regime will show, however, the animosity towards Bolshevism was the only common point between the two sides. The Church and the larger part of the Lithuanian society appreciated only the Nazi-provided possibility to escape the Soviet regime. Otherwise, they had no common interests with the Nazist ideology and practice.[74]

After the establishment of the Nazi regime, it was not long before the first complications began in its relations with the Lithuanian Church. During its meeting on August 6-7, 1941, the Lithuanian Bishops' Conference prepared a request for the Nazi Commissar-General. The bishops asked the Nazis to stop interfering with religious teaching in the schools and to allow the apostolic nuncio to return to Lithuania. The Commissar-General, however, refused to receive the representatives of the Bishops' Conference. Soon the Nazis announced that there was only one weekly lesson of religious instruction permissible. The delegation of the following Lithuanian Bishops' Conference (October 7-8, 1941) to the Nazi Commissar-General intended to request the cessation of the terror against the Jews, but met the same fate.[75] On March, 22, 1942, the Gestapo arrested Vilnius' Archbishop R. Jalbrzykovski. In the summer of 1942, the Nazi Commissar-General ordered the salaries of teachers of religion, and of theology-philosophy faculty at Kaunas University to be cut off. Besides that, the Nazis kept church buildings and monasteries under surveillance, and closed some churches[76] as well as Vilnius' priestly seminary. Despite the Nazi anti-religious policy, neither the hierarchy of the Catholic Church nor the clergy ceased its activities or conceded to the oppressive decisions. After the arrest of Archbishop R. Jalbrzykowski, Bishop M. Reinys took over

---

74. Streikus, *Sovietų valdžios antibažnytinė politika*, 61, 66.
75. Bružas, "Karo metai," 18-20.
76. The Nazis tried to conceal the actual reasons and intentions of their repressive decisions. For example, in the winter of 1942, they closed some churches under the pretext of the danger of typhus epidemic, whereas theatres, cinemas and the other places of mass attendance were left open. See Arvydas Bružas, "Karo metai," 19; Vaišnora, *Nepriklausomybės ir okupaciniais laikais*, 149.

the ruling of Vilnius archdiocese. He succeeded in reopening Vilnius' seminary, which soon received as new rector Ladas Tulaba, the future rector of the Lithuanian college of St. Casimir in Rome.[77]

As we will see in the following sections, the intention of the Lithuanian Bishops' Conference of October 7-8, 1941, to request the Nazi Commissar-General the cessation of terror against the Jews was not the only Lithuanian initiative regarding Nazi anti-Semitic policy. This policy revealed 'extremes' in the country. On the one hand, a number of Lithuanian activists and even institutions participated in the extermination of the Jews.[78] The Lithuanian public and security police as well as some rural district officials and mayors contributed to the slaughter by collecting demographic data about the Lithuanian Jews, and later by arresting and transporting them to camps. Special responsibility fell on the chief of the public police, Vytautas Reivytis, who prepared and disseminated orders to arrest the Jews. An important role in the extermination was played by the so-called battalions of defence of national labour (*tautinio darbo apsaugos batalionai*). Twenty battalions were comprised of up to eight thousand men in total. Approximately half of those battalions participated in the extermination process. The battalion of Antanas Impulevičius was the most ruthless: it killed Jews not only in Lithuania but also in Belarusian territory.[79] On the other hand, Nazi anti-Semitic policy revealed the other 'extreme' in the country – those private citizens and individual families who helped Jews, harboured them as fugitives and in many cases were punished by the Nazis. A substantial part of the Lithuanian clergy also tried to help persecuted Jews in various ways, for example, by defending Jews through the message of homilies, housing them in shelters for children, or providing aid through the so-called Fund of Freedom. As a result, some of those priests were sent to concentration camps.[80] Apart from the 'extremes', the majority of Lithuanian inhabitants were against the extermination of Jews and nicknamed its Lithuanian participants pejoratively as *žydšaudžiai* – 'Jew-shooters'.[81]

---

77. Vasiliauskienė, "Arkivyskupo Mečislovo Reinio," 7.
78. Atamukas, *Lietuvos Žydų kelias*, 235.
79. *Naujausi nacių režimo nusikaltimų tyrimai Lietuvoje* [The Newest Investigation of Crimes of the Nazi Regime in Lithuania] (September 23, 2004) The International Commission for the Evaluation of the Crimes of the Nazi and Soviet Occupation Regimes in Lithuania. http://www.komisija.lt/lt/2_3.php#2081 (access July 12, 2005).
80. Dauknys, *The Resistance of the Catholic Church*, 38-39; Atamukas, *Lietuvos Žydų kelias*, 279; Savasis, *The War Against God in Lithuania*, 23.
81. *Holokaustas Lietuvoje* [Holocaust in Lithuania] Second World War 1939-1945. http://antraspasaulinis.vhost.lt/content.php?article.136 (access July 12, 2005).

What was the reaction of various Lithuanian authorities to the anti-Semitic policy? In July, 1941, the rector of Kaunas University, Antanas Purėnas, the Dean of the Construction Faculty, Steponas Kolupaila, medical practitioners Elena Kutorgienė, J. Staugaitis and V. Kairiūkštis, together with several other concerned persons, asked the Nazi authorities to stop the extermination of Jews. In response, the Nazis threatened the appellants with the same fate that awaited the Jews.[82] In the Summer of 1941, the former defence minister of the Lithuanian provisional government and former commander-in-chief of the Lithuanian army, Stasys Raštikis, also stood up for the Jews. After he had received a visit from a couple of Jewish officials, S. Raštikis addressed the Nazi commander and – in the name of the Lithuanian government and society – expressed concern and dissatisfaction about the persecution and extermination of Lithuanian Jews, as well as asking for the cessation of anti-Semitic actions. More than a year later, on September 9, 1942, former Lithuanian president, Kazys Grinius, together with the ministers of agriculture – priest Mykolas Krupavičius and Jonas Aleksa – in their joint memorandum to the Reich commissar-general in Lithuania and other Nazi officials noted that the Lithuanian nation was against the German colonisation of Lithuania and the measures taken against Lithuanian Jews. In response to the memorandum, M. Krupavičius and J. Aleksa were arrested and taken to a concentration camp. The elderly ex-president K. Grinius was deported to Suvalkija, a region inside the territory of Lithuania.[83]

As has already been mentioned, the Lithuanian Church authorities also intervened in favour of Jews. Having heard about the massacre, Archbishop J. Skvireckas, together with Bishop V. Brizgys, and the prelate K. Šaulys, expressed their protest to the Nazi Commissar-General by declaring that Jews were Lithuanian citizens and their killing was against all laws. On October 7-8, 1941, the Commissar-General refused to receive the previously-mentioned delegation of the Bishop's Conference and argued that the issue of the Jews concerned Germany and not Lithuania.[84] One day after the Nazi massacre in the ghetto of Kaunas, on October 28-29, 1941, the representative of the Lithuanian Bishops' Conference, Bishop V. Brizgys, addressed the Lithuanian Assessor-General, P. Kubiliūnas, and asked his intervention to stop the extermination of Jews.

---

82. Atamukas, *Lietuvos Žydų kelias*, 277.
83. *Ibid.*, 245.
84. Dauknys, *The Resistance of the Catholic Church*, 38-39.

Unfortunately, none of those appeals could stop anti-Semitic terror.[85] According to the data of a Lithuanian Jew and historian, Solomonas Atamukas, from 240,000 Jews who lived in Lithuania in June 1941, 170,000-180,000 were killed by the end of 1941 – beginning of 1942.[86]

After the Vatican had learned about the Nazist repression in Lithuania, it tried diplomatic action to help those arrested or deported. The Nazis mostly ignored the Vatican's efforts, however. The Vatican tried to guarantee the succession of the Church hierarchy and made some changes in the Lithuanian episcopacy. In June, 1942, Pius XII appointed Bishop Teofilius Matulionis[87] as successor to the recently deceased Bishop of Kaišiadorys, Juozas Kukta.[88] In August, 1942, through the nuntio in Berlin, the Vatican addressed the Lithuanian bishops, asking them to choose a candidate for the diocese of Telšiai as successor of the deceased bishop, Justinas Staugaitis.[89] The Vatican did not get any response from the Lithuanian bishops, however.[90] Therefore, on January 21, 1944, Pius XII himself appointed Bishop Vincentas Borisevičius[91] Bishop of Telšiai and nominated priest Pranciškus Ramanauskas, as his assistant bishop.[92] During the Nazi – as during the first Soviet – occupation, Pius XII showed his support by sending his heartening wishes and apostolic blessing to the Lithuanian bishops on specific occasions like anniversaries or illnesses. The Lithuanian seminarians received some theological books as the Pope's personal present.[93]

Meanwhile, the tension between the Nazis and the Lithuanian Church was growing. The Lithuanian Bishops' Conference of October 6-8, 1942, prepared a document concerning Church land, youth mobilisation for

85. Atamukas, *Lietuvos Žydų kelias*, 245.
86. *Ibid.*, 234-235.
87. T. Matulionis: b. July 4, 1873 (Kudoriškis, dioc. of Samogitia), ord. March 17, 1900, cons. February 9, 1929, impeded. See *Annuario Pontificio* (1950) 218.
88. J. Kukta: b. February 3, 1873 (Trakiniai, archdioc. of Kaunas), el. April 5, 1926. See *Annuario Pontificio* (1942) 173. V. Spengla indicated the year 1943 when Pius XII appointed bishop T. Matulionis to administer Kaišiadorys diocese instead of J. Kukta. See Vidas Spengla, "Skelbiau krikščionių tikėjimo tiesas ir moralę. Pagal vyskupo Teofiliaus Matulionio bylą KGB archyve [I Was Preaching the Truths and Morality of the Christian Faith. An Account Following the Case of Bishop Teofilius Matulionis in the KGB Archive]," *Katalikų pasaulis* [The Catholic World] 5 (1997) 12.
89. J. Staugaitis: b. November 17, 1866 (Tupikai, dioc. of Seinai), el. April 5, 1926. See *Annuario Pontificio* (1942) 279.
90. The response might have been hindered by the occupation regime.
91. V. Borisevičius: b. November 23, 1887 (Benbrinkai, dioc. of Vilkaviškis), ord. May 29, 1910, cons. March 10, 1940. See *Annuario Pontificio* (1948) 361.
92. Vaišnora, "Nepriklausomybės ir okupaciniais laikais," 149.
93. Viktoras Pavalkis, "Bažnyčia Lietuvoje ir Vatikanas 1940-1945 [The Church in Lithuania and the Vatican]," *Aidai* [Echoes] 6 (1973) 245-249.

labour to the Reich as well as restoration of the Catholic press and organisations. In response, several signatories of the document were punished by deportation to East Prussia. Besides the petitions, the hierarchy's protest and non-submission to the Nazi anti-religious repression were expressed by disobedience to their orders: in 1943 the Nazi government failed to get the Church's support for mobilisation of Lithuanians to the Nazi military subunits. By refusing the demand of the Chief of Kaunas' Gestapo to issue a pastoral letter asking Lithuanian youth to register into the SS (*Schutzstaffel*) legion, Kaunas' Archbishop J. Skvireckas hindered the Nazi attempt to organise the SS legion in Lithuania.[94] On February 20 the Chief of German Security Police, Karl Jäger, and *Untersturmführer* Paul Müller, responsible for the Catholic Church affairs in this establishment, visited the curia of Kaunas archdiocese. Following Bishop V. Brizgys, the witness of the meeting, Bishop J. Skvireckas told Nazi officials that their demand for clerical help for mobilisation was humiliating in regard to soldiers themselves: mobilisation was not a Church affair. Instead, J. Skvireckas expressed his expectation for the Nazi army to defeat the Bolshevic army and for the Church to try to defeat the Bolshevic spirit. A similar motive for the refusal to request priests' encouragement of the believers not to boycott mobilisation to the German military subunits was given by Archbishop M. Reinys.[95] Besides the Nazi attempt to form military units, the tension between the Church and the German government was increased by the Nazi decision to consolidate the carrying out of the registration of civilians. On July 12, 1943, Archbishop J. Skvireckas wrote to the commissar-general that the civil registering was nothing positive in the fight against Bolshevism. Instead, it sustained the remnants of the Bolshevic regime.[96]

From the beginning of their occupation, the Nazis had treated the Catholic Church in Lithuania rudely, disregarding its addresses and

---

94. Bružas, "Karo metai," 18-20; Dauknys, *The Resistance of the Catholic Church*, 38-39.

95. The Archbishop, in the meanwhile, was not only disobeying the Nazis, but also publicly expressed his anti-communist thoughts. During the Nazi occupation, the newspapers *Naujoji Lietuva* [New Lithuania] and *Karys* [Soldier] contained about ten of his articles, dedicated to the criticism of Bolshevism. Later, Archbishop M. Reinys' publicistic activity became one of the main accusations in the criminal case against him. Public pronouncements of other Church hierarchs were also often inspired by anti-communist criticism especially of its anti-religious convictions. Bishop V. Borisevičius' first pastoral letter to the believers of Telšiai diocese, publicised on August 8, 1943, was dedicated solely to this topic. See Streikus, *Sovietų valdžios antibažnytinė politika*, 63-65; Zugger, *The Forgotten*, 344.

96. Streikus, *Sovietų valdžios antibažnytinė politika*, 65.

applications. However, because there was no sign of widespread anti-Nazi resistance based on religious establishments, the occupation authorities did not hurry to carry out open and violent repression. Due to various disagreements, however, the tension between the Lithuanian Catholic Church and the Nazi policy grew steadily worse. Finally, in 1943, the firm stand of the Church on certain issues became unacceptable to the Nazis, and they began open and violent repression by closing the universities, arresting 46 eminent Lithuanian intellectuals, with two priests among them, and arresting people by taking them straight from the churches.[97]

IV. From Nazi Occupation to Soviet Annexation

This wave of Nazi violence did not last: the summer of 1944 brought the Nazi occupation to an end, leaving the *Ostplan* unfulfilled. The Bishop Conference's decision to convoke the second Lithuanian Eucharistic Congress in summer 1944 failed too. In view of the Congress that was meant to revive spiritual life suppressed by the occupations, a preparatory committee was established, a pastoral letter, signed by all Lithuanian bishops, was published, and a project of the Lithuanian Catholic greeting to Pius XII was prepared. The war front approached faster than expected, however, and the Congress did not take place.[98] From July 1944 on, the battle raged in the movements of the front-line and in Lithuania itself. Each belligerent took along in its retreat the populations that were at the scenes of operation. 200,000 Lithuanians were transported to Germany, some of whom preferred this transfer to falling under Soviet rule again. While the front-line was approaching and the Soviets were returning, thousands of Lithuanians fled to the West, together with three bishops, J. Skvireckas, V. Brizgys and V. Padolskis, and approximately 250 priests.[99] Just as the first Soviet occupation had been stopped by the war events, so did the Nazi occupation: the Soviet army gradually pushed out the Nazis and reoccupied the countries.[100] After the three years of Nazi occupation (summer 1941 – autumn 1944,

---

97. Bružas, "Karo metai," 18, 20; Dauknys, *The Resistance of the Catholic Church*, 38; Misiunas and Taagepera (eds.), *The Baltic States*, 52-53.
98. Streikus, *Sovietų valdžios antibažnytinė politika*, 65-66.
99. Chélini, *L'Église sous Pie XII*, 159; Vaišnora, "Nepriklausomybės ir okupaciniais laikais," 149.
100. Chélini, *L'Église sous Pie XII*, 157. Since November, 1942, the Nazi army was gradually thrown back from the territory of the Soviet Union.

while a part of Lithuania was already re-occupied by the Soviet army in July 1944), all three Baltic states were exhausted by war and occupation as well as losing approximately 20% of their population.[101]

After the Nazi occupation the activity of the Lithuanian Catholic Church was considerably restrained. Nevertheless, according to some sources, the situation of the Catholic Church in Lithuania was better during the Nazi occupation than during the first Soviet occupation.[102] Generally, as G. Adriányi puts it, "die dreijährige deutsche Besetzung Litauens (...) während des Zweiten Weltkrieges bedeutete nur eine Atempause, denn mit der zweiten Besetzung Litauens durch die Sowjetarmee (1944) kehrten die früheren Verhältnisse wieder ein."[103] Some facts point to greater religious freedom during the Nazi occupation in comparison to the first Soviet occupation. For example, the Nazis restricted but did not suppress the teaching of religion, nor did they ban chaplains' work in prisons, hospitals and schools. Nevertheless, even during the period that G. Adriányi termed as "Atempause", the Lithuanian Catholic Church and the nation itself faced the problem of survival. Besides that, the greater religious freedom can be explained by the war situation, when the Nazis had other priorities.

Selective Bibliography

Gabriel Adriányi, *Geschichte der Kirche Osteuropas im 20. Jahrhundert* (Paderborn/München/Wien/Zürich: Ferdinand Schöningh, 1992).
Solomonas Atamukas, *Lietuvos Žydų kelias: Nuo XIV amžiaus iki XX a. pabaigos* [The Journey of Lithuanian Jews from the 14th until the 20th centuries] (Vilnius: Alma Littera, 1998).
Trevor Beeson, *Discretion and Valour: Religious Conditions in Russia and Eastern Europe*, Fontana Books, 27 (Glasgow: Collins, 1975).
Vincentas Brizgys, *Katalikų Bažnyčia Lietuvoje: Pirmoje rusų okupacijoje 1940-1941 M. Vokiečių okupacijoje 1941-1944 M.* [The Catholic Church in Lithuania: The First Russian Occupation 1940-1941. The German Occupation 1941-1944] (Chicago: Draugo, 1977).

101. In total more than 200,000 inhabitants of Lithuania were killed during the Nazi occupation. See Tininis, *Sovietinė Lietuva ir jos veikėjai*, 23.
102. For example, following V. Vaišnora, during the Nazi occupation the situation of the Catholic Church was slightly easier (Vaišnora, "Nepriklausomybės ir okupaciniais laikais," 149). "Bien que les trois années de l'occupation allemande (1941-1944) ne furent pas aussi cruelles, néanmoins elles furent pour notre peuple un véritable chemin de Croix." Kaslas, *La Lithuanie et la Seconde Guerre Mondiale*, 206.
103. Gabriel Adriányi, *Geschichte der Kirche Osteuropas im 20. Jahrhundert* (Paderborn/München/Wien/Zürich: Ferdinand Schöningh, 1992) 37.

Jean Chélini, *L'Église sous Pie XII: La tourmente (1939-1945)* (Paris: Fayard, 1983).
"Communism's Struggle with Religion in Lithuania," *Lituanus* 9 (1963) no. 1, 2-17.
Pranas Dauknys, *The Resistance of the Catholic Church in Lithuania against Religious Persecution*. Dissertatio ad Lauream in facultate S. Theologiae apud Pontificiam Universitatem S. Thomae de Urbe (Rome, 1984).
Holokaustas Lietuvoje [Holocaust in Lithuania] Second World War 1939-1945. http://antraspasaulinis.vhost.lt/content.php?article.136 (access July 12, 2005).
Boris Iwanow (ed.), *Religion in the USSR*, Institute for the Study of the USSR, Series I, 59 (Munich, 1960).
Bronis Kaslas, *La Lithuanie et la Seconde Guerre Mondiale: Recueil des documents* (Paris: G. P. Maisonneuve et Larose, 1981).
Vilius Kavaliauskas, *Suokalbis* [Plot] (Vilnius: Lituanus, 1989).
Walter Kolarz, *Religion in the Soviet Union* (London/New York: Macmillan/St. Martin's Press, 1961).
Regina Laukaitytė, *Lietuvos vienuolijos XX amžiuje* [Lithuanian Monastic Orders in the 20th Century]. Lietuvos Istorijos Institutas [Lithuanian Historical Institute] (2002). http://vienuolijos.iwebland.com (access June 25, 2004).
Romuald J. Misiunas and Rein Taagepera (eds.), *The Baltic States: Years of Dependence 1940-1980. Estonia, Latvia, Lithuania* (London: C. Hurst & Co., 1983).
Vilma Narkutė, *Catholicism versus Communism: The Confrontation between the Roman Catholic Church and the Soviet Regime in the Case of Lithuania (1940-1978)* (unpublished doctoral dissertation, Faculty of Theology, K.U.Leuven, Leuven, 2005).
Naujausi nacių režimo nusikaltimų tyrimai Lietuvoje [The Newest Investigation of Crimes of the Nazi Regime in Lithuania] (September 23, 2004) The International Commission for the Evaluation of the Crimes of the Nazi and Soviet Occupation Regimes in Lithuania. http://www.komisija.lt/lt/2_3.php#2081 (access July 12, 2005).
Viktoras Pavalkis, "Bažnyčia Lietuvoje ir Vatikanas 1940-1945 [The Church in Lithuania and the Vatican]", *Aidai* [Echoes] 6 (1973) 245-249.
Gediminas Rudis (ed.), *Lietuvos gyventojų trėmimai 1941, 1945-1952 m.* [The Deportations of Lithuanian Inhabitants, 1941 and 1945-1952] (Vilnius: Mokslo ir enciklopedijų leidykla, 1994).
J. Savasis, *The War against God in Lithuania* (New York: Manyland Books, 1966).
"Selected Documentary Material on the Lithuanian Resistance Movement against Totalitarianism 1940-1960," *Lituanus* 8 (1962) nos. 1-2, 41-60.
Hansjakob Stehle, *Eastern Politics of the Vatican, 1917-1979*, trans. Sandra Smith (Athens, OH/London: Ohio University Press, 1981).
Arūnas Streikus, *Sovietų valdžios antibažnytinė politika Lietuvoje (1944-1990)* [The Anti-Church Policy of the Soviet Government in Lithuania, 1944-1990] (Vilnius: Lietuvos gyventojų genocido ir rezistencijos tyrimo centras, 2002).

Vytautas Tininis, *Sovietinė Lietuva ir jos veikėjai* [Soviet Lithuania and its Statesmen] (Vilnius: Enciklopedija, 1994).
K. Valančius, *Lietuvos Valstybės Konstitucijos* [The Constitutions of the Lithuanian State] (Vilnius, 1989).
Christopher Lawrence Zugger, *The Forgotten: Catholics of the Soviet Empire from Lenin through Stalin* (Syracuse, NY: Syracuse University Press, 2001).

Catholicism in the Low Countries During the Second World War
Belgium and the Netherlands:
a Comparative Approach

Lieve Gevers

Belgium and the Netherlands, known as the 'Low countries', have in part a common, and in part a very divergent history. In the 15th century they evolved into a kind of political unity as the 'Seventeen provinces' within the Duchy of Burgundy. From the second half of the 16th century the religious wars drove them apart. The Northern part became an independent Protestant dominated country, the 'United Dutch provinces', the Catholic 'Southern Netherlands' remained incorporated in the Habsburg Empire. After the fall of Napoleon, from 1815 till 1830, the great powers united these two territories again in the 'United Kingdom of the Netherlands', governed by the King of Orange, William I. The religious and cultural differences that had grown between the Northern and the Southern Netherlands throughout the centuries, seemed nonetheless too strong to allow such a union. In 1830 the people of the South, the Belgians, argued for their independence and established their own nation, the Kingdom of Belgium. Since then Belgium and the Netherlands became two separate nations, although mutual contacts and influences continued to exist to a certain extent.

I. Introduction

This essay will be focused on the situation and the attitude of the Catholic population and Church in both countries at the time of the Second World War. It is conceived as a comparative study, based on the actual research. We will mainly deal with the institutional-political developments: the religious policy of the German occupier and the reactions towards the war events by the Catholic Episcopal hierarchy, in particular by its primates, Cardinal-Archbishop Jozef Ernest Van Roey in Belgium and Archbishop Johannes de Jong in the Netherlands. We will also deal with the evolution of the political position of Catholicism. This approach offers the best starting point for a comparative approach and is also the most heavily studied topic. To a lesser extent we will also pay attention to the attitude of the clergy and the Catholic population. However, religious life will only be touched upon in this essay, since scientific research on this question is still very limited and disparate.

A chronological treatment seems to be the best approach because the war events offer the logical framework for our exposé. We will start with a description of the historical context: the installation of the occupying regime and the position of the Roman Catholic Church in the pre-war society. We will then turn to the evolving phases during the war. Finally, we will look at developments in the immediate aftermath of the war period, as far as they can be perceived as after-effects of the war. Our comparative study of Belgium and the Netherlands should make clear the similarities and differences between both countries. We will try to elucidate these in our conclusion.

II. The Occupation

After the invasion and a short period of fighting (the campaign lasted for 18 days) the Belgian King Leopold III accepted the capitulation on May 28th 1940. A few days earlier the Belgian government had fled the country and left Belgium under the leadership of the highest officials in the ministry departments, the Secretary Generals. This caused a heavy conflict with the King. Indeed, the government wanted to pursue the struggle from abroad together with the other allies. The King on the other hand refused to accompany the government: he wanted to stay in the country, take a neutral stance and share, as he said, the fate of his soldiers and people. Hitler placed Belgium under a military regime, the *Militärverwaltung*. The SS had no formal direct power over the country, but Himmler succeeded gradually to gain political and police control. Meanwhile though, the Belgian administrative structures remained intact, with most public servants, mayors and policemen keeping their positions under the leadership of the Secretary Generals. According to international law (Convention of The Hague) they were bound to loyal co-operation with the occupier as far as its directives did not affect national legislation. In this state of tension many Belgian authorities adhered to a policy which is generally called 'the policy of the lesser evil', which intended to preserve as much as possible of the national identity, but also involved compromises with the occupying regime.[1]

The situation in the Netherlands differed from the Belgian in several ways. Since the Netherlands had not been involved in the First World War the German invasion (as in Belgium on May 10th 1940) caused complete consternation among the Dutch rulers and population. Since the 19th century the idea of neutrality had been deeply rooted in the society producing a misleading feeling of security. The Dutch Queen Wilhelmina launched a fierce protest against the German invaders and fled the country together with her government, after the quick defeat (within five days) of the Dutch troops. The Germans established a civilian regime, a *Zivilverwaltung*, headed by *Reichskommissar* A. Seyss-Inquart, on which the Nazi-party and the SS had a direct influence. He governed the country with four other *Kommissare*. On the other hand, similar to Belgium, the lower governmental and judicial levels were kept intact in the hands of the Dutch and continued to function as before. Due to that, as well as to the relatively friendly behaviour of the Germans in the first months of the occupation, and the seemingly unavoidable German victory, the majority of the population tried to pursue their usual way of life as well as they could, once they had overcome their fear of the first moments of invasion. They tended, as in Belgium, to an attitude of acceptance and to accommodation to the new situation.[2]

III. The Catholic Church before the War

What was the position of the Catholic Churches in the given context? For a better understanding of this position we refer briefly to the pre-war period. The Belgian Church was a firmly established institution and had a strong moral power. The ecclesiastical structure contained six

---

1. Herman Balthazar, "België onder Duitse bezetting 10 mei 1940-8 september 1944," *Algemene Geschiedenis der Nederlanden*, 15 (Haarlem: Fibula-Van Dishoeck, 1982) 29-51; Etienne Verhoeyen, *België bezet, 1940-1944: Een synthese* (Brussel: BRTN-Instructieve Omroep, 1993) 9-84.
2. J. C. H. Blom, "Nederland onder Duitse bezetting 10 mei 1940-5 mei 1945," *Algemene Geschiedenis der Nederlanden*, 15, 55-61; J. C. H. Blom, *Crisis, bezetting en herstel: Tien studies over Nederland 1930-1950* (Den Haag: Universitaire Pers Rotterdam, 1989) 56-64.

dioceses: Brugge (Bruges) and Gent in the northern, Flemish (Dutch-speaking) part of the country, Namur and Tournai in the southern Walloon (French-speaking) part of the country and furthermore two dioceses which covered a part of both Flanders and Wallonia: Liège and Mechelen (Malines). Mechelen, situated in the centre of the country, was an archdiocese, governed by the Primate of the Belgian church province, Cardinal-Archbishop Van Roey. Catholicism was the very predominant religion in Belgium; in 1920 still 98% of the people were baptized, though not every one of them was a practising Catholic. Only about 0.5 to 1% was Protestant and other religions were even smaller. The relationship between the Catholic Church and the State was a favourable one. The Church was on the one hand independent and free of state control, but on the other hand enjoyed state support, for instance in the payment of the clergy. Secular and regular clergy were strongly established. They recruited largely from the widespread network of Catholic educational institutions as well as from different thriving Catholic youth movements, especially in Flanders. Catholicism had indeed a stronger hold in Flanders, with a rural background than in traditionally more industrialized Wallonia. The strong position of the Catholic Church was also reflected in politics. Since the last quarter of the 19th century the Catholic party governed the country. As a consequence of the introduction of universal suffrage though, Catholics had to share their power with other parties in coalition governments from 1921 on.[3]

Notwithstanding its apparent strength, the Catholic institute was constantly being threatened from outside as well from inside. Since the 19th century the Church had been challenged by a hostile anticlerical Liberalism and the rise of Socialism. In the interwar period a new danger came from ultra-nationalist, right wing and new order tendencies. Some sections of Catholic opinion were attracted to those movements to such extent that they began to organize themselves in separate political parties that thus affected a unified Catholic political front. In Flanders, this threat came from a radical minority wing in the predominantly Catholic Flemish movement. Since the 1920's Flemish nationalists had propagated a separatist anti-Belgian order, and evolved further in the 1930's in an anti-democratic and fascist direction. This tendency found its political expression in the 'Verbond van Dietsche Nationaal Solidaristen' (Verdinaso, League of Old Dutch National Solidarists), established in 1931, and in the (more influential) 'Vlaamsch Nationaal Verbond' (VNV, Flemish

---

3. Roger Aubert, *150 ans de vie des églises* (Bruxelles: Paul Legrain, 1980).

National League), established in 1933. In the French-speaking part of the country the danger came from the Rexist party. The Rex movement had emerged from the integral-Catholic, anti-Liberal and corporate tendency within the Catholic Action and evolved to a new order formation, which led in 1935 to a conflict and a break with the Catholic party.

The bishops counteracted these Catholic dissident movements. In 1936, after the overwhelming elective success of the extremist parties they pronounced a common statement in which they condemned both Communism and right wing totalitarianism and stressed that democracy was the best regime to guarantee liberty for the Church. By doing this they weakened not only VNV and Rex but also the position of the promoters of a more authoritarian and corporate society model within the Catholic Party itself. The bishops, in contrast, supported the Christian democratic tendency within the party and the Christian Workers movement. The issuing of the papal encyclical *Mit brennender Sorge* in 1937 and the speech of the Belgian Cardinal-Archbishop in 1938, which underscored the irreconcilable relationship between Christianity and the racist Nazi ideology, contributed further to the reinforcement of the Christian democratic tendency within Belgian Catholic opinion. So, on the eve of the war, the Catholic hierarchy in Belgium turned down a new order regime out of motives of both church interests as well as a rejection in principle of the Nazi ideology.[4]

In the Netherlands the Catholic Church held a strong minority position in a Protestant dominated country.[5] In 1930 about 36.5% of the

---

4. Griet Van Haver, *Onmacht der verdeelden: Katholieken in Vlaanderen tussen demokratie en fascisme 1929-1940* (Berchem: EPO, 1983); Emmanuel Gerard, *De Katholieke partij in crisis: Partijpolitiek leven in België (1918-1940)* (Leuven: Kritak, 1985); Lode Wils, *Honderd jaar Vlaamse beweging*. 2: *Geschiedenis van het Davidsfonds 1914 tot 1936* (Leuven: Davidsfonds, 1985); Lode Wils, *Honderd jaar Vlaamse beweging*. 3: *Geschiedenis van het Davidsfonds in en rond Wereldoorlog II* (Leuven: Davidsfonds, 1989); Emmanuel Gerard, "Aanpassing in crisistijd (1921-1944)," *De christelijke arbeidersbeweging in België 1891-1991*, ed. Emmanuel Gerard, vol. 1, Kadoc-Studies, 11 (Leuven: Universitaire Pers, 1991) 172-243; Lieve Gevers, "Voor God, vaderland en moedertaal: Kerk en natievorming in België, 1830-1940," *Cahiers d'histoire du temps présent: Bijdragen tot de eigentijdse geschiedenis* 3 (1999) 27-53.

5. The paragraphs on the Netherlands in the interwar period mainly based on: L. J. Rogier, *Katholieke herleving: Geschiedenis van katholiek Nederland sinds 1853* ('s-Gravenhage: Pax, 1956) 540-580; L. M. H. Joosten, *Katholieken & fascisme in Nederland, 1920-1940* (Utrecht: Hes Publishers, ²1982); J. A. Bornewasser, *Katholieke Volkspartij 1945-1980*. Band I: *Herkomst en groei (tot 1963)* (Nijmegen: Valkhof Pers, 1995) 7-106; J. P. de Valk, *Roomser dan de paus? Studies over de betrekkingen tussen de Heilige Stoel en het Nederlands katholicisme 1815-1940* (Nijmegen: Valkhof Pers, 1998) 307-335; Paul Luykx, *Andere katholieken: Opstellen over Nederlandse katholieken in de twintigste eeuw* (Nijmegen: SUN, 2000) 9-41, 62-76, 117-150, 211-283.

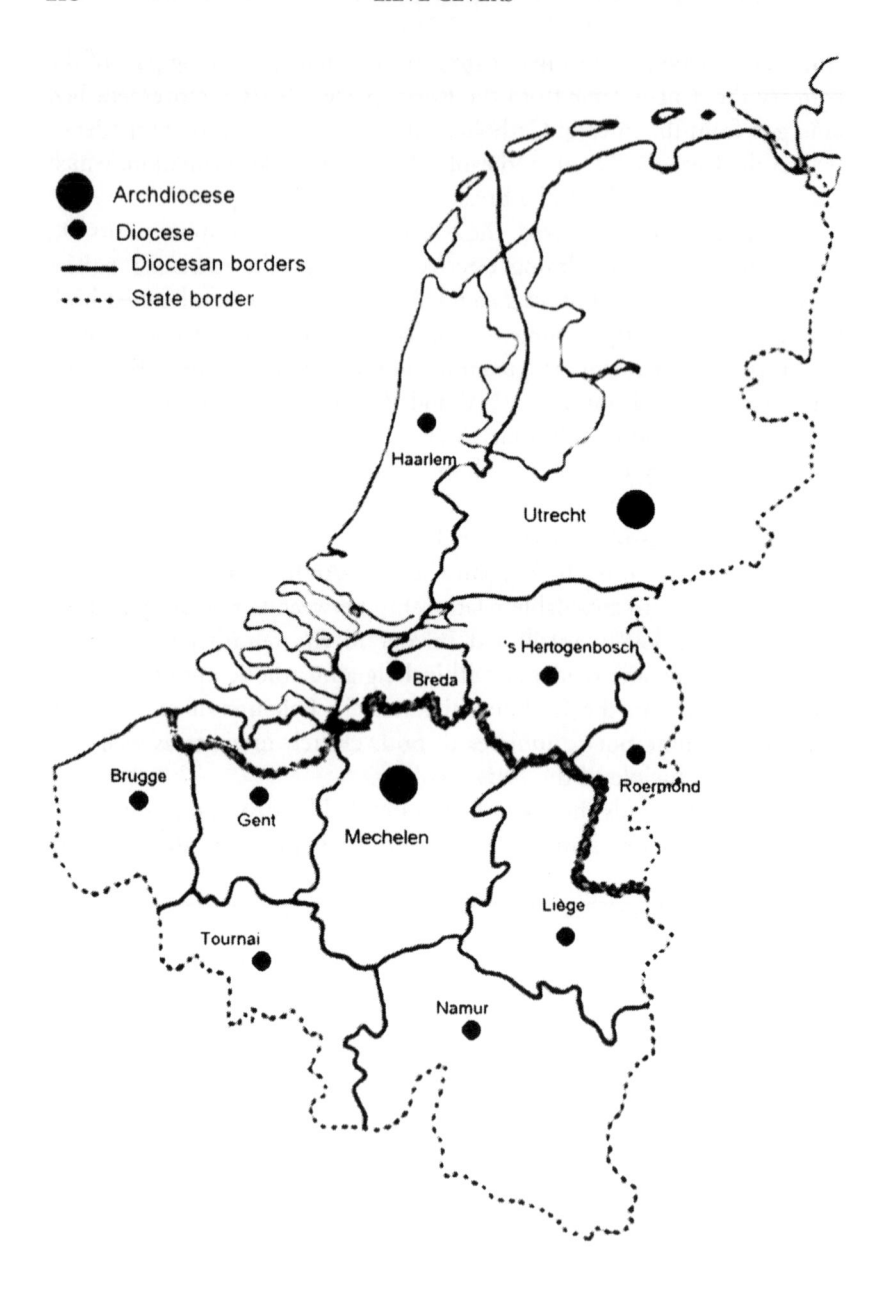

Dioceses in Belgium and the Netherlands

population was Catholic, 48% Protestant, 1.5 belonged to non-Christian religions and 14% was non-religious. Catholics lived predominantly in the Southern part of the country, beneath the large rivers of the Rhine and Meuse, mainly the provinces of Brabant and Limburg. Since the re-establishment of the Catholic hierarchy in 1853 the Dutch Church province consisted of five dioceses: Haarlem, Breda, Den Bosch ('s-Hertogenbosch), Roermond and the archdiocese of Utrecht, governed since 1935 by Archbishop De Jong. In the 19th century the Church had been characterized by a strong ultramontane Roman-oriented tendency. At the same time they were loyal to the fatherland and to the monarchy, notwithstanding the suspicious perception of their Protestant co-citizens. Since the end of the 19th century they had tried to overcome their feeling of being discriminated against by the establishment of a network of educational, cultural and social-economic institutions. As in Belgium, Catholic Action contributed to a further strengthening of this Catholic subsystem in the interwar period, especially among the youth.

The Catholic social organizations held a corporative view on society, according to the papal encyclical *Rerum Novarum*. It was seen as an alternative to both the Liberal and Socialist answers to capitalism. Due to their resentment towards the liberal system the bishops and Catholic conservative leaders objected until the beginning of the 20th century to the Church's participation in political life. Only after the introduction of universal suffrage in 1917 was the 'Roomsch Katholieke Staatspartij' (RKSP, Roman Catholic State Party) established. Until the 1950's the bishops and the Catholic leadership succeeded in imposing the 'holy' duty to vote for this party on the great majority of the Catholic population.

The need to form a unified political bloc was a factor of stability in the 1930's because it prevented the emergence of important dissident political movements among the Catholic population. In 1933 the bishops strengthened the already existing predominant fierce anti-Communist stance of their flock by repeated condemnation of Socialism and Communism: people voting for those parties would no longer receive sacraments. In 1934 and 1936 the bishops uttered the same warnings against Catholics who wished to support the 'Nationaal Socialistische Beweging' (NSB, National Socialist Movement), being the only extreme right-wing party in the Netherlands with a significant electoral success in those years (8% in 1935). As a consequence the NSB failed to gain a substantial electoral basis among the Catholic population. Admittedly there was some Catholic support for extreme right wing National Socialist groupings in the 1930's. Relatively, the most important of these was the 'Zwart Front' (Black Front), in the first months of 1940: renamed the 'Nationaal Front' (National Front), a political formation recruiting mainly among Catholic intellectuals. It propagated anti-Semitism and an authoritarian-corporate state, but it remained so marginal that it never gained a seat in the parliament. The bishops never condemned the National Front because they didn't perceive it as a real danger. The dissident threat among Catholics came more from left-wing tendencies, which gathered their forces in 1933 in the 'Katholiek-Democratische Partij' (Catholic-Democratic Party) and reacted against the shortcomings in the social policy of the Catholic Party. This danger was countered in 1936 by the order of the leadership of the Catholic labour movement to vote for the Catholic Party. In short: the unity of the Catholic party was never seriously threatened.

The question remains whether in the 1930's the democratic parliamentary system was contested from inside the Catholic party. Wasn't the Catholic preference for corporatism leverage for support of fascism? Regarding this issue authors point at the difference that should be made between social and political corporatism. Proposals of some Catholic politicians, such as C. Romme in the 1930's, for a corporate-authoritarian reorganization of the state remained unanswered in a broader Catholic circle. The mainstream of the Catholic politicians and population continued to support a "strong and sound democracy" over a dictatorial system. On the other hand the tendency to social corporatism was even enhanced by the encyclical *Quadragesimo anno* in 1931. It was successful in establishing consultation structures in economic life. But they had little to do with fascist ideology because they were meant to function in the private sphere, with no the interference from the state. In fact, Catholics mostly adhered to a kind of religious inspired totalitarianism that offered an alternative to the totalitarian systems of Communism and National Socialism. It was not political, but spiritual in nature, and led to mobilization campaigns in order to regain the world for Christ as the 'Actie voor God' in the Netherlands and the anti-Communist offensive movement in Flanders.

IV. Accommodation, Expectation and Presence

During the first year of the Belgian occupation the relationship between the Belgian church authorities and the occupying regime was characterized by a kind of mutual reservation and a willingness not to offend each other.[6] The Germans feared the Church and its influence. Church authorities and clergy could continue to perform their duties and religious activities could continue, in so far as they were not disturbed by war events. On the other hand the occupying regime did restrain public activities of the Church, such as processions and other religious manifestations. The bishops in their turn also tried to avoid irritating the Germans in order to protect their well established institution. They tended at the same time, as most of the clergy did, to ignore the occupying force as far as possible. Therefore, at the beginning of the occupation direct clashes between the church authorities and the occupier were limited: a first conflict swirled around the appointment of professors at the Catholic University of Leuven (Louvain), a second around the celebration of the national holiday on July 21st. In both cases Van Roey did not give in to the German demands and the Germans resigned themselves to the situation.

There was a very close relationship between Cardinal Van Roey and Leopold III. In his first pastoral letter after the invasion (issued in May 1940) Van Roey defended the decision of the King to remain in the country and urged his flock to prayer and acceptance of the situation. His colleague of Liège, Bishop Louis-Joseph Kerkhofs spread quite another message at the same time. He expressed his sympathy with the Belgian government continuing to resist the occupier from abroad. At the same time the Cardinal seemed to have hoped in the first year of occupation and in the light of the overwhelming and seemingly permanent victory of Germany, just as the King did, that Belgium and its Church would be enabled to continue to play a certain political role within the new order framework of a Europe dominated by Germany. He was informed about the royal project for a revision of the constitution in order to create a

6. Main works on the Catholic Church in Belgium on which the next paragraphs are based: *Le Cardinal Van Roey et l'occupation allemande en Belgique: Actes et documents publiés par le chanoine Leclef* (Bruxelles: Ad. Goemaere, 1945); *Le diocèse de Tournai sous l'occupation allemande par les professeurs du séminaire de Tournai* (Tournai: Casterman, 1946); Alain Dantoing, "La hiérarchie catholique et la Belgique sous l'occupation allemande," *Revue du Nord* 60, no. 237 (avril-mai 1978) 311-330; Joseph Kempeneers, *Le Cardinal Van Roey et l'Ordre nouveau* (Gembloux: Duculot, 1982); Rudi Van Doorslaer, "De Kerk en de katholieke zuil in de Tweede Wereldoorlog," *Kultuurleven: Maandblad voor kultuur en samenleving* 55, no. 9 (1988) 791-797; Etienne Verhoeyen, "Tussen verzet en collaboratie: Katholieken onder Duitse bezetting," *Kultuurleven: Maandblad voor kultuur en samenleving* 55, no. 9 (1988) 787-790; Alain Dantoing, *La 'collaboration' du Cardinal: L'Église de Belgique dans la guerre 40* (Bruxelles: De Boeck, 1991); Robrecht Boudens, *Kardinaal Van Roey en de Tweede Wereldoorlog* (Averbode: Altiora, 1997); Fabrice Maerten, Frans Selleslagh and Mark Van den Wijngaert (eds.), *Entre la peste et le choléra: Vie et attitudes des catholiques belges sous l'occupation* (Gerpinnes: Quorum, 1999).

semi-autonomous, neutral and Catholic inspired Belgian authoritarian regime under the leadership of the King and he very probably seems to have supported that idea. The same concern for an active role of the church within the new order structures became apparent when Van Roey did not object to the decision of the Flemish wing of the Christian trade union in November 1940 to join the unified new order trade union, the 'Unie van Hand- en Geestesarbeiders' (UHGA, Union of Manual and Intellectual Workers), in order to keep its power position on the social front. But the hope for a kind of active role within the new structures was soon destroyed when Germany gradually made more manifest its desire for complete control. The royal plan was deadlocked by Hitler in November 1940.

The attitude of the Belgian church authorities in the first year of the war can be evaluated as tending mostly to accommodation and presence. In this policy two motives were prevalent: the protection of the interests and the power position of the church as well as a deep attachment to the King and the Belgian nation. In fact, the bishops maintained this attitude until the end of the war. But gradually, as German repressive power grew stronger and the war events took another course, the feeling of resignation and acceptance that was prevalent in the first months of the war made way for a firmer antagonist stance.

As in Belgium, so the church structures and the ecclesiastical activities in the Netherlands were left intact after the invasion.[7] The Germans avoided open conflict with the churches because they feared it could have repercussions on the population. The attitude of the Catholic bishops in the first months of the occupation was comparable to that of other administrative, political and ecclesiastical authorities: they took a stance of reserved, moderate and expectant accommodation to the new

---

7. Main works on the attitude of the Catholic Church in the Netherlands in the Second World War used in next paragraphs: S. Stokman, *Het verzet van de Nederlandsche bisschoppen tegen nationaal-socialisme en Duitse tyrannie: Herderlijke brieven, instructies en andere documenten* (Utrecht: Spectrum, 1945); S. Stokman, *De katholieke arbeidersbeweging in oorlogstijd* (Utrecht/Brussel: Spectrum, 1946); H. W. F. Aukes, *Kardinaal de Jong* (Antwerpen/Utrecht: Spectrum, 1956); Rogier, *Katholieke herleving*, 580-603; L. de Jong, *Het koninkrijk der Nederlanden in de Tweede Wereldoorlog*, 14 vols. ('s-Gravenhage/Leiden: Martinus Nijhoff, 1969-1994), *passim*; A. F. Manning, "De Nederlandse katholieken in de eerste jaren van de Duitse bezetting," *Jaarboek Katholiek Documentatiecentrum* 18 (1978) 105-129; Blom, *Crisis, bezetting en herstel*, 56-163; J. M. Snoek, *De Nederlandse kerken en de joden 1940-1945: De protesten bij Seyss-Inquart. Hulp aan joodse onderduikers. De motieven voor hulpverlening* (Kampen: J. H. Kok, 1990); Ton H. M. van Schaik, *Aartsbisschop in oorlogstijd: Een portret van kardinaal De Jong (1885-1955)* (Baarn: Gooi en Sticht, 1996) 41-72; Luykx, *Andere katholieken*, 284-313.

authorities. They tried to proceed in the normal way. Their first concern was to keep intact the established network of Catholic organizations. The primate of Utrecht, Archbishop De Jong, refused to react in a forthcoming way to the first public conciliatory statement of *Reichskommissar* Seyss Inquart in June 1940. On the other hand, in that same summer the bishops and the Catholic Party remained remarkably silent about the Catholic support for the 'Nederlandsche Unie' (Dutch Union). This new political formation, founded in July 24 1940, can be considered as a form of aggressive and active accommodation. In the given context it wanted to create a new élan and solidarity among the Dutch people in order to establish an organic Dutch society. The 'Nederlandsche Unie' was not in favour of collaboration with the Germans and even detested the 'traitors' of the NSB but it wanted to guarantee a respectable position for the fatherland in a German ruled society. In December 1941 the 'Nederlandsche Unie' was to be dissolved by the Germans who had been unable to force it to take a more pro-German direction. Many members of the Union then joined the resistance. However, in the first months of its existence, the new party scored an overwhelming success, especially in the Catholic provinces of Brabant and Limburg. It was an expression of the latent frustrations among the population from the period before the war, as well as regarding the backward position of those Catholic regions within the central administration in Holland as regarding the feeling that the worn out democratic institutions no longer functioned as they should.

The lack of clear episcopal guidance in the first months of the war, to which people had been accustomed for decades, made them turn away from the traditional Catholic party and make their own political choice for the 'Nederlandsche Unie'. The bishops did not condemn such a choice. But they were soon aware of the danger it could involve. Yet on August 20th 1940 they warned their clergy that no Catholic organizations could be dissolved without their permission. They were not prepared to sacrifice the hard-earned established network of Catholic organizations on the altar of a 'national solidarity on a broader base'. The preservation of the Catholic organizational structure would remain one of their first concerns during the whole course of the war. Till the end of 1940, however, this did not involve a rejection of the idea that Catholic organizations could accommodate to the New Order structures. Indeed, in October and November 1940 Catholic social organizations such as the 'Algemeene Katholieke Werkgevers Vereeniging' (AKWV, General Catholic Union of Employers) and the 'Roomsch-

Katholiek Werkliedenverbond' (RKWV, Roman Catholic Union of Workers) were still considering their loyal cooperation in a corporate German dominated society, with the restriction though that they wanted to retain their Catholic identity.

V. Increasing Antagonism

Notwithstanding their tendency to accommodation, the Belgian bishops took a firmly hostile stance towards the collaboration movements from the first year of the war. In Flanders the collaboration movements were the VNV and the smaller 'SS-Vlaanderen' (SS-Flanders), in the French speaking part of the country it was mainly the Belgian Rex party.[8] The predominantly Catholic following of those movements was an extra incentive for the Episcopal hostility: the bishops refused to allow these Catholic dissidents to play any political role. Yet in the summer of 1940 Van Roey took a manifestly hostile attitude towards the Flemish nationalist VNV, and at the end of 1940 he also distanced himself from the Belgian Rex movement. In their first common pastoral letter of October 1940 the bishops stressed the duty of steady love for the fatherland, within the limits of the necessary obedience to the occupying regime. They also incited their flock to national solidarity and political passivity and warned them to avoid discussions that could evoke discord among the people and endanger the future of the country. The latter part of the letter could be understood as a condemnation of collaboration with the occupying forces.

In 1941 the conflict with the collaboration movements became more vehement and manifest. In the first months of the year the bishops took measures against their misuse of religious offices for political ends. For instance, they prohibited solemn funeral ceremonies for the leader of Verdinaso, who had been killed at the beginning of the war in Abbeville. In the next years they gave similar orders regarding funeral services for military volunteers killed on the Eastern front. In the spring of 1941 they refused communion to new order members in uniform. As a reaction the collaboration press censured the 'cassocked scum' and fulminated against clerical interference in politics. Indeed, in the background another struggle was going on. The Catholic social organizations fought

---

8. Bruno De Wever, *Greep naar de macht: Vlaams-nationalisme en nieuwe orde* (Tielt: Lannoo, 1994); Martin Conway, *Collaboratie in België: Léon Degrelle en het Rexisme, 1940-1944* (Groot Bijgaarden: Globe, 1994).

in vain for the preservation of their autonomy within new order structures. In the summer of 1941 the Flemish wing of the Christian Workers movement lost the uneven battle within the UHGA. As a consequence Cardinal Van Roey, in a speech on July 19, 1941, for the first time publicly denounced collaboration with the occupying regime: Catholics were forbidden to collaborate with a regime affecting the rights of conscience and the freedom of the Church. In August 1941 the Flemish Catholic Workers Organization withdrew, with the Cardinal's consent, from the UHGA and refused any further co-operation.[9]

The large majority of the clergy also rejected collaboration. Of course, Catholicism and Nazism shared a common feeling of fierce anti-Communism and a common preference for a corporate, even an autocratic order of society. The traditional strong link between the Flemish clergy and the Flemish movement could have been an additional motive to kindle sympathy for the German regime.[10] But, as already mentioned, before the war the bishops had successfully counteracted fascist tendencies within Catholic opinion. They could not, however, prevent a minority of the clergy (most probably a very small minority of 2 to 3%) from choosing the side of collaboration in 1940 in Flanders as well in Wallonia. A few of them, such as Cyriel Verschaeve, a priest of the province of West-Flanders, even presented himself as a figurehead of the collaboration. Inevitably, these priests were frequently reprimanded by their bishops.[11]

The evolution in the Netherlands was quite similar, though there were also important differences. Firstly, there was hardly any affinity between the Catholic population and the most important collaboration movement, the NSB.[12] Further on, the bishops took a more manifest stance of resistance and impressed more severe measures on their flock.

---

9. Dantoing, "La hiérarchie catholique," 317-319; Jozef Mampuys, "De christelijke vakbeweging," *De christelijke arbeidersbeweging*, ed. Gerard, vol. 2, 147-271; Guy Leemans, "Des voies divergentes: Péripéties communautaires au sein de la C.S.C. des années 1940-1941," *Entre la peste et le choléra*, ed. Maerten, Selleslagh and Van den Wijngaert, 49-62.

10. Lieve Gevers and Louis Vos, "Kerk en nationalisme in Vlaanderen in de 19de en 20ste eeuw," *Is God een Turk? Nationalisme en religie*, ed. Roger Burggraeve, et al. (Leuven: Davidsfonds, 1995) 33-64; Lieve Gevers, "The Catholic Church and the Flemish Movement," *Nationalism in Belgium: Shifting Identities, 1789-1995*, ed. Kas Deprez and Louis Vos (Hampshire/London: Macmillan Press, 1998) 110-118.

11. Mark Van den Wijngaert, "L'église et les catholiques sous l'occupation: L'angle belge," *Entre la peste et le cholera*, 17-18; Romain Vanlandschoot, "La tentative de Cyriel Verschaeve pour réconcilier national-socialisme et christianisme (1941-1942)," *ibid.*, 166-174.

12. Van Schaik, *Aartsbisschop in oorlogstijd*, 65-66; Luykx, *Andere katholieken*, 288.

From October 1940 on, tensions arose between the Catholic Church and the collaboration movement NSB. In a common letter the bishops issued on the occasion of the closing of the Willibrord year, they stressed the merits of the Catholic organizations and the devotion of the Catholic population for the fatherland. Their cautious patriotic terminology and their antagonist statement of "sound social order" against "unsound unchristian principles" angered both the German occupier and the NSB. The letter could not be made public in the newspapers, nor in the Catholic radio broadcast. In November 1940 the Catholic social organizations affirmed the guideline, existing since 1936, suggesting that their members could not belong to the NSB. On January 13, 1941 the bishops also reconsidered their disciplinary measures of 1936 against the NSB and made them even stricter. In a pastoral letter they ordered that not only the leadership but also the members of the NSB should be refused the sacraments. The following March the bishops took distance from the National Socialist recourse organization 'Winterhulp' (Winter Aid).

The German authorities perceived the episcopal letter of January 1941 as a declaration of war against National Socialism. As in Belgium the Germans tried to gain full control of the confessional social organizations in the course of 1941: they had to merge into German controlled centralized structures or would be abolished. And as in Belgium the Dutch bishops encouraged the dissolution of the Catholic organizations rather than give up their confessional autonomy and identity. The Catholic Party, the Catholic Broadcast, the Catholic social and related organizations disappeared one after another in the course of 1941. On the occasion of the National Socialist seizure of power over the Catholic Workers Organization (RKWV) the bishops launched a public protest in a common pastoral letter, dated July 25th 1941. It was read from the pulpit on August 3, notwithstanding the German intimidation against Archbishop De Jong. The pastoral letter had the same tenor as the oral protest of the Belgian Cardinal. It pressed charges against the affection of the freedom of the Catholic social and cultural organizations and ordered the faithful to resign from membership of Nazi-dominated institutions. At the same time the bishops extended the disciplinary measure of refusal of sacraments to all members of National Socialist umbrella organizations.[13]

13. Stokman, *Het verzet van de Nederlandsche bisschoppen*, 24-83; Stokman, *De katholieke arbeidersbeweging*, 9-124; Rogier, *Katholieke herleving*, 593-598; Manning, *De Nederlandse katholieken*; Luykx, *Andere katholieken*, 285-289.

Some Catholic activities nonetheless were allowed to continue. Catholic schools, for instance, were able to continue their teaching. The Dutch bishops in their turn accepted some degree of collaboration for the Catholic press. Sometimes the activities went on in another form. This was the case for Catholic youth organizations: they were brought under the umbrella of the Catholic Action because the Germans did not dare to touch upon strict religious activities. Religious life was able to continue as well, almost without hindrance until the end of the war. All the same, in 1941 the scene had moved from a certain degree of accommodation to antagonism. Soon it would turn into confrontation.

VI. Clashes between the Church and the Occupying Regime

1942 was a turning point in the relationship between the Church authorities and the occupying regime. The Belgian Cardinal Van Roey, along with many others, became convinced that the Germans would not win the war and that eventually a liberal-democratic regime would be restored. It can be concluded from his pastoral letter of February 1, 1942 that at that time he had abandoned the idea of accommodation between the occupying and occupied, but that he wanted to raise hopes for a more promising perspective. The first condition for a just and lasting peace, the Archbishop contended, to the strong dismay of the Germans, was the restoration of the fatherland in its independence and integrity. Moreover in March 1942, in a speech to the Catholic women's federation, he made clear that he not only condemned the Nazi regime in order to protect the interests of the church, but also out of principle. He pointed at the irreducible antagonism between "a morality based on force and on the professed superiority of race and a morality based on the value of the human person."[14] Also from 1942, the Dutch bishops turned on to a more explicit rejection in principle of the Nazi regime, as will be demonstrated later on.

At the same time, the increasing repressive measures of the Nazi-regime, led to almost continuous disputes and clashes between the occupying force and the Catholic hierarchy and clergy. In fact these frictions revolved around two major questions: the Jewish question and the forced labour requirement and, related to these two issues, the growing involvement of the clergy and ecclesiastical institutions in resistance activities.

---

14. Dantoing, "La hiérarchie catholique," 319; Van Doorslaer, "De Kerk en de katholieke zuil," 795.

1. The Persecution of the Jews

The attitude of the Dutch bishops to the persecution of the Jews was most striking. Archbishop De Jong, especially, objected to it on principle.[15] Certainly, in comparison with the Dutch Protestant Churches, the bishops reacted relatively late. Indeed, some years passed before De Jong could persuade his fellow bishops of the Southern part of the country (Den Bosch, Breda and Roermond) to speak up openly against the anti-Jewish measures. In the meantime, since June 1940, the Protestant Churches had established among themselves a consultative body, the 'Convent van Kerken' (Convent of Churches), in order to exchange views and promote possible common actions in the face of the new circumstances. The Dutch Reformed ('Nederlandse Hervormde Kerk') and the Reformed Churches ('Gereformeerde Kerken van Nederland') took a prominent position in the Convent. The Convent was also joined by six smaller Protestant denominations. Anti-Semitism was one of the first discussion points dealt with in the Convent. On October 24, 1940 it directed a written protest to the *Reichskommissar* against the expulsion of Jews from the administration. In March 1941, on the occasion of the worker strike in Amsterdam, a new letter was sent to the Secretary Generals in order to file a complaint against the growing insecurity of the people with regard to their legal position, especially of the Jews. German intimidation (several Protestant leaders had been arrested) and internal discord silenced the protests against anti-Semitic measures in the next months.

In October 1941 the Catholic Church became involved when Archbishop De Jong willingly accepted the invitation to join the Convent. This seemingly created a new dynamism. The Convent had been renamed about that time to 'Interkerkelijk Overleg' (IKO, Deliberation between the Churches), and was granted an audience with Seyss Inquart in February 1942. The representatives of the Dutch Reformed, the Reformed and the Catholic Churches made known to the *Reichskommissar* their Christian inspired rejection of anti-Semitism and pleaded for

---

15. On the Dutch Catholic Church and the persecution of Jews: Stokman, *Het verzet van de Nederlandsche bisschoppen*, 114-118; Aukes, *Kardinaal de Jong*, 336-448; A. P. M. Cammaert, *Het verborgen front: Geschiedenis van de georganiseerde illegaliteit in de provincie Limburg tijdens de Tweede Wereldoorlog* (Leeuwarden/Mechelen: Eisma, 1994) 369-457; Ton H. M. van Schaik, *Vertrouwde vreemden: Betrekkingen tussen katholieken en joden in Nederland 1930-1999* (Baarn: Ten Have, 1992) 13-53; Van Schaik, *Aartsbisschop in oorlogstijd*, 53-64; Snoek, *De Nederlandse kerken*, 74-111; Luykx, *Andere katholieken*, 306-311. See also Peter Romijn, "De oorlog (1940-1945)," *Geschiedenis van de joden in Nederland*, ed. J. C. H. Blom, R. G. Fuks-Mansfeld, I. Schöffer (Amsterdam: Balans, 1995) 313-347.

mercy for the Jewish people. They got a negative response. On 11 July, when the mass deportations of Jews were in progress, the Protestant and Catholic Churches sent a telegraphic protest to the German authorities and planned to launch a public protest from the pulpit. The German promise that Christian baptized Jews would be spared prevented the Dutch Reformed Church from acting in this way. The Reformed and Catholic Churches did not, however, bend to this concession and had the protest read out in their churches on July 26, 1942. The Catholic Church was especially hard hit by the subsequent German retaliation measures: 213 Catholic baptized Jews were arrested and many of them taken to concentration camps, among them several religious men and women, such as the Carmelite sister and philosopher Edith Stein. She died soon after her transportation to Auschwitz. The mass deportations continued unremittingly until September 1943.

In February 1943 the Churches again sent a letter to the *Reichskommissar* in order to denounce the massive and manifold repression of the people: the persecution of the Jews, the forced labour in Germany, the brutal imposition of an ideology, the effect on freedom of education, the killing of hostages, the taking into captivity of many people, among others also ecclesiastics. The protest was once more read from the Catholic pulpits on February 21, 1943 (this time also the Dutch Reformed Church participated in the action while the Reformed Church refused to do so). In his pastoral letter De Jong talked at length about the fate of the Jews as well as of the young people deported to Germany as forced labourers. He gave clear directives to his flock: it was impermissible in conscience to participate in repressive actions, even if a refusal would involve sacrifices. This message was taken seriously by a (eventually limited) number of policemen and civil authorities. Generally speaking, the pastoral letter enhanced among Catholic believers the willingness to avoid the *Arbeitseinsatz* by going into hiding.[16]

Unlike their Dutch colleagues, the Belgian bishops did not pronounce an open protest against the persecution of the Jews.[17] Cardinal

---

16. Snoek, *De Nederlandse kerken*, 34-111.
17. On the Belgian Church and the persecution of the Jews: *Le Cardinal Van Roey et l'occupation*, 229-246; Dantoing, "La hiérarchie catholique en Belgique," 319-321; Lieven Saerens, "L'attitude du clergé catholique belge à l'égard du judaïsme (1918-1940)," *Les juifs de Belgique: De l'immigration au génocide, 1925-1945*, ed. Rudi Van Doorslaer, et al. (Bruxelles: Centre de recherches et d'études historiques de la seconde guerre mondiale, 1994) 11-15; Mark Van den Wijngaert, "Les catholiques belges et les juifs durant l'occupation," *ibid.*, 121-127; Lieven Saerens, *Vreemdelingen in een wereldstad: Een geschiedenis van Antwerpen en zijn Joodse bevolking (1880-1944)* (Tielt: Lannoo, 2000) 487-758; Florence

Van Roey was upset by the anti-Jewish measures being enforced by the Germans as we know from several letters he wrote to Rome. He was aware of the public protest of bishops and priests in France and Norway (very probably also in the Netherlands) and seemingly he considered to acting in the same way, especially since the massive deportations began in July 1942 from his episcopal town Mechelen. But eventually he preferred to choose – like the Vatican – the way of silent diplomacy and private actions. Via his personal secretary Edmond Leclef, he urgently requested the German authorities to mitigate their policy. The *Militärverwaltung* told the Cardinal that he should send his request to the Gestapo, upon which he concluded further insistence would be in vain. His intention was that by avoiding an open protest he could possibly at least save the Belgian and Catholic baptised Jews. He was also convinced that any protest might have endangered Jewish children hiding in Catholic institutions. As head of the Belgian Catholic community he felt responsible for Catholic believers and the interests of his Church, and should therefore do nothing to jeopardize these.

The Cardinal intervened with the German authorities, always through his personal secretary, to the benefit of dozens of Jews, although with little success. He made believers and clergy understand that he appreciated their help to Jewish people, but he refused to take the responsibility for their acts and never publicly approved of them. He was very probably not personally involved in rescue operations, though he must have been aware of René Ceuppens' (the secretary of the Archbishopric) active involvement in them. On the other hand, Van Roey did provide Jewish children with material goods and opened an account of 3 million francs in favour of the Belgian Relief Committee for the Jews.[18] Anyway, regarding the restrained official attitude towards an ecclesiastical involvement in rescue operations, the attitude of the Dutch and Belgian archbishops seems to have been rather similar. Archbishop De Jong also took a very reserved stance towards the involvement of his clergy in such operations, due to his responsible position as Primate of his Church.[19]

Matteazzi, "L'attitude du clergé face à la Shoa dans le diocèse de Liège," *Entre la peste et le choléra*, 177-207; Lieven Saerens, "L'aide des catholiques aux juifs dans l'archevêché de Malines," *ibid.*, 208-240; Maxime Steinberg, "Le silence de l'Église et les actes des chrétiens face à la solution finale en Belgique occupée," *ibid.*, 241-262; Geneviève Thyange, "L' abbé Joseph André et l'aide aux juifs à Namur," *ibid.*, 263-275. See also the contribution of Lieven Saerens in this book, "The Attitude of the Belgian Catholic Church towards the Persecution of Jews," 243-281.

18. Saerens, *Vreemdelingen*, 722-728; Saerens, "L'aide des catholiques," 220-229.
19. Luykx, *Andere katholieken*, 305.

The other Belgian bishops supported with this policy of silence and private interventions, except for Monsignor Kerkhofs, the bishop of Liège (a diocese covering the provinces Limburg and Liège), who clearly did more than that. Indeed, Kerkhofs was the cornerstone in the important aid given by the clergy in this diocese to the Jews. At his insistence Catholic institutions became refuge places for many Jewish children, some of whom were sent by the bishop personally. The Bishop also provided refuge for the Jewish rabbi of Liège and his family. Kerkhofs's close collaborator, a professor of the grand seminary of Liège got involved, at the bishops' request, in a clandestine network for relief of Jewish people.[20] Here again we find a remarkable parallelism with the Netherlands. There it was also the bishop of the province of Limburg (Bishop G. Lemmens of the diocese of Roermond) and his diocesan functionaries who took the lead in rescue operations. Moreover, the exemplary model of the bishops, both in the dioceses of Roermond and Liège, was an important incentive for the clergy to follow suit.[21] As a consequence, a relatively high number of the Liège clergy fell victim to German repression. The Malines primate consequently watched with distress the resistance activities of the bishop of Liège: he reproached him for putting the Catholic population, the clergy as well as the interests of the Church at risk. Kerkhofs reckoned with the fears of his primate in the sense that he also renounced launching a public protest against the deportations.

2. Forced Labour

Since 1942 the conflict regarding forced labour placed a severe strain on the relations between the Belgian bishops and the German authorities. In Belgium the measures for forced labour were taken in two steps. Since March and April 1942 the Germans imposed forced labour in the country itself and from October 1942 they started with the deportations of required labour forces to Germany. In May 1942 the question aroused a first heavy confrontation between the occupier and the Catholic hierarchy. The bishops sent a protest which, to German dismay, also became widely known among the population in general. In the next months the bishops insisted on several occasions on the abolishment or a mitigation of the *Arbeitseinsatz*. Finally, when all diplomatic efforts seemed to be

---

20. Florence Matteazzi, "L'attitude du clergé."
21. Cammaert, *Het verborgen front*, 477ff; Luykx, *Andere katholieken*, 303-304; Van Schaik, *Aartsbisschop in oorlogstijd*, 66.

exhausted and the requisitions became even more massive in character, the bishops launched a common fierce protest in March 1943. Actually, it was the only common public protest of the Belgian episcopate against the occupying regime during the whole course of the war. The bishops stigmatized the requisition of young people as a violation of human liberty and dignity, forcing them moreover to cooperate with the enemy against the interests of their own fatherland. The German justification that the labour force was needed to defend European civilization against Communism was rejected by them as a fallacy. In fact, the bishops argued, the occupier himself violated the fundamental principles of every civilization. This protest answered the expectations of the people and was received by them with great enthusiasm. The episcopal letter was also an encouragement to Catholic people, especially clergy and religious orders, to continue to provide refuge for people dodging deportation. Moreover, it clearly signified a final breach in the relationship between the occupying and ecclesiastical authorities.[22]

The Netherlands shows the same pattern of increasing confrontation between the Catholic bishops and the occupying regime regarding the *Arbeitsansatz*. Until 1942, only unemployed people had been affected by the obligation of forced labour in Germany. From March 1942 on, the measure was extended to people already in employment, thus threatening a large part of the male population. In April 1942 the bishops issued a pastoral letter in order to warn the parents and the young people of the danger of National Socialist influence in the *Arbeidsdienst*. Indeed, like the Belgian bishops, in the previous years they had tried in vain to send priests to Germany to give spiritual assistance to the labourers. The Dutch bishops stressed that the Nazi-ideology should be rejected in principle because it fundamentally contradicted Christianity and was a severe threat to Christian belief and morals. They advised the people to evade the summons by all possible means. In the same month the archbishop made known that Dutch functionaries were not allowed to cooperate with the recruitment of the workers.[23]

As in Belgium, the problem reached its apogee in the spring of 1943. The joint protest of the Churches mentioned earlier, read from the pulpit on February 21, 1943, among others against forced labour, had been to no avail. On the contrary, in order to answer the increased need for workers

22. *Le Cardinal Van Roey et l'occupation allemande*, 115-162; Dantoing, "La hiérarchie catholique et la Belgique," 321-324.
23. Stokman, *Het verzet van de Nederlandsche bisschoppen*, 118-127; Aukes, *Kardinaal de Jong*, 403-407, 425-448; Snoek, *De Nederlandse kerken*, 101-111.

in Germany, the German authorities decided in April 1943 to summon again those who had been released as prisoners of war. This measure caused strong resistance among the population. The Protestant Churches remained silent on this occasion; Archbishop De Jong in his turn once more reacted fiercely. On May 12, 1943 the Dutch bishops issued a pastoral letter against forced labour which has been called "one of the strongest documents written in those years."[24] In fact, the letter contained the same ideas as the letter of the Belgian bishops, but they were expressed in an even sharper and more explicit way. The bishops called the deportation of labourers "a cruel injustice against all human and divine laws:" people were not only prevented from working for their own country; they were even forced to help the enemy. At the same time the bishops burst the National Socialist myth that all Christians had to fight Bolshevism. In fact, they proclaimed, only Christianity, being suffocated by National Socialism was the adequate answer to Communism. The faithful were called on to react to the situation with "a crusade of prayer." The same day Archbishop De Jong issued a directive to the functionaries not to cooperate with the deportation of recalcitrant people, unless their lives were at stake. As in Belgium these episcopal guidelines encouraged a number of people to resist the German measures and to go into hiding underground.

VII. Church and Resistance

In the meantime a substantial part of the secular and regular clergy became engaged in resistance activities. As for those who collaborated it is difficult to come to an exact assessment of their numbers. It is thought that about 20% of the Belgian clergy was involved in the resistance, and that the number might reach to about 37% if also help to Jewish people is included. As a consequence the occupier turned from a rather reserved attitude towards the clergy at the beginning of the war to an ever harsher regime of repression, with a significant increase of arrests since 1942. There were important regional differences though: the Antwerp clergy, for instance, seems to have been much less involved in rescue operations than the clergy of Brussels, the Dutch speaking clergy less than the French speaking clergy.[25] The activities they were involved

---

24. Van Schaik, *Aartsbisschop in oorlogstijd*, 62.
25. Saerens, *Vreemdelingen*, 716-722; Saerens, "L'aide des catholiques," 209-219. See further the detailed study in this book of Lieven Saerens, "The Attitude of the Belgian Catholic Church towards the Persecution of Jews," 243-281.

in could vary from ideological resistance (for instance in their preaching) to armed resistance as well as in helping people in need (forced labourers, Jews and other 'illegal persons' such as stranded allied pilots).[26]

Giving assistance to illegal people was the predominant resistance activity carried out by the clergy, but the younger male clergy also got involved in various kinds of political or military resistance. They were also understandably inclined towards non-violent actions, contributing for instance to the clandestine press or to information services. They showed an obvious preference to get engaged (almost unanimously) in the right-wing and patriotic resistance, rather than in left-wing anticlerical organizations. The right-wing arm of Belgian resistance was dominated by ardent adherents of Leopold III and ex-soldiers and had its military arm in the Secret Army. The left-wing Independence Front was controlled by the Communist Party and pursued its armed resistance with the partisan-army. A small minority (less than 10%) of the clergy got engaged, with the silent consent of their bishops, in the armed resistance, often by providing spiritual assistance to the Secret Army. Among Catholic laypeople, the Catholic Workers Youth ('Katholieke Arbeidersjeugd', KAJ – 'Jeunesse Ouvrière Chrétienne', JOC) played a distinguished role in the resistance, especially by hiding forced labourers and Jews. Members of that organization also pursued a moralizing mission among the forced labourers in Germany.[27]

With the changing tide of the war, the partisans started to fight the collaborationists in a more active way. As a consequence in 1943 and 1944 Belgium was confronted with a kind of civil war, with bloody assaults on supporters of the occupying regime by partisan groups, and German acts of retaliation against members of the resistance as well as innocent civilians. In this atmosphere of terror and contra-terror, foreshadowing post-war politics, hundreds of people were killed. The parti-

26. Several contributions in Selleslagh and Van den Wijngaert, *Entre la peste et le cholera*: Van den Wijngaert, "L'église et les catholiques," 15-17; Anne-Sophie De Sutter, "Le clergé régulier dans les provinces de Namur et de Luxembourg," 77-90; Eddy Louchez, "Les congrégations religieuses sous l'occupation," 91-126; Fabrice Maerten, "Le clergé du diocèse de Tournai face à l'occupation: la voie étroite," 127-165.
27. Frans Hugaerts (ed.), *De K.A.J., haard van verzet* (Gent: Reinaert uitgaven – Het Volk, 1989); Louis Vos with the collaboration of Paul Wynants and André Tihon, "De christelijke arbeidersjeugd," *De christelijke arbeidersbeweging*, ed. Emmanuel Gerard, vol. 2, 412-483; Pieter Lagrou, *The Legacy of Nazi Occupation: Patriotic Memory and National Recovery in Western Europe, 1945-1965* (Cambridge: Cambridge University Press, 2000) 144-150; Leen Alaerts, *Door eigen werk sterk: Geschiedenis van de kajotters en kajotsters in Vlaanderen 1924-1967* (Leuven: Kadoc-K.U.Leuven, 2004) 273-345.

san operations sometimes deteriorated to mere banditry, tending to loot and harass people under cover of resistance acts. In January 1943 Cardinal Van Roey warned against those deviations from pure resistance. He condemned the assaults on collaborationists as endangering the people because of the German retaliation. His message was badly received from both sides though. The collaborationists objected to the letter of the cardinal, because it did not condemn the intrinsic evil of the partisan assaults, the resistance fighters in their turn took the letter as a negative stance towards their struggle. In the last year of the war the cardinal gave active support to the resistance by appointing a head chaplain in the spring of 1944, to be responsible for the chaplain service in the Secret Army.[28]

Regarding the Netherlands we are less well informed on the involvement of the clergy in the resistance, especially of members of religious orders. That the latter contributed to resistance operations may be demonstrated by the example of the Carmelite Professor of Nijmegen Titus Brandsma. As spiritual advisor of the Association of Dutch Catholic Journalists ('Nederlandse Katholieke Journalistenvereniging'), he inspired the Catholic press to resistance against National Socialism. When in January 1942 he paid a visit to the editorial boards of the Catholic newspapers in order the convince them to refuse publication of NSB-advertisements, he was arrested by the Germans and taken to Dachau where he died. Among the secular clergy it was mostly the younger chaplains who were involved in resistance activities, according to the more active role they used to play in Catholic social organizations.[29] But, as in Belgium, there seem to have been apparent differences between the dioceses, dependent on the attitude of the respective bishops. We have already referred to the different attitudes in this regard of the Archbishop of Utrecht and the Bishop of Roermond.

Many Catholic laymen and women were also involved in (mainly humanitarian) resistance activities. It appears though that, again as in Belgium, Catholics were numerically under represented in resistance

28. Dantoing, "La hiérarchie catholique," 321; Jos Bouveroux, *Terreur in oorlogstijd: Het Limburgse drama* (Antwerpen: Nederlandsche boekhandel, ²1984); Wils, *Honderd jaar Vlaamse beweging. 3: Geschiedenis van het Davidsfonds in en rond Wereldoorlog II*, 232-236, 254-255.

29. H. W. F. Aukes, *Het leven van Titus Brandsma* (Antwerpen: Spectrum, 1961); Van Schaik, *Aartsbisschop in oorlogstijd*, 59; Herman Pijfers and Jan Roes, *Memoriale: Katholiek leven in Nederland in de twintigste eeuw* (Zwolle: Waanders, 1996) 160-163; Luykx, *Andere katholieken*, 301-306.

ranks.[30] This might be explained by the fact that the predominantly Catholic southern part of the Netherlands was liberated in September 1944, while the mainly Protestant northern part still had to endure the harsh repression until May 1945, a period in which resistance activities reached their peak. Another, more general possible reason might be that Catholics felt less inclined to join a resistance organization, because their Church continued to provide them with an organizational structure. Recent research points out that Jews had more chance of survival in the more Catholic communities, and less in the more Protestant Reformed communities.[31] Certainly, Catholics played a significant role in Dutch resistance groups. It is important to mention, for instance, the active involvement of Catholic ex-members of the 'Nederlandsche Unie' in the plans made in the hostage camp of Sint-Michielsgestel for the rebuilding of the 'new Netherlands' after the liberation. They published their views in, among others, the clandestine periodical *Christofoor*.[32]

VIII. Restoration and Renewal

Allied forces liberated Belgian territory in the first days of September 1944, so that the Belgian government was able to return from its London exile on September 8. Political life took on its normal shape, however, only after the German capitulation on May 8, 1945. The first post-war elections took place in January 1946. The pre-war balance of power seemed to have withstood the storm of the war. The newly formed Christian People's Party ('Christelijke Volkspartij', CVP) got 42% of the votes (its predecessor, the Catholic Party 32% in 1939) while the Belgian Socialist Party obtained 31% (30% in 1939). Most remarkable was the success of the Belgian Communist Party (12% against 6% in 1939).[33]

30. Luykx, *Andere katholieken*, 301-306; Wils, *Honderd jaar Vlaamse beweging*, 252-254.
31. Marnix Croes and Peter Tammes, *'Gif laten wij niet voortbestaan': Een onderzoek naar de overlevingskansen van joden in de Nederlandse gemeenten 1940-1945* (Amsterdam: Aksant, 2004).
32. Jan Bank, *Opkomst en ondergang van de Nederlandse volksbeweging (NVB)* (Deventer: Kluwer, 1978) 15-38.
33. Els Witte, "Tussen restauratie en vernieuwing: Een introductie op de Belgische politieke evolutie tussen 1944 en 1950," *Tussen restauratie en vernieuwing: Aspecten van de naoorlogse Belgische politiek (1944-1950)*, ed. E. Witte, J. C. Burgelman and P. Stouthuysen (Brussel: VUB-Press, 1989) 13-52.

In the Netherlands, the transition from war to peace was more problematic due to the allied offensive being halted by the Germans in the autumn of 1944, half way the Dutch territory. The south of the country was liberated on September 5, 1944, but the North and North-West remained under German occupation and had to suffer a hard winter of starvation and repression before the final German capitulation in May 1945. In the meantime, the liberated south of the country was initially ruled by an Allied Military Authority, and even after the end of the war political life only gradually returned to normal. The first elections were organized in May 1946. They resulted in a restoration of the pre-war political parties, although they were somewhat restyled. The Catholic People's Party ('Katholieke Volkspartij', KVP), the heir of the pre-war Roman Catholic State Party became the largest party with 32 seats in parliament (2 more than in 1937) and as a consequence obtained the initiative for the formation of a new government. The Dutch Communists could not validate their spectacular electoral success (10 seats as opposed to 3 in 1937), and were – unlike in Belgium – kept out of the government. For the next twelve years, until 1958, the Netherlands was ruled by coalitions of the KVP and the renewed and enlarged Socialist party, the Party of Labour ('Partij van de Arbeid', PvdA), the heir of the pre-war Social Democratic Worker's Party ('Sociaal Democratische Arbeiderspartij', SDAP).[34]

The recovery of the traditional parties was less obvious than it seemed though. In the last years of the war, plans had been forged for a profound reform of Dutch political life, based on the euphoria of national union. Reformers wanted to overcome the old cleavages of religion and class. Young Catholic intellectuals, gathering around the review *Christofoor*, had met in the resistance with Socialist contemporaries. Together they had elaborated a political platform based on the concept of personalist socialism, inspired by the French writers and philosophers of the review *Esprit*, especially by Jacques Maritain and Emmanuel Mounier. This innovatory train of thought resulted in the summer of 1945 in the founding of a new movement, the Dutch People's Movement ('Nederlandsche Volksbeweging', NVB). It directed an invitation to the different parties to break down the walls between the political fractions and to unite in one progressive people's party (a party of

---

[34]. J. Bosmans, "Het maatschappelijk-politieke leven in Nederland 1945-1980," *Algemene Geschiedenis der Nederlanden*, 15 (Haarlem: Fibula-Van Dishoeck, 1982) 269-295.

the so-called 'doorbraak', breakthrough). But such a 'doorbraakpartij' never reached fruition. Eventually Catholics and Socialists entered the electoral campaign in 1946 with both their own party and program. The PvdA profiled itself as the party best suited for collaboration between Catholics and Socialists on the basis of a social progressive project. It was successful in attracting a number of Catholics, resulting in the establishment within the PvdA of a faction with its own name and identity, known as the Catholic Work Community ('Katholieke Werkgemeenschap', KWG). This ended the monopolist position of the Catholic Party, as the only one rallying all Catholics.[35]

But the desired unification process between the parties (the 'doorbraak') remained, as mentioned, far below expectations. At the explicit insistence of the Dutch bishops the restoration of the Catholic organizations had taken a start from 1944 on, preventing at the same time trade-union collaboration between Catholics, Protestants and Socialists. During the electoral campaign of 1946 the bishops once again made clear that they rejected any collaboration transcending the old polarization. They forbade membership of Socialist organizations to Catholics, and ordered their flock from the pulpit that they should vote for the KVP. The progressive 'doorbraak'-Catholics of the Catholic Work Community experienced the victory of the Catholic Party over the PvdA as a bitter disappointment.[36]

Even so, the revival of the political pillars did not hinge on a mere restoration of the pre-war situation. The promoters of the KVP understood all too well that a profound renovation of the traditional Catholic party was badly needed. Indeed, the new KVP, founded in December 1944, showed an inclination to innovation and radicalism, as expressed by a party leader: "progressive in a Catholic direction." Apart from a new name, the renewal was reflected in more fundamental options: the party should be based on a concrete program, not merely on principles, it should be a 'people's' party, not merely a 'state' party, it should be independent from the Church hierarchy and advocate a progressive socio-economic policy. This progressive orientation encouraged some of the former 'doorbraak'-Catholics to return to the Catholic party.

---

35. Rogier, *Katholieke herleving*, 604-633; Bank, *Opkomst en ondergang*, 38ff.
36. Bornewasser, *Katholieke Volkspartij*, 118-168; Walter Goddijn, Jan Jacobs and Gérard van Tillo, *Tot vrijheid geroepen: Katholieken in Nederland 1945-2000* (Baarn: Ten Have, 1999) 31-41.

But the tide of renewal disappeared rather quickly. The hope that the renewed KVP might attract non-Catholic voters on the basis of its program proved to be an illusion. In reality it functioned again as merely a party of and for Catholics. Moreover, through the loss of left-wing Catholics to the PvdA, it was difficult for the party to keep up its progressive course. From 1948 on, political problems such as the Indonesian question and the Cold War, contributed to reinforcing the right-wing leaning in the party yet again. The notorious letter of the Dutch bishops, issued in 1954 (called the 'mandement'), was both a sign and confirmation of the still vivid authoritarian clericalism in the Dutch Roman Catholic community of the early fifties. It called to mind the interdiction of membership of Socialist organizations, and explicitly condemned the left-wing Catholics of the Catholic Work Community. Nonetheless, the negative and critical reception of the Episcopal letter in some Catholic circles demonstrated that the law-abiding attitude of the Catholic 'flock' had begun to wane. Latently a critical and ecumenical lay-movement was emerging, that would manifest itself overtly in the second half of the fifties.[37]

In Belgium there was shortly after the war also a new antifascist wind blowing within Catholic political circles. In the French speaking part of the country, in Brussels and Wallonia, a group of progressive Catholic intellectuals and trade union workers wanted to get rid of the tutelage of the bishops and the conservative leaders of the Catholic party. During the war they had worked together with Socialists in the resistance and they wanted to continue this cooperation in a unified workers party and trade union. This plan was rejected by the Socialists so that they founded a political party of their own in June 1945, the 'Union Démocratique belge' (UDB, Belgian Democratic Union) on the base of a Christian inspired, but pluralist oriented socially progressive program.[38]

But as in the Netherlands, the movement to break down the walls between the parties was not a success. The great majority of the Catholic public opinion wanted the renewal to be limited to the traditional Catholic party itself. In August 1945 a new Christian People's Party ('Christelijke Volkspartij', CVP – 'Parti Social-Chrétien', PSC), was

---

37. Rogier, *Katholieke herleving*, 605-633; Goddijn, Jacobs and Van Tillo, *Tot vrijheid geroepen*, 40-44, 85-93.
38. Witte, "Tussen restauratie en vernieuwing," 18; Jean-Louis Jadoulle, "The Milieu of Left Wing Catholics in Belgium (1940s-1950s)," *Left Catholicism 1943-1955: Catholics and Society in Western Europe at the point of Liberation*, ed. Gerard-Rainer Horn and Emmanuel Gerard, Kadoc-Studies, 25 (Leuven: University Press, 2001) 102-117.

founded, proclaiming rejuvenation, unity and progress as key notions of its program. Christian inspiration and the personalist ideas of Maritain and Mounier were, as for Catholics in the Netherlands, the ideological basis for the new party and also in Belgium the party wanted to abandon its confessional character and take an autonomous stance towards the ecclesiastical hierarchy. There was a wish for a strongly centralized party, with less autonomy for the constituting social organizations and a good understanding between Flemings and Walloons. The Social Pact of 1944, providing a settlement between trade unions and employers for peaceful deliberation of social conflicts and for the generalization of social security provisions, favoured the new social climate in Belgium.[39]

Eventually though, as in the Netherlands, restoration would set the tone in the Belgian post war politics rather than renewal. The traditional party system and the pillarization were maintained, also in trade-unionism. Attempts at a 'doorbraak', like that by UDB, were countered by the conservative reactions of the bishops, and most of Catholic public opinion. The Catholic hierarchy was not inclined either to give up its influence on politics and were not always prepared to respect the claimed autonomy of the Catholic party. Soon after the war, therefore, the spirit of renewal tending to open mindedness and democratization was silenced and counterbalanced by a defensive overtone of Catholic mobilisation and party discipline. As in the Netherlands this evolution was enhanced by the Cold War, but as opposed to the neighbouring country the conservative turn in the Belgian Catholic opinion was to be seen as directly linked to the heritage of the war.

Indeed, the war had Belgium saddled with two venomous gifts. The first one was the problem of punishing the collaborators to which, significantly, in Flanders is not referred to as 'the purge', but as 'the repression'. The second was the royal question, namely the discussion about the political position of the King. Until the end of the fifties, both problems dominated the political agenda, and caused a polarisation between two groups of the Belgian population. Their huge impact and the near impossibility of finding solutions for them, were mainly due to the fact

39. M. Van den Wijngaert, *Ontstaan en stichting van de C.V.P.-P.S.C.: De lange weg naar het kerstprogramma* (Antwerpen/Amsterdam: De Nederlandsche Boekhandel, 1976); Emmanuel Gerard, "Van katholieke partij naar CVP," *Tussen staat en maatschappij: 1945/1995 Christen-democratie in België*, ed. Wilfried Dewachter, et al. (Tielt: Lannoo, 1995) 25-26. On the evolution of the Christian Workers Movement: Gerard (ed.), *De christelijke arbeidersbeweging*; Patrick Pasture, *Kerk, politiek en sociale actie: De unieke positie van de christelijke arbeidersbeweging in België 1944-1973*, Hiva-reeks, 14 (Leuven: Garant, 1992).

that in those years the ideological and community cleavages coincided. There was a Catholic Front opposing an anti-Catholic (Socialist/Liberal) one, and the majority of the (predominantly Catholic) Dutch-speaking population in Flanders, was confronted with a majority of the (mainly Socialist or Liberal) French-speaking population in Brussels and Wallonia. Within the scope of this contribution we can only briefly discuss these after-effects of the war.

IX. The After-Effects of the War

Belgium and the Netherlands dealt with the war in very different ways. In the Netherlands the political elites rather quickly succeeded in reaching a consensus that the war events should not overshadow the future. The resistance groups accepted they would play no independent role in post-war politics while the Communist party was excluded from governmental power. After an outburst of popular fury and numerous arrests in the first days of the liberation the legal authorities gained supervision over the purge of collaborators with a rather short delay. The purge was moderate and evolved in a relatively orderly and swift manner.[40]

The Catholic and Protestant Churches, still convening in the 'Interkerkelijk Overleg', played an important role in spreading among the population a readiness to clemency. Archbishop De Jong repeatedly warned against uncontrolled acts of revenge against collaborators. He denounced the degrading conditions in the internment camps and exhorted his flock in 1946 to receive released prisoners in a caring way. Among the churches in the Netherlands, the Catholic Church was probably most kindly disposed to the release and resettlement of political detainees, just like the Catholic politicians tended more to a policy of clemency than their Socialist coalition partners. Nonetheless, there were only minor differences in the policy between parties regarding the resistance and the purge. The Dutch Catholics, Protestants and Socialists were almost on the same wavelength.[41] Moreover the Catholic Church had benefited from the war as it strengthened its position within the nation.[42]

---

40. Peter Romijn, *Snel, streng en rechtvaardig: Politiek beleid inzake de bestraffing en reclassering van 'foute' Nederlanders 1945-1955* (Houten: De Haan, 1989) *passim*, on the attitude of the Churches in particular: 225-242; Lagrou, *The Legacy*, 59-77, 241-250.
41. Romijn, *Snel, streng en rechtvaardig*, 18.
42. Rogier, *Katholieke herleving*, 624-625; Van Schaik, *Aartsbisschop in oorlogstijd*, 73-74.

Belgium had a much greater problem in digesting the war. The resistance movements, especially the partisans, were in command in the gulf of terror and arrests of alleged collaborators in September 1944 and again in May 1945. The government had to make great efforts to disarm the resistance and to take control again. Almost immediately the political parties and public opinion were divided on the way the purge should be dealt with. The Catholic, predominantly Dutch speaking opinion denounced the acts of violence and insisted on a just and human treatment of the collaborators. The anti-clerical, predominantly French speaking part of the population on the contrary claimed an even harsher approach in the purge. In the first post-war years anti-clerical governments containing Socialists, Communists and representatives of the resistance conducted a policy of severe punishment of those who had collaborated. From 1947, when the power position of the Communist party was affected by the Cold War, the policy was considerably mitigated: thousands of prisoners were released and resettled. This was due to the Christian People's Party, entering the government in March 1947 together with the Socialists. In the following years the success of the CVP was steadily growing. In 1950 the party even won the absolute majority of the votes, so that it could govern the country alone.[43]

Logically, the Belgian bishops joined the claims of Catholic opinion. In several pastoral letters in 1945 and 1946 they made clear that the punishment of the collaborators should be just, but also that the punishment was the responsibility of the legal state authorities alone. They rejected any repression that was based on feelings of hatred and revenge of an inflamed mob, and condemned severely the maltreatment of almost innocent civilians and the inhumane conditions in the prisoner-camps. On the occasion of the Holy Year in 1950 Van Roey asked mercy for those who were still suffering from the purge and he repeated the same appeal in 1959. The archbishop also reacted sympathetically on demands made by people in detention or their families, and tried through personal interventions to alleviate their suffering, or to obtain release from prison. Also many members of the diocesan clergy or different religious orders

---

43. Wils, *Honderd jaar Vlaamse beweging*. 3: *Geschiedenis van het Davidsfonds in en rond Wereldoorlog II*, 251-254; Kris Hoflack and Luc Huyse, "De afrekening met de vrienden van de vijand," *De democratie heruitgevonden: Oud en nieuw in politiek België 1944/1950*, ed. Luc Huyse and Kris Hoflack (Leuven: Van Halewyck, 1995) 27-44; Pieter Lagrou, "Verzet en naoorlogse politiek," *ibid.*, 45-68; Lagrou, *The Legacy*, 47-58. See also José Gotovitch and Chantal Kesteloot (eds.), *Collaboration, répression: Un passé qui résiste* (Bruxelles: Labor, 2002).

tried to help people afflicted by the purge. On the other hand, Van Roey rejected explicitly the justification, brought forward by ex-fighters at the Eastern front or ex-members of VNV, that their collaboration had been motivated by Christian inspired anti-Communism or even, that they had merely obeyed the guidelines of the Church. The bishops, in their handling of the purge were criticized from two sides. Anti-Catholic left-wing circles blamed their efforts for clemency as taking sides with the collaborators; Flemish-Nationalists on the other hand were embittered because the Church should not have protested in a sufficient way against the unjust treatment of the victims of the repression.[44]

Post-war Belgium not only was torn apart because of the problem of the repression, but also because of the royal question. Leopold III had remained in his palace in Laeken as a prisoner of war until 1944, but shortly before the liberation he and his family had been taken in captivity to Germany. After the German capitulation the question arose whether or not he could return as a legal monarch to his country. The dividing lines between those who were in favour of the return of the king and those who were against it, coincided with the positions taken in the dossier of the repression. The French speaking anti-Catholic opinion opposed the return of the King, because it accused him of having accommodated too readily the enemy or even collaborating with him. The Flemish Catholic opinion and the Belgian episcopate on the other hand, were strongly in favour of a return of the King. To find a solution a referendum was organized in 1950, resulting in an overall majority of Belgian voters in favour of the King's return. If divided according to linguistic lines though, only a minority of French-speakers had cast a positive vote. When in the next parliamentary elections of 1950 the CVP got the absolute majority so that it could form a one party government, it decided to ask the King to return. Violent demonstrations in Wallonia brought the country to the brink of a civil war, which could only be prevented by the abdication of Leopold III and his succession to the throne by his son Boudeoin.[45]

The ideological confrontation between Catholics and non-Catholics remained the dominant issue in Belgian politics until the end of the 1950's. In 1954 the Catholic party, still the largest one in Belgium, was

44. Boudens, *Kardinaal Van Roey*, 106-141.
45. Paul Theunissen, *1950: ontknoping van de koningskwestie* (Antwerpen/Amsterdam: De Nederlandsche Boekhandel, 1984); M. Van den Wijngaert, *Een koning geloofd, gelaakt, verloochend*. Vol. 1: *De evolutie van de katholieke opinie* (Leuven/Amersfoort: Acco, 1984).

forced into opposition by an anti-Catholic coalition of Socialists and Liberals. It immediately took measures in the education system that were felt by the Catholics as a declaration of war against their secondary schools. The school-war ended in 1958 with, again, an electoral victory of the CVP and subsequently with an ideological pacification. Only by the end of the fifties, also linked to the waning of the Cold War, did the Church and the Catholic opinion abandon its defensive attitude, so that the forces of renewal within the community of faithful got the chance to manifest itself freely. In Flanders the review *De Maand* (The Month), founded by lay people, would become the rallying point for intellectuals advocating an open form of Catholicism.[46]

X. Conclusion: Similarities and Differences between Belgium and the Netherlands

Though the pre-war Roman Catholic Church in the Netherlands was relatively weaker than in Belgium there are nevertheless apparent similarities in the way Catholics addressed the rise of right-wing tendencies in the 1930's. In both countries a part of the Catholic population felt seduced by them, in both countries the bishops fought those tendencies for reasons of self-preservation (the political unity of the Catholic population and the freedom of the Church within the democratic structures), as well as out of a rejection in principle of fascism. 1936 was an important year in that regard. The Episcopal directives discouraged the majority of the Catholic population from being seduced by the call of the right-wing revolution. There were nonetheless also important differences between both countries. The minority position of the Dutch Catholics had made them more docile towards their ecclesiastical leaders so that the Dutch bishops did not face real problems in order to keep them in the right political fold. The Belgian Church on the contrary was the victim of its own success. Notwithstanding its strong, seemingly unthreatened power position, the authority of the bishops and the Catholic party was internally contested, in Flanders as well as in the French speaking part of the country, by a considerable extreme

46. Gevers and Vos, "Kerk en nationalisme in Vlaanderen;" Gevers, "The Catholic Church and the Flemish movement;" Lieve Gevers, "Kerkelijke ontwikkelingen in Vlaanderen in het licht van Vaticanum II: De stem van het lekenblad 'De Maand' (1958-1971)," *Trajecta: Tijdschrift voor de geschiedenis van het katholiek leven in de Nederlanden* 5, no. 3 (1996) 275-296.

right-wing tendency of the Catholic rank and file. Even among those who remained loyal to the Catholic party, a right-wing minority favoured political corporatism, apparently more than in the Netherlands. Indeed, the warnings of the Belgian episcopate in 1936 were intended to silence political corporate tendencies both inside and outside the party.

The analysis of the war itself has made evident a remarkable parallelism between both countries, regarding both the policy of the German authorities towards the Church and the reactions of Church authorities. We discerned three phases in this evolution. During the first year of the war the Germans still showed some respect to the Church and left a certain level of autonomy to the confessional organizations. The bishops of both countries tended to an attitude of accommodation and expectation. They tried to ignore as well as possible the occupying regime and keep the Catholic organizations intact. However, Cardinal Van Roey showed more readiness to an active form of accommodation, or as we called it, a policy of presence. The Dutch bishops were more passive, they did not condemn forms of active accommodation as the 'Nederlandsche Unie' but they did not encourage it either. In October 1940 both hierarchies turned from a rather resigned, to a more able-bodied patriotic discourse and to a concealed critic of the collaboration.

This was a harbinger of the second phase, a phase of growing antagonism which lasted from ca. December 1940-January 1941 to the beginning of 1942. The hierarchies now clearly condemned the collaboration movements. Cardinal Van Roey pointed at the "grave inadmissibility" to support the collaboration and ordered his priests to refuse Holy Communion to new order members in uniform. Archbishop De Jong went a step further when he refused all sacraments to members of collaborative organizations. At the same time, and related to this, the bishops lost their battle for an autonomous position of the confessional network, especially of the Catholic Workers organization. It resulted, in the summer of 1941, in a public protest issued by Cardinal Van Roey in Belgium and by the common episcopacy in the Netherlands. Social organizations refused further cooperation within new order structures and went underground.

From the spring of 1942, a third period set in, in which clashes between the Germans and the ecclesiastical authorities became the rule. From that time on both hierarchies on several occasions denounced explicitly the irreconcilability between Christianity and the Nazi-ideology. We have pointed at two major questions which caused constant friction: the increased persecution of people, especially the Jews and the forced labour conscripts. Regarding the persecution of the Jews the Dutch and the Belgian primates chose a different approach. De Jong, in consent with the Protestant Churches and the other bishops, launched in July 1942 and in February 1943 a public protest against the treatment of the Jewish population and ordered the faithful not to cooperate with this policy. Van Roey followed a policy of silent diplomacy and private interventions. Regarding forced labour the Belgian Cardinal also tried diplomatic efforts in order to alter the situation. In March 1943 the Belgian bishops finally launched a formal public protest. In the meantime the Dutch bishops had addressed the question in two pastoral letters, in April 1942 and February 1943. In May 1943 a fierce pastoral protest was again read from the pulpit. It contained the same ideas as had been expressed by the Belgian episcopate, but the Dutch bishops were also then more explicit in their directive to the faithful to resist against the execution of the measures. In short, certainly in the last phase, the differences between both episcopates are more striking than the similarities.

What then were the similarities, what the differences? There was firstly a striking parallelism in the evolution of the stresses and the goals of the policy of both episcopacies. We can also notice a strong congruence in their motivations, being a mixture of ecclesiastical self-preservation, pastoral concern for the well-being of the faithful and a rejection in principle of the anti-Christian and inhuman Nazi-ideology. Both the archbishops of Utrecht and Malines demonstrated a deep feeling of responsibility towards the problems caused by the holocaust: they were well aware of the fact that their Church was one of the only remaining institutions to which the Jewish people could turn. But in order to reach their goals – here begins the difference – both used conscientiously another strategy. Archbishop De Jong preferred an expressive policy, with public protests against the oppressor and stringent moral appeals to the faithful. Van Roey chose for an instrumental approach of diplomacy and was cautious about forcing people to take on an often dangerous responsibility.

This difference can in part be explained by the manifest other personalities of the two archbishops, the one being more close-lipped and pragmatic (in popular speech: 'the Silent'), the other more a man of principle, straightforward in his statements (in popular speech: 'the Iron John'). But very probably there was something more going on than just a different strategy and personality. Notwithstanding the similarity in their motivations, we cannot disguise that both primates were on a different wavelength regarding their convictions and priorities. The attitude of Van Roey in the first year of the war demonstrates that he didn't reject in principle an autocratic regime, as long as it did recognize the rights of the Church. His condemnations in principle of Nazism shortly before and during the war were rather abstract and did not explicitly mention the Jews. Notwithstanding his concern about the holocaust, in his reactions towards the occupying regime he tended to give priority to the interests of the Church, the Catholic population and the fatherland. De Jong's priorities were on a different level. From the first year of the war he felt sympathy for public protests against the ongoing anti-Semitic measures. As far as we can assess, he showed a stronger moral indignation over the discriminatory policy than his Belgian counterpart. In his statements he was very explicit: he not only mentioned the injuries against the Dutch people, but in particular also those against the Jews. His awareness that public protests were in vain and that they might put at risk the Catholic population did not hold him back from his conviction that he himself and the Church as such had to speak up.

Moreover both episcopacies faced very different circumstances. Next to conviction and personality, they provide an additional explanation for the divergent attitude of both archbishops. There was first of all the different position of the kingdom. Leopold's decision to remain in the country was contestable. His reputation was the more badly damaged by his marriage in 1941 with Liliane Baels, especially within resistance circles. Van Roey remained always solidly behind the King. In the meanwhile Queen Wilhelmina, exiled with her government in London, acquired the status of the head of Dutch resistance. Secondly, the Germans established a *Zivilverwaltung* in the Netherlands that involved immediate control of the nation by the Nazi-party and the Gestapo, while the *Militärverwaltung* in Belgium left some room for autonomy for the Belgian civil authorities, and only indirect – though as we have mentioned gradually more – control to the Gestapo. Both factors were significant for the different ways the Church authorities addressed the war situation. They were probably conducive to the Belgian Cardinal to tend more to active accommodation at the beginning of the war and to diplomatic interventions in the following years. Archbishop De Jong had little to expect from such interventions. As a last resort he had to turn to immediate appeals to the people. The pre-war conditions should also be taken into consideration. As mentioned, in the 1930's new order tendencies got a stronger response among the Catholic population in Belgium than in the Netherlands. Also during the war the Flemish-nationalist and Rexist collaboration movements could still reckon with active support or had at least some sympathy among a significant minority among the Belgian population. It might explain the less stringent measures of Van Roey towards members of those movements out of pastoral concern. The refusal of sacraments would have deprived many devoted Catholics, even clergy, of spiritual assistance. Finally, regarding the attitude of the Dutch bishops, one should point at the evident influence of the Protestant Churches, with their strong tradition of a policy of principle and witnessing. Indeed, one of the gains of the war for the churches in the Netherlands was the growth of ecumenical openness within the 'Interkerkelijk Beraad'.

A final question remains to be answered. What has been the effect of the different strategies used by both the Belgian and the Dutch bishops? John F. Morley in his *Vatican Diplomacy and the Jews During the Holocaust, 1939-1943* uses an elucidating twofold criterion in order to assess the success or failure of the Vatican diplomacy. Success or failure, the author states, should be evaluated "not only by the amount of lives it saved or did not save, but also by the application of its own criterion that it should be the moral voice defending rights of all men."[47] Applying those criteria to the episcopal policy in the Low Countries, it is evident that Archbishop De Jong answered the second criterion better than his Belgian colleague (and than Pius XII, to De Jong's "painful amazement"[48]). Whether this involved the saving of more lives is another question. Without any doubt, De Jongs' fierce statements made his flock clearly aware of the problem and exhorted a number of them to act accordingly. But they also incited the Germans to retaliation acts against his Church and against Jews. People obeying his moral directives were often taken into captivity. For that reason some of his advisers and other Dutch bishops sometimes questioned his approach. The dramatic consequences of the episcopal letter of 1942 in the neighbouring country very probably also motivated the 'silence' of Van Roey on the Jewish question. It is a fact that in the Netherlands relatively more Jews felt victim to the holocaust than in Belgium.[49] Whether this fact can be related to the silence or the speaking up of the church authorities though, is impossible to say. It remains a difficult and open question to which historical research does not have an adequate answer yet, supposing it ever shall.

47. John F. Morley, *Vatican Diplomacy and the Jews during the Holocaust, 1939-1943* (New York: KTAV, 1980) 6.
48. Van Schaik, *Aartsbisschop in oorlogstijd*, 62-64.
49. Blom, *Crisis, bezetting en herstel*, 136-137.

Selective Bibliography

H. W. F. Aukes, *Kardinaal de Jong* (Antwerpen/Utrecht: Spectrum, 1956).
J. C. H. Blom, *Crisis, bezetting en herstel: Tien studies over Nederland, 1930-1950* (Den Haag: Universitaire Pers Rotterdam, 1989).
J. A. Bornewasser, *Katholieke Volkspartij 1945-1980*. Band I: *Herkomst en groei (tot 1963)* (Nijmegen: Valkhof Pers, 1995).
Alain Dantoing, "La hiérarchie catholique et la Belgique sous l'occupation allemande," *Revue du Nord* 60, no. 237 (avril-mai 1978) 311-330.
Alain Dantoing, *La 'collaboration' du cardinal: L'Église de Belgique dans la guerre 40* (Bruxelles: De Boeck, 1991).
Kas Deprez and Louis Vos (eds.), *Nationalism in Belgium: Shifting Identities, 1789-1995* (Hampshire/London: Macmillan Press, 1998).
Emmanuel Gerard (ed.), *De christelijke arbeidersbeweging in België, 1891-1991*. 2 vols., Kadoc-Studies, 11 (Leuven: Universitaire Pers, 1991).
Emmanuel Gerard, *De Katholieke partij in crisis: Partijpolitiek leven in België (1918-1940)* (Leuven: Kritak, 1985).
Walter Goddijn, Jan Jacobs and Gérard van Tillo, *Tot vrijheid geroepen: Katholieken in Nederland 1945-2000* (Baarn: Ten Have, 1999).
José Gotovitch and Chantal Kesteloot (eds.), *Collaboration, répression: Un passé qui résiste* (Bruxelles: Labor, 2002).
Luc Huyse and Kris Hoflack (eds.), *De democratie heruitgevonden: Oud en nieuw in politiek België 1944/1950* (Leuven: Van Halewyck, 1995).
Pieter Lagrou, *The Legacy of Nazi Occupation: Patriotic Memory and National Recovery in Western Europe, 1945-1965* (Cambridge: Cambridge University Press, 2000).
Paul Luykx, *Andere katholieken: Opstellen over Nederlandse katholieken in de twintigste eeuw* (Nijmegen: SUN, 2000).
Fabrice Maerten, Frans Selleslagh and Marc Van den Wijngaert (eds.), *Entre la peste et le choléra: Vie et attitudes des catholiques belges sous l'occupation* (Gerpinnes: Quorum, 1999).
L. J. Rogier, *Katholieke herleving: Geschiedenis van Katholiek Nederland sinds 1853* ('s-Gravenhage: Pax, ²1956).
Peter Romijn, *Snel, streng en rechtvaardig: Politiek beleid inzake de bestraffing en reclassering van 'foute' Nederlanders, 1945-1955* (Houten: Den Haan, 1989).
J. M. Snoek, *De Nederlandse kerken en de joden, 1940-1945: De protesten bij Seyss-Inquart. Hulp aan joodse onderduikers. De motieven voor hulpverlening* (Kampen: Kok, 1990).
S. Stokman, *Het verzet van de Nederlandsche Bisschoppen tegen nationaal-socialisme en Duitsche tyrannie* (Utrecht: Spectrum, 1945).
Mark Van den Wijngaert, *Een koning geloofd, gelaakt, verloochend*. Vol. 1: *De evolutie van de katholieke opinie* (Leuven/Amersfoort: Acco, 1984).
Mark Van den Wijngaert, *Ontstaan en stichting van de C.V.P.-P.S.C.: De lange weg naar het kerstprogramma* (Antwerpen/Amsterdam: De Nederlandsche Boekhandel, 1976).
Ton H. M. van Schaik, *Aartsbisschop in oorlogstijd: Een portret van kardinaal Jong (1885-1955)* (Baarn: Gooi en Sticht, 1996).

Ton H. M. van Schaik, *Vertrouwde vreemden: Betrekkingen tussen katholieken en joden in Nederland 1930-1999* (Baarn: Ten Have, 1992).
Etienne Verhoeyen, *België bezet, 1940-1944: Een synthese* (Brussel: BRTN-Instructieve Omroep, 1993).
Lode Wils, *Honderd jaar Vlaamse beweging. 3. Geschiedenis van het Davidsfonds in en rond Wereldoorlog II* (Leuven: Davidsfonds, 1989).

The Attitude of the Belgian Catholic Church towards the Persecution of Jews

Lieven Saerens[1]

Before the Second World War, the predominant attitude of the Belgian Church and Belgian Catholics in general was one of ambivalence. Physical violence, such as that which occurred during *Kristallnacht*, was rejected; psychological violence (i.e. anti-Semitic legislation), on the other hand, was generally tolerated. It is noteworthy that the Protestant churches in Belgium, which formed a very small minority amongst churches, openly expressed their sympathy for the Jewish community through letters and public meetings in 1933 and 1938. Such open sympathy was not to be found in the public actions of the highest Belgian Catholic church authority, Cardinal Van Roey. Like the rest of the Catholic world, Van Roey was of the opinion that many protested against the persecution of Jews in Germany while ignoring the persecution of Catholics in Russia, Spain, and Mexico. In 1938, he closed down the 'Katholiek Bureau voor Israël' (KBI, Catholic Bureau for Israel), whose sole purpose was to combat prejudices against Jews amongst Catholics. Officially, the reason for the closure was the claim that the KBI was responsible for "fanning the flames" around the touchy matter of anti-Semitism.[2]

---

1. Mainly based on: Lieven Saerens, "L'aide des catholiques aux juifs dans l'archevêché de Malines," *Entre la peste et le choléra: Vie et attitudes des catholiques belges sous l'occupation*, ed. Fabrice Maerten, Frans Selleslagh and Mark Van den Wijngaert (Bruxelles/Louvain-la-Neuve: SOMA/Quorum/Aura, 1999) 208-240; Lieven Saerens, *Vreemdelingen in een wereldstad (1880-1944): Een geschiedenis van Antwerpen en zijn joodse bevolking* (Tielt: Lannoo, 2000) 711-732; Lieven Saerens, "Die Hilfe für Juden in Belgien," *Solidarität und Hilfe für Juden während der NS-Zeit. Regionalstudien 4: Slowakei, Bulgarien, Serbien, Kroatien mit Bosnien und Herzegowina, Belgien, Italien*, ed. Wolfgang Benz and Juliane Wetzel (Berlin: Metropol Verlag, 2004) 193-280.
2. Lieven Saerens, "The Attitude of the Belgian Roman Catholic Clergy toward the Jews Prior to the Occupation," *Belgium and the Holocaust*, ed. Dan Michman (Jerusalem: Yad Vashem, 1998) 159-194.

I. Introduction: The Jews in Belgium[3]

When the Germans occupied Belgium in May 1940 a large number of Jews fled the country. Additionally, around 8,000 Jews with German nationality were deported to France by the Belgian government as so-called 'suspects'. As a result of this, the prewar number of 70,000 to 75,000 Jews living in Belgium was greatly reduced. During the occupation the Germans succeeded in listing about 55,700 Jews. There were only four regios containing more than 1,000 Jews: the regio of Brussels (province of Brabant), the regio of Antwerp (province of Antwerp), the regio of Liège (province of Liège) and the regio of Charleroi (province of Hainaut). In Gent (province of East Flanders) about 250 Jews lived. (For a short synopsis of the Belgian geographical situation: cf. infra).

Table 1: Number of Jews in Belgium ca. April 1942

Antwerp and the Antwerp greater metropolitan area	21,277	(38.36%)
Brussels and the Brussels greater metropolitan area	29,134	(52.53%)
Liège and the Liège greater metropolitan area	2,081	(3.75%)
Charleroi and the Charleroi greater metropolitan area	1,064	(1.91%)
Gent and the Gent greater metropolitan area	257	(0.46%)
Rest of the country	1,645	(2.96%)
Total	55,458	(100%)

During the war, Belgium was ruled by a German military government (*Militärverwaltung*), while the Netherlands was governed by a German civil government (*Zivilverwaltung*, i.e. SS-government). Since the Belgian Government had fled abroad at the time of the German invasion, the Belgian Secretary Generals were the highest remaining authorities in the country. In contrast to some neighbouring countries the Belgian Secretary Generals refused to respond to the German request to adopt anti-Jewish regulations (see below, 'the policy of the lesser evil'). This resulted in the Germans promulgating the regulations themselves. From October 1940 onwards the first anti-Jewish measures were applied. In total, the military government promulgated eighteen anti-Jewish regulations; for contravention of each there was a punishment of imprisonment or a fine in cases of non-compliance. The anti-Jewish policy of the occupying authority was based on four principles. First,

---

3. Saerens, *Vreemdelingen in een wereldstad*, 499-504, 546-554.

Jews were defined: who is Jewish? On the basis of this definition, Jews were listed in 1940 in the Jewish register, so their places of residence were known. A second principle was economic disablement: the closure of certain vocations to Jews, such as law; the liquidation of the trade in diamonds, etc. The third principle was the marking of Jews: the Star of David badge was introduced in June 1942. Finally, beginning in the summer of 1942, deportation was introduced.

The anti-Jewish measures were promulgated by the *Militärverwaltung* and published in the German *Verordnungsblatt*. The actual deportation of the Jews was coordinated by the Sipo-SD (SS), with the help of German *Feldgendarmen* and Belgian collaborators. The first Belgian convoy of Jews left from Mechelen (the Dossin-barracks) to Auschwitz on 4th August 1942. The Germans transported 24,608 Jews altogether, which is about 44% of the registered Jewish population.

In general, the German authorities followed the so-called 'policy of the lesser evil'. They wished the persecutions to take place as quietly as possible, and were above all concerned with expediting cooperation of the Belgian authorities and institutions, at national, provincial, and local levels. The 'policy of the lesser evil' meant in this regard that the German authorities promulgated their own anti-Jewish regulations, but left the carrying out of these regulations to the local Belgian authorities. Secondly, carrying out this policy meant, concretely, that during the razzias and deportations, for a very long time the Jews of Belgian nationality were spared. They were, at the time, only 6% of the total population of Jews. Approximately half of the Jewish population was of Polish origin. We will also see instances in which the Belgian Catholic Church, in particular Cardinal Van Roey, seemed to follow the ratio of the 'policy of the lesser evil'.

Yet, before the war a secularization process had set in among the Jewish people. This process was even stronger than the secularisation process that took shape among the Belgian population. It is likely that more than half of the Jews living in Belgium were freethinking. Nonetheless, Jewish religious life retained an important place, as was demonstrated by the traditional costumes at Jewish ceremonies, although at the same time there were important regional differences. We can make a comparison for instance between Brussels and Antwerp, where most of the Jews lived. The secular trend was stronger in Brussels where, for example, there were no Jewish schools. In Antwerp, on the other hand, there were many synagogues, religious schools, and other Jewish educational institutions. One can say that there was in Antwerp a very strong orthodox stream, but this may not be overestimated. Most of the pictures of Antwerp Jews show them dressed in the modern way. It is only after World War II, after a third wave of immigration by Eastern European Jews, that the image of Chassidic Jews began to predominate in Antwerp.[4]

As was demonstrated by the historian Jean-Philippe Schreiber, religious life within the Jewish Community in Belgium went on in a 'normal' way during the occupation. This was partly due to the Belgian legal framework that, according to the Convention of The Hague, impeded any intervention from the German occupying forces. As a result of the Belgian constitution of 1831 which provided for freedom and equality of religion, (most) Jewish communities were recognized by the Belgian state and were granted a title similar to that of the Church fabric. They were legally protected and to a certain extent sponsored by the Belgian state. This implied that contacts existed between the Jewish religious communities and the Belgian authorities, in particular the board of Directors of Religious affairs of the ministry of Justice, led by the secretary general.[5]

Also granted legal status was the Central Israeli Consistory of Belgium, established in 1832, almost immediately after Belgian independence (1830), and that was the official representation of the Jewish community. The Consistory was composed of representatives of the different rites. We can distinguish three important rites: the Dutch/Holland rite (the so-called reformed Jews), the orthodox rite (practised by the so-called traditional Jews, especially East-European and more particularly Polish Jews) and the Sephardim or Portuguese rite (professed by the levanter Jews from Italy, Turkey and so on). This last rite clearly constituted a minority. The task of the Consistory was to represent and to defend the financial interests of the cult towards the civil authorities, in the first place the Ministry of Justice. Furthermore it had to approve the appointments of rabbis and the yearly budgets of the synagogues.

---

4. Saerens, *Vreemdelingen in een wereldstad*, passim.
5. Jean-Philippe Schreiber, "Tussen traditionele en verplichte gemeenschap," *De curatoren van het getto: De Vereniging van de joden in België tijdens de nazi-bezetting*, ed. Rudi Van Doorslaer and Jean-Philippe Schreiber (Tielt: Lannoo, 2004) 71-110; French edition: Jean-Philippe Schreiber, "Entre communauté traditionnelle et communauté obligatoire," *Les curateurs du ghetto: L'Association des Juifs en Belgique sous l'occupation nazie*, ed. Rudi Van Doorslaer and Jean-Philippe Schreiber (Bruxelles: Labor, 2004) 91-140.

The Germans (the Sipo-SD) showed no interest in working with the Consistory and the Jewish religious communities. They preferred to create a new Jewish organisation. At the end of 1941 the 'Jodenvereeniging in België'/'Association des Juifs de Belgique' (JVB/AJB, Association for Jews in Belgium) had been established. In contrast to the Jewish religious communities and the Central Israeli Consistory of Belgium, the JVB/AJB promoted the interests of the Jews not towards the Belgian, but to the German authorities. In 1942 some Jewish resistants, who were opposed to the JVB/AJB, founded the resistance movement 'Joodsch Verdedigingscomiteit'/'Comité de Défense des Juifs' (JVC/CDJ, Committee for the Defense of Jews). The JVC/CDJ would save thousands of Jews.

All Jews were forced to become members of the 'Jodenvereeniging in België' (JVB/AJB). The aim of the JVB/AJB was to "promote" the "emigration" of the Jews. It also supervised the Jewish educational system and the Jewish social security system, although in fact these organisations fell under the jurisdiction of the Secretary General of the Ministry of Internal Affairs and Public Health, while the Jewish educational system was in the competence of the Ministry of Education. By the establishment of the JVB/AJB the Germans tried to abolish the Israeli communities and to incorporate them into the JVB/AJB. In other words, they hoped the JVB/AJB would eventually coordinate both Jewish social and religious life. But this plan turned out to be of no avail. To be sure, the board of the JVB/AJB created six committees in January 1942: a committee for Religion in addition to the committees for Charity and Social affairs, Education, Emigration, Finances and Culture. But the committee for Religion never became operative. In August 1942 four departments replaced the committees: Finances, Social Assistance, Education and Administration. No new department of Religion was founded. So, finally the JVB/AJB never proceeded to a systematic abolishment of the existing Jewish communities.[6]

Yet, at the end of September 1940 the Central Israeli Consistory of Belgium resumed its activities. At the end of the same year the Jewish religious communities continued their traditional tasks as well, such as covering the cost of funerals for Jews. Also religious offices proceeded as usual, not only in the synagogues, but even in the prison of

---

6. Schreiber, "Tussen traditionele en verplichte gemeenschap," 84-86.

Forest/Vorst (Brussels) where, until 1943, services were organized for Jewish criminals, imprisoned by Belgian juridical authorities. And in Antwerp, for example, until about 1941 Jewish teachers were still paid by the Antwerp city government. Moreover, during the whole course of the war, in celebration of Jewish Easter, the Jews were provided with unleavened bread ('matse'), baked by the famous Antwerp biscuit plant Parein, among others. Alongside this, the most prominent Antwerp Jewish 'matse-bakery', Enelka's Matzos Factory, was allowed to continue its activities until at least 1942. Later, a Jewish people's kitchen in Brussels provided ritual kosher meals until at least March 1944. In May 1943 Jewish women still went to the 'mikvah', ritual-bathing house in Brussels.[7]

Of course, since the deportations to the 'East' had removed so many Jews, the above-mentioned situation referred to only a minority – be it a relatively considerable minority of several thousands[8] – of Jews who could legally pursue their lives, such as functionaries of the JVB/AJB, employees in Jewish religious communities and funeral undertakings, Jews with a specific nationality, like the Belgian, Hungarian and Turkish Jews (until the end of September 1943), partners of a 'mixed' marriage, people enlisted on the so-called 'German-Palestinian' exchange program, persons having earned some merits for Belgium, etc.[9] The majority of the Jews were deported or went in to hiding, thus becoming 'illegal'. There are nonetheless examples of hidden Jews celebrating Jewish feasts and receiving 'matze' from the people hiding them (among them a number of Catholic clergy).

The so-called deportations to the 'East' were carried out in conjunction with raids from the summer of 1942 onwards. This affected the visits to synagogues. In September 1942 Salomon Van den Berg, one of the Brussels members of the general board of the AJB, wrote in his diary: "Les raffles ont continué de plus belle, des centaines de familles sont dans le désespoir. Entre temps, nous avons eu la Nouvelle Année. Celle-ci a été fêtée très tristement. La synagogue était presque vide, et pour la première fois sans doute depuis son existence, il n'y a pas eu de sermon. Le Grand Rabbin a eu peur de voir mal interpréter n'importe quel sermon qu'il aurait pu prononcer, et il a préféré s'abstenir complètement.

---

7. Schreiber, "Tussen traditionele en verplichte gemeenschap," 79, 82, 92-94.
8. Still in January 1944 the number wanting 'matse' was assessed by the Head Rabbi as between 5,000 and 10,000 (*ibid.*, 93).
9. *Ibid.*, 109.

Les gens ont eu peur de se rendre à la synagogue de peur qu'on ne vienne les y prendre."[10]

Salomon Van den Berg gave a description of the situation in Brussels. In Antwerp, however, the situation had already worsened prior to the deportations, and local religious life already had been affected. More than a year earlier, especially in April 1941, a pogrom had broken out. Collaborating Flemish organisations set fire to the house of a chief Rabbi and two synagogues. Talmuds and Thoras were torn to pieces and then burned on the streets together with other religious articles. Furthermore, hundreds of shop-windows were broken. Exactly one year later, in April 1942, the Antwerp bench of Aldermen decided to comply with the request of the Germans to cancel the housing-allowance of the minister of the Israeli worship. The neighbourhood of the Antwerp Synagogues remained in a state of unrest after the 1941 progrom. In June 1942 the Mayor of Antwerp asked his Chief of Police to organise police supervision around the synagogues on Saturday afternoons. "Jewish persons" had complained "at having been attacked and religious subjects having been damaged," he said.[11]

In autumn 1943 the local Antwerp section of the JVB/AJB was liquidated. At the same time the activities of the Jewish religious communities ceased. The same happened in Liège, Charleroi, Gent, Ostend, Mons and Arlon. On the other hand, the Brussels local section of the JVB/AJB and the Israeli religious community could continue their activity more or less during the whole course of the occupation.[12]

Unlike the Catholic Churches of France and the Netherlands, the hierarchy of the Belgian Catholic Church never took a public position against the persecution of Jews during the occupation. This did not, however, prevent clergy, cloister members, and Catholic institutions from taking their responsibility in helping Jews. Such help ranged from the writing of recommendations for Jews who came to Belgian dioceses for help, and the production of false baptism and identity documents along with the baptism of Jews with the intention of preventing deportations, to providing accommodation or finding hiding places for those hiding, providing them with food stamps, or smuggling them out of the country. Some in the church responded with

---

10. SOMA (AB 207): Salomon Van den Berg, *Journal de guerre* (unpublished manuscript).
11. Saerens, *Vreemdelingen in een wereldstad, passim.*
12. Schreiber, "Tussen traditionele en verplichte gemeenschap," 95-106.

rather noteworthy efforts to help the victims, such as "a sister from Turnhout" (province of Antwerp) who is reported to have married a Jew in a civil wedding.

My analysis of the attitude of the Belgian Catholic Church will be primarily concerned with the secular (diocesan) clergy. I shall only be able to provide short accounts of the extremely worthy efforts of cloistered clergy such as those of the Benedictine Henry (cloistered name Bruno) Reynders, born in the Brussels community of Ixelles/Elsene, who is reported to have saved 307 Jewish children.[13] I shall be particularly concerned with the general attitudes of the secular clergy in the archdiocese Mechelen, with a distinction between the provinces of Antwerp (a Flemish province) and (Walloon and Flemish) Brabant. I shall also briefly treat the dioceses of Liège and Tournai, which were also home to many Jews, concentrated in Charleroi (diocese Tournai) and Liège.

Map of Belgian dioceses and provinces

13. [Johannes Blum], *Père Bruno Reynders: Juste des nations* (Bruxelles: Le Carrefour de la Cité, 1993).

For the sake of context I will provide a short synopsis of the Belgian geographical situation. Belgium is divided into French-speaking and Dutch-(Flemish-)speaking territories. At the time of World War II, the Dutch-speaking provinces were: Antwerp, West Flanders, East Flanders, and Limburg; the French-speaking provinces were: Hainaut, Liège, Namur, and Luxembourg. The province Brabant was composed of a Dutch-speaking (the Leuven/Louvain district), a French-speaking (Nivelles), and a bilingual, but primarily French-speaking, part (the Brussels district). The archdiocese of Mechelen consisted of the provinces of Antwerp and Brabant together; the diocese of Liège consisted of the provinces of Liège and Limburg; and the diocese of Namur consisted of the provinces of Namur and Luxembourg. In addition to these were the dioceses of Tournai (i.e the province of Hainaut), Bruges (Brugge; the province of West Flanders), and Gent (the province of East Flanders).

II. Statistical Information Regarding Belgian Resistance and Aid to the Jewish Community[14]

A distinction must be made between French-speaking (including Brussels) and Dutch-speaking Belgium when discussing the Belgian resistance in general during the Second World War. All previous research indicates a much larger presence of resistance in French-speaking (and the Brussels area) Belgium. Of the underground papers that appeared during the occupation, at least 567,415 (or 73.19%) were written in French, 141 (or 24.86%) were in Dutch, and 11 (1.94%) were bilingual. Two of these French underground papers appeared in Flanders. During the first months of war, the numeric discrepancy was even greater: of a total of 95 underground papers, only seven (7.36%) were in Dutch, compared to 79 (83.15%) in French and nine (9.47%) which were bilingual.[15]

This trend can also be noted amongst Catholic clergy. In French-speaking Belgium and in Brussels, the call for some form of resistance seems to have been seen by many clergy as a self-evident duty. Many participated in the resistance movement 'Geheime Leger'/'Armée Secrète' (the Secret Army) and intelligence-gathering organizations such as

---

14. See also: Lieven Saerens, "De Antwerpse verzetspers en de jodenvervolging," *Tegendruk: De geheime pers tijdens de Tweede Wereldoorlog* (Antwerpen: AMSAB-ISG/SOMA-CEGES/Erfgoeddeel Stad Antwerpen/Stad Antwerpen/Universiteit Gent, 2004) 145-164.
15. Etienne Verhoeyen and Nico Wouters, "Verzet (Tweede Wereldoorlog)," *Nieuwe Encyclopedie van de Vlaamse Beweging* (Tielt: Lannoo, 1998) 3292-3297.

Socrates, which also provided assistance for Belgian 'work-resisters'. In Dutch-speaking Belgium, such resistance was much less outspoken. One of the indications of this comes to light in an analysis of the number of diocesan priests arrested by the German authorities, 400 in total.[16] The distribution amongst the different provinces – with Brabant split into the districts of Brussels, Louvain, and Nivelles – is as follows:

Table 2: Belgian diocesan priests arrested by the Germans during World War II

Hainaut		82 (20.50%)
Liège		73 (18.25%)
Brabant		61 (15.25%)
- Brussels district	40 (10.00%)	
- Louvain district	11 (2.75%)	
- Nivelles district	10 (2.50%)	
Luxembourg		42 (10.50%)
Namur		39 (9.75%)
Bruges		35 (8.75%)
Gent		30 (7.50%)
Antwerp		26 (6.50%)
Limburg		12 (3.00%)
Total		400 (100%)

This indicates that 286 (or 71.50%) of the priests arrested by the German authorities were from the French-speaking region or from Brussels, compared to 114 (28.50%) from the Dutch-speaking region.

In the general issue of aid to the Jewish community, there is also a marked difference between the French-speaking and Dutch-speaking regions of Belgium. One first set of available statistics regarding this difference is found in the 1990 publication *Liste der 1978 ermittelten Retterinnen und Retter jüdischer Menschen in Belgien im Zeitraum 1940-1945*. This is the report of the initiative of the 'Hulde Comité van de Joden van België aan hun Helden en Redders' (Homage Committee of the Jews of Belgium to their Heroes and Rescuers) from 1978, during a mass meeting in Brussels to honour all Belgian 'helpers'.

---

16. The number of 400 is based on the book of Edmond Leclef and concerns only those diocesan priests who were arrested for a long period of time: Edmond Leclef, *Le Cardinal Van Roey et l'occupation allemande en Belgique* (Bruxelles: Ad. Goemaere, 1945) 339-347.

THE BELGIAN CATHOLIC CHURCH AND THE PERSECUTION OF JEWS 253

A total of 2,966 'helpers' were honoured. Addresses were provided for 2,290. The 676 others (22.79%) were reported as "ohne Ortsangabe" ("without address") or lived outside the country. They will not be taken into account in the following short analysis. If we leave aside Brussels for a moment, it is obvious at a first glance that a large majority of 'helpers' was from the French-speaking region: 960 (or 41.92%). There is also a remarkably small number of 'helpers' from Antwerp. 152 'helpers' were from the area then classified as Antwerp and its greater metropolitan region, or 6.63% of the total. The statistic for Brussels is of an entirely different order. For Brussels and its greater metropolitan area, the number of 'helpers' is as large as 718, or 31.35% of the total – nearly five times the number of those reported from Antwerp. Of course, the Brussels statistic must be somewhat relativized given the fact that the population of Brussels at that time was larger.[17]

Table 3: "Liste der 1978 ermittelten Retterinnen und Retter jüdischer Menschen in Belgien im Zeitraum 1940-1945"

French-speaking provinces and French-speaking Brabant:		960 (41.92%)
Dutch-speaking Brabant and the Brussels area:		904 (39.47%)
* Brussels and the Brussels greater metropolitan area:	718 (31.35%)	
The province of Antwerp		260 (11.35%)
* Antwerp and the Antwerp greater metropolitan area:	152 (6.63%)	
East Flanders		86 (3.75%)
Limburg		34 (1.48%)
West Flanders		46 (2.00%)
Total		2,290 (100%)

The fact that aid to Jews in the Brussels and French-speaking areas was significantly greater was confirmed by a 1994 list of 165 organizations, colleges, and colonies which provided care for Jewish children during the occupation.[18] (No location was published for seven of these institutions, so we will not include them in our account.) More than 70%

17. Saerens, "Die Hilfe für Juden in Belgien," 231-232.
18. Viviane Teitelbaum-Hirsch, *Les larmes sous le masque: Enfants cachés* (Bruxelles: Labor, 1994).

of the institutions named were situated in the districts of Brussels and Nivelles and the provinces Hainaut and Namur, compared to less than 11% in the provinces of Antwerp, Limburg, East Flanders and West Flanders. If the Brussels district is not accounted for, the district of Louvain (6.33%) is the region in Flanders providing the most assistance. The area providing by far the greatest assistance is the larger metropolitan region of Brussels, where at least 42 institutions (26.58%) provided assistance. Only one institution is listed for the greater metropolitan area of Antwerp.

Table 4: Number of institutions providing help for Jewish children

1. Brabant	76 =	48.10%
- Brussels District	54 =	34.18%
* Brussels and Brussels greater metropolitan area	42 =	26.58%
- Nivelles District	12 =	7.59%
- Louvain	10 =	6.33%
2. Hainaut	28 =	17.72%
3. Namur	20 =	12.66%
4. Liège	11 =	6.96%
5. Luxembourg	6 =	3.80%
6. West Flanders	6 =	3.80%
7. East Flanders	4 =	2.53%
8. Antwerp	4 =	2.53%
- Antwerp district	2 =	1.27%
* Antwerp and Antwerp greater metropolitan area	1 =	0.63%
- Mechelen district	2 =	1.27%
- Turnhout district	0 =	0.00%
9. Limburg	3 =	1.90%
Total	158 =	100 %

I have analysed new sources of data to determine whether they confirm this analysis. More specifically, my study was aimed at analysing one specific group: secular clergy members. One of the primary reasons for this choice is the extensive resources on this group, including an extensive questionnaire, available at the 'Studie- en Documentatiecentrum Oorlog en Hedendaagse Maatschappij' (SOMA, Centre for Historical Research and Documentation on War and Contemporary Society).[19] In the current study it will also be possible to take Mechelen into account.

19. "Enquête Kerk en clerus tijdens de bezetting" (SOMA, nrs. AA 1217-1218 and 1449).

Mechelen was not only the seat of the archdiocese, but also the city from which the deportation trains departed. The performance of Cardinal Van Roey, it seems to us, also yields further explanation regarding the differences in assistance provided in Brussels and Antwerp.

The conclusions drawn from the lists of the 'Hulde Comité' and Viviane Teitelbaum-Hirsch are confirmed by my analysis of the questionnaire organized by SOMA during the period of 1977-1982 – approximately forty years after the period concerned.[20] The questionnaire regarded the attitudes and activities of the secular clergy during the occupation. Questions F1 and F2 of the questionnaire explicitly deal with the issue of assistance to the Jewish community. The archdiocese Mechelen also organized a questionnaire-based inquiry in 1945 regarding 'war events', amongst both the secular and regular clergy (that is, clergy members who have taken on orders). It is not easily comparable with the SOMA inquiry, partially because the secular clergy was not explicitly asked to respond further regarding assistance to Jews.

III. The Archdiocese of Mechelen

1. General Survey

Only the reports regarding the secular clergy from the archdiocese inquiry of 1945 have so far been recovered, and these only partially. More specifically, what has been recovered is the part which deals with parish clergy – which does not include, for example, the clergy working in educational institutions. The Archive of the Archdiocese of Mechelen possesses 100 reports on local parishes. For the province of Brabant, nearly all parishes are represented; 87 of the reports deal with Brabant (22 on the Brussels district, 39 on the Louvain district, and 26 on the Nivelles district). The additional 13 reports deal with the provinces of Luxembourg (two) and Antwerp (eleven, of which eight deal with the Mechelen district, two deal with the Turnhout district, and one deals with the Antwerp district). In addition to the fact that these reports do not explicitly ask about assistance to the Jewish community, the reports are also somewhat unrepresentative for this study for a further reason: the 'Jewish centre', 'the Brussels metropolitan area', was almost unrepresented with only five

---

20. Historians agree that it is a highly representative inquiry. Mark Van den Wijngaert, *Een koning geloofd, gelaakt en verloochend: De evolutie van de stemming onder de katholieke bevolking ten aanzien van Leopold III tijdens de bezetting (1940-1944)* (Leuven: Acco, 1984).

reports dealing with it. Two of the five parishes in the Brussels area reported assistance to Jews: Laken (parish of Notre-Dame) and Schaerbeek (parish of Saint John and Saint Nicholas). The parishes of Tienen and Zoutleeuw in the Louvain district also report assistance to Jews. Of the eleven parishes in Antwerp, on the other hand, not a single one reports such help. In addition to the 100 reports in the Archdiocesan archive, we were able to locate 71 additional reports in the University Archive of the 'Universitaire Faculteiten Sint-Ignatius' (UFSIA, Antwerp) regarding the Archdiocesan inquiry. These deal with all of the parishes in the province of Antwerp: two are from the Mechelen district, 30 from the Turnhout district, and 39 from the Antwerp district. Not a single report mentioned clerical assistance to Jews, which is particularly noteworthy since no less than 20 dossiers dealt with parishes in the larger Antwerp metropolitan area, also an important Jewish population centre.[21]

In the total of 82 (i.e. 11+71) reports located from the province of Antwerp, then, not a single clergy member mentioned assistance to Jews, while four of the 87 clergy in Brabant did indeed do so, even though they were not asked about this issue. To what extent can these statistics be regarded as providing a picture of the actual situation? And to what extent are the Brussels statistics – however small the sample group it covers – representative? Can we conclude that since two of the five clergy from the greater Brussels region spontaneously mentioned their assistance, around 40% of the Brussels clergy in general assisted Jews in need? The SOMA inquiry provides more decisive information.

300 clergy members answered the SOMA questionnaire.[22] These were, specifically, those who actively exercised their profession as secular clergy within Belgium during the time of the occupation. Of 183 questioned who had been priests in the province of Brabant during the Second World War, 78 (or 42.62%) had offered assistance to Jews. A large majority of these 78 *actively* aided Jews in hiding. (By active aid I understand: finding hiding places for Jews, providing them with (stolen) food stamps, making false identity cards, or smuggling Jews out of the country.) For the province of Antwerp, there were 117 questionnaires maintained for use in the study. Fifteen (12.82%) of these offered assistance to Jews, of which nine (7.69%) were *actively* involved in aiding Jews in hiding: five from the city of Antwerp and four from Mechelen.

21. Saerens, *Vreemdelingen in een wereldstad*, 714-715.
22. See above, note 19.

Table 5: Secular clergy's assistance to Jews in archdiocese Mechelen (based upon the SOMA inquiry)

Brabant		
1. General		
Total number questioned:	183	
Assisted Jews:	78	= 42.62%
2. Nivelles District		
Total number questioned:	36	
Assisted Jews:	19	= 52.78%
3. Brussels District		
Total number questioned:	111	
Assisted Jews:	54	= 48.65%
Number questioned in greater Brussels metropolitan area:	94	
Assisted Jews:	48	= 51.06%
4. Louvain District		
Total number questioned:	36	
Assisted Jews:	5	= 13.89%
Antwerp		
1. General		
Total number questioned:	117	
Assisted Jews:	15	= 12.82%
2. Mechelen District		
Total number questioned:	27	
Assisted Jews:	5	= 18.52%
Number questioned in the city of Mechelen:	19	
Assisted Jews:	5	= 26.32%
3. Antwerp District		
Total number questioned:	59	
Assisted Jews:	9	= 15.25%
Number questioned in greater Antwerp metropolitan area:	39	
Assisted Jews:	8	= 20.51%
4. Turnhout District		
Total number questioned:	31	
Assisted Jews:	1	= 3.23%

It is noteworthy that not a single priest questioned in the province of Antwerp indicated assistance to the Jewish community by means of the school with which he was associated. In Brabant, 22 of the 80 (27.50%) replied affirmatively in this regard.

The SOMA inquiry seems to indicate that those who offered assistance in Antwerp were far less 'organized' than their counterparts in Brussels, where it was possible to construct a number of 'networks'. The smaller amount of help provided in Antwerp is implied by the fact that three priests in Brussels who indicated that they had offered no assistance to Jews referred to such assistance provided by some of their colleagues. Not a single priest in the region of Antwerp referred to other colleagues assisting.

2. 'Organized' Assistance in the Brussels Region

Although in Brussels, slightly more than 50% of those questioned provided help to the Jewish community, the high degree of commitment among the clergy in Anderlecht (particularly Kuregem) and Schaerbeek is particularly noteworthy (both Brussels district). These are neighbourhoods where particularly large concentrations of Jews lived, situated near the Brussels North and South stations respectively. Eight of eleven priests in Anderlecht and eight of thirteen in Schaerbeek questioned provided assistance, significantly more than half. Also significant for the Brussels region is the participation of a number of parishioners or, as has been reported, the participation of nearly the "whole parish" in assisting.

One of the first to show concern for the fate of converted Jews was Georges Meunier, pastor of Saint John and Saint Nicholas in Schaerbeek. As early as 29 September, 1941, he had written a letter to Cardinal Van Roey, showing his support for the cause of Jews converted to Catholicism: "A number of my [converted Jewish] parishioners and a few others are terribly worried about the situation," he wrote. The letter was written in response to a message from one of his parishioners, not named, a council member in the community of Schaerbeek connected to the Commission for Public Relief, that the Germans were considering requiring the Belgian communities to have their Jews do 'dirty work' without the necessary tools and implements, such as the cleaning of sewers. According to Meunier, it was possible that Jews would even be required to wear the Star of David (this was in September 1941). Meunier wished Van Roey to ask the Belgian authorities to request ("or even demand") that the converted Jews be exempted from such tasks: "The Belgians first – but possibly also our poor brothers of Dutch origin… or 'stateless' or Russian – or even Austrian – German, Polish… how many of them have not eminently served our country? How the Christian sentiments of our people will be wounded if one debases also these 'Christians' who have renounced their Judaism and the 'tares' of Israel…" He proposed providing a stamp for the identity cards of converted Jews: a Christian cross or a symbol of their parish.

George Meunier and his assistant pastor, Armand Spruyt (born in Antwerp), became veritable specialists in baptising Jews, according to Meunier's testimony in 1945: "They both incessantly provided instruction to these lost and shepherdless sheep." Between 1939 and 1944 they baptised no less than 160. Their assistance went even further than this. 22 Jewish children were provided with shelter by Miss Fernande Henrard from the rue Dupont in Schaerbeek. In addition, "countless" Jews came to request advice or to ask for a safe hiding place for their children. The parish priests placed them in monasteries, sanatoria, colleges, and centres for handicapped children, or with individuals. Most found shelter in Brabant, but some were also sheltered in Lanaken in Limburg, or Farnieres in Luxembourg. Cooperation also came from the 'Werk der Speelpleinen Brussel' (Playground Initiative Brussels), a project of the priest Edward Froidure. The 'Werk der Speelpleinen Brussel' provided for some Jewish children's summer vacations and provided them with food. According to his statement in 1987, Froidure saved about 100 Jewish children.[24]

George Meunier's 1945 account describes "a secret association" of priests "devoted to saving Jews," which convened a number of times at the national offices of the 'Jeunesse Ouvrière Chrétienne'/'Katholieke Arbeidersjeugd' (JOC/KAJ, Catholic Workers' Youth). This association had twelve active members, including Meunier and Armand Spruyt, as well as the Schaerbeek priest Antoon De Breucker, the Namur priest Joseph André, and the Benedictine Paul Démann from the Mont César Abbey in Louvain, himself a Jewish convert.

The KAJ/JOC also cooperated with the 'Joodsch Verdedigingscomité'/'Comité de Défense des Juifs'. The discrepancy between Antwerp and Brussels, and even more, that between Flanders and Wallonia – is quite apparent here. The JOC provided for at least 58 children through its 'Rustoorden voor Verzwakte Kinderen' (Children's Sanatoria) in Dworp and Braine-l'Alleud (in Brabant), Leffe-lez-Dinant and Schaltin (Namur), Banneux (Luxembourg), and Lauwe (West Flanders). The JOC/KAJ even established an information centre for Jewish families, which provided parents with contact information of "people who can help find a place for their children." The KAJ organization 'Boerenhulp voor Stadskinderen' (Farmers' Assistance for Urban Children) also cooperated, which, according to a report of the KAJ published directly

---

23. Jo Gerard, *Interview historique de l'abbé Froidure* (Bruxelles: Pierre H. Wouters, 1987).

after the war, kept 500 Jewish children out of the hands of the German authorities. The assistance given to Jews by the KAJ/JOC branches is worthy of further research. From an inquiry carried out directly after the war, and conducted by the KAJ/JOC itself, regarding the resistance activities of its own members, which asked explicitly about assistance offered to Jews by the Dutch-speaking wing, the following appears to be the case. None of the seven KAJ-branches of the Antwerp League had offered assistance to Jews. The Brussels League had offered assistance, although only to a limited extent. Three of the completed 16 questionnaire forms mentioned some assistance.[24]

But let us return to Schaerbeek, where, besides Georges Meunier and Armand Spruyt, Antoon De Breucker was also active. He was from Bocholt in Limburg and, after a period of teaching in Brussels, became assistant pastor of the parish of Saint Mary in Schaerbeek in October 1938. Along with a few other parishioners, he committed himself from 1942 on to saving Jewish children. Just as Meunier and Spruyt did, he cooperated with Fernande Henrard, a teacher connected with De Breucker's project 'L'Ami des Pauvres' (Friend of the Poor). He also worked together with the director of the nearby home 'Notre Foyer' (Our Home), Madeleine de Roo. According to a post-war account of De Breucker, together they helped 250 Jewish children to hide. Most of these children were provided with shelter in diverse places within the province. About 40 stayed in Schaerbeek and the surroundings, trusted to individuals or to religious institutions such as the Sisters of Charity of Saint Vincent de Paul. De Breucker also provided false identity cards. He also cooperated with the Benedictine Bruno Reynders, connected to the Abbey of Mont César in Louvain.

As already mentioned, the Kuregem clergy (district Brussels) was deeply committed to assisting in the situation the Jews found themselves in. The parish priests of Our Lady Immaculate here played a noteworthy role: pastor Jan De Ridder and assistant pastors Victor Verbiest, Leonard Bernaerts (born in the province of Antwerp) and Jan Bruylandts. Bruylandts is reported to have helped approximately 80 Jews. The parish house was transformed into a hiding place, from which Jews could be brought to safe houses located around Brussels and Mechelen. It is reported that these parish clergy, with the aid of "the people and the community administration of Anderlecht," hid thirteen Jewish boys from a Jewish children's home, among other things. Moreover, they were

---

24. Saerens, *Vreemdelingen in een wereldstad*, 718.

also involved in a raid on 20 May, 1943, at the Sisters of the Holy Saviour in Kuregem, in which about ten Jewish girls were released and taken into hiding. In addition, the teachers from the nearby College of Our Lady actively assisted Jews. Not only were Jewish children taken in, but a few priests functioning as teachers were able to help Jews escape the official round-ups of Jews.

When looking at the other towns in the Brussels area, we come across the assistant pastor in Forest/Vorst, Albert Zech and the Franciscan Sisters for the Dissemination of Faith in Forest. Furthermore, there was a person designated specifically for the responsibility of hiding Jews at the office of the parish of Saint Alix in Woluwe Saint-Pierre/Sint-Pieters-Woluwe. According to the account of assistant pastor Jean Massion, the "whole" parish cooperated in hiding Jews. Some priests who provided assistance were actively aided by their family members, all from the Brussels area. This occurred in the case of the assistant pastor of Saint Susan in Schaerbeek, Adriaan Vermeesch, whose sister cooperated in initiatives with the assistant pastor of Saint Nicholas in Brussels, Arnold Gillessen. And after the arrest of the assistant pastor of Saint Michael and Saint Gudule in Brussels, Joseph Weeghmans, the arrestee's own sister provided assistance to Jews.

3. 'Organized' Help in the Antwerp Region

For the greater metropolitan region of Antwerp, there is, as mentioned, evidence of five clergy members who can be described as 'active helpers' – in the sense of their involvement in the hiding of Jews. Two of these provided help only to individuals. Constant Goethals, assistant pastor of the Cathedral of Our Lady, placed "a Jewish girl" in a nunnery. "I visited her regularly. After the war I did not hear any more from her." Emiel Van der Kerken, a teacher at the College of Saint John Berchmans, hid "a mother with two children." "She fled out of fear." A third Antwerp clergy member was somewhat vague in his answer. Jacques Heuvelmans, assistant pastor of the parish of Saint Catherine in Antwerp-Kiel, responded to the question as to whether he had helped Jews: "Yes, by strengthening them and supplying provisions."

Jacques Heuvelmans indicates no cooperation with others, while two other Antwerp clergy did, allowing us to consider their assistance to Jews as more or less "organized." Gilbert Van Dormael, born in the district Louvain and teacher at the Saint Edmund College in Antwerp, lived, according to his own account, in the middle of the "Jewish quarter." During nights, reported Van Dormael, he witnessed from the school, together with the school director, a colleague, and a couple who lived there, "many raids upon Jews." In this period, he cooperated with the "Sisters of the Left Bank" to help shelter Jewish children. He mentioned no help from his colleagues. He mentioned also that the Sisters of the Union with the Sacred Heart on Zurenborg told him at a certain moment that they housed Jewish children as residents. It is unclear whether Van Dormael also cooperated with this effort, or whether it was the information from the sisters that moved him to begin assisting children.

Apparently, Gilbert Van Dormael, at the time of the SOMA inquiry, was still quite moved by the war drama. He added to his questionnaire a handwritten *Belevenissen in het Jodenkwartier van Antwerpen* (Experiences in the Jewish Quarter in Antwerp). This document is important in that it provides afresh a view of what bystanders could see and hear at the time razzias (or raids) took place: "We [Van Dormael and the residents of the school] witnessed there the inhuman deportation of Jews. This happened mostly at night. People heard screaming coming from the street. The Germans (abductors) called out to us, ordering us to draw back and close the windows, and they pointed their guns at us … The Jews were taken away in a 'moving truck' into which they were pushed. Men, women, elderly, young children … I saw them once throw a child above the heads of those occupying a full moving truck. The poor victims cried from fear and pounded the walls of the truck. They were taken to the barracks in Mechelen."

The assistant pastor of Saint Anthony in Antwerp, Lodewijk De Pauw (born in Mechelen), was also involved in what can be described as "organized" action. From his own account, he helped a few young people by finding an address where they could hide, and later providing falsified baptismal certificates. He also placed children in schools who were hiding with a number of his acquaintances and also provided falsified baptismal certificates for them. Finally, his signature was also requested by a member of the Daughters of Wisdom in the 'Italiëlei' in Antwerp for five falsified baptismal certificates.

It is quite remarkable that neither of the two priests included in the SOMA inquiry who were stationed at the Antwerp parish of Saint Joseph mentioned any form of assistance to Jews. Neither did either of the two mention any assistance on the part of colleagues. This parish was situated in the middle of the "Jewish neighbourhood," in a situation similar to the Brussels parishes of Kuregem and Anderlecht.[25]

The significantly lesser assistance of the Antwerp clergy is confirmed by the homage list published in 1963 by Ephraïm Schmidt which mentions 97 "'true friends during time of need' from Antwerp and the surrounding communities."[26] Three of these are mentioned as priests, but subsequent analysis reveals that only one held a function in Antwerp, namely pastor Simons. This is most likely Corneel Simons, pastor of the parish of Saint Willibrord in Borgerhout, likewise in the middle of the "Jewish neighbourhood." The other two priests had functions in Mechelen, namely the secretary of the archdiocese Mechelen, René Ceuppens, and the assistant pastor of the parish of Saints Peter and Paul, Gustaaf Du Moulin, of Jewish origin and at the time a trustee of the already mentioned 'Katholiek Bureau voor Israël' (KBI). They were not the only ones in Mechelen who assisted Jews. Of the nineteen inquired from Mechelen – including Ceuppens – five responded positively to the question as to whether they had assisted Jews: in other words, 26.31%, more than the "flattering" figure for Antwerp of 20.15%. (In fact only 5 Antwerp priests, 12.82%, *actively* gave help.)

René Ceuppens (born in Louvain), according to the inquiry, was in contact with Ida Sterno, responsible in the 'Joodsch Verdedigingscomiteit'/'Comité de Défense des Juifs' for sheltering Jewish children. He also opened his house for the temporary shelter of Jewish children.

---

25. Is the lack of help to be explained by the 16 June 1942 arrest of Edward Salman, assistant pastor of the parish of Saint Joseph? On 15 December, 1942, assistant pastor Armand Cassiers was also arrested. However, in the Brussels area, clergy were regularly arrested, and this did not prevent clergy there from assisting Jews. On 21 May 1941, Joseph Weeghmans, assistant pastor of Saint Gudule in Brussels, was arrested. Decades afterwards, Weeghmans remained just as strident: "For the Jews: I tried to help in the chances I had, and they (*"les boches,"* i.e. the Germans) knew it – a number of different 'interrogators' visited me. Once I was stopped, my sister helped the Jews and others, and was eventually stopped herself, but that is another issue, and she is now deceased." Also his colleague, Pierre Meert helped Jews, in spite of the fact that he seemed to be somewhat influenced by the stereotype of "the rich Jew." He was assistant pastor at Saint Gudule since 30 April 1942. To the question, "resistance?," he answered: "Housed and hid Jews," and in the further, more specific question, "Assistance to Jews?," he specified: "Yes and hid them without accepting compensation even though they're loaded with money and jewels." And when, on 22 December 1943, the previously mentioned Victor Verbiest, assistant pastor of Kuregem, was arrested, the help provided Jews by his confraters was not abated; much to the contrary.

26. Ephraïm Schmidt, *L'histoire des juifs à Anvers (Antwerpen)* (Antwerpen: Ontwikkeling, [1969]).

Fernand Cammaert, a professor at the Saint Joseph seminary, also provided housing for Jews. Those living in the neighbourhood of the Dossin-barracks, a neighbourhood of Mechelen, were particularly involved in offering assistance to Jewish children. The Franciscan Missionary Sisters of Mary were a 'centre of assistance activity' in this neighbourhood, who also received the help of Victor Heylen, who taught at the Major Seminary of Mechelen. We can also mention in this regard Albert Dierckx, a teacher at the Saint Rombout College, who "as a neighbour of the Dossin barracks" organized a service for "very young Jewish children." Both Heylen and Dierckx were from the Antwerp Kempen region, Rijkevorsel and Turnhout respectively.

4. "Mechelen: City of Cardinal Van Roey, and of the Dossin barracks"[27]

Cardinal Van Roey, born in Vorselaar, was also a son of the Antwerp Kempen region. In the first years of the occupation, he maintained a circumspect relation to the Germans. From the middle of 1942 on, this relation became more characterized by enmity.[28]

As we have seen, Van Roey had shown little concern for the persecution of Jews in the German Reich before the Belgian occupation. But during the occupation, Van Roey was not indifferent to the anti-Jewish measures. In December 1940, when Jews who had settled in Antwerp after 1938 were deported to Limburg, "he attempted, in a modest way, to come to their help." Afterwards, he received a letter on 29 December 1940 from the head rabbi Salomon Ullmann, which thanked him "for steps which Your Eminence took, in an attempt to better the position of those affected by the deportation measures in Antwerp."[29]

It was particularly the drama that took place after July 1942, literally under his own nose, which struck Van Roey. This is apparent from the work published by his private secretary Edmond Leclef directly after the war, *Le Cardinal Van Roey et l'occupation allemande en Belgique* (Brussels, 1945), and his correspondence, kept at the archive of the archdiocese. We were unable to find many of the letters cited by Leclef in the archives of the archdiocese. Neither were the letters to the papal nuncio mentioned by Leclef, included in the Vatican-authorized publication *Actes et*

---

27. *Le Flambeau* (organ of the 'Joodsch Verdedigingscomiteit'/'Comité de Défense des Juifs'), March, 1943.
28. Alain Dantoing, *La 'collaboration' du Cardinal: L'Église de Belgique dans la guerre 40* (Bruxelles: De Boeck/Wesmael, 1991).
29. Leclef, *Le Cardinal Van Roey*, 229-230.

Documents du Saint Siège relatifs à la Seconde Guerre mondiale (11 volumes, Vatican, 1965-1981). From the non-systematically organized correspondence of the archdiocese Mechelen, we reconstructed 70 dossiers with requests for intervention on behalf of Jews. The dossiers concern more than 100 persons.[30]

The data of the requests for intervention reflect the general tempo of the persecution of Jews in Belgium:

Table 6: Chronological overview of the number of intervention requests (based on the archive of Cardinal Van Roey)

	1940	1941	1942	1943	1944
January				4	
February				1	
March			1	1	
April					1
May			4		
June		2	1	1	3
July			3	2	1
August			13	2	
September		1	7	1	
October	1	1	4	4	
November		1	2	2	
Dececmber			4		
Total[31]	1	5	39	18	5

Van Roey wanted no personal contact with the German occupying force. He did appoint a few mediators, such as his private secretary Edmond Leclef and honorary cannon Pieter Willem Van der Elst, pastor in Uccle/Ukkel (district Brussels). Leclef was born and brought up in Antwerp, and came from a conservative-bourgeois milieu. The seventy dossiers we reconstructed regarding interventions on behalf of Jews, were interventions by Leclef himself. An analysis of the dossiers makes it apparent that Leclef took steps for most, if not all, of the cases. The vast majority of the dossiers (at least 46, or 65.71%) dealt with converted and/or Belgian Jews and/or mixed marriages (marriages with a Belgian Catholic and Jewish partners). No less than 30 dossiers deal with converted Jews.

---

30. Saerens, *Vreemdelingen in een wereldstad*, 722-728.
31. Two of the 70 dossiers were not dated.

Twenty dealt with mixed marriages (we include two betrothals), and in eleven of these cases, the Jewish partner had converted to Catholicism. Sixteen dossiers mention explicitly that the Jews were of Belgian nationality, of which seven referred to persons who had neither converted nor were partners in a mixed marriage.

In 32 of the 70 dossiers, letters of recommendation and/or letters testifying to a personal intervention of non-Jews were found, forty in total. Clergy wrote twenty, mostly recommendations. Others were letters written by friends, close acquaintances, or colleagues of the party involved, most of them written on the initiative of the writer him/herself. There are also two others, one by a lawyer and one by a physician, who supported their clients.

In the dossiers, two periods can be distinguished. The first period, from circa June 1941 to June 1942, contains requests to be exempted from anti-Semitic measures such as listing in the register of Jews and the wearing of the Star of David. All requests, seven in total, relate to converted, and mostly Belgian, Jews. The requirement to wear the star of David since June 1942 resulted in a particular problem for converted Jews when they went to mass: "How can we go to church and to communion, when we walk around with this sign that says 'Jew' stuck on our clothes?"

Most of the requests for help and protection were of course made during the period of deportations, as is apparent from the table with the chronological summary of the number of interventions. "Since the month of July 1942, the persecution took on unheard-of proportions," Van Roey's private secretary, Edmond Leclef, recalled: "Every day, a certain number of Jews, regardless of age or gender, was called together from all corners of the country to Mechelen, where they were brought to the barracks of Dossin, provided with blankets and food for fourteen days."[32]

The 'Jodenvereeniging in België'/'Association des Juifs de Belgique' (JVB/AJB), established by the German occupiers in late 1941 was, according to a memo of king Leopold III, the first to hear from the Gestapo that "all Jews under 40 years old, regardless of nationality, would be transported with their families to Eastern Europe before the first of September." For the older Jews, "camps" were provided between Mechelen and Evere (province of Brabant). According to the memo, the JVB/AJB decided to request an audience with Cardinal Van Roey for

---

32. Leclef, *Le Cardinal Van Roey*, 230.

the head rabbi of Belgium, also their current president, Salomon Ullmann. Delegates of the JVB/AJB were also sent to the Royal Palace and to the Secretary-General of Justice, Gaston Schuind.[33]

Nothing yet has been found in the archives of the archdiocese regarding a discussion between Van Roey and Ullmann. The archive of the Royal Palace does contain a dictated memo for the king, written by his adjunct-cabinet chief Gobert d'Aspremont-Lynden, in which a report is given regarding the discussion with the representative of the 'Jodenvereeniging in België'/'Association des Juifs de Belgique' (JVB/AJB), Raymond Wolff. According to Wolff, the JVB/AJB desired "primarily an intervention on behalf of Jews *with Belgian nationality*," "who number 3,500 out of 50,000." According to Wolff, the situation still appeared "hopeless," since "the question depended exclusively on the Gestapo, and was entirely independent of the *Militärverwaltung*." Wolff's only hope was with an intervention by the Cardinal.[34]

The elderly deacon and pastor of Saint-Gilles (district Brussels), Gaspard Simons, also had hope of an intervention on the part of Van Roey. On 2 August 1942, he wrote to the Cardinal, "flooded" as he was with requests for "demarches" (measures). He believed to have heard that Van Roey had procured an exemption for Belgian Jews. He pointed out that even a woman who had recently given birth and was seriously ill had been forced to go to Mechelen, "with the perspective of being separated, husband, wife, and children, each taken in a different direction."[35]

In contrast to what Gaspard Simons had thought, Van Roey contacted the German authorities for the first time only on the next day, 3 August 1942, by sending Edmond Leclef. Leclef went to the *Militärverwaltung* and was received by Dr. Rudolf Leiber, head of the police and *Feldgendarmerie*. He suggested four categories for exemption (it is not clear as to what degree these categories were the result of discussion with the head rabbi): Catholics of Jewish origin; Jews with Belgian nationality; Jews married to Catholics; "Jewish girls who, far from their families, would be exposed to great danger."[36]

Edmond Leclef was unable to obtain an acceptable exception for converted and baptized Jews: "Dr. Leiber answered that Berlin had no regards for the issue of religion and only took race into consideration."

33. Saerens, *Vreemdelingen in een wereldstad*, 725.
34. *Ibid.*
35. *Ibid.*
36. Leclef, *Le Cardinal Van Roey*, 231.

Leiber did give him "the guarantee" that Jews of *Belgian nationality* (cf. the 'policy of the lesser evil') would not be deported, nor would Jews under 17, or above 40. "He did add that the *Militärverwaltung* was not responsible for the measure, nor for its execution, and that only the Gestapo was authorized in this matter."[37]

A day later, 4 August 1942, the day that the first deportation trains left Mechelen, a disappointed Van Roey wrote to the secretary of state in Rome, Cardinal Maglione: "The treatment which Jews must undergo at this moment is truly inhuman and moves everyone to sympathy and indignation; Catholics of Jewish origin are also subject to these measures. I have tried to attain mitigation of the measures, but have unhappily accomplished nothing."[38]

Edmond Leclef was immediately confronted with two flagrant infringements of the assurances he had verbally received from Dr. Rudolf Leiber. He went twice, on 10 and 12 August 1942, to the *Kreiskommandantur* of Mechelen, where a certain Lieutenant Marcus received him. On the second occasion, Marcus interrupted him almost immediately, and concluded: "We can do nothing for the Jews. Go directly to the Gestapo, although I don't believe you have of a chance of accomplishing anything…" Leclef then lost his patience, and spoke pointedly: "(…) I do not in any way doubt your good faith, nor that of Dr. Leiber. Only I cannot understand that officers like yourselves sweep aside or excuse the illegalities, injustices and indecencies committed by the Gestapo." Although Leclef was informed, for the second time, that the Gestapo had the last word on deportations, he did not go to this authority: "The Cardinal [Van Roey], informed of this discussion, was also of the judgement that further efforts were useless."[39]

Van Roey had therefore resigned himself almost immediately to the fact that converted Jews would not be spared deportation. Neither could Jews in mixed marriages be assumed safe. Nonetheless, Jews in certain quarters appreciated the steps which Cardinal Van Roey had taken. In particular, the (actually non-official) 'Centraal Israëlitisch Consistorie van België' (Central Israeli Consistory of Belgium), whose headquarters at the moment were established in Antwerp, was grateful. Van Roey received a letter from the 'Centraal Israëlitisch Consistorie' dated 12 August, thanking him "for the good will and sympathy Your Eminence

37. Leclef, *Le Cardinal Van Roey*, 231.
38. *Ibid.*, 232.
39. *Ibid.*, 233.

has showed on the occasion of the sad circumstances in our dear country in which the Jewish population now finds itself."[40] We add that, according to the statement of the Antwerp JVB/AJB functionary Maurice Benedictus, around August/September 1942, Van Roey came to intervene with the Antwerp Catholic mayor Léon Delwaide regarding the cooperation of the Antwerp police in raids on Jews.[41] Another notable JVB/AJB figure, Salomon Van den Berg (from Brussels), seemed to have fewer positive words regarding Van Roey. Benedictus, who was himself 'involved' with deportations and ultimately fled the country, gave his opinion on Van Roey in an official memo for the Belgian government in London. Van den Berg expressed his own opinion in a personal diary. This is found in the context of his describing the performance of the Belgian authorities on behalf of Jews of Belgian nationality, being a Belgian Jew himself. If he was being honest with himself, it seems, the intervention should not be over-evaluated. In the beginning of 1943 Van den Berg noted: "Until now, the Belgians are not worried, but there are so few who have enough respect for the king and government [sic] to be motivated to do enough for the Jews so they could honestly say they had done all they could. I know that they can't change much, that they do what they can, but it is isn't enough. *It seems to me that in the other war [World War I], Archbishop Mercier carried more authority*".[42]

When Salomon Van den Berg wrote this passage in his diary, the first deportations and razzias of the summer of 1942 had already occurred. Van Roey never publicly condemned the razzias and deportations. He seems also to have been informed of such public condemnations by the Catholic hierarchy and clergy in other countries. From the archive of Cardinal Van Roey, one may conclude that he knew about the episcopal letter of 6 September 1942 of the French archbishop of Lyon, Cardinal Gerlier, and the protest of the Norwegian priests in November of the same year. He most likely also knew of the episcopal letter of the French archbishop of Toulouse, Msgr. Saliège, of 23 August 1942. Saliège's letter was broadcast by BBC radio. An important witness, Paul Struye, later a Belgian minister of Justice, leaves little doubt as to the reach of the BBC into Belgium. "In spite of the ban by the occupying authorities and the rigorous condemnations and sanctions, it seems that nearly all Belgians

---

40. Leclef, *Le Cardinal Van Roey*, 234.
41. Saerens, *Vreemdelingen in een wereldstad*, 617, 726.
42. Maxime Steinberg, *L'étoile et le fusil*. Vol. II: *1942. Les cent jours de la déportation des juifs de Belgique* (Bruxelles: Vie Ouvrière, 1984) 166 (my italics, LS).

keep up with the London broadcasts, either by listening themselves, or by hearing about them from others."[43]

In spite of Van Roey's 'silence', he had nonetheless condemned "the doctrine of blood and race" a few months earlier, on 4 March 1942, in "a speech." The content of the speech continues the trend of his pre-war general line on the issue: a rather theoretical and heavily spiritual message that does not mention anti-Semitism or the persecution of Jews specifically.[44] Furthermore, it seems that Van Roey had once considered explicitly and publicly protesting against the deportations. This is at least mentioned in a letter of 21 September 1942 written by the Liège attorney and 'rescuer' Albert Van den Berg to the Liège Bishop Kerkhofs:[45] "His eminence [Van Roey] has considered whether he would protest what is happening to the Jews. He has decided to do nothing." According to Van den Berg, Van Roey ultimately had three reasons for not protesting against the treatment of Jews:

– The Germans had declared that they were only concerned with the Jews of the German Reich, including Poland, Silesia, Ukraine, Yugoslavia, and Austria. The Belgian and Dutch Jews, then, had nothing to fear. [cf. the 'policy of lesser evil', L.S.]
– The occupying forces seemed to take no account of previous protests.
– Van Roey feared that protest would result only in harm to the (hidden) Jewish children.[46]

The avoidance of public protest did not prevent Van Roey, via his private secretary Edmond Leclef, from intervening in a number of individual requests for help. This is also apparent from a letter to Cardinal Maglione of 18 December 1942, in which Van Roey describes the drama and hopelessness of the situation: "Since I wrote you on 4 August, the arrests and deportations of Jews have incessantly continued, and I don't believe many are left in Belgian territory. These measures were carried out with a brutality and cruelty that have filled the Belgian people with a deep disgust. I have intervened in a number of cases, but in general to no avail. Even the converted and baptised Jews

---

43. Saerens, *Vreemdelingen in een wereldstad*, 727; Paul Struye, *L'évolution du sentiment public en Belgique sous l'occupation allemande: Documents pour servir à l'histoire de l'occupation allemande en Belgique* (Bruxelles: Lumière, 1945) 48.
44. Saerens, *Vreemdelingen in een wereldstad*, 727.
45. About Albert Van den Berg and Kerkhofs, see *infra*.
46. Léon Papeleux, "Le réseau Van den Berg qui sauva des centaines de juifs," *La Vie Wallonne*, 1981, no. 375-376, 129-208.

were not spared." The replies to these two letters to Maglione are not known.[47]

What then, was the result of the individual interventions of Van Roey? Let us examine the 70 reconstructed dossiers. 47 dossiers deal with requests for exemption from "required employment," or were on behalf of persons who were arrested, confined to the Dossin-barracks, or had already been deported. 31 of these 70 dossiers deal with persons in the Dossin-barracks or (temporarily) in jails elsewhere in Belgium. In total, these 31 dossiers deal with 52 persons. For at least 35 persons (67.30%) the attempt at help had no success: they all were deported. The other 17 persons are dealt with in 14 dossiers, of which 7 dossiers deal with mixed marriages. Two dossiers deal not only with Belgians, but also point out that the concerned parties themselves, or else their sons, had fought in May 1940 with the Belgian army. King Leopold III and the Queen mother Elisabeth had involved themselves in some way or other in at least three other dossiers, by means of cabinet and secretariat, respectively. Of the 80 or so detainees for whom the king had intervened, at least 80% were actually deported. In general, the result of the initiatives of the cabinets of Leopold III and the archbishop was extremely poor. The cabinet of the Queen mother Elisabeth achieved somewhat better results, without being a resounding success. Not only did it intervene for 419 persons – significantly more than in the cases of Van Roey and the king –, the deportation percentage was also lower: (at least) 232 of the 419 persons (55.37%) were deported.[48]

IV. Liège: Bishop Kerkhofs's Hand in Organizing Assistance[49]

As mentioned, the diocese of Liège consisted of the Dutch-speaking province of Limburg and the French-speaking province of Liège. A few thousand Jews lived in the province Liège, primarily in the city of Liège, the seat of the diocese. Fewer than a hundred Jews lived in Limburg, spread over a number of cities and villages, too small a number to make it worth including the province of Limburg in our analyses.

---

47. Leclef, *Le Cardinal Van Roey*, 234.
48. Saerens, *Vreemdelingen in een wereldstad*, 728.
49. For further information: Florence Matteazzi, "L'attitude du clergé face à la Shoa dans le diocèse de Liège," *Entre la peste et le choléra*, ed. Maerten, Selleslagh and Van den Wijngaert, 177-207.

Louis Joseph Kerkhofs, born in Limburg, was the Bishop of Liège since 1927. He had held a particular interest and concern for the Jewish people throughout his life, though sometimes his main interest was in converting them to the Catholic faith. In 1924, a branch of the 'Aartsbroederschap tot Gebed voor de Bekering van Israël' (Brotherhood for Prayer for the Conversion of Israel) was established in Liège, an organization founded in 1904 in Paris. The branch in Liège was headed by Msgr. Louis De Gruyter. Kerkhofs (like the Bishop of Namur, Msgr. Heylen, born and raised in Flanders) supported the Liège branch. At the end of the 1920's, this led to the announcement of a number of 'prayer days' in Liège for the conversion of Israel.

Let us first examine the results of the SOMA inquiry.[50]

Table 7: Secular clergy's assistance to Jews in province Liège (based upon the SOMA inquiury)

1. General	
Total number questioned:	80
Assisted Jews:	29 = 36.25%
2. Liège-District	
Total number questioned:	41
Assisted Jews:	14 = 34.14%
3. Verviers-District	
Total number questioned:	21
Assisted Jews	7 = 33.33%
4. Huy-District	
Total number questioned:	18
Assisted Jews	8 = 44.48%

The statistics show that in the province of Liège, the amount of assistance given to Jews was three times the amount provided in Antwerp. In the greater metropolitan region of the city of Liège, twice the amount of assistance was provided as was given in the Antwerp metropolitan region, where significantly more Jews were residing at the time. Furthermore, two priests who had not assisted Jews spontaneously mentioned help provided by their colleagues. I might add that in Liège it is also quite remarkable that a number of seminary students – who at the time were not ordained and whom I have thus left out of the statistical account – were

---

50. See above, note 19.

also involved in actively aiding Jews. For six (25%) of the 24 seminarians involved in the inquiry, this was the case. It was not easy for seminary students to assist Jews; nearly all seminary students from other dioceses answered, in the question with regard to assisting Jews, that this was nearly "impossible," since seminaries were "closed communities," without any feel for the outside world. Apparently there was quite another "spirit" in the Liège seminary, which is not surprising, since one of the central figures in organizing and inspiring help for the Jews was the priest André Meunier, who had taught at the seminary in Liège since 1930.

The SOMA inquiry only provides a short look at the phenomenon of assistance for Jews in the case of Liège. It must be added that many other priests in Liège were involved in other forms of resistance, and were in principle prepared to aid Jews. "I simply did not have the opportunity to help Jews," answered the assistant pastor of Hodimat, François Schils, who was also the local head of the 'Geheim Leger'/ 'Armée Secrète'.

A very important particularity in the case of Liège is the fact that, unlike Cardinal Van Roey, Bishop Kerkhofs himself developed initiatives for aiding Jews. Also indicative of Liège is how many priests there referred to the heroic posture of Cardinal Mercier during the First World War. The Liège priest Louis de Lamotte put it thus: "The position on the matter of Cardinal Van Roey? People do say 'he's not Mercier,' but no one dares say more than this." De Lamotte was himself the friend of a Jewish doctor, and provided a number of false baptism certificates for Jews. The assistant pastor of Vierset-Barse, Lucien Marichal, who had helped a Jewish girl, responded in the SOMA questionnaire: "Mercier would have protested against the deportation of Jews; but the one cardinal is not the other… But [on the other hand] Msgr. Kerkhofs was very admirable."

Kerkhofs personally sheltered a Liège rabbi, Joseph Lepkifker, pretending he was his secretary. Lepkifker's wife and youngest son were brought to the Saint Joseph home for the elderly of the Sisters of Mercy, directed by Sister Lutgarde, Kerkhof's niece. When it became too dangerous there, Kerkhofs brought the rabbi's wife and son to the Sisters of Bonsecours, a small cloister in Liège. Later, Joseph Lepkifker and his oldest son Mendel were sheltered by the above-mentioned Msgr. Louis De Gruyter, inspirer of the Liège branch of the 'Aartsbroederschap tot Gebed voor de Bekering van Israël'. In the meantime, Kerkhofs had, in August 1942, also asked the Catholic school camp of Stoumont to take in Jewish children.

Following the example of Cardinal Van Roey, Kerkhofs did not clearly or openly protest against the persecutions. However, it seems to me no coincidence that on 15 October, 1942, he urged the clergy of his diocese to aid "the children in the city who are most endangered and needy." This was during the time that the deportations were taking place and can be interpreted as an implicit plea to help the persecuted Jewish children.

In addition, Kerkhofs contacted a number of laymen who were particularly involved in assisting Jews. The so-called Albert Vandenberg-Georges Fosny network was begun with this initiative of Kerkhofs. At first glance, this network appears to be a kind of 'family business'; Vandenberg and Fosny were brothers-in-law. Vandenberg was an attorney who was quite active in the parish of Saint-Christophe. Fosny was a Catholic industrialist, who had been active in the fight against fascism before the war. Both men were assisted in their initiatives of helping the Jews, by Berthe Vandenkieboom, Fonsny's niece, and by Pierre Coune, Vandenberg's secretary. However, this was not only a 'family-run' initiative; it was a larger network. At a certain moment, cooperation was brought about with the groups situated around the Namur priest Joseph André, the Brussels priest Antoon De Breucker and the Louvain Benedictine Bruno Reynders. In total, Fosny and Vandenberg were able to save 229 Jews, including about 80 children. As already mentioned, De Breucker helped hide 250 Jewish children. Reynders helped at least 307 Jews, including more than 200 children. André is reported to have saved 240 Jews, including 180 children. In total, all these groups, which were primarily active in the French-speaking region of the country, are reported to have saved more than 1,300 Jews.

During 1942, furthermore, a strong cooperative bond developed between Vandenberg-Fosny and the JVC/CDJ, which had been founded that same year, in which the Liège priest Emile Boufflette was active. In Liège, sometimes known as "la cité ardente," during these difficult years, the religious and socio-political prejudices that had so characterized the pre-war years were pushed into the background. Or, as the Liège resistance paper *Churchill Gazette* wrote, "We repeat, we do not defend the Jews upon religious grounds. These discussions are not particularly relevant at this time." Not only was so-called neighbourly love the foundation of these sentiments, but also a form of patriotism, and more specifically, the fact that the Germans were seen as the common enemy.

V. Diocese of Tournai

Before the war an important number of the Tournai clergy sympathised with the New Order (fascist) party Rex. But during the war most of the Tournai clergy joined the (right-wing) resistance. Since January 1940 the bishop of Tournai was Louis Delmotte. His attitude towards the German authorities was similar to that of Cardinal Van Roey.[51]

The case of the diocese of Tournai's attitude towards the persecution of the Jews needs further investigation. The following figures are only based on the SOMA-enquiry.[52]

Table 8: Secular clergy's assistance to Jews in province Hainaut (based upon the SOMA inquiry)

1. General	
Total number questioned:	79
Assisted Jews:	36 = 45.56%
2. Tournai-District	
Total number questioned:	22
Assisted Jews:	9 = 40.90%
3. Charleroi-District	
Total number questioned:	34
Assisted Jews	17 = 50.00%
4. Mons-District	
Total number questioned:	23
Assisted Jews	10 = 43.47%

The statistics show that in the province of Hainaut, the amount of assistance given to Jews was nearly four times the amount provided in the province of Antwerp. In the larger metropolitan region of the city of Charleroi, more than twice the amount of assistance was provided as in the Antwerp metropolitan region, where significantly more Jews were residing at the time. In contrast to Antwerp, nearly all the Charleroi priests – as well as priests in Liège and Brussels – *actively* helped Jews. Furthermore, six priests who had not assisted Jews spontaneously mentioned help provided by their colleagues or others. As I said, not a sin-

---

51. Fabrice Maerten, "Le clergé du diocèse de Tournai face à l'occupation: la voie étroite," *Entre la peste et le choléra*, ed. Maerten, Selleslagh and Van den Wijngaert, 127-165.
52. See above, note 19.

gle priest in the province of Antwerp associated with a school indicated assistance to the Jewish community in their institutes. In Hainaut, 14 of the 42 (33.33%) replied affirmatively in this regard.

With regard to Tournai it has also to be mentioned that particularly all of the members of the local ('collaborating') JVB/AJB were also members of the local (resisting) JVC/CDJ. This is another reason why so many Jews were saved in the bishopric of Tournai. Further research should disclose how far the local JVC/CDJ worked together with the local priests.

VI. Conclusion

In spite of its great prestige, the Belgian Church did not publicly protest against the persecution of Jews; it protested no more than the Belgian secretary-general, or Pope Pius XII, for example. The hesitation of the Pope ultimately meant that within 'monolithic' Catholicism, there was decidedly no 'Catholic message' in this regard. Partially as a result of this, reactions of the Catholic Church differed from country to country. The church hierarchy saw itself between the horns of a difficult dilemma: public silence, and so (perhaps) saving lives; or speaking out, but (perhaps) risking lives. Partially because of his fear for the fate of Jewish children in hiding, Van Roey did not speak out. This is very strange, because for other matters like the employment of Belgian forced labour in Germany Van Roey publicly protested. These forced labourers where not Jews, but only Belgians. Van Roey also publicly protested against the plunder of the church bells – in fact the plunder of 'dead material'.

The outcry from the 'Joodsch Verdedigingscomiteit'/'Comité de Défense des Juifs', the Jewish resistance movement, was unfortunately left unanswered. The fact that the trains in which the Jews were being deported departed from Mechelen elicited the following comment from the 'Joodsch Verdedigingscomiteit'/'Comité de Défense des Juifs': "Mechelen, the city of Cardinal Van Roey, but also the city of the Dossin barracks ... The carillon of the cathedral Saint Rombout is not loud enough to stifle the cries of the tortured victims."[53]

Van Roey's attitude was consistent with the so-called 'policy of the lesser evil'. As long as Jews naturalized as Belgians and the converted Jews who were one's fellow (Belgian) Catholics were not touched, silence followed. This principle was shared with at least a portion of the

---

53. *Le Flambeau*, March 1943.

leadership of the Jewish community in Belgium, which was nearly all of Belgian nationality. This might have been why the archdiocese resigned itself so quickly to the notion that nothing could be done for the converted non-Belgian Jews.

Although the archdiocese was informed at least twice that the Gestapo held the ultimate authority on deportations, like the cabinet of King Leopold III, it did not turn to this authority. It was, first of all, discouraged by the *Militärverwaltung* about the possible outcome; and for 'traditional diplomacy' it seemed less than evident that it was safe to take the step of approaching the "coarse" Gestapo, which had engaged in "illegalities, injustices, and atrocities." The personal intervention of the Cardinal was primarily limited to a number of individual dossiers. It was primarily in a few, occasional cases of mixed marriages that Van Roey seems, at a first glance, to have had a small, relative success. However, the occupying authorities did not in practice deport partners in mixed marriages anyway. So in this sense, one can speak with even more difficulty of a 'relative success'.

The public 'silence' of the cardinal, as well as the continuing anti-Semitism in broad segments of the Belgian Catholic public, did not prevent a very large number of clergy and faithful from actively helping their fellow Jewish citizens in hiding. Van Roey was aware of this assistance and was in favour of it, but he did not take such an initiative himself: instead he gave the faithful a free hand to give their help. Another fact is remarkable considering the cardinal's passivity. The largest female religious congregation in Flanders, the 'Sisters of Vorselaar', never helped Jews.[54] Van Roey himself was originally from Vorselaar and even visited the superiors of Vorselaar regularly. It thus seems obvious that Van Roey never instructed the sisters to help Jews.

The phenomenon of active assistance provided by Christians to Jews was not limited to Belgium. This also occurred, for example, in France. In both Belgium and France, the Church possessed an impressive network of congregations and confessional schools, which had the extra room necessary to provide a haven for the needy. Moreover, clergy were more experienced in dealing with people in need, they had extensive contact networks at their disposal, and knew which parishioners were trustworthy.[55]

54. Raf Vanderstraeten and Marij Preneel, *175 jaar Zusters der Christelijke Scholen Vorselaar: 1820-1995* (Vorselaar/Leuven: KADOC, 1996).
55. Susan Zuccotti, *The Holocaust, the French and the Jews* (New York: Basic Books, 1993).

In hindsight, only conjecture is possible concerning the effect of public protest. It is possible that more clergy and faithful would have engaged themselves in aiding Jews. In this context, there was a remarkable difference between the Antwerp region on the one hand and Brussels, Liège and Charleroi regions on the other. For Brussels, the duty of aiding Jews seems to have been rather self-evident, so public protest did not seem necessary. For Antwerp, the situation was apparently different. That 'indignation' about the razzias and deportations was shown in steadily greater segments of the Antwerp population is clear, but the actual step toward providing active assistance seems to have been a less self-evident choice in Antwerp. For some clergy, assisting the Jews was even considered an impossible sacrifice.

The difference between Flanders on the one hand and Brussels and Wallonia on the other was evidently not – to use in this context an emotionally charged word – 'ethnic' in nature. It was due mainly to place, circumstances and context, more particularly the history of those regions and peoples in ideological, political, cultural and economic respect. For instance, the priest Armand Spruyt and Bishop Kerkhofs, who were the figureheads of the rescue operations in connection with the Jews in Brussels and Liège respectively, were both born and bred in Flanders.

The smaller amount of aid in Antwerp – and the 'collaboration' with the Germans by the Antwerp municipal authorities also had consequences for the number of deported Jews. In Brussels 37% of the Jewish population was deported; in Liège 34% and in Charleroi 38%. The number of deported Jews in Antwerp was of another dimension: there more than 65% was deported. The result approached the extremely high deportation figure of the Netherlands (about 74%). (In France 25 to 30% of the Jewish population was deported.)

There is no unilateral explanation to be given for the smaller amount of aid provided in Antwerp. A number of conclusions can be drawn, and hypotheses formulated. An analysis of the general opinions of the population of Antwerp regarding Jews in the 1930's shows that there was apparently, in the pre-war metropolis, a high degree of intolerance, which would have the effect of weakening the resistance and opposition to anti-Jewish measures. It must also be underlined that, concerning the persecution of the Jews, the Antwerp municipal government did almost anything the German authorities asked for. In the summer of 1942 the Antwerp police even arrested more than 2,000 Jews, who were deported to the Dossin-barracks in Mechelen (and later on to Auschwitz).

At least some of the Antwerp clergy were aware of this level of intolerance: "The Jews have never been liked ... in Antwerp," said one priest. This of course does not mean that the rest of the country was free of anti-Semitism. Quite the contrary was true of Brussels, but anti-Semitism seems at least to have penetrated less deeply there.

The degree to which Antwerp clergy members were more prone to anti-Semitic sentiments remains an open question. It is plausible that they were less apt to support the Jews themselves since they were confronted with such a large segment of the population with anti-Semitic and passive attitudes. That is, it seems that in Antwerp it took more courage to immediately and spontaneously offer help. This had the effect of creating a vicious circle. Sociological studies have shown a number of times that some are more likely to actually offer help in circumstances when a reference group possessing some degree of authority which shares their values explicitly calls on them to help. Churches and church authorities are often cited as examples of such reference groups. But amongst the church authorities themselves, apparently some priests, unconsciously, needed directives from their hierarchical governing structure, as the situation in Antwerp seems to suggest. In addition to this, because of a lack of a moral example, but this time on the part of their local clergy (and local city government), fewer parishioners in Antwerp were likely to aid their Jewish neighbours. In Brussels there were even a few mentions of assistance provided by "whole" parishes. Also in Liège and Charleroi similar actions were found. References to such broad-scale help in Antwerp have not been found.

There are, in addition to this, a number of other possible explanations for the situation in Antwerp. The Antwerp branch of the 'Joodsch Verdedigingscomiteit'/'Comité de Défense des Juifs', an organization with which Catholics cooperated, was slow to react. It only began functioning in earnest in 1943, by the time that most of Antwerp's Jewish population had already either fled or been deported. Furthermore, Antwerp missed, during the crucial period of the deportations, an outspoken catholic underground paper, like *La Libre Belgique* in Brussels, *De Vrijschutter* in Halle (district Brussels) and *Churchill Gazette* in Liège, which explicitly protested against the deportations. What is also noteworthy in the case of Antwerp, but just as significant, is the greater boldness of the occupying authorities in their efforts against not only the Jews, but also all who aided them. In Antwerp, when Jews in hiding were discovered by the authorities, not only the Jews, but also those sheltering them were arrested. This made assistance to Jews in Antwerp a risky endeavour, and was not the case in the rest of the country.

Although our analysis has emphasized so-called 'organized' aid, aid in general was usually informal. In many cases, help came spontaneously, from neighbours, in-laws, business relations, friends, and colleagues. But most likely it was usually the Jews themselves who took the first step, often approaching persons with whom they had little or no acquaintance, in order to request help for themselves or their children. Those actively helping formed a minority of the Belgian population; but success in hiding was also dependent on the 'tacit cooperation of the Belgian street'. Some who aided did so in explicit obedience of the so-called Christian doctrine of 'love for one's neighbour'. Others referred to their patriotism, and more specifically, to the fact that they saw the Germans as their common enemy. A few saw their aid as a continuation of their pre-war struggle against anti-Semitism and racism.

During the occupation, a large portion of the Belgian Catholic population engaged in "une belle forme de résistance" (a beautiful form of resistance) in their assistance of Jews, children in particular. This resistance was most prominent in the Brussels and French-speaking regions.[56] The post-war words of thanks brought by Ida Sterno to René Ceuppens, secretary of the archdiocese, do history justice: "(...) [I] can only respond with my homage and recognition (...) of the people and the Church, thanks to whom a great many children were saved from even more terrible suffering. We do not forget that the majority of our children were left with Catholic families and in institutions led by monks and priests."[57]

---

56. The difference between French-speaking and Dutch-speaking Belgium – between the Walloon and Flemish part of Belgium – can certainly not be reduced to the different geographical situation. (In the Walloon part are more woods and 'mountains', which would facilitate going into hiding). At the time – from October 1942 onwards – that Belgian (i.e. not Jewish!) 'work-resisters' went into hiding on a large scale, they could do so as easily in Dutch-speaking Belgium as in French-speaking Belgium (Bob Moore, *Victims and Survivors: The Nazi Persecution of the Jews in the Netherlands. 1940-1945* [London: Arnold, 1997]. Neither the presence nor the non-presence of Jews was of importance. In the French-speaking province of Namur lived (nearly) no Jews, nevertheless many found shelter there (Geneviève Thyange, "L'abbé Joseph André et l'aide aux Juifs à Namur," *Entre la peste et le choléra*, ed. Maerten, Selleslagh and Van den Wijngaert, 263-275). The Dutch-speaking provinces of Limburg and West Flanders had practically no Jews either. But contrary to Namur, only a very small number of Jews could hide there.

57. Saerens, "L'aide des catholiques aux juifs dans l'archevêché de Malines," 236-237.

Selective Bibliography

[Johannes Blum], *Père Bruno Reynders: Juste des nations* (Bruxelles: Le Carrefour de la Cité, 1993).

Edmond Leclef, *Le Cardinal Van Roey et l'occupation allemande en Belgique* (Bruxelles: Ad. Goemaere, 1945).

Fabrice Maerten, *Du murmure au grondement: La résistance politique et idéologique dans la province de Hainaut pendant la Seconde Guerre mondiale (mai 1940-septembre 1944)*, Analectes d'histoire du Hainaut, 7, 3 vols. (Mons: Hanonia, 1999).

Florence Matteazzi, "L'attitude du clergé face à la Shoa dans le diocèse de Liège," *Entre la peste et le choléra: Vie et attitudes des catholiques belges sous l'occupation*, ed. Fabrice Maerten, Frans Selleslagh and Mark Van den Wijngaert (Bruxelles/Louvain-la-Neuve: SOMA/Quorum/Aura, 1999) 177-207.

Léon Papeleux, "Le réseau Van den Berg qui sauva des centaines de juifs," *La Vie Wallonne*, 1981, no. 375-376, 129-208.

Lieven Saerens, "The Attitude of the Belgian Roman Catholic Clergy toward the Jews Prior to the Occupation," *Belgium and the Holocaust*, ed. Dan Michman (Jerusalem: Yad Vashem, 1998) 159-194.

Lieven Saerens, "L' aide des catholiques aux juifs dans l'archevêché de Malines," *Entre la peste et le choléra: Vie et attitudes des catholiques belges sous l'occupation*, ed. Fabrice Maerten, Frans Selleslagh and Mark Van den Wijngaert (Bruxelles/Louvain-la-Neuve: SOMA/Quorum/Aura, 1999) 208-240.

Lieven Saerens, *Vreemdelingen in een wereldstad (1880-1944): Een geschiedenis van Antwerpen en zijn joodse bevolking* (Tielt: Lannoo, 2000).

Lieven Saerens, "Die Hilfe für Juden in Belgien," *Solidarität und Hilfe für Juden während der NS-Zeit. Regionalstudien 4: Slowakei, Bulgarien, Serbien, Kroatien mit Bosnien und Herzegowina, Belgien, Italien*, ed. Wolfgang Benz and Juliane Wetzel (Berlin: Metropol Verlag, 2004) 193-280.

Lieven Saerens, "De Antwerpse verzetspers en de jodenvervolging," *Tegendruk: De geheime pers tijdens de Tweede Wereldoorlog* (Antwerpen: AMSAB-ISG/SOMA-CEGES/Erfgoeddeel Stad Antwerpen/Stad Antwerpen/Universiteit Gent, 2004) 145-164.

Ephraïm Schmidt, *L'histoire des juifs à Anvers (Antwerpen)* (Antwerpen: Ontwikkeling, [1969]).

Jean-Philippe Schreiber, "Tussen traditionele en verplichte gemeenschap," *De curatoren van het getto: De Vereniging van de joden in België tijdens de nazibezetting*, ed. Rudi Van Doorslaer and Jean-Philippe Schreiber (Tielt: Lannoo, 2004) 71-110.

Jean-Philippe Schreiber, "Entre communauté traditionnelle et communauté obligatoire," *Les curateurs du ghetto: L'Association des Juifs en Belgique sous l'occupation nazie*, ed. Rudi Van Doorslaer and Jean-Philippe Schreiber (Bruxelles: Labor, 2004) 91-140.

Maxime Steinberg, *L'étoile et le fusil*. 4 vols. (Bruxelles: Vie Ouvrière, 1983-1986).

Viviane Teitelbaum-Hirsch, *Les larmes sous le masque: Enfants cachés* (Bruxelles: Labor, 1994).

Christian Social Movements Confronted with Fascism in Europe
Consistency, Continuity, or Flexibility in Principles, Strategies, and Tactics towards Social and Economic Democracy

Patrick Pasture

I. The Organized Catholic Church, or the Catholic Milieu: Some Preliminary Observations

The Catholic Church is not just the hierarchy but, certainly from a post-Vatican II perspective, also the community of the faithful, the 'people of God' in Hans Küng's seminal expression. It can be argued that this includes the Catholic social movements and parties, which became important actors in continental European societies from the late nineteenth century onwards. However, the exact position of these movements and parties within the Church was not always clear: nevertheless, they should be situated at the outer edge of the Christian community.[1] Some of them explicitly identified themselves with the interests of the Church, but this was by no means always the case. Some parties and movements, on the contrary, even explicitly distanced themselves from a clerical and even from a neat 'confessional' or denominational stance, even if they were essentially composed of Catholics and were inspired by Catholic social teachings. The latter was certainly the case of many Christian trade unions, for example, which followed the 'German' model of an interdenominational and politically neutral Christian organization.[2] In addition, Christian Democratic parties and movements after World War II defined themselves, as opposed to some pre-war Catholic parties, as not being clerical. That was most clearly the case in

---

1. Compare the model of J. M. G. Thurlings, *De wankele zuil: Nederlandse katholieken tussen assimilatie en pluralisme* (Deventer: Van Loghum Slaterus, 1978).
2. See Michael Schneider, *Die christlichen Gewerkschaften 1894-1933* (Bonn: Neue Gesellschaft, 1982) and Eric D. Brose, *Christian Labor and the Politics of Frustration in Imperial Germany* (Baltimore: Catholic University Press, 1985). For a broader perspective see Patrick Pasture, *Histoire du syndicalisme chrétien international: La difficile recherche d'une troisième voie* (Paris: L'Harmattan, 1999) chapter 1.

Germany, Italy, and France, as well as in Belgium. However, even those prewar Catholic parties, with the possible exception of the Dutch Catholic Party, refused to consider themselves as bare expressions of the interests of the Catholic Church.[3]

On the other hand, the position of the Catholic hierarchy towards organized Catholicism was most ambiguous. In fact, the hierarchy rarely favoured, in fact it rather barely tolerated, Catholics to organize politically, be it in parties or unions. Moreover, the position of local or national episcopacies and of the Vatican could diverge considerably. The ambivalent attitude of the Catholic ecclesiastical authorities was closely connected with their attitude towards political democracy. In general, the Church in the interwar period did not really favour democracy, even if it accepted democratic political systems, as it did with dictatorships and Ancien Regime monarchies as well; one can fairly state that, so long as its immediate and spiritual interests were recognized and safeguarded, the Church preferred an authoritarian regime. In that sense, the Catholic authorities only reluctantly supported Catholic or Christian Democratic social movements and they did so only if that was in the immediate interests of the Church. Moreover, as these organizations were led by laypersons and stressed their autonomy, they challenged the clerical order and authority. Catholic Action, still regarded by some as an expression of the 'emancipation' and the recognition of the laity by the clerical Church,[4] in fact can be viewed as exactly the opposite. As the leaders of the Christian Democratic movements in Italy and Belgium correctly emphasized in their disputes with Catholic Action, it was much more a strategy of the hier-

---

3. For the origins of this choice see Statys N. Kalyvas, *The Rise of Christian Democracy in Europe* (Ithaca, NJ/London: Cornell University Press, 1996), who gives ample illustrations and references. Since the 1980s, the literature on Christian democracy has become vast. A recent assessment in Wolfram Kaiser, "Review Article: Christian Democracy in Twentieth Century Europe," *Journal of Contemporary History* 39, no. 1 (2004) 127-135. Recent titles include the double volume of Wolfram Kaiser and Helmut Wohnout (eds.), *Political Catholicism in Europe 1918-45* (London: Routledge, 2004) and Michael Gehler and Wolfram Kaiser (eds.), *Christian Democracy in Europe since 1945* (London: Routledge, 2004); Thomas Kselman and Joseph A. Buttigieg (eds.), *European Christian Democracy: Historical Legacies and Comparative Perspectives* (Notre Dame, IN: University of Notre Dame Press, 2003) (not included in Kaiser's review article); and Emiel Lamberts (ed.), *Christian Democracy in the European Union (1945-1995)* (Leuven: Leuven University Press, 1997).

4. E.g. Martin Conway, "Introduction," *Political Catholicism in Europe, 1918-1965*, ed. Martin Conway and Tom Buchanan (Oxford: Oxford University Press, 1996) 22.

archy to regain control over the laity,[5] even if it was also, as modern scholars agree, a manifestation of Catholic lay militancy.

However, the attitude of the hierarchy towards Catholic political and social movements was not necessarily negative. On the contrary, since the various Culture Wars of the 1870s[6] and especially after the so-called 'turn of the Church to the people' after *Rerum novarum*,[7] such movements for tactical and strategic reasons could also enjoy the support of the Church. Clerics were often involved in organizing Catholic parties and unions. The Belgian Christian unions, for example, had benefited greatly from the activities of Father G.-C. Rutten who, incidentally, stressed the political neutral stance of the union and supported the German model of a politically neutral and interdenominational trade unionism. The French Christian trade union originated largely from an initiative from the Vatican, which – incidentally bypassing the French episcopacy – asked the Brothers of the Christian Schools to promote Christian trade unionism in France. Some clerics became influential political leaders, such as Msgr. Ignaz Seipel, the Austrian chancellor (1922-24 and 1926-29), and Msgr. Tiso, the president of the Nazi puppet State of Slovakia (1939-45). In Austria as well as in the Netherlands, the Catholic clergy was particularly active in organizing the political and social associations.[8]

The attitudes of the Catholic Church towards interwar political systems have received considerable scholarly attention in recent years. In this article, the attitude of the Church towards political democracy and the impact of World War II only offers a general framework and is not

---

5. Emmanuel Gerard, "Adaptation en temps de crise (1921-1944)," *Histoire du mouvement ouvrier chrétien en Belgique*, ed. Emmanuel Gerard and Paul Wynants, KADOC-Studies, 16 (Leuven: Leuven University Press, 1994) vol. 1, 174-245, p. 187; Staf Hellemans, *Strijd om de moderniteit: Sociale bewegingen en verzuiling in Europa sinds 1800*, KADOC-Studies, 10 (Leuven: Leuven University Press, 1990) 174-221. See also Jean-Marie Mayeur, *Catholicisme social et Démocratie chrétienne: Principes romains, expériences françaises* (Paris: Cerf, 1986); Pierre Milza and Serge Bernstein, *Le fascisme italien 1919-1945* (Paris: Seuil, 1980) 158-172.

6. Christopher Clark and Wolfram Kaiser (eds.), *Culture Wars: Secular-Catholic Conflict in Nineteenth-Century Europe* (Cambridge: Cambridge University Press, 2003).

7. Emiel Lamberts (ed.), *Een kantelend tijdperk: De wending van de Kerk naar het volk in Noord-West Europa / Une époque en mutation: Le catholicisme social dans le Nord-Ouest de l'Europe / Ein Zeitalter im Umbruch: Die Wende der Kirche zum Volk im nord-westlichen Europa (1890-1910)*, KADOC-Studies, 13 (Leuven: Leuven University Press, 1992).

8. See esp. Kalyvas, *The Rise of Christian Democracy*; Patrick Pasture, "Between Cross and Class: Christian Labour in Europe 1840-2000," *Between Cross and Class: Comparative Histories of Christian Labour in Europe 1840-2000*, ed. Lex Heerma van Voss, Patrick Pasture and Jan De Maeyer, International and Comparative Social History, 8 (Berne/New York: Peter Lang, 2005) 9-48.

the primary subject. Instead, I intend to look at the position of the Church in its wider organizational components, in particular within the labour movement – the movements for Catholic employers, farmers and the middle-class will only be briefly touched upon – towards social and economic democracy; these last two, however, cannot be disconnected from the political context for several reasons. It is to be expected that Christian social movements played a vanguard role in the shaping of the Churches' ideas, especially on social and economic matters.[9]

Social and economic democracy are largely postwar concepts. Alternatives are (neo-)corporatism and industrial organization. In the interwar period, one can summarize corporatism as a political ideology or vision of the State that aimed at reorganizing society by associating socio-economic corporations, consisting of employers and workers, to the political, economic and social decision-making process.[10] In its authoritarian and political expressions (State corporatism), these corporations would substitute the elected parliament, in more democratic forms they would simply be associated with it and operate alongside parliament. Two questions remain though, the main problem being the authority of the corporate organization and, in some cases, of the employers' organizations in social and economic matters compared to parliament. Secondly, for interwar contemporaries, associations of workers (unions) and employers could be regarded as expressions of the civil society and as democratic per se; they would, then, reject historians' criticisms about their anti-democratic stance.[11] Other key issues in a corporatist organization were the power of the State, the recognition of right to strike, and the freedom of association and affiliation, and thus the nature of the corporations – voluntary associations consisting of separate free and independent unions of workers and employers, or unitary organizations with compulsory affiliation and considered as an executive

---

9. Kees van Kersbergen, *Social Capitalism: A Study of Christian Democracy and the Welfare State* (London: Routledge, 1995).

10. Compare Frans van Waarden, "Introduction: Crisis, Corporatism and Continuity," *Organizing Business for War: Corporatist Economic Organization during the Second World War*, ed. Wyn Grant, Jan Nekkers and Frans van Waarden (New York/Oxford: Berg, 1991) 1-19, esp. 12-13; Dirk Luyten, *Ideologisch debat en politieke strijd over het corporatisme tijdens het interbellum in België* (Brussel: Koninklijke Academie voor Wetenschappen, Letteren en Schone Kunsten van België: Klasse der Letteren, 1996) and id., *Ideologie en praktijk van het corporatisme tijdens de Tweede Wereldoorlog* (Brussel: VUB-Press, 1997).

11. See Peter Heyrman, Patrick Pasture and Geert Vermote (eds.), *Civil Society and Democracy: An Historical View* (Proceedings of the International Conference Leuven/Brussel, 28-29 November 2003, forthcoming).

branch of the State. In most authoritarian corporatist systems, as in Nazism, the corporations were intended as executing instances of a centralized socio-economic policy. In more democratic State systems corporations functioned independently from the central State power. The latter was the traditional Christian view, the former the Fascist version, although, as we will see, the difference was not always obvious for the contemporaries (nor, I would like to add, for some later historians). The main question in this chapter then is if the experiences with Fascism and occupation in continental Europe, modified the attitudes of the Catholic Church, in its widest meaning, towards political and socio-economic democracy, i.e. the role and authority of the trade unions (hence the issue of freedom of association) and the role of the State in the organization of work (i.e. mainly industrial relations).

For this purpose, I do not believe one should isolate the years 1940 to 1945 and to single out the 'Occupation' period, as is the perspective of the ESF project. I consider a wider period, which may end around 1945 with the defeat of Nazi Germany and the democratic reconstruction of Western Europe, but which certainly began much earlier, in fact it would begin with Mussolini's seizure of power in Italy in 1922. Indeed, the case of Italy in some respects most reveals the attitudes of the Catholic world in the first half of the twentieth century towards a political system of omnipresent authoritarian State. Moreover, it provoked Catholics to develop their views on the relationship between Church and State, and the codetermination of the workers in the political as well as the social and economic system. The main encyclical about Church/State relations of the interwar period, *Quadragesimo anno*, for example, cannot – and definitely should not – be understood without proper reference to the existing Fascist regime in Rome. For similar reasons, I will not only look at occupied countries, but will also include the Italian, German and Austrian cases.

II. Italy, the Ominous Example

The case of Italy has already been intensively studied, so I can limit myself here to some reminders. The manner in which the Vatican sacrificed the 'Partito Populare and the Confederazione Italiano del Lavore' (CIL), the 'white' trade union close to the PPI, is particularly illustrative of the fundamental attitude of the Roman Catholic hierarchy towards the interwar political situation and would be repeated later on in Germany and Austria. The Church apparently displayed few regrets in withdrawing its support for the Christian Democratic party and unions in order to save the Catholic Action and the educational activities of the Church, and eventually reach an agreement about Church-State relations, which led to the conclusion of the Lateran Treaty (1929).[12] This policy was largely supported in European Catholic milieus, though there were some notable exceptions, to which we will return in a moment. However, we need first to look in some more detail to the political system introduced by Mussolini.

Italian Fascism was not just a dictatorship, but a political ideology that aimed at controlling the whole society. It was a truly totalitarian enterprise. In that sense, the historical compromise of the Vatican with Mussolini was indeed a compromise, even if the balance was uneven. In Italian Fascism, the State aimed to control everything. However, practice was sometimes different from the ideology or the discourse, as is apparent in the Italian Fascist socio-economic organization. In the socio-economic field, a corporatist system was introduced, based on Fascist corporations. From 1923 (the Palazzo Chigi agreement), and 1925 (the Palazzo Vidoni Pact), the Fascist unions were the only organizations to be recognized by the employers of Confindustria as the sole representatives of labour. The labour laws of 1926 and 1927 sealed the fate of free trade unionism and democratic industrial relations. In 1930, a National Council of Corporations was established and in the major sectors of the economy, supposedly self-regulating corporations were created, although a nationwide corporatist organization of the economy could never be implemented. In fact, as far as they functioned, the employers and big business, and not the State, controlled the corporations, as they determined economic policy if these corporations did not exist.[13] Some steps were taken to implement a Fascist Welfare State, in particular via family allowances and some other indirect wages (end-of-the-year bonuses, severance pay), the organization by the Fascist Party's welfare agencies ('Ente Opere Assentenziali', EOAs) of health camps for young children and the running of a winter relief program, and the organization and centralization of leisure and recreation activities under the framework of the 'Opera Nazionale Dopolavore' (OND),

---

12. Compare Martin Conway, "The Age of Christian Democracy: The Frontiers of Success and Failure," *European Christian Democracy*, ed. Kselman and Buttigieg, 43-67.
13. Eduard R. Tannenbaum, *Fascism in Italy: Society and Culture 1922-1945* (London: Allen Lane, 1972) 100ff.

initially set up within the Ministry of National Economy but from 1927 onwards an auxiliary of the Fascist party.

The Italian 'model' engendered much sympathy among Catholics. In Italy itself large sections of the Catholic community were allied behind the Fascist ambitions already in the early 1920s, while after the conclusion of the Lateran agreements in 1929 conciliation with the Catholic Church appeared complete. Most historians nowadays agree that this conciliation was "probably the most important contribution to the consolidation of the Fascist government in power," which brought Mussolini and his regime "a tremendous internal and international prestige."[14] In the first place, it killed off Catholic anti-Fascist agitation, at least temporally. Moreover, clergy and bishops gave their full support to the Fascist party and to many of its economic and social policies. What attracted Catholics particularly in the socio-economic sphere was, apart from obvious anti-Bolshevism, the introduction of corporatism, seen as a co-operation between the social classes, which responded to very deep Catholic aspirations.

At least one faction within the Catholic world, however, appeared not to be fooled. The fate of the CIL woke up the international Christian labour movement, and provoked a reaction from the International Federation of Christian Trade Unions (better known under its French acronym CISC, 'Confédération Internationale des Syndicats Chrétiens'). This labour international warned against Fascism in its publications and opposed the Italian Fascist syndicalists at the International Labour Organization (ILO), e.g. by voting and arguing against the recognition of the Italian workers' delegations at the international labour conferences.[15] This reaction focussed on the imposed trade union unity and the abolition and persecution of the Christian trade unions. Hence, the CISC turned into the champion of trade union freedom and of freedom of association in general, to which the Christian unions were all the more sensitive since they themselves had to fight for recognition by the State, the employers and the bourgeoisie – often particularly the Catholic establishment – as well as by the Socialist labour movement,

---

14. Quotations from Philip Morgan, *Italian Fascism 1919-1945* (Houndmills/London: Macmillan, 1995) 96. See also Richard J. Wolff, "Italy: Catholics, the Clergy and the Church – Complex Reactions to Fascism," *Catholics, the State and the European Radical Right, 1919-1945*, ed. Richard J. Wolff and Jörg K. Hoensch (Highland Lakes, NJ: Atlantic Research, 1987) 137-157; John F. Pollard, *The Vatican and Italian Fascism, 1929-32: A Study in Conflict* (Cambridge: Cambridge University Press, 1985); John Pollard, "Italy," *Political Catholicism*, ed. Conway and Buchanan, 69-96.

15. See Pasture, *Histoire*, 124-127.

something which they did not fail to emphasize.[16] In Germany, already in January 1923 the Italian case worked as a warning against Hitler.[17] In the absence of an international organization of Catholic parties and given the widespread sympathy for Mussolini, the Catholic parties, most of which were dominated by conservative Catholics and thus often sympathetic to Mussolini, did not react in a similar way. In progressive and Christian-Democratic milieus, however, the PPI received much sympathy. Exiled in France, Great Britain and the USA, the PPI leader Don Sturzo became a martyr and a very influential Catholic critic of totalitarianism and an advocate of the Christian Democratic cause.[18]

III. A Corporatist Trap? Germany and Austria

With the economic crisis of the 1930s, corporatism became more popular than ever in the Catholic world and beyond. Particularly influential were some Austrian radical Catholic thinkers such as Karl Lugmayer, Anton Orel and Johannes Ude. The most radical advocates of corporatism, like the Austrian corporatist Othmar Spahn, aimed at replacing parliamentary democracy by a corporatist structure based on economic corporations uniting employers. However, corporatism was not a well-outlined theory.

Spahn's ideas, that influenced many right-wing Catholics and social movements (such as the 'Heimwehr' in Austria), were combated by, among others, the German solidarist school of Heinrich Pesch and also the young German Jesuit Oswald von Nell-Breuning, who argued for a corporatist order at branch level and who admitted State interven-

---

16. Particularly important for the CISC was the judicial fight of the CISC and its general secretary P. J. S. Serrarens to be recognized as genuine workers' representatives in the ILO. See Abdul-Karim Tikriti, *Tripartism and the International Labour Organisation: A Study of the Legal Concept: Its Origins, Function and Evolution in the Law of Nations* (Stockholm: Almqvist & Wiksell Int., 1982) 201-206 and Pasture, *Histoire du syndicalisme chrétien international*, 117-119.

17. See William L. Patch, "Fascism, Catholic Corporatism, and the Christian Trade Unions of Germany, Austria and France," *Between Cross and Class*, ed. Heerma van Voss, Pasture and De Maeyer, 173-202, esp. 174-175, 178; William L. Patch, *Christian Trade Unions in the Weimar Republic, 1918-1933: The Failure of "Corporate Pluralism"* (New Haven, CT/London: Yale University Press, 1985) and Schneider, *Die christlichen Gewerkschaften*.

18. Jean-Dominique Durand, *L'Europe de la Démocratie chrétienne* (Bruxelles: Complexe, 1995) 127-129; Gabriele de Rosa (ed.), *Luigi Sturzo e la democrazia europea* (Bari: Laterza, 1990); Griet Van Haver, *Onmacht der verdeelden: Katholieken in Vlaanderen tussen demokratie en fascisme, 1929-1940* (Berchem: EPO, 1983).

tion to facilitate the market mechanism. Nell-Breuning was one of the members of the so-called Königswinter Circle, a group of Catholic social thinkers close to the German Catholic labor movement, which also included Gustav Gundlach, Götz Briefs and Otto Brauer.[19] The Jesuit largely influenced the encyclical *Quadragesimo anno* (1931), of which he wrote the basic canvas. Heralded by some (until this day) as a major step in the development of the Catholic social doctrine, it received mitigated reactions at the time of issue. Nell-Breuning later admitted that some passages, particularly those regarding the role of the State, could be interpreted in different ways.[20] Moreover, Pius XI (in a passage added by the Pope himself) spoke out in favourable terms about the Italian Fascist system ("Anyone who gives even slight attention to the matter will easily see what the obvious advantages are in the system," QA 91), even if he admitted that the Fascist State "is substituting itself for free activity" and that "it rather serves particular political ends than leads to the reconstruction and promotion of a better social order" (QA 95). Among the more reserved reactions, one should note that of P. J. S. Serrarens, Secretary General of the CISC, who saw the danger that a corporatist order based on some ideas of the encyclical could be established while ignoring freedom. In general, the Christian labour movement "issued respectful public commentary [re QA] and moved on to other issues" (W. Patch). The introduction of a corporatist regime in Austria showed how much these hesitations were justified, even if the encyclical recognized the importance of free unions (QA 29-36).

In those years of crisis and transition (1929, 1930 and 1931), however, many conservative Catholics as well as Protestants endorsed anti-democratic corporatist ideals. Even within the Christian labour movement, particularly among public sector and white-collar workers, many showed an astonishing lack of clarity in respect to corporatism and Fascism. Even Christian trade unionists such as the Dutch Protestant Herman Amelink praised the virtues of Italian Fascism in its anti-Marxist

---

19. Oswald von Nell-Breuning, "Der Königswinterer Kreis und sein Anteil an 'Quadragesimo anno'," *Wie sozial ist die Kirche? Leistung und Versagen der katholischen Soziallehre* (Düsseldorf: Patmos, 1972) 99-104; Gotthard Klein, *Der Volksverein für das katholische Deutschland, 1890-1933* (Paderborn: Schöningh, 1996) 285-290; Patch, "Catholic Social Movements."
20. Nell-Breuning, "Königswinterer Kreis," 110-112, and "Octogesimo anno," also in *Wie sozial ist die Kirche?*, 121-122. These and the following statements (including the quotations from QA) are inspired by Patch, "Catholic Social Movements," although my interpretation of QA is far more critical.

action and in stabilizing the social order.[21] However, the Christian trade union movement in general maintained its own line of conduct.

The pressure rose, however. In Germany the triple strategy of the Christian blue collar workers' unions followed in their fight against Nazism failed. This had been based on three main concepts: (1) forbidding Fascist propaganda, (2) underscoring the incompatibility between Nazism and the principles of the Christian labour movement, and (3) emphasizing their patriotic character as an alternative to both the internationalism of the Socialists and the extreme nationalism of the Nazis. Indeed, some important ambiguities remained, which do much to explain why this strategy was not successful. For example, the Christian workers' unions did not distance themselves clearly from the white collar union DHV (in itself not a Christian union, however, but it was nevertheless part of the 'Deutsche Gewerkschaftsbund', an anti-Socialist trade union alliance, and even of the Christian trade international of white collar workers).[22] Sympathy towards Fascism was widespread, especially among the Catholic, and even more so among the Evangelical workers' leagues (Katholische and Evangelische Arbeitervereine KAB and EAB).[23] On 17 March 1933 the Christian unions adopted a new program for "corporatist self-administration" drafted by Theo Brauer, a former trade union expert and Professor at the Technical University of Karlsruhe, who also led the negotiations with the (Socialist) Free Union leaders about a possible merger to forestall *Gleichschaltung* by the regime. In fact, they still hoped to preserve the essential features of free trade unionism in the new regime and to have the value of religion recognized. On 2 May 1933,

21. Report of the 30th meeting of the Bureau of the CISC, Paris, 26-27 January 1931 (Leuven, KADOC, CMT Archives, no. 15); Pasture, *Histoire*, 160. It did not prevent him from being declared *persona non grata* by the Italian and later German governments. Paul Werkman, "Amelink, Herman," *Biografisch Woordenboek van het Socialisme en de Arbeidersbeweging in Nederland* (BWSA), ed. P. J. Meertens (†), et al., http://www.iisg.nl/bwsa/bios/amelink.html.

22. I will not engage in a discussion on the responsibility of the Christian labor movement in the collapse of the Weimar Republic and the seize of power of Hitler. See the different – on this issue opposing – publications of William Patch and Michael Schneider (already quoted). In a letter to his Austrian colleague Johannes Staud, the leader of the German Christian unions Bernhard Otte clearly outlined his triple strategy against the Fascists as well as the dilemmas he faced. See Otte to Staud, 3 May 1932 (Bundesarchiv Koblenz, *Kleine Erwerbungen* 461-5, Bernard Otte Papers, 205-296), quoted and discussed in Pasture, *Histoire*, 160-162 (also by Patch and Schneider).

23. See Claus Haffert, *Die katholischen Arbeitervereine Westdeutschlands in der Weimarer Republik* (Essen: Klartext, 1994); Norbert Friedrich, "Zwischen allen Stühlen? Zur Geschichte der protestantischen Arbeiterbewegung zwischen Kaiserreich und früher Bundesrepublik," *Christliche Arbeiterbewegung in Europa 1850-1950*, ed. Claudia Hiepel and Mark Ruff (Stuttgart: Kohlhammer, 2003) 42-63.

the Nazis seized control over the Socialist unions, a move which was sanctioned by the leaders of the Christian unions, who agreed to join the German Labour Front.[24] They argued that they might still be able to influence the Nazi labour policy. The CISC, however, expelled the German Christian unionists and did not recognize the legitimacy of German delegations at the international labor conference in Geneva in June, even though the German Christian trade union leader and the then resigning CISC President (!) Bernhard Otte, was part of the delegation.[25]

A similar tragedy occurred in Austria. Large factions of the Catholic social movement, including the Christian Social Party under the leadership of Msgr. Ignace Seipel, already in the later 1920s associated with the fascist, anti-parliamentary Heimwehr movement. The Christian labour movement opposed the rapprochement, especially after the 'Heimwehr' in 1929 created its own unions (*Unabhängige Gewerkschaften*), but, numerously insignificant, it was not able to resist. In 1927 the Christian labour movement even felt compelled to support the government's severe repression of the general strike. Incidentally, the Austrian Christian labour movement in 1923, although advocating its support for parliamentary democracy, had already adopted a corporatist program according to which the corporations (*Berufstände*) "within their sphere should be granted a corresponding legislative, administrative and judicial sovereignty."[26] Anti-Semitism was widespread – the anti-Semitism of the founder and political leader of the Christian labour movement Leopold Kunschak was particularly notorious[27] – and obsessed by the bitter opposition with the virulently anticlerical Socialists,[28] the Austrian Christian labour movement by and large endorsed the Dollfuß' coup of March 1933, motivated at least partly as a reaction to Nazi influence. Subsequently it also sanctioned the suppression of the Socialist revolt of February 1934, as well as the gradual implementation of a corporatist social order, in which the Christian trade unions received a primary role

24. Patch, "Catholic Social Movements"; Schneider, *Die christlichen Gewerkschaften*.
25. Pasture, *Histoire*, 160-171.
26. Quotations according to the translation of Patch, "Catholic Social Movements," 10 (orig. *Das Linzer Programm der christlichen Arbeiter Österreichs*, ed. Dr. Karl Lugmayer, Vienna, 1924). See also Anton Pelinka, *Stand oder Klasse? Die Christliche Arbeiterbewegung Österreichs 1933 bis 1938* (Vienna: Europa-Verlag, 1972).
27. B. F. Pauley, *From Prejudice to Persecution: A History of Austrian Anti-Semitism* (Chapel Hill, NC/London: The University of North Carolina Press, 1992) 158-163.
28. Pieter van Duin and Zuzana Poláčková, "'Against the red industrial terror!': The Struggle of Christian Trade Unions in Austria and Czechoslovakia against Socialist Trade Union and Workplace Domination, 1918-1925," *Between Cross and Class*, ed. Heerma van Voss, Pasture and De Maeyer, 127-172.

alongside the Heimwehr although they had never represented more than 10 per cent of the organized workforce.

Only isolated voices were raised against this evolution, among which we nevertheless note the Christian trade union confederation's president Franz Spalowsky and its chaplain Father Rudolf Hausleitner.[29] Other Catholic social movements, such as the Catholic Action and the Catholic university students of the Cartellverband, of which both Seipel and Dollfuß were former members, displayed far more sympathy to the new regime. Even if some prominent Catholics, such as President Miklas and the president of the Catholic People's League Aigner, were critical of Dollfuß' authoritarianism, they supported the creation of a corporatist regime in Austria, which considered itself Catholic and explicitly referred to papal encyclicals. Father Hausleitner was one of the few who argued that the new constitution was not consistent with *Quadragesimo anno*. The Vatican, incidentally, did not speak out on the matter, but silence can be as eloquent, particularly considering that Dollfuß successfully negotiated a concordat with the Vatican. It was signed the same day as the chancellor declared the end of the Republic and the creation of the Austro-Fascist Bundesstaat Österreich (1 May 1934).[30]

Within the corporatist order, however, Austrian Christian labour leaders, systematically referring to *Quadragesimo anno*, tried to preserve a number of their principles and in particular to limit public (State) authority and preserve 'self-government'. At the same time, one may note a certain rapprochement with Socialists, notwithstanding the fact that the movement supported the government repression of the Socialist uprising of February 1934 and even mobilized its militia in support. In the 'transition period' between the coup of Dollfuß and the installation of the new constitution, attempts were made to ally the Socialists behind a corporatist model. After the uprising, Christian labour leaders showed some sympathy towards the Socialists, something they did not do for Nazis. That the ranks of the Austrian labour federation inflated, indicates that many Socialist workers sought and probably also received some social protection from the new institution, which may well have contributed to a détente between Christians and Socialists.[31] After the

---

29. Pasture, *Histoire*, 175.
30. Erika Weinzierl, "Austria: Church, State, Politics and Ideology, 1918-1938," *Catholics, the State and the European Radical Right*, ed. Wolff and Hoensch, 5-30.
31. Patch, "Catholic Social Movements"; Pelinka, *Stand oder Klasse?*; Ludwig Reichhold, *Geschichte der christlichen Gewerkschaften Österreichs* (Vienna: Verlag des ÖGB, 1987, 483ff. (there is some discussion between Reichhold and Pelinka on this subject).

assassination of Dollfuß, while the episcopacy began to criticize the fascist tendencies in the corporatist State and education (Fascism was considered as an Italian import product),[32] breathing space for labour action increased, and under the impulse of Spalowsky also a new socio-cultural Christian workers organization was created as a safe haven for Christian unionists. Relations with the CISC also improved.[33] Under threat of a Nazi invasion, talks were resumed with Socialists to reinforce the regime against a German invasion, but it was too late. The *Anschluss*, welcomed by large factions of the population and of the Church – notoriously by Archbishop Innitzer –, put an end to any possibility of the survival of the Christian labour movement, which felt itself victim to a similar persecution as the Socialists.[34]

Unlike the Nazi regime, the Austrian corporatist system received widespread support in Catholic and even Protestant milieus throughout Europe. Even many Christian labour and trade union leaders expressed their admiration, or at least their sympathy, for Dollfuß and the creation of a Christian, corporatist State: there was support also in Belgium and the Netherlands. The CISC, however, was probably the sole major international Christian organization that declared the Austrian constitution to be irreconcilable with Catholic social teaching and in particular with *Quadragesimo anno*. Its argumentation is interesting in more than one respect. In its eyes, according to the encyclical the State should withdraw as much as possible from interfering in the economy, which was exactly the opposite of what the Dollfuß administration was involved in. Concerning the alleged Catholic character of the Austrian Constitution which, in its preamble, stated that all rights came from God, the secretary general of the CISC Serrarens argued that the Christian State had first to be a constitutional State (un *état de droit*). Although the federation expressed words of 'understanding' for the difficult situation they were in, the CISC consequently expelled the Austrian Christian trade unionists from its ranks and denied the unitary labor federation the right to represent the workers at the international labour conferences, even if this federation and its delegation in Geneva were presided

---

32. Weinzierl, "Austria."
33. Pasture, *Histoire*, 180-182; Reichhold, *Geschichte der christlichen Gewerkschaften Österreichs*, 536ff. See also Weinzierl, "Austria."
34. Reichhold, *Geschichte der christlichen Gewerkschaften*, 559ff; Everhard Holtmann, *Zwischen Unterdrückung und Befriedung: Sozialistische Arbeiterbewegung und autoritäres Regime in Österreich 1933-1938* (Vienna: Verlag für Geschichte und Politik, 1978) 233ff.; Pelinka, *Stand oder Klasse?*, esp. 172-181.

over by Johann Staud, the (former) general secretary of the Austrian Christian trade union federation.[35]

Among Catholics and Protestants throughout Europe, tensions existed between advocates of an authoritarian corporate State and those who defended basic democratic liberties and considered corporatism as a way of transcending class antagonism and restraining, not increasing State interference in the economy. Catholic employers organizations in particular often advocated economic corporatism as a way of limiting both union power and State intervention. They (rightly) believed that a corporatist organization would give the employers a greater direct voice in the political and socio-economic decision-making process.[36] Some even argued for authoritarian political corporatism. However, it is also apparent that the demarcations are not always clear, and many intermediate positions existed. Mainstream blue-collar workers' Christian unions defended some form of industrial organization in which freedom of association remained safeguarded. They did agree, however, with far-reaching competencies for the industrial corporations and defended compulsory collective agreements that limited the right to strike – at least if employers were bound by them and lock-outs forbidden as well.[37] However, they distanced themselves from forms of corporatism that did not respect freedom of association and that gave the primary role in the organization of the economy to a centralized State. To highlight this difference, for example, the Belgian and French Christian unions avoided the use of the word corporatism altogether in the thirties, and spoke of "le syndicat libre dans la profession organisée" (free trade unionism in the industrial organization) or "industrial organization," linking up with the nineteenth-century terminology.[38]

---

35. Cf. Pasture, *Histoire*, 171-182.
36. E.g., for Belgium, Luyten, *Ideologisch debat en politieke strijd*.
37. Paul Werkman, "'Een voorbehoedmiddel voor openlijke strijd'. Het CNV en de collectieve arbeidsovereenkomst voor de Tweede Wereldoorlog," *Collectief geregeld: Uit de geschiedenis van de CAO*, ed. Luuk Brug and Harry Peer (Amsterdam: Vakbondshistorische Vereniging/FNV-Pers, 1993) 27-39; Luyten, *Ideologisch debat en politieke strijd*, esp. 105-130.
38. Jean-Pierre Le Crom, *Syndicats, nous-voilà! Vichy et le corporatisme* (Paris: L'Atelier, 1995) 86-91; Michel Launay, *La C.F.T.C.: Origines et développement 1919-1940* (Paris: Éditions de la Sorbonne, 1986); Jozef Mampuys, "Quadragesimo Anno, corporatisme en de christelijke vakbeweging (1930-1940)," *De Gids op maatschappelijk gebied*, 75, no. 5 (1984) 395-418; Luyten, *Ideologisch debat en politieke strijd*, 105-130. The latter author, however, emphasizes the ambiguities of the doctrine of the Belgian Christian labor movement.

If we seem to have dwelled on the attitude of the Christian movements towards Fascism in the 1920s and 1930s, it is because the same issues were at stake in the years 1940-1944. Indeed, only in this way can we hope to ascertain the importance and the significance of the period of war and German occupation of much of Europe. Apart from the particularity of the Christian communities being confronted with a foreign invader, they soon faced the same dilemmas as were evident in the 1930s: they were confronted not only with an 'alien' invasion and regime, but also with a political and economic regime that not only had some frightening features, but in many ways looked appealing as well. Nowhere was this clearer than in Vichy France.

IV. Temptation and Resistance in Vichy France

French Catholics were politically deeply divided. By far most of them, however, in the 1930s rejected the Front populaire. Also the Christian trade union confederation CFTC ('Confédération Française des Travaileurs Chrétiens') joined the opposition to Léon Blum's Socialist-Communist government, though it limited itself to democratic forms of resistance, denouncing in particular leftist monopolistic policies in the sphere of labour. It benefited greatly from its nuanced stance, offering a credible social alternative.[39] Notwithstanding the virulent anti-Communist atmosphere, stirred up by the hierarchy, a Social Catholic movement gradually developed, supported by prominent intellectuals (Maritain, Mounier, Mauriac, Marcel, Sangnier, Schuman) and movements such as the Jesuit 'Action Populaire', the 'Jeune République', and the 'Nouvelles Équipes Françaises' surrounding the daily *L'Aube*; there were some initiatives for Catholic-Left co-operation as well. These Social Catholics defended social progress and democratic values and informed the French public about the dangers of Fascism. They were wary about supporting Franco's insurrection and the Spanish civil war. Not all Catholics supported the Spanish bishops' exhortations for a new crusade; many shared the CISC's difficulties in choosing sides.[40] Nevertheless, Catholics in particular at the eve of the outbreak of war still considered bolshevism as a far greater threat than Hitler at their frontiers (French Protestants in contrast seemed more aware of the nature of

39. Launay, *La C.F.T.C.*
40. Pasture, *Histoire*, 186-188.

Nazism). Guidance from the Vatican was crudely lacking, for Pius XI warnings against Fascism (notwithstanding *Mit brennender Sorge*) were submerged in the anti-Communist discourse and his successor Pius XII (for whatever motives) remained painfully mute.[41]

When the German army quickly defeated the French and a collaborationist regime was installed in the South, the Catholic hierarchy and the large majority of the Catholic establishment, while opposing the Nazis in the occupied zone, sided with Marshall Pétain and gave their total loyalty and support to the Vichy regime, putting their hopes on the *Révolution nationale* that would restore the alliance between throne and altar, or just hoping that they could exercise a moderating influence from within an authoritarian but Catholic regime rather than undergoing a full German occupation, or in the conviction that this was the best way of defending the Church's and the population's (not to be equated!) interests; after the experience of the Front populaire the sacrifice of 'democracy' certainly was not deeply deplored.[42] Most Catholics adopted a similar attitude. Protestants showed more restraint towards the totalitarian regime with its obvious Catholic outlook. Only gradually would the Catholic bishops distance themselves somewhat from the regime and some elements of its totalitarian policies, among other things the persecution of the Jews, although on the whole they never denounced their allegiance with the 'legitimate power' of Vichy and in particular Marshall Pétain. A minority of Catholics though, mainly in 'Christian-Democratic' circles, refused to follow suit and even went on to play an active part in the Resistance, notwithstanding the opposition of their bishops.[43]

For many Catholics, the new situation also offered opportunities for social and economic reform in accordance with Catholic principles – although there were considerable divergences as to the concrete form of the organization of the economy. The 'Action Populaire' of the Jesuit Father Desbuquois, an important Social Catholic think-tank, as well as

---

41. It goes without saying that the literature on this issue is vast. Instead of the often polemical literature, one may rather refer to the nuanced and (perhaps overly though) emphatic assessment of Philippe Chenaux, *Pie XII: Diplomate et Pasteur* (Paris: Cerf, 2003).

42. W. D. Halls, *Politics, Society and Christianity in Vichy France* (Oxford: Berg, 1995) 384 and Jacques Duquesne, *Les Catholiques français sous l'occupation* (Paris: Grasset, 1996, 3rd ed.) and the major syntheses of French Catholicism.

43. Cf. extensively Bernard Comte, *L'honneur et la conscience: Catholiques français en résistance (1940-1944)* (Paris: Éd. de l'Atelier, 1998); Halls, *Politics, Society and Christianity*, 199-222; Duquesne, *Les Catholiques français sous l'Occupation*, 134ff. (and passim).

the *Cité nouvelle* now promoted an authoritarian State, founded on the values of work and family. Many other Social Catholics agreed to collaborate with the social and economic legislation of Pétain as well. Even the Dominicans succumbed to the fascination of the Marshall, although Father Lebret and his association 'Économie et Humanisme' would eventually change course after 1942.[44]

The Vichy government had extensive plans for a reorganization of the French economy and the organization of work occupied a central place in them.[45] Putting an end to class warfare was a cornerstone of the Marshall's objectives who nevertheless, in his own words, heralded labour as "the chief source of national wealth" (11 June 1940). Initially Pétain expressed some reassuring words towards the leaders of the CFTC regarding the rights of the unions.[46] However, what he had in mind was a State-directed corporatist social order. The law of 16 August 1940 on "the provisional organization of the industrial production" led to the dissolution of all national organizations of employers and employees. The law foresaw initially only the dissolution of the national confederations, but these, the CFTC in the first place, decided to put an end to all activities, also at branch and local level. Per branch of industry *comités d'organisation* (industrial committees) were created. In response to the vigorous opposition this proposal arose, the unions were associated with the preparations of the new order, but their demands for recognition of union plurality and the right to appoint members to these committees was not granted. The 'Charte du Travail' (Labour Act), issued on 26 October 1941, imposed one single, national, obligatory union for employers and workers in the 29 industrial branches.[47]

Although some union leaders – Pétain's Labour minister René Bélin was a former leader of the main (reformist) union CGT ('Confédération Générale du Travail') – were willing to collaborate with the Vichy proposals, the main Christian trade union leaders Gaston Tessier, Secretary General, and Jules Zirnheld, the CFTC-President, refuted them from the outset. They appealed, unsuccessfully, to the Conseil d'État, as well

---

44. Cf. Denis Pelletier, *Économie et Humanisme: De l'utopie communautaire au combat pour le Tiers-monde 1941-1966* (Paris: Cerf, 1996) 22-53.
45. See the excellent analysis of Le Crom, *Syndicats, nous-voilà!*, as well as Halls, *Politics, Society and Christianity*, 241-268.
46. Halls, *Politics, Society and Christianity*, 245; Duquesne, *Les Catholiques français sous l'Occupation*, 239.
47. See Le Crom, *Syndicats, nous voilà!*, 105-166; Duquesne, *Les Catholiques français sous l'Occupation*, 239-255; Adrian Rossiter, "Business and Corporatism in Vichy France," *Organizing Business for War*, ed. Grant, Nekkers and van Waarden, 195-224.

as to the bishops, in particular Msgr. Liénart of Lille. Although Msgr. Liénart was one of the most ardent supporters and a personal friend of Pétain, he had repeatedly backed the CFTC rights in the past.[48] The bishops indeed intervened on behalf of the CFTC and supported its position, but eventually in a statement of the ACA ('Assemblée des Cardinaux et Archevêques') of 22 October 1942, they maintained obedience to the law, however without formally endorsing the *syndicat unique*. Incidentally, the episcopacy's stand was less ambiguous and therefore much stronger regarding the (refusal of the) unification of youth movements.[49] Anyway, many Social Catholics continued to support the social policy of Vichy, including the Charte du Travail, among whom were Father Gustave Desbuquois of the 'Action Populaire' and Eugène Duthoit, president of the *Semaines sociales*. Even the 'Ligue Ouvrière Chrétienne' (LOC), the extension of the JOC for workers families, did not explicitly denounce the social policy of the Vichy government.[50]

Remarkably, the CFTC leaders in the Resistance reacted jointly with the non-collaborationist CGT. Already in February 1940, activists of the CGT and the CFTC published a common *Bulletin*, and in July 1940 Gaston Tessier wrote a letter to his CGT colleague Léon Jouhaux to consult on a common attitude towards Vichy. On 15 October 1940 nine CGT and three CFTC leaders (Gaston Tessier, Jules Zirnheld and Maurice Bouladoux) signed a manifesto – the *Manifeste des douze* – with the principles on which they all agreed, including freedom of association and freedom from government interference – implicitly referring to *Rerum novarum* – presented as a 'natural right'.[51] Subsequently, many Christian trade unionists as well as Christian Democrats of different

---

48. For example in 1927-29 in the Mathon-case, which had provoked a formal recognition of the CFTC by the Vatican, and in 1936 against the monopolizing ambitions of the CGT. See Launay, *La C.F.T.C.*, 109-205, 217-222; Val Lorwin, *The French Labor Movement* (Cambridge, MA: Harvard University Press, 1954), 54-65; Bruno Béthouart, "La naissance du syndicalisme chrétien dans le Pas-de-Calais (1913-1939)," *International Review of Social History* 40 (1995) 75-95.

49. Halls, *Politics, Society and Christianity*, 269-310.

50. Michel Chauvière, "1945, les contradictions de l'entrée du MPF en politique," *Chrétiens et ouvriers en France 1937-1970*, ed. Bruno Duriez, et al. (Paris: Éd. de l'Atelier, 2001) 230-244; Halls, *Politics, Society and Christianity*; Michel Chauvière and Bruno Duriez (eds.), *Les mouvements familiaux populaires et ruraux: Naissance, développement, mutations, 1939-1955*, Les cahiers du GRMF, 1 (Villeneuve d'Ascq: GRMF, 1983).

51. Le Crom, *Vichy, nous voilà!*, 187-194; Duquesne, *Les Catholiques français sous l'Occupation*, 239ff.; Alya Aglan, "Des syndicalistes dans la Résistance," *Vingtième siècle* 67 (July-Sept. 2000) 119-127; Jean-Pierre Le Crom, "Syndicalisme et Résistance," *La Résistance et les Français: Villes, centres et logiques de décision. Colloque de Cachan*, ed. L. Douzou, et al. (Paris: IHTP, 1995) 397-415.

alliances and associations joined the Resistance and played a prominent role in it. The consequences of this attitude, against the explicit demands of the episcopacy, should not be underestimated. It not only granted the Christian trade unions recognition and esteem after the war – both in the world of labour and in the Catholic community – and contributed greatly to the political co-operation with Socialists, but might also have helped to 'save' the Catholic community and indeed the episcopacy from post-war revenge.

It should be observed, however, that while the Vichy's reforms in the industrial field provoked fierce opposition from important factions of the Catholic community, this was less the case with other domains. The corporatist organization of agriculture, which incidentally largely would survive the Liberation, met with almost unanimous support. Eventual fears about excessive State control were compensated by the paramount position occupied by members of the Catholic-inspired 'Union Nationale des Syndicats Agricoles' and the 'Jeunesse Agricole Chrétienne' JAC in the corporatist administration. The measures to promote the family received general approval and support even from Christian-Democratic milieus. It should be noted, however, that the policy of unification of social organizations was not applied in this field. The LOC – from 1942 'Mouvement Populaire des Familles' MPF –, the main mass family organization, was allowed to function also according to the Gounot Law of 29 December 1940 that instituted the 'Fédération Nationale des Familles Françaises' (National Federation of French Families). Regarding youth organizations, sport, and education, the Church vigorously opposed unification and State control.[52]

In sum, the attitudes of the Catholic Church were ambiguous. While there was widespread and general opposition to the Nazis, Marshal Pétain exercised a strong fascination upon many Catholics, in the first place among the episcopacy, even among the most socially oriented bishops. A mitigated view on corporatism was, in part, responsible for this. Even if all measures of the regime were not equally appreciated – the persecution of the Jews and the attempts to impose unified and State dominated social organizations were generally, albeit not unanimously and as vigorously, opposed – the episcopacy and higher clergy maintained their support and sympathy, although from 1942 onwards they did retreat somewhat from their initial over-commitment. Among

---

52. Halls, *Politics and Christianity*, 255ff; Duquesne, *Les Catholiques français sous l'occupation*.

the Christian Democrats, the lower clergy and the ordinary flock, many increasingly resisted the temptation, turned their backs on Pétain, and even joined the Resistance where they were involved together with non-Christians.

Because of Vichy, the situation of French Catholics is somewhat peculiar. Belgium and the Netherlands show different forms of reaction towards the occupation and offer possibilities for an interesting comparison.

V. On the Test: Between Opposition and Temptation in the Netherlands

Although industrial relations were controlled, and strikes and lockouts forbidden, the unions in the Netherlands initially adopted a cautious stance towards the German occupation. Anticipating an imposed unification according to the model of the German *Arbeitsfront*, some initiatives were taken to create a union front or a unitary trade union structure, both on the initiative of the Liberal and the Socialist unions. However, on 16 July 1940 the 'Dienststelle für Soziale Verwaltung', or 'Dienststelle Hellwig', 'replaced' the president of the Social Democratic union NVV ('Nederlands Vakverbond') by a Dutch Nazi, H. J. Woudenberg. In contrast, the Catholic, (Protestant) Christian and liberal unions only had to cope with some apparently union-friendly German 'observers' and remained, at least for the moment, autonomous.[53] The Catholic labour movement even saw in the German occupation an opportunity to realize its ambition of a corporatist industrial organization; it seems to be generally accepted that the Catholics, including the Catholic workers' organization, in the first year of the occupation were prepared to collaborate with the Germans as the 'legitimate authority'. Convinced that the war was lost and democracy buried, they believed resistance to be futile, and compliance to be in the general interest.[54]

---

53. Both the observers to the Catholic and the Protestant unions were seen as fairly decent in the given circumstances. Hans Righart and Joop Scheerman, "Het Rooms-Katholiek Werklieden Verbond en de Duitse bezetter mei 1940 – augustus 1941," *Jaarboek voor de geschiedenis van socialisme en arbeidersbeweging in Nederland 1978* (Nijmegen: Socialistiese Uitgeverij Nijmegen SUN, 1978) 251-252; Siegfried Stokman, *De katholieke arbeidersbeweging in oorlogstijd* (Brussel: Het Spectrum, 1946) 21; Jan-Jacob Van Dijk and Paul Werkman, *Door geweld gedwongen: Het CNV in oorlogstijd* (Utrecht: CNV, [1995]) 35.

54. Righart and Scheerman, "Het Rooms-Katholiek Werklieden Verbond," 245-263.

The Catholic Party, for example, sat back and watched itself being led to the slaughter. Party vice-president P. J. Witteman declared "parliamentary democracy was never a principle of our party, but a guideline."[55] However, the episcopacy and in particular Archbishop De Jong – who in his own words at that time refused to be "a second Innitzer" – opted for a firm stance and opposed in particular any attempt to disband Catholic social organizations.[56]

In August 1940, the Dutch Catholic workers' movement drafted its own plan for a corporatist social order, in which the defence of the workers' interests would be entrusted to corporations.[57] The trade unions would lose many of their functions and would collaborate in unitary federations, but they would be able to elect representatives in these corporations; moral action would be developed by the collateral organizations (in particular the Catholic *standsorganisatie*). However, this plan was rejected by both the Germans and the Protestant unions. The leadership of the Catholic labour movement and in particular its president A. C. de Bruijn, who was briefly imprisoned and liberated on the intercession of the 'Dienststelle Hellwig' and apparently lost faith in the good outcome of the war, was more and more drawn into the corporatist philosophy. After a 'study trip' to Germany in November 1940, to which the Dutch union leaders were more or less 'morally enforced' to participate, De Bruijn commented positively about the German socio-economic order. He also supported the 'Nederlandsche Unie', an attempt to create a unitary political organization, as well as the National Committee for Economic Organization, better known as the Woltersom Organization, a committee consisting of industrialists to co-ordinate all sectors of trade and industry.[58] De Bruijn hoped that representatives of the unions would also participate in the Woltersom Organization, but that was an illusion. Incidentally, also the CNV, that rejected the corporatist ideology and the Catholic plans in that respect, initially welcomed the Woltersom Organization, but it soon changed its mind.[59]

55. *De Tijd*, 22 July 1940, quoted in A. F. Manning, "De Nederlandse katholieken in de eerste jaren van de Duitse bezetting," *Jaarboek van het Katholiek Documentatie Centrum* 1978 (Nijmegen: Dekker & Van de Vegt, 1978) 123 (translation P. P.).
56. Quoted in Manning, "Nederlandse katholieken," 108.
57. Cf. Manning, "Nederlandse katholieken" and Righart and Scheerman, "Het Rooms-Katholiek Werklieden Verbond."
58. David Barnouw and Jan Nekkers, "The Netherlands: State Corporatism against the State," *Organizing Business for War*, ed. Grant, Nekkers and Van Waarden, 137-162.
59. At least H. Amelink did. See Van Dijk and Werkman, *Door geweld gedwongen*, 51-52. In contrast to the latter authors, I believe Amelink's position before the war had been sometimes ambiguous. See Pasture, *Histoire*, 159.

From early 1941, the climate in the Netherlands changed, and pressures towards nazification increased, as did the resistance against it, both in Catholic and Protestant milieus. In January 1941 the Catholic bishops, solicited by the Catholic workers' movement, explicitly ordered that even passive members of National-Socialist organizations, included the NVV – seen as part of the Nazi party – should be refused the sacraments, and also a Catholic burial. The bishops also contacted the Vatican, "influential relations in Germany," and Hermann Goering.[60] The process of *Gleichschaltung*, that had started in education in the summer of 1940, gained momentum in the spring and summer of 1941 with, among other things, the unification and nazification of the press (including union-related newspapers). On 30 June 1940, political parties were forbidden and many prominent opinion leaders arrested, among whom were the Protestant trade union leaders Herman Amelink and CNV president Antoon Stapelkamp. On 25 July 1941, the Catholic and Christian unions were placed under the authority of Woudenberg. However, all the members of the committees of both unions resigned and most ordinary members returned their affiliation cards; Catholics were forbidden by the episcopacy to remain affiliated. Consequently, the Protestant and Christian unions were dissolved and integrated in the NVV. Particularly painful was that many NVV committee members gave their support to this operation, sometimes even with some enthusiasm for the 'unification'. In contrast to (blue collar) workers, Christian farmers, market gardeners and particularly the self-employed, however, were far less ready to resist the pressures towards *Gleichschaltung*.[61] Incidentally, also the employers' organizations, federated in early 1941, were dissolved.[62]

In the years between the dissolution and the Liberation, several plans for the postwar economic organization were drafted. Protestant and Catholic workers harked back to prewar plans of a public industrial organization, but there was much discussion and debate on the degree of State responsibility and the relationship between industrial

60. Righart and Scheerman, "Het Rooms-Katholiek Werklieden Verbond," 258; *Het verzet van de Nederlandse bisschoppen tegen nationaal-socialisme en Duitse tyrannie: Herderlijke brieven, instructies en andere documenten*, ed. S. Stokman (Utrecht: Het Spectrum, 1945) 183, 184.
61. Arno Bornebroek, *De strijd voor harmonie: De geschiedenis van de Industrie- en Voedingsbond CNV 1896-1996* (Amsterdam: IISG, 1996) 221-237; Van Dijk and Werkman, *Door geweld gedwongen*; Manning, "Nederlandse katholieken."
62. Maarten van Bottenburg, et al., *'Aan den arbeid!': In de wandelgangen van de Stichting van de Arbeid 1945-1995* (Amsterdam: Bert Bakker, 1995) 29.

and political (parliamentary) decision-making. There were also several contacts between the leaders of the Catholic and Christian unions with other Christian organizations as well as with the dismissed president of the NVV Evert Kupers. The Germans, on the other hand, were dissatisfied with the lack of success of the NVV and were looking for ways to create a new organization that would unite all workers, possibly a Dutch Labour Front. While the president of the Catholic union A. C. de Bruijn still was 'peddling' with his plans dated of August 1940, Kupers continued to argue for some form of unitary union after the war, although he soon accepted the existence of three – just and only three – union federations: the Socialist, Catholic and Protestant ones, excluding newcomers such as the largely Communist Unitary Trade Union ('Eenheidsvakcentrale'). In the course of 1943, these three agreed to form a 'union' or federation after the war, which would respect the autonomy of each. At some date in 1943, a blueprint of a social organization was also drafted which gave extensive executive powers to a public organization of labour. Such an idea was never realized, but the discussions in the 'Hacke-circle', named after the general director of the labour inspectorate A. W. H. Hacke who had taken the initiative in these discussions, laid the basis of the postwar Foundation of Labour, a joint body, under private law, with equal representation of workers and employers, which was to become the main advisory body on social and labour policy in postwar Netherlands.[63]

VI. 'The Sorrow of Belgium'

In Belgium, before the outbreak of war, the Christian unions had decided to dissolve themselves in the event of a German victory. However, while those unionists who had escaped to France wished to comply with the prewar decisions, already in June 1940 most leaders of the Christian trade unions in occupied territory had decided to resume their union activities.[64]

63. Van Bottenburg, *et al.*, '*Aan den arbeid!*', 29.
64. On the Christian trade unions during the Occupation and the attempts to create a unitary union, and the consequences of these attempts, see Alain Dantoing, *La 'collaboration' du cardinal: L'Église de Belgique dans la Guerre 40* (Bruxelles: De Boeck, 1991); Luyten, *Ideologie en praktijk*, 29-109; Jozef Mampuys, "Le syndicalisme chrétien," *Histoire du mouvement ouvrier chrétien en Belgique*, ed. Gerard and Wynants, vol. 2, 151-277; Jean Neuville, *La CSC en l'an 40: Le déchirement et la difficile reconstruction de l'Unité* (Bruxelles: Vie ouvrière, 1988); Wouter Steenhaut, "De Unie van Hand- en

Moreover, conservative employers tried to realize their plans for an authoritarian new political and social order built around King Leopold III. Convinced that the war was lost and democracy had come to an end, they found support from Catholic employers and Christian Democratic leaders. The notorious manifesto on the corporatist order, for example, drafted in August 1940 by Catholic employers and labour leaders such as P. W. Segers, general secretary of the political organization of the Christian workers ACW/LNTC ('Algemeen Christelijk Werkersverbond'/'Ligue Nationale des Travailleurs Chrétiens'), and August Cool, secretary of the Christian Trade Union Confederation CSC ('Algemeen Christelijk Vakverbond'/'Confédération des Syndicats Chrétiens'), argued for the abolishment of the party system and a reform of the parliamentary regime, that should be replaced by a Catholic-corporatist order based upon compulsory organization for workers and employers – which implied the end of free and autonomous trade unionism –, in which strikes and lock-outs would be forbidden. While the Christian unionists did not finally approve the Manifesto, attempts were indeed made to realize a unitary trade union movement between the Socialist and Christian unions together with the Flemish-Nationalist and Fascist union Arbeidsorde. Some proponents of these plans hoped to prevent worse regulations being introduced by the German occupier; particularly the Flemish Christian unions, fearing competition in the new order from the (still virtually non-existent though) Arbeidsorde, reckoned that they could safeguard their dominant position in a unified or federated structure set up on their own terms. In the final event, however, both Arbeidsorde and the 'Dienststelle Hellwig' refused these proposals.

In November 1940, the 'Dienststelle Hellwig' in collaboration with the internationally renowned Socialist Party leader Hendrik De Man decided to create a centralized unified trade union, the 'Union des Travailleurs Manuels et Intellectuels'/'Unie van Hand- en Geestesarbeiders' (UTMI).[65] At first, the branch unions would be allowed to function separately, but eventually they would also have to merge. Notwithstanding the opposition of CSC president Henri Pauwels, the majority, mainly Flemish, Christian union leaders – having received the 'green light' from Archbishop Card. Van Roey – agreed to collaborate with the UTMI, hoping in practice to dominate this unified structure and at

---

Geestesarbeiders: Een onderzoek naar het optreden van de vakbonden in de bezettingsjaren 1940-1944," Unpublished PhD thesis, Gent University, 1983.

65. Steenhaut, "De Unie van Hand- en Geestesarbeiders."

least to maintain a way of propagating Catholic social and moral views among the workers. A minority of mainly Walloon unionists under the leadership of Pauwels, who disagreed with the course the CSC had been taking since May 1940, however, refused to follow suit and put an end to their trade union activities. Several months later, when the German occupation forces began to intervene very directly in the unified union, collaboration was hampered and on 18 July 1941 the majority of the Christian unionists also withdrew from the UTMI; only a few Christian unionists, among whom were the presidents of the powerful Christian textiles workers' union and of the Flemish white collar workers' union, who both turned out to be convinced Nazis, took the step to total 'collaboration' with the occupiers. After they had withdrawn from the UTMI, the 'majority' and the 'minority' came together again, but the wounds inflicted by the split took many years and considerable pressure from the archbishop to heal.

In the following years, the CSC secretly reflected on postwar reconstruction. It remained in contact with the other social actors, in particular (equally underground) Socialist union leaders and Catholic employers. In 1943, the CSC concluded an agreement with the Catholic employers that reverted to prewar views on industrial organization and economic codetermination of the unions, but which foresaw bans on strikes and lock-outs; more than the so-called 'social pact', to which the Catholic community was barely associated, it contained the basis of the Christian trade union views on the social and economic organization for the postwar period.[66] In the plans developed within the underground movement 'Le Ralliement Social Belge' (Groupe Demain), rooted in Catholic Action – to which also union leaders as Henri Pauwels participated –, there was even talk of unitary trade union structures, with collateral organizations for moral education, and 'factory councils' to enhance class collaboration at plant level. Some Catholic employers continued to promote outright reactionary corporatist reforms. The president of the Catholic employers federation Henri Velge in October 1944 largely reiterated his corporatist views in his blueprint of a statutory

66. Luyten, *Ideologie en praktijk*, 233-235, 243-250. On the attitude of the Christian labour movement towards the Social Pact see Patrick Pasture, "Liefde na datum: De christelijke arbeidersbeweging en het sociaal pact," *Het sociaal pact van 1944: Oorsprong, betekenis en gevolgen*, ed. Dirk Luyten and Guy Vanthemsche (Brussel: VUB Press, 1995) 305-323; Patrick Pasture, "The April 1944 'Social Pact' in Belgium and its Significance for the Post-War Welfare State," *Journal of Contemporary History* 28, no. 3 (1993) 695-714.

organization of the industry. In his "lessons of the war" he took great pains though to distance the industrial organization as he saw it from authoritarianism or dictatorship, arguing that legislative power should remain exclusively in the hands of parliament and should not be conferred to the industrial associations or industrial councils – though he left an opening after the system had proved its worth and after a change of the Constitution. He emphasized freedom of association, the public and representative character of the professional associations and the promotion of the "general interest" as goals of the industrial organization. Illustrative of his state of mind is that he saw no contradiction in that unitary industrial associations with compulsory membership would replace the existing trade unions and the members of the associations and councils were appointed by the King (the executive).[67] His proposals inspired the decree installing the preliminary industrial organization of 16 November 1944, which indeed did not contain any dispositions regarding unions' representation in the industrial councils.[68] This 'preliminary industrial organization', however, was completely replaced by the Industrial Organization Act of 20 September 1948.

The history of the attitude of the Christian social organizations in Belgium and The Netherlands reveals some astonishing, even disenchanting parallels. Particularly the attitude of the Catholics during the first year of the German occupation – cf. the corporatist plans of De Bruijn in The Netherlands and of Segers and Cool in Belgium – shows how ambiguous their attitude towards corporatism and democracy really was. The right to strike and even freedom of organization were quite easily sacrificed, and their ban was integrated in their own blueprints of an ideal society. Obviously, not only a 'policy of lesser evil' can explain their attitude and politics, nor even a real existing opportunity to grasp the chances to retain or gain authority in the new order that was often considered inevitable in any case. One has to conclude that in the context of war and occupation the Christian labour movement in both countries – to a large extent even including in Wallonia – believed that a corporatist system would put an end to class warfare and was able to introduce a just social and political order and to maintain possibilities for the

---

67. Henri Velge, *L'organisation professionnelle: les leçons de la guerre* (Tournai: Casterman, 1944).
68. Guy Vanthemsche, "De Belgische patronale groeperingen in een belangrijke mutatieperiode (1944-1946): De reorganisaties op het sectoriële vlak," *Belgisch Tijdschrift voor Filologie en Geschiedenis* 57 (1989) 299-337; Luyten, "The 'policy of the lesser evil'," 178-179.

Catholic apostolate as well.[69] It seems that the lessons of Italy, Austria and Germany did not penetrate so deeply after all. However, nazification and total *Gleichschaltung* finally went one step too far.

VII. After the War: Lessons Learned?

After the war, the political and trade union landscape was profoundly altered, even if on closer sight the elements of continuity would soon prevail over the renewal. Can we conclude that the war and the occupation modified the attitude of the Christian communities towards the social and economic order? The Christmas message of Pius XII in 1944 illustrates perhaps less a fundamental change in attitude than a continuing ambivalence towards democracy in the Vatican. Indeed, if the Pope nominally accepted the "democratic ideal of liberty and equality," he still warned against "the whims of the masses." In 1948 he even expressed doubts about the Declaration of Human Rights.[70] Our question, however, is: what about the Catholic lay social movements?

A first element in answering such a question is that the position of the Christians in society and in particular organized Christianity (unions especially) had changed. This can be seen most clearly in the former Fascist countries, where confessional trade unions, for example, were not restored. Catholics as well as Protestants joined unitary organizations, such as the ÖGB ('Österreichischer Gewerkschaftsbund') in Austria, the CGIL ('Confederazione Generale Italiana del Lavoro') in Italy and, later, the DGB ('Deutscher Gewerkschaftsbund') in Germany. Their motives for joining were diverse, but without doubt, it was a deliberate decision, taken voluntarily, even wholeheartedly.[71] The drive

---

69. Compare the conclusions of Luyten, *Ideologisch debat en politieke strijd* and id., *Ideologie en praktijk* for Belgium, and Righart and Scheerman, "Het Rooms-Katholiek Werklieden Verbond" for The Netherlands.

70. Cf. Étienne Fouilloux, "Intransigence catholique et monde moderne," *Revue d'histoire ecclésiastique* 96, nos. 1-2 (2001) 71-87 (esp. 79) (English quotations from Pius XII' 1944 Christmas message from http://www.catholicculture.org/docs/). A different view in Chenaux, *Pie XII*, 305-309.

71. See Patrick Pasture, "Window of Opportunities or *trompe l'œil*?: The Myth of Labor Unity in Western Europe after 1944," *Transnational Moments of Change: Europe 1945, 1968, 1989*, ed. Gerd-Rainer Horn and Padraic Kenney (Lanham, MD: Rowman & Littlefield, 2004) 27-49. Compare Andrea Ciampani and Massimiliano Valente, "The Social and Political Dynamics of Christian Workers in Unified Trade Union Movements: The Experiences of Italy and West-Germany after World War II," *Between Cross and Class*, ed. Heerma van Voss, Pasture and De Maeyer, 203-224.

for unity was not restricted to workers' organizations and unions. Also at a political level Christian Democrats supported parties that were not based on confession or Church allegiance, although in the end the Christian Democratic parties that arose, apart from the MRP ('Mouvement Républicain Populaire') in France, retained a definite Christian identity and remained largely tied to the Churches, if not according to their statutes then at least in the perception of their voters, their adversaries and, last but not least, the Catholic hierarchy as well. For Catholics, however, the acceptance of political and trade union unity appears a major change only at first sight: one should remember that in the nineteenth century, before the papacies of Leo XIII and Pius IX increased the grip of the Catholic Church upon social and political organizations, this was their 'natural condition'.[72] Protestants, be it Lutherans or Reformed, never shared the Catholic obligation to organize on a confessional basis. Incidentally, within the Catholic world after the war it was particularly those organizations influenced by Catholic Action that, from an apostolic perspective, chose to open their ranks to non-Christians. The most radical example of this remarkable development was undoubtedly the French 'Mouvement Populaire des Familles', which eventually was even transformed into a left-radical, revolutionary party.[73] This 'paradox of the apostolate' was one of the most amazing expressions of the new spirit of the times.[74]

It is equally important to observe that in the case of encompassing unified trade union structures for workers, collateral organizations (such as the ACLI in Italy, the KAB in Germany, and to a certain extent also the ÖAAB in Austria) undertook the moral education of the Catholic workers. Moreover, when the Cold War resumed in 1947, the unity shattered, leading to separations (as in Italy) or fractionalization (as in Austria). In the countries where Christian social organizations (unions in particular) only had to suspend their activities for three to four years – and not ten or more years as in Italy, Austria and Germany – they

72. Cf. Pasture, "Between Cross and Class."
73. Joseph Debès, *Naissance de l'Action Catholique Ouvrière* (Paris: Vie Ouvrière, 1982); Chauvière and Duriez (eds.), *Les mouvements familiaux populaires et ruraux*; Louis Guéry, Bruno Duriez and Georges Tamborini (eds.), *Une politique de l'agir: Stratégie et pédagogie du Mouvement Populaire des Familles*, Les cahiers du GRMF, 10 (Villeneuve d'Ascq: GRMF, 1997). Similar developments occurred in Switzerland and (Francophone) Belgium.
74. See extensively Patrick Pasture, *Kerk, politiek en sociale actie: De unieke positie van de christelijke arbeidersbeweging in België (1944-1973)* (Leuven/Apeldoorn: Garant, 1992) chapter 4. A short discussion also in id., "Modèles internationaux d'action ouvrière catholique," *Chrétiens et ouvriers en France*, ed. Duriez, et al., 245-257.

resumed their work and refused proposals to merge with non-Christian organizations.[75]

Essential in both cases is the recognition of plurality, and the willingness to collaborate on a systematic basis with non-Christian social organizations, which was expressed in the new social arrangements regarding welfare and industrial relations after the war. This recognition of plurality considerably extended the prewar recognition of freedom of organization, a principle still used though in the defence of the right of Christians to organize separately against Socialists' pressures towards unification. In this respect, the Catholic social movements were again ahead of the hierarchy, although explicit reactions against the new situation were rare. Reluctance to accept the new situation was expressed sometimes in closed circles,[76] and in the explicit episcopal support for so-called 'deconfessionalized' Christian Democratic parties as in Belgium. It must be admitted though that the Christian Democrats themselves were not always as straight about their position, as was demonstrated in 1954 in the supportive reactions of Catholic and even (in fact more positive) Protestant unions in the Netherlands and also in Belgium, when the Dutch bishops in their notorious 'Mandement' reiterated their ban on Catholics to adhere to non-Catholic organizations (which, however, in the longer term contributed to the distancing of the Catholic labour movement from the episcopacy).[77]

The postwar evolution of the Church should not obliterate the fact that the attitude of Christians, including even labour organizations, towards Fascist and authoritarian corporatism had been often ambiguous, to say the least.[78] While in some cases the demand for pluralism

75. On this subject see Pasture, "Window of opportunities."
76. Cf. the reaction of Pius XII to the formation of the CGIL expressed in a secret audience to the Belgian Christian trade union leader August Cool in March 1947 as reported in a document for the 70th 'bis' meeting of the Office (Bureau) of the CISC, Paris, 4 June 1947 (Leuven, KADOC, Archives CISC, no. 16). The report of the meeting in the *Osservatore Romano* dd. 28 March 1947 does not mention the discussion on this subject.
77. On this Mandement see inter alia Hans Righart, "'De ene ongedeelde KAB', vrome wens of werkelijkheid?," *Katholieke arbeidersbeweging: Studies over KAB en NKV in de economische en politieke ontwikkeling van Nederland na 1945*, ed. Jan Roes (Baarn: KDC, 1985) 103ff.; Ed Simons and Lodewijk Winkeler, *Het verraad der clercken: Intellectuelen en hun rol in de ontwikkelingen van het Nederlandse katholicisme na 1945* (Baarn: Arbor, 1987) 80ff.; Wentholt, *Arbeidersbeweging*, 103-106. On its reception in Belgium Pasture, *Kerk*, 228-229 and Patrick Pasture, "Diverging Paths: The Development of Catholic Labour Organisations in France, The Netherlands and Belgium since 1945," *Revue d'histoire ecclésiastique* 87, no. 1 (1994) 54-90.
78. There should be no doubt, as occasionally has been noted above as well, that Catholic employers, farmers and middle class organizations often were even more ambiguous – if not blatantly sympathetic – to some forms of authoritarianism and Fascism.

and the fight for freedom of organization that the Christian trade unions particularly experienced stimulated the growth of a democratic consciousness, that for example P. J. S. Serrarens displayed, the absence of pluralism and openness of many socialists also created bitterness and hatred, and the sense of revenge, as is apparent in the Austrian and Slovakian cases.[79] Already in the 1930s and certainly in 1940, it became apparent that Christian labour leaders, even the well informed ones, easily agreed to collaborate with Fascist regimes. Certainly, this was in part inspired by a strategy of survival and by the prospect that in the new order they might have the opportunity to play an important role and escape from their position as a despised minority. From the latter perspective they were not, as a rule, hindered by the oppression of their Socialist competitors, which illustrates the big gap between both labour movements as well as the lack of mutual recognition and plurality. This was most obvious in Austria and Germany, but also in the Netherlands, where to my knowledge Christian Churches and unions in July 1940 did not act against the occupation of the NVV, while they were allowed to continue their activities more or less undisturbed. The Belgium case too illustrates the importance of tactical/ strategic power deliberations, even if they were different from the other cases just mentioned. The involvement of many Christian labour leaders in 1940 with extreme authoritarian corporatist models – P. W. Segers in Belgium, A. C. de Bruijn in the Netherlands –, however, illustrates how deeply corporatist ideology had 'corrupted' the minds, and shows that notwithstanding the warnings of, among others, CISC general secretary P. J. S. Serrarens, the lessons of the 1930s were not always taken to heart, far from it in fact. In the 1920s and '30s the CISC, thanks to outstanding leaders such as its Dutch Secretary General P. J. S. Serrarens and its French President Jules Zirnheld, functioned as a strong beacon; its disappearance in 1940 was cruelly felt. Even after the liberation proposals were sometimes drafted that contained severe restrictions on democratic social action and in particular the right to strike and the freedom of association.

79. See e.g. Wilfried de Waal, "Betriebsterror und christliche Gewerkschaften (Das Entstehen des Antiterrorgesetzes)," Ph.D. dissertation (University of Vienna, 1979) and Pieter van Duin and Zuzana Poláčková, "'Against the red industrial terror!': The Struggle of Christian Trade Unions in Austria and Czechoslovakia against Socialist Trade Union and Workplace Domination, 1918-1925," *Between Cross and Class*, ed. Heerma van Voss, Pasture and De Maeyer, 127-171, for Austria and Czechoslovakia, and compare with Carl Strikwerda, *A House Divided: Mass Politics and the Origins of Pluralism: Catholicism, Socialism and Flemish Nationalism in Nineteenth Century Belgium* (Lanham, MD: Rowman & Littlefield, 1997) for Belgium.

Nevertheless, at least in France, Belgium and the Netherlands the Christian labour movement during the difficult years of the war, and in particular the blue collar trade unions (in general white collar worker unions as well as middle class and peasant workers resisted far less), were not drawn into collaboration with the occupying forces.[80] Even in the Axis countries the Christian labour movements, surely because of the persecution they fell victim to, also found the way to the opposition and resistance against Fascism and occupation. In this way the Christian labour movements, even in Belgium, appeared not to have been tainted by the Fascist experiences, and were therefore able to engage fully in the postwar democratic reconstruction. In Germany, this was less evident and this was one of the reasons (though probably not the most important one) for not reconstructing a proper Christian trade union organization and for joining a unitary trade union federation. In France, in contrast, the Christian unions contributed greatly to 'save' a Church tarnished by its commitment to Pétain.

Selective Bibliography

Martin Conway and Tom Buchanan (eds.), *Political Catholicism in Europe, 1918-1965* (Oxford: Oxford University Press, 1996).
Emmanuel Gerard and Paul Wynants (eds.), *Histoire du mouvement ouvrier chrétien en Belgique* (Leuven: Leuven University Press, 1994).
Wyn Grant, Jan Nekkers and Frans van Waarden (eds.), *Organizing Business for War: Corporatist Economic Organization during the Second World War* (New York/Oxford: Berg, 1991).
W. D. Halls, *Politics, Society and Christianity in Vichy France* (Oxford: Berg, 1995).
Lex Heerma van Voss, Patrick Pasture and Jan De Maeyer (eds.), *Between Cross and Class: Comparative Histories of Christian Labour in Europe 1840-2000*, International and Comparative Social History, 8 (Berne/New York: Peter Lang, 2005).
Claudia Hiepel and Mark Ruff (eds.), *Christliche Arbeiterbewegung in Europa 1850-1950* (Stuttgart: Kohlhammer, 2003).
Wolfram Kaiser and Helmut Wohnout (eds.), *Political Catholicism in Europe 1918-45* (London: Routledge, 2004).
Jean-Pierre Le Crom, *Syndicats, nous-voilà! Vichy et le corporatisme* (Paris: L'Atelier, 1995).
Dirk Luyten, *Ideologie en praktijk van het corporatisme tijdens de Tweede Wereldoorlog* (Brussel: VUB-Press, 1997).

---

80. At least in the countries under review. What exactly happened in some Eastern European countries as Hungary and Czechoslovakia is unclear to me. The Christian union of German workers in Czechoslovakia certainly supported the Anschluss. Pasture, *Histoire*, 201-203.

Dirk Luyten, *Ideologisch debat en politieke strijd over het corporatisme tijdens het interbellum in België* (Brussel: Koninklijke Academie voor Wetenschappen, Letteren en Schone Kunsten van België: Klasse der Letteren, 1996).

Patrick Pasture, *Histoire du syndicalisme chrétien international: La difficile recherche d'une troisième voie* (Paris: L'Harmattan, 1999).

William L. Patch, *Christian Trade Unions in the Weimar Republic, 1918-1933: The Failure of "Corporate Pluralism"* (New Haven, CT/London: Yale University Press, 1985).

Anton Pelinka, *Stand oder Klasse? Die Christliche Arbeiterbewegung Österreichs 1933 bis 1938* (Vienna: Europa-Verlag, 1972).

Michael Schneider, *Die christlichen Gewerkschaften 1894-1933* (Bonn: Neue Gesellschaft, 1982).

Griet Van Haver, *Onmacht der verdeelden: Katholieken in Vlaanderen tussen demokratie en fascisme, 1929-1940* (Berchem: EPO, 1983).

Richard J. Wolff and Jörg K. Hoensch (eds.), *Catholics, the State and the European Radical Right, 1919-1945* (Highland Lakes, NJ: Atlantic Research, 1987).

The Roman "non possumus" and the Attitude of Bishop Alois Hudal towards the National Socialist Ideological Aberrations

*Johan Ickx**

I. Introduction

In its January edition of 1937, a German monthly for Catholic youngsters, *Die Aufrechten*, presented two closely connected news-items on the same page: "Syllabus gegen den Nazionalsozialismus?" and "Bischof Hudals Buch im Dritten Reich verboten!" The editor commented that, according to a well-informed source in Rome, a high-ranking theologian and a "German bishop" (the name of whom he knew but did not want to release for understandable reasons) were charged with the elaboration of a "Syllabus" in which the National Socialist heresy and other totalitarian ideologies were to be exposed. One statement, contained in this Syllabus, would have been: "Nicht durch den Führer und nicht durch die Blutfahne sind wir mit Gott verbunden, sondern durch Jesus Christus."[1]

Either the theologian or the Bishop the monthly referred to was one of the most controversial Vatican prelates at that time, Alois Hudal. Our contribution will deal with the complex personality of this Austrian prelate. He is certainly not the easiest topic to write about: apart from his numerous publications, his sermons and articles, the archival material Hudal left to the Austro-German Church of Santa Maria dell'Anima alone, amounts to no less than 90 files[2] and testifies to his wide indus-

---

* The present paper was prepared for the Workshop of the European Science Foundation in Ljubljana (Slovenia) June 6-8, 2002 and presented there as a lecture. Although the text has been edited for publication, nothing new has been added and literature published after that date was not taken into account.

1. *Die Aufrechten*, Sonntag 10. Januar, 1937, 2. Beiblatt, [p. 2].
2. Cf. Hans Spatzenegger, "Das Archiv von Santa Maria dell'Anima in Rom," *Römische Historische Mitteilungen* 25 (1983) 163. After our appointment as the archivist of Santa Maria dell'Anima, the Rector, Msgr. DDr. Richard Mathes, gave us instructions to prepare the material in Hudal's files in order to facilitate the work of a Scientific Commission charged with the research on the material for the coming years. After a first scrutiny, three observations can be made: first, in the past the archival material had been

try as a Rector of this foundation, as a Consultor in the service of the Holy Office, and as a Bishop who held some very personal political beliefs, and who was not afraid of taking political action.

It is not our intention however, to introduce new archival evidence in this contribution. We want to shed some light on the complex personality of Bishop Hudal, simply by making ample use of evidence to be found in some of his own writings and in the existing literature about him. We will also use unbiased testimony about some heretofore unknown actions he took during the war years. Our attempt may not resolve the ambiguities associated with Alois Hudal, but I hope it will at least make a modest contribution to reaching an unbiased and truly historical interpretation of the personality and the activities of this high-ranking Austrian cleric.

II. An Austrian in the Service of the Holy See

Little is known about Hudal's genealogical background. He was born in Graz on May 31, 1885[3] and although Hudal calls himself a *Grenzlanddeutscher*, he may be considered of Slovenian descent. Ordained a priest on July 19, 1908, he worked as a chaplain for some time. In 1911 he became a Doctor in Theology in Graz. In that same year he went to Rome for the first time in his life, entering the Pontifical College of Santa Maria dell'Anima, where he was a chaplain from 1911 till 1913, attending courses in Old Testament at the Biblical Institute. There, in 1913, he took his second doctoral degree, on *Die religiösen und sittlichen Ideen des Spruchbuches*. This dissertation was published in 1914.[4]

---

used by people who had (un)supervised access and did not always treat the material with care; second, some material has disappeared; third, documents that belonged in the files of Hudal, were found in the archives of his successors and were collected, which resulted in the addition of another file to the 90 already existing.

3. There is not much systematic biographical material available, and the most authoritative German, Austrian and Catholic biographical dictionaries do not even mention his name. We found these data in Markus Langer, *Alois Hudal: Bischof zwischen Kirche und Hakenkreuz: Versuch einer Biographie* [Diss.] (Wien 1995) 6-11; Albrecht Weiland, *Der Campo Santo Teutonico in Rom und seine Grabdenkmäler*, Römische Quartalschrift für christliche Altertumskunde und Kirchengeschichte, 43. Supplementenheft, I (Rom/Freiburg/Wien: Herder, 1988) 521-522 and F. C. Benedict, *Fürsten der Kirche: Begegnungen und Erinnerungen* (Wien, 1950) 127-130, 157-158.

4. Alois Hudal, *Die religiösen und sittlichen Ideen des Spruchbuches: Kritisch-exegetische Studie*, Scripta Pontificii Instituti Biblici, 20 (Rom: Istituto Biblico Papale, 1914).

In 1914 Hudal presented his *Habilitationsschrift* for the chair of Old Testament and Oriental Languages, at the University of Graz, thus obtaining the right to lecture in German universities. In those years he acted as a vice president of the seminary of Graz and in the last period of the Great War he served as a Chaplain in the German army. In 1919 he started lecturing at his old university. During his professorship in Graz, Hudal founded the *Katholikentage* in the Steiermark. In 1923, while becoming an Ordinary professor, he was appointed as Rector of Santa Maria dell'Anima.

For the second time Alois Hudal arrived in Rome where he would stay for the rest of his life. In 1929 he was appointed as a Consultor of the Holy Office, a task he would exercise until his death. When the Archbishop of Vienna, Cardinal Pfiffl, died in April 1932, Hudal had been hoping to be appointed as his successor, but this dream was never realized. The Austrian government, which from May 1932 was led by Chancellor Engelbert Dollfuß, objected to his nomination because, according to Langer, Hudal was too "nationalistic."[5] Theodor Innitzer became the new Archbishop of Vienna, and Hudal was ordained Titular Bishop of Ela *i.p.i.* on June 1, 1933, by Cardinal Eugenio Pacelli, Cardinal Protector of the Anima. After the death of the former Cardinal Protector, Cardinal Merry del Val, Cardinal Pacelli, the future Pius XII, who had been Apostolic Nuncio in Bavaria, Prussia, and Germany, had been appointed to this (honorific) task.

Along with other representatives of the Roman Curia, Hudal took part in the negotiations that led to the Concordat of the Holy See with the Austrian Government as well as with Berlin, in 1933.[6] The Austrian prelate would soon prove to have some very personal ideas about the future of the German speaking nations. It must be left to future researchers to determine to what extent Hudal, working for the Holy Office at that time, took part in the efforts of the central Dicasteries of the Catholic Church in order to withstand the National Socialist threat on an ideological level. Nevertheless, it seems to me that, especially given what follows, he was better prepared than anyone else and better

---

5. Langer, *Alois Hudal: Bischof zwischen Kirche und Hakenkreuz*, 11, based on information received from Bishop Dr. Kostelecky in 1992. There is reason to be sceptical about this, not only because it is third-hand information, but also because of the good relationship Hudal enjoyed with Cardinal Innitzer, even after he was appointed in Vienna.

6. The Concordat between the Holy See and the Government of the Third Reich is one of the central themes in a recent debate; cf. Ronald J. Rychlak, "Goldhagen v. Pius XII," *First Things*, no. 124 (2002) 40-41.

placed to deal with such sensitive issues. A look at Hudal's position on the issues of Racism and the Jewish question will perhaps provide a glimpse into his ideological orientation and his aims.

III. Hudal against National Socialism

Hudal's writings show that he did in fact fight against what he considered to be the errors of National Socialism. He even took several initiatives in order to urge the Vatican authorities to publicly denounce them. His first initiative goes back as far as 1934. Hudal described this "*Syllabus*-project" not only in his *Römische Tagebücher*,[7] there is also a letter to the Allied Intelligence in Rome, written immediately after the liberation and still extant in the Records of the Office of Strategic Services.[8]

Hudal's fight began in 1934. During an audience with Pius XI, he urged the Holy Father to prepare a solemn condemnation, in the form of an Encyclical or a Syllabus, of the errors of the main political ideologies existing in those days, including among others a clear pronouncement against the ideas of the Rosenberg and Streicher group. The Syllabus should condemn the following concepts: *any* totalitarian form of government, which suppresses the concept of individual freedom; the radical racial doctrine, which disintegrates the unity of the human race; a radical form of nationalism, which gives primacy to the positivistic law

---

7. Alois C. Hudal, *Römische Tagebücher: Lebensbeichte eines alten Bischofs* (Graz/Stuttgart: Stocker, 1976) 120-122. It is interesting to read the various comments and critiques that followed its publication: Elisabeth Kovács, "Alois C. Hudal, Römische Tagebücher...," *Mitteilungen des Instituts für Österreichische Geschichtsforschung* 4 (1970) 389-390; Franz Wasner, "Torso aus der Anima: Zu Bischof Hudals Memoiren," *Theologisch-praktische Quartalschrift* 126 (1978) 1, 57-67; Ludwig Volk, "Hudal, Alois C.: Römische Tagebücher," *Stimmen der Zeit* 102 (1977) 789-790; Josef Lenzenweger, "Hudal, Alois C. Römische Tagebücher," *Theologische Revue* 74 (1978) 96-100; Wolfgang Stump, "Hudal, Alois C. Römische Tagebücher," *Römische Quartalschrift* 73 (1978) 132-135.

8. "I may add that, as the first theologian and bishop of the whole world, I handed to Pope Pius XI on his request a *Pro Memoria* on the fundaments of NS already in November 1934 (!), after I had returned from a tour of lectures in Germany. Especially at Trier I had spoken on "*Rome and the German People.*" My proposal to the Holy Father was the following: to condemn by a Papal statement issued in Rome the following haresies [sic] as dangerous for our epoch: Radical nationalism, racism and state totalitarism. I am sorry that my proposal could not be carried out for reasons I am not entitled to judge" *(A Word on my Book "The Fundaments of National Socialism"* – Report of 2 September 1944, USNA, RG 226, Records of the Office of Strategic Services, 95157 – the text is accessible on the internet: http://web.archive.org/web/*/http://www.home.earthlink.net/~velid/cf/fundaments.html).

system of a State or a Nation over natural law, according to the false statement (of Machiavelli, taken over by Lenin, Stalin and Hitler): "Right is what benefits one's own people."

Hudal asserts that this was the first proposal of its kind to be made by any Bishop. Pope Pius XI would have submitted the *'dubium'* of the opportuneness of a Syllabus to the Holy Office. Hudal, writing his memoirs almost half a century later, dwells upon the fact that Germany and Austria could have been spared a lot if, in 1934, an anathema had been pronounced against these errors.[9] Nowhere in his memoirs however, does he explain what exactly happened to the proposal or why it was never taken up. Only the archives of the Secretariat of State and of the Holy Office can provide an answer to this question, but they are not yet open for historical research.

According to Hudal, a second phase began in 1935,[10] when a Commission was set up by the Holy Office to deal with the substance of a condemnation of the National Socialist ideology of race, of radical nationalism and of the totalitarian principles of Communism. The members of this Commission were, according to Hudal, several Jesuit Fathers from the Pontifical Gregorian University. Though their identities have not yet been discovered, it is known that at that time Willem Arendt, S.J. and Pedro Vidal, S.J., were working in the Holy Office as consultors, and Alberto Vaccari, S.J., and Sebastian Tromp, S.J., as qualificators.[11] It is possible that still other Jesuit theologians were involved as collaborators, e.g. Heinrich Lennerz, Arthur Vermeersch or Franz Hürth.[12] Also taking

---

9. This might prove to be an important psychological factor to explain Hudal's attitude towards German and Austrian war criminals, as we will see. Cf. already his report of 1944: "I am sure that the German people, Austria and other nations that had to feel the cruel consequences of these false doctrines, could have [been] spared much, had the ban as I proposed, in time been thrown against these doctrines which to whole Europe have brought so much disaster. The salvation of mankind lies in the courage to fight ruthlessly against the error even at the cost of present sacrifices" (*A Word on my Book "The Fundaments of National Socialism"* – cf. previous note).
10. Hudal, *Römische Tagebücher*, 121.
11. *Annuario Pontificio* (Città del Vaticano, 1936) 660.
12. For the list of other Jesuit theologians in that period: *Pontificia Universitas Gregoriana: Catalogus professorum et auditorum. Anno scolastico 1933-1934* (Romae: P.U. Gregoriana, 1934) 9-11; *Anno scolastico 1934-1935* (Romae: P.U. Gregoriana, 1935) 9-13; *Anno scolastico 1935-1936* (Romae: P. U. Gregoriana, 1936) 33-37. It would seem obvious that the Jesuits involved were native German speakers, or at least were familiar with the language. It is possible that the following Professors at the Gregorian University were involved: Sebastian Tromp, S.J., Professor of Fundamental Theology, Heinrich Lennerz, S.J., Professor of Dogmatics, Arthur Vermeersch, S.J., and Franz Hürth, S.J., Professors of Moral Theology. Thanks to Dott.sa Lydia Salviucci, Archivist of the Pontifical Gregorian University, for providing the necessary data. Arthur Vermeersch has been one of

part were Msgr. Ernesto Ruffini, Secretary of the Congregation of Studies (today known as the Congregation for Catholic Education), and the Master General of the Dominicans, Father Martin Stanislas Gillet.[13] The Commission worked intensively, until the project was suddenly cancelled. Hudal claims that it was the Secretary of State, also a member of the Holy Office, Cardinal Marchetti Selvaggiani, who considered an open attack on the National Socialist regime to be inopportune, because it might have had negative consequences for the position of the Catholics in Italy, where the Fascist party was increasingly dependent on Berlin. So Cardinal Selvaggiani's position perhaps might provide at least a partial explanation for what is generally called and often denounced as the "silence" of the later Pope Pius XII. Indeed, instead of a clear statement in the form of a *formal condemnation*, preference was given to what Hudal calls *Nadelstich-politik*, publishing critical commentaries in *L'Osservatore Romano*, or condemning National Socialist writings.

Some of the titles in the *Index librorum prohibitorum* prove that indeed the Holy Office was concerned about the ideology of the Third Reich. For example, Alfred Rosenberg's *Der Mythus des 20. Jahrhunderts* and his *An die Dunkelmänner unserer Zeit: Eine Antwort auf die Angriffe gegen den "Mythus des 20. Jahrhundert"* were condemned by Decrees of February 7, 1934[14] and of July 17, 1935[15] respectively. Whereas the delation of the *Mythus* of Rosenberg was of a "Dutch hand,"[16] Hudal claims

---

the most influential Catholic moral theologians of the first half of the twentieth century. Franz Hürth, successor of Arthur Vermeersch, taught for thirty years in Valkenburg (Netherlands), and then was appointed in 1934 at the Gregoriana. Both Vermeersch and Hürth contributed to the defense of the Encyclical *Casti Connubii* by the German bishops in 1933 in reaction to the "Gesetz zur Verhütung von Erbkranken." Without a doubt these two Jesuits constituted something of a think-tank for the Holy Office in the field of Catholic morals. See Ingrid Richter, *Katholizismus und Eugenik in der Weimarer Republik und im Dritten Reich: Zwischen Sittlichkeitsform und Rassenhygiene*, Veröffentlichungen der Kommission für Zeitgeschichte, Reihe B: Forschungen, 88 (Paderborn: Schöningh, 2001) 381-387.

13. As "Maestro Generale" of the Dominican Order, Father Gillet gave a public speech in November 1932, in which he warned against seeking a solution to the problems of mankind in both the nationalistic and internationalistic political currents. Martin S. Gillet, *L'Église Catholique et les relations internationales: Discours prononcé à Rome pour l'inauguration solennelle du nouvel "Angelicum"* (Rome: P. U. S. Thomae de Urbe, 1933).

14. *Index librorum prohibitorum Ss.mi D.N. Pii PP. XII iussu editus* (Romae: Typis poliglottis Vaticanis, 1940) 418. For the text of the Decree, see: *Acta Apostolicae Sedis: Commentarium officiale*, Vol. 26, Ser. II, vol. 1 (Roma, 1934) 93.

15. *Index librorum prohibitorum* (1940) 418. The Decree was published in: *Acta Apostolicae Sedis: Commentarium officiale*, Vol. 27, Ser. II, vol. 2 (Roma, 1935) 304-305.

16. Hudal, *Römische Tagebücher*, 119-120.

responsibility for the rest:[17] *An die Dunkelmänner* by Rosenberg, and the writings of Ernst Bergmann: *Die deutsche Nationalkirche*, condemned by Decree of February 7, 1934,[18] and *Die natürliche Geistlehre*, condemned by Decree of November, 17, 1937.[19] A denunciation of the works of Nietzsche was unsuccessful.[20]

Hudal himself had from different sides to cope with problems of copyright, publication rights and editorial interference, as well as with mere censure. A cursory glance at the list of his works that were condemned by National Socialist and Fascist party censors, shows that the bishop has been treated quite ruthlessly by them. His academic speeches, assembled in *Tatkatholizismus* (Graz 1923) were burned; in December 1935 both his books, *Deutsches Volk und christliches Abendland* (Innsbruck, 1935) and *Der Vatikan und die modernen Staaten* (Innsbruck, 1935), were taken off the market in Germany because – as the press asserted – his works criticised the ideas of Rosenberg, which formed an essential part of National Socialist doctrine.[21] Some time later, *Rom, Christentum und deutsches Volk* (Innsbruck, two editions in 1935) and the Vienna edition of *Deutsches Volk und christliches Abendland* (Wien, 1935) were burned; *Der Vatikan und die modernen Staaten*, that had already been taken off the market, was also burned by the Nazis and the Italian translation was never to become public.[22] His *Nietzsche und die moderne Welt* (Wien, 1937) was confiscated by the Italian Secret Service. Much

17. Hudal, *Römische Tagebücher*, 120.
18. *Index librorum prohibitorum* (1940) 46. For the text of the Decree, see: *Acta Apostolicae Sedis: Commentarium officiale*, Vol. 26, Ser. II, vol. 1 (Roma, 1934) 94.
19. *Index librorum prohibitorum* (1940) 46. For the text of the Decree, see: *Acta Apostolicae Sedis: Commentarium officiale*, Vol. 30, Ser. II, vol. 4 (Roma, 1937) 471.
20. Hudal, *Römische Tagebücher*, 120.
21. "Werke Bischof Hudals in Deutschland beschlagnahmt," *Grazer Mittag*, December 14, 1935.
22. The fate of the Italian translation of this work, *Il Vaticano e gli Stati moderni (note di diritto concordatario)* (Roma, [Tipografia della Pace], 1937), is interesting. On the inside cover of the copy preserved in the Anima, Hudal wrote: "Abgelehnt vom Vatikan als 'nicht opportun,' fast alle Exemplare vernichtet durch Fascisten beim Verlag – Sic transit gloria mundi! Grottaferrata, 14.II.63." The book received the *Imprimatur* of Archbishop Aloysius Traglia, Vice Regent of the Vicariate of Rome on July 25, 1937 and the Italian translation was the work of Paolo Savino, former *Aiutante di Studio* of the Third Section of the Congregation of Studies, and at that time President of the Academia Pontificia, better known as the Pontifical School for Diplomats. The question is raised as to who removed the Italian translation of the work from sale: given that the *imprimatur* had been granted by a high Church authority, it could only have been the Holy Office or the Secretariat of State. According to Hudal, it was the latter (cf. Hudal, *Römische Tagebücher*, 121). This offers a new element to the interpretation of the relationship between Hudal and Pacelli, who was at that time Secretary of State and Cardinal Protector of the Anima.

later, during the war, his *Das Vermächtnis unserer Gefallenen: Religion und Nation*, the text of a sermon delivered at the Anima Church in 1943, was publicly burned in Anagni.[23] The intriguing question is: why was Hudal such a problem?

IV. Hudal on Racial Theory and the Jewish Question

In 1936, an article by Hudal, published by *Eichingers Zeitungsdienst* (Vienna), caused controversy. At the last minute Hudal had in vain tried to prevent its publication, because some 116 lines were left out. The omitted lines had left no doubt about Hudal's position precisely with regard to National Socialism – they were published afterwards in *L'Osservatore Romano*, in a comment on the incident. National Socialism, Hudal stated in the censored passage, was, if considered in its *first* program, undoubtedly not identical to Bolshevism, even if many elements of its general organization were identical. National Socialism – judged by the program, which continued to serve as the basis for the movement – had a positive Christian foundation. But not a few enemies of true revealed religion took advantage of the existing ambiguity with regard to Catholicism and religion, to enter the Party, in order to demolish and destroy the foundation of the Christian Religion in the same way the Bolshevists had done in Russia and in other countries.[24] This was not what the Party wanted to hear.

The opposition he met with, did not discourage Hudal from publishing, in July 1936, his most famous work: *Die Grundlagen des National Sozialismus*,[25] which immediately became a best-seller and in which he developed similar views. As the title suggests, this book is a fundamental theoretical work. The author aimed to bridge what seemed to separate Christendom and National Socialism – at least according to the existing literature, which seems to see only this aspect in Hudal's magnum opus. Hudal's book also treats topics such as race and Judaism, themes he had been dealing with publicly for quite some time, for

---

23. For more details see: Hudal, *Römische Tagebücher*, 180-184 and his report of 1944 (cf. n. 8).

24. "La storia di un articolo e di una mistificazione," *L'Osservatore Romano*, October 23, 1936, 2.

25. We will use the fifth edition: Alois Hudal, *Die Grundlagen des National Sozialismus: Eine ideengeschichtliche Untersuchung von katholischer Warte* (Leipzig/Wien: Günther, ⁵1937). The first edition was of July 1936. The work was reprinted in 1982 (Bremen: Faksimile-Verlag).

example, in a public lecture held in Vienna, in the spring of 1936. Hudal had left no doubt about his feelings:

> Wenn das Problem des Rasseneinflusses auf die Religion erörtert wird, muss deshalb vor jeder einseitigen radikalen Stellungnahme gewarnt werden, die man heute unter dem Einfluss des Antisemitismus gegenüber der Geschichte und Literatur des Alten Testamentes findet. Die angebliche Unverträglichkeit der alttestamentlichen Religion mit "deutscher Frömmigkeit," die heute zu einem eigentlichen Mythos des Blutes ausgebaut wird, gehört in das Gebiet der Geschichtsklitterung. […] Dieser Versuch, alles Geistesleben aus unausrottbaren Rasseinstinkten abzuleiten, Geist und Glaube zu Funktionen des Blutes herabzuwürdigen und jede Rassenmischung als minderwertig zu brandmarken, führt über Gobineau, Renan, Delitzsch und Chamberlain hinein in die antisemitistischen Phantastereien unserer Tage, die besonders in Dinter und Fritzsch ihre Propheten und Dogmatiker erhalten haben. Dabei vergisst man völlig, dass der religiöse Gehalt des Alten Testamentes nur Wegbereitung war, um erst im Christentum vollendet und teilweise aufgehoben zu werden, dass also sein religiöser und sittlicher Wert nur ein relativer sein konnte, der bestimmten Kulturverhältnissen angepasst war. Eine Zerreißung des Bandes zwischen Altem und Neuem Testament aus Gründen der Rassenlehre bedeutet für beide das Ende, denn ihr Zusammenhang ist nicht nur ein geschichtlicher sondern organischer. Ein von allem "Jüdischen" gereinigtes Evangelium bleibt eine Utopie und wäre eben kein Evangelium mehr.[26]

In his *Grundlagen* Hudal insisted on this argument when, after citing the names of the North-African giants of the patristic times, he claimed that:

> Rassenmäßig das Problem betrachtet, ergibt sich die überraschende Feststellung, dass überhaupt die bedeutendsten Persönlichkeiten, von denen auf die Weiterbildung des abendländischen Christentums in den ersten und entscheidenden Jahrhunderten die stärksten Anregungen ausgegangen sind, nicht rein-, sondern gemischtrassig waren. Wir haben ganz ähnliche Erscheinungen auf dem Gebiete der Profankultur der Antike, […] In allen Jahrhunderten finden wir im abendländischen Christentum ein Zusammenarbeiten der Rassen und Nationen, denn nur auf diesem Wege konnte eine Weltkirche trotz vieler Gegensätze innerhalb der Menschheitsgruppen sich entfalten.[27]

---

26. Alois Hudal, *Das Problem des Rasseneinflusses in der Entwicklung des abendländischen Christentums: Vortrag im Kulturbund – Wien, Oesterreichische Gruppe des Verbandes für kulturelle Zusammenarbeit (Fédération des Unions intellectuelles) am 17. März 1936* (Roma: [Tipografia della Pace], 1936) 15-17. See also: Hudal, *Die Grundlagen des National Sozialismus*, 101-102.

27. Hudal, *Die Grundlagen des National Sozialismus*, 110.

Hudal's purpose becomes even more clear when we hear his conclusion:

> Wer in der Rasse das einzige kulturbindende Prinzip sieht, muß folgerichtig das Christentum ablehnen, weil seine erste Träger einer fremden Rasse angehörten.[28]

Eugenics was another sensitive issue Hudal took into consideration. In fact, where an over-emphasis on the importance of race led to a distancing of the German people from Christianity, in the hygienic-social field "erscheint als Folge, die Ausscheidung der erkrankten Masse durch Eheverbote und Sterilisation."[29] Hudal obviously defended the Catholic position on eugenics and conjugal ethics, citing *Casti Connubii* and documents of the Holy Office,[30] in particular that of March 21, 1931 on sexual education and genetics, which condemned all non-natural practices within marriage.[31]

Hansjakob Stehle argues that Hudal tried to build a bridge between National Socialism and the Catholic Church, as a means to counteract Bolshevism. According to Stehle, Hudal was of the opinion that National Socialism "only" had to abandon the anti-Christian aspects of its ideology and to free itself from the "false" anti-Semitism of "rassischer Überspitzung."[32] Indeed, Hudal did not present the Catholic Church to National Socialism on a silver platter. The German Catholics were prepared to march with National Socialists, under condition however that National Socialism would abandon all concepts that were unacceptable to a true Catholic, e.g. its attitude towards the Jews as a consequence of its racial theories.

The success of Hudal's writings was entirely due to the convincingly straightforward way in which he wrote down his own convictions. In connection with what Hudal had to say on the Nürnberger racial laws, Markus Langer argues that Hudal applied a specific "scientific" method, that is, he cited the various anti-Jewish arguments in order to reject them one after the other, asserting in the same immediate context that, as a Catholic, he would condemn "*any*" injustice." At the same time –

---

28. Hudal, *Die Grundlagen des National Sozialismus*, 115.
29. *Ibid.*, 123.
30. *Ibid.*, 134.
31. *Acta Apostolicae Sedis: Commentarium Officiale, Annus XXIII* (Città del Vaticano, 1931) 118-119.
32. Hansjakob Stehle, *Geheimdiplomatie im Vatikan: Die Päpste und die Kommunisten* (Zürich: Benziger, 1993) 170. And also: Langer, *Alois Hudal: Bischof zwischen Kirche und Hakenkreuz*, 75.

according to Langer – Hudal stuck directly or indirectly to the doctrine of the NSDAP while, on the other hand – always according to Langer – Hudal's chapter on anti-Semitism in particular provoked disputes within the Church itself.[33] In the eyes of Hudal, the Jewish question was an "auf das Reich übertragenes ostdeutsches Grenzlandproblem."[34] There might be merit to Langer's opinions, but I would like to be more precise in the interpretation of Hudals' own thoughts.

Hudal detects roots of anti-Semitic sentiment that date back to the 19th century, identifying two different tenors in the anti-Semitic movement: one in agreement with racial terminology, another consisting in the mere concept of *Volkstümern*. In the first case, anti-Semitism might result in a direct attack against any Jewish person simply because he is of another race. As to the second, the Jewish never were a 'people', and even in their own ranks there was a difference between those who assimilated with the local population and those who did not. According to Hudal, it came as a shock to German Jews to be, suddenly, treated as a distinct and single ethnic group, something for which they were not psychologically prepared. Jews, Hudal argued, did not consider themselves as forming one ethnic group, and moreover he contradicts the myth – current in his time – of the Jews forming some secret society: "obschon ihre Gegner glauben, sie hätten es mit einem auf Not und Tod verschworenen 'Geheimbund' zu tun."[35]

Hudal thus clearly contradicts some main issues of National Socialist ideology and propaganda. According to Hudal's reasoning, precisely stressing the racial question completely changes the whole Jewish question:[36] "scientific" studies on race did not concern themselves with the opinions on, or the position of the Jew as an individual in relation to the State or the "host country," but only with the question of "blood," this being the only, "mystical" foundation of his basic attitude:

> Erst dadurch ist das ganze Judenproblem in Parteikreisen volkstümlich geworden und in Rosenbergs "Mythus des 20. Jahrhunderts" zum großen Thema deutscher Zukunft gemacht worden [...] Obwohl die objektive Forschung noch in einem Wald unentschiedener Fragen steckt, werden bereits nach einem a priori-Schema Eigenschaften verteilt, wobei niemand gewisse seelische Rasseneigentümlichkeiten und Veranlagungen leugnen möchte. Ein höchst verwickeltes Problem soll

---

33. Langer, *Alois Hudal: Bischof zwischen Kirche und Hakenkreuz*, 74.
34. *Ibid.*, 75.
35. Hudal, *Die Grundlagen des National Sozialismus*, 82.
36. "Die Akzentverlegung auf die Rassenfrage hat die Lage geändert," *ibid.*, 83.

im Nationalsozialismus scheinbar eine höchst einfache Lösung finden. So ist das ethnische Problem in ein moralisches verwandelt; einer Rasse werden als solcher moralische Defekte als konstitutive Mitgift überbunden.[37]

On the other hand, Hudal comments on the increasing presence of Jewish people in all sectors of society, and being perceived as a threat to young unemployed Germans. In his opinion, the presence of Jews in positions of power or influence was indeed in disproportion to their total number. It was easy to foresee, Hudal concludes, the danger: such a situation could drive many young people to embrace a dangerous radicalism.[38] It would be remiss of me not to mention how Hudal also repeats the popular beliefs about Jews that were current in many Catholic circles, expressing suspicion towards the Jewish people, or at least, towards Jewish individuals, but:

> das Schicksal der Juden unter den Völkern und damit das Judenproblem überhaupt kann in letzter Hinsicht nicht bloß aus dem Tatbestand einer anderen Rasse oder nur aus der POLITISCHEN Sphäre erklärt werden, sondern bedarf notwendig auch einer theologischen Orientierung, um nicht im Bestreben, das eigene Volkstum zu schützen, zu ungerechten Anschauungen zu kommen, die nicht bloß der Wahrheit, sondern auch der rein menschlichen Humanität widersprechen würden.[39]

V. The Hidden Agenda of *Die Grundlagen*

It is surprising that Stehle and Langer did not take the Syllabus project into consideration when assessing Hudal's work, as it would have certainly affected their reading of it. For example, how was it possible that a Bishop of the Roman Catholic Church would ask the Holy Father himself to condemn publicly the heretical components of certain ideologies in 1934-35, and then directly or indirectly himself propagate the same heretical components only a few years later? It is quite possible that Hudal wanted to make known publicly part of the material he composed for a "Syllabus" in his *Grundlagen*. In my opinion, when looking at the way he deals with race, the Jewish question, genetics and sterilization, Hudal's concise and methodical way of listing various

---

37. Hudal, *Die Grundlagen des National Sozialismus*, 83-84.
38. Ibid., 87.
39. Ibid., 93.

examples – the "scientific" approach Langer discovered in the *Grundlagen* – corresponds to the typical style of the Consultor's *votum*. It is a style that proceeds by commenting on 'propositions' in such a way that it makes the author's own, sometimes hidden agenda emerge, emphasizing what is in favour and leaving out what is not, never offending the opponent, acknowledging that he may have a point but at the same time emphasizing that other priorities are at stake. And last but not least: unyielding when Roman Catholic principles are involved.

Langer points out that, in his critique on anti-Semitism, Hudal refers only to a few and less significant exponents of the NSDAP. Even if this were true, it would be possible to explain this by the problems he faced from Rosenberg and the official National Socialist press, and also by his position in the Vatican, being an Austrian Bishop in service of the Holy See. Hudal deliberately seeks to avoid, whenever possible, an open attack against highly placed members of the Party, although, as already noted, he does not hesitate to openly attack Rosenberg in essential parts of his *Grundlagen*, another fact not mentioned by Langer.[40]

Hudal certainly was not a supporter of the National Socialist methods of repression, and of its denigration of the human person, although this is exactly the impression created by historians for more than half a century. In fact, anyone reading the *Grundlagen* from beginning to end would not doubt Hudal's position *vis-à-vis* National Socialism. He clearly explains that, as long as it remains a socio-political theory, it may belong to the sphere of political debate, but he concludes his book with a clear warning: "when National Socialism coincides with a new philosophy of life which is exalted to the level of a dogma, in which an over-abundance of errors of the last decades are gathered into a dazzling and, to the youth particularly, fascinating myth; in such a case to remain silent and to wait would equal an approval [of its errors] and at the same time a denial of the Faith. The Church can renounce associations and organisations, even the economic support of the State, painful as it would be. Even if in an over-organised state-management those means were snatched away from religion the Church could never renounce its eternal mandate to give leadership and to be and remain the tower of light for the Truth in peaceful and even more so in tumultuous times, just as nowadays. The words of the Apostle prevail: 'One shall obey God more than man' and also that other phrase that Rome, so often in

---

40. Cf. Hudal, *Die Grundlagen des National Sozialismus*, 53-55, 64 (on positive Christendom): 67, 71.

the course of the centuries has uttered against numerous heresies, 'non possumus!'"[41] The attack on the Nazi ideology is irrefutable. Remark how Hudal accuses the Nazis between the lines of depriving the Church of its organisations and associations and how he uses the precise word "Führergabe." At the end of the paragraph (the closing paragraph of his book) there is the vehement "Non possumus!," a clear abjuration of the Nazi ideology. These *Grundlagen*, with personal dedications written by Hudal, were presented to Hitler on October 8, 1936, by the Vienna Ambassador Franz von Papen.[42]

As could be expected, the National Socialist censors had difficulty finding an acceptable line in Hudal's book. On December 21, 1936, the Press Office of the German Reich announced that the Commission charged by the Party with censorship, after "several" examinations, forbade circulation of the book in the whole of the Reich.[43] Some days later a similar announcement was made in Czechoslovakia.[44] The book's enormous success in Austria was only to be halted immediately after the *Anschluss*. The German censor had to proceed in this way because Hudal's book was not the innocent factum of an author desiring to make known his personal view on National Socialism. Its redaction fitted into a larger context, and was written in response to an invitation from others, among them von Papen. Recent scholarship has proven beyond doubt that the idea to compose *Die Grundlagen* was not that of Hudal alone, as was and is commonly believed.[45]

---

41. "Ist aber der Nationalsozialismus gleichbedeutend mit einer neuen, zum Dogma erhobenen Weltanschauung, in der eine Überfülle von Irrwegen vergangener Jahrzehnte zu einem blendenden, besonders die Jugend faszinierenden Mythos zusammengebaut sind, dann würde Schweigen und Warten eine Zustimmung und Verleugnung des Glaubens sein. Die Kirche kann auf Vereine und Organisationen verzichten, selbst auf die wirtschaftliche Unterstützung des Staates, so schmerzlich es auch wäre, wenn in einem überorganisierten Staatswesen diese Mittel der Religion entrissen würden, allein sie kann niemals auf ihre ewige Führergabe verzichten, der Leuchtturm der Wahrheit zu sein und zu bleiben in ruhigen, noch mehr in stürmisch bewegten Zeiten, wie es die Gegenwart ist. Da gilt ein Apostelwort: "Man muß Gott mehr gehorchen als den Menschen," und jenes, das Rom so oft im Laufe der Jahrhunderte gegen zahlreiche Irrtümer gesprochen hat: Non possumus!" Hudal, *Die Grundlagen des National Sozialismus*, 253.

42. Wolfgang Dierker, *Himmlers Glaubenskrieger: Der Sicherheitsdienst der SS und seine Religionspolitik 1933-1941*, Veröffentlichungen der Kommission für Zeitgeschichte, Reihe B: Forschungen, Band 92 (Paderborn/München/Wien/Zürich: Schöningh, 2002) 232, n. 111.

43. *Prager Presse*, Prag, December 22, 1936. Whereas Goebbels, Bormann and Rosenberg condemned Hudal's book without hesitation or delay, Rudolf Heß, on the other hand, proposed (without success) to let it serve to irritate the ranks of the Party (thus destroying Hudal's credit forever); Dierker, *Himmlers Glaubenskrieger*, 232 (see also n. 112).

44. *Das Echo*, Wien 13 Januar 1937.

45. Langer, *Alois Hudal: Bischof zwischen Kirche und Hakenkreuz*, 76-81.

In his book *Himmlers Glaubenskrieger*, Wolfgang Dierker observes that, around July 1936, Adolf Hitler had to consider, in one way or another, a rapprochement with the Catholic Church, while he wanted to support the anti-communist campaign of the Spanish General Franco.[46] The German episcopate supported Franco openly because he guaranteed the cessation of widespread atrocities against the clergy in Spain. In this regard, in a Pastoral Letter issued on August 19, 1936, the German Bishops asked that the acts of defamation and restriction of the clergy be ended, stating that "the communist threat in Spain could only be overcome by the Christian faith and not by philosophies of life "die sich lediglich aus dem Blute und dem Zeitcharakter ergeben."[47] This is seen as a call for a peaceful and united collaboration of State and Church to gain victory over communism. It was as much a warning to National Socialists: it was dangerous to ignore the Catholics as they did.

Initially, the National Socialist regime responded positively to this invitation; the Secret Service had to cease its prosecution of regular and secular clergymen. It was precisely in the midst of this political play that Franz von Papen, Hitler's special ambassador in Vienna, who had won a first major diplomatic victory in the so-called *Juli-Abkommen*, realised that the annexation of predominantly Catholic Austria could exercise a positive effect on National Socialist Germany. It was Ambassador von Papen – no hardliner of National Socialism – who invited Hudal to write a book about National Socialism from a Christian point of view, in order to smooth the way for a possible understanding between National Socialism and Catholicism.[48]

Dierker's research shows that when the Secret Service later sequestered the personal files of von Papen, they were to discover that Hudal, responding to the wishes of the ambassador, made many corrections and additions to his book.[49] This brings us to the real aim of Hudal's work. Considering the antecedents of both von Papen and the

---

46. Dierker, *Himmlers Glaubenskrieger*, 230
47. Pastoral Letter of the German Episcopate, August 19, 1936, cited by Dierker, *Himmlers Glaubenskrieger*, 230.
48. *Ibid.*, 232. According to Hudal, in his report from 1944, the book wanted to provide guiding in two important matters of conscience that existed among German speaking Catholics in those days: "May a German Catholic without affecting his religious conscience join Nazi organisations or is he obliged to fight [it] as adversary to Christianity?" and "How is it possible that in Austria Nazism is opposed by the Church whereas the Vatican concludes a Concordate with the Nazi party in Germany" (*A Word on my Book "The Fundaments of National Socialism"* – cf. note 8).
49. Dierker, *Himmlers Glaubenskrieger*, 232, n. 108.

Austrian prelate, it could be asked if those men really wanted to build *a bridge* on which Catholics and National Socialists could meet halfway. If the principles set forth in *Die Grundlagen* were to be accepted by the party, little would be left of "genuine" National Socialist doctrine, which, according to Hudal, was not a German, but a "Latin" invention – his own analysis in the report of 1944 already mentioned, be it circumstantial, is worth citing: "I was able to prove that Nazism cannot be compared with a common party. It is rather a movement of the German middle classes, particularly of their intellectual ranks and not a movement of German peasants, much less of the working class. It is in a certain sense the result of the cultural decadence of German spiritual life in the 19th century tied up with the names of Hegel, Feuerbach, Nietzsche and Hackel. By means of the oldest Nazi program of the Iglau party conference in 1933 I was able to demonstrate that not Hitler but a printer immigrated from Poland to Mahrisch-Trubau in 1902 – his name is Burschowski (Jew?) –is the founder of National Socialism and that above all its decisive doctrines – race, totalitarianism – are not of German but of French and Italian origin (Gobineau, Machiavelli) [...] The final result of my inquiries was the following one: There are two currents in NS, a left one (radical) and a right one (Conservative), either fighting for supremacy. There are moreover *two ideas* to be found which as such mean something positive: *nation and socialism*. If separated, however, from religion and conscience they run the risk of ending in a radical movement to which nothing is sacrosanct. Supernationalism necessarily leads to the doctrine of the superman, the *Herrenvolk*, and to the oppression of all other nations in the sense of ancient paganism; socialism if not dominated and mitigated by religion, leads to the dictatorship of the proletariate, to class combat and at least to anarchy."[50]

VI. The Reception of Hudal's Ideas on National Socialism

The Secret Service of the Reich was of course greatly alarmed by Hudal's publication. The *Sicherheitsdienst*, in a report about *Die neue Taktik des politischen Katholizismus*, was most offended by Hudal's comparing those in the National Socialist Movement who didn't belong to a Church with Marxists: "Hudal aber meint mit dem Marxismus den EIGENTLICHEN Nationalsozialismus, sucht so dem Volke Sand in die

---

50. *A Word on my Book "The Fundaments of National Socialism"*, cf. n. 8.

Augen zu streuen und in die Reihen seiner Gegner einzudringen."[51] It is obvious by the reaction of the *Sicherheitsdienst* that they considered Hudal to be an instrument of the Holy See. His activities over the previous year were seen as a new strategy, directed by Rome, to reconcile Church and State.[52] The *Sicherheitsdienst* was so conditioned by these suspicions, that they interpreted the critique on Hudal's book by Cardinal Innitzer of Vienna and by the Prince-Bishop of Salzburg, Waitz, as either a mere mistake in the Church's tactics, or as part of a systematic "Jesuitical" plot.

In reality, not only the leaders of the NSDAP, but also some of the highest church officials distanced themselves from the book and, thereby, from Hudal's concept of an acceptable form of National Socialism. The Austrian bishops were not the only ones to suddenly show themselves sceptical of Hudal's *Grundlagen*.[53] One cannot ignore the fact that, at least officially, no support whatsoever was given to the publication of the book. In fact it was heavily condemned. Hudal, who had given a voice to the Church's censures of National Socialism, would himself also be censored by the Catholic Church. In an article published in October 1936 in *L'Osservatore Romano*, the Holy See denied any responsibility or co-involvement with the publication of *Die Grundlagen*.[54] His dignity as a Bishop, and the fear of possible reactions in the Reich, preserved him from the worst: a formal prohibition of his book.[55]

It is obvious that this negative reaction had nothing to do with Hudal's chapters on the Jewish question or on genetics. It had, I presume, everything to do with his obvious attempt not so much to build a bridge between National Socialism and Christianity, but to Christianize National Socialism altogether. This politically motivated choice and somewhat startling ideological position was at the time not only a theoretical and political illusion, but also an error, given the fact that National Socialist leaders would not abandon their radical positions on race and the Jewish question. The Vatican considered Hudal's line of

---

51. Dierker, *Himmlers Glaubenskrieger*, 233.
52. *Ibid.*, 233.
53. Cf. the report of 1944: "After the war I shall publish all documents and letters concerned in my possession in an epilogue of my book, among them the positive judgments of the Vienna Cardinal, who gave me the imprimatur, as well as of Chancellor Schuschnigg, who by no means checked the publication in Austria."
54. Hudal, *Römische Tagebücher*, 129.
55. Hudal's personal commentary, cited in: Langer, *Alois Hudal: Bischof zwischen Kirche und Hakenkreuz*, 95: "[…] von Pius XI. mit dem Index bedroht, was nur unterblieb mit Rücksicht auf meine bischöfliche Stellung und eventuelle Rückwirkungen im 3. Reich, dem gegenüber Kardinalssekretär Pacelli eine mildere Haltung einnahm."

thinking "inopportune" because a majority within the German episcopacy obviously did not want to get involved in National Socialism. All this is consistent with the reaction of the Secretary of State: as Hudal noted in his memoirs, Pacelli explained to him that, if Church policy in the Reich had been friendly to the Vatican, the opinion on his book would have been positive. Pacelli detested the NS Movement, not only on account of its opposition to the Church, but also on the account of its total disregard of natural law.[56]

Another striking and even more intriguing episode is that of Hudal's *Nietzsche und die moderne Welt*, a treatise based on a lecture Hudal delivered on April 13, 1937. Notwithstanding the cool reactions to his *Grundlagen*, and the negative consequences for himself, the Anima Rector accepted the invitation of the *Wiener Kulturbund* to give a lecture on this theme. As he had done earlier in 1936, he would speak his mind before the Austrian cultural and political elite. Explaining the basic concepts of Nietzsche's philosophy to his audience, Hudal attempted to show that National Socialism was based on Nietzschian principles in the same way as Russian Bolshevism. He inveighed against the *Deutsche Glaubensbewegung*, the new 'church' of the Reich, founded by Jakob Wilhelm Hauer.

> Der Hass gegen das Christentum und Rom, den ungezählte Bücher und Zeitschriften der deutschen Glaubensbewegung in das deutsche Volk gerade seit Herbst 1936 hineintragen, ist keineswegs schwächer als jener der Pamphletliteratur des russischen Bolschewismus [...] Die deutsche Glaubensbewegung ist ebenso wie der Bolschewismus eine GOTTLOSENBEWEGUNG, auch wenn ihre Anhänger nicht den Mut haben, sich als solche öffentlich vor dem Staate zu bekennen. Was sie Gott nennen, hat mit einem wirklichen Gottesbegriff nichts zu tun, ist kein persönliches Wesen, keine Wirklichkeit über das menschliche Sein hinaus, sondern eine Selbstvergöttlichung von Blut, Rasse und Nation, also von bedingten Werten die niemals ewig sein können [...].[57]

Let it be important that modern culture "auch auf den Werten von Nation, Rasse und Boden aufbaut," this can only be the case while these are "vielen Fragen tragende Kräfte," not because they are "letzte sittliche Normen."[58]

---

56. Hudal, *Römische Tagebücher*, 131: "Der päpstliche Staatssekretär Pacelli erklärte mir, wenn die Kirchenpolitik im Reich vatikanfreundlich würde, wäre auch das Urteil über mein Buch günstig." See also on this account the version of H. Jansen, who unfortunately neglected to quote his sources: Hans Jansen, *De zwijgende Paus? Protest van Pius XII en zijn medewerkers tegen de jodenvervolging in Europa* (Kampen: Kok, 2002) 183.
57. Alois Hudal, *Nietzsche und die moderne Welt* (Rome, 1937) 44-45.
58. *Ibid.*, 45.

The Bishop warned that one could not fight politically against Russia and at the same time go along with Russian Bolshevism on the ideological level.[59] He asked his audience some decisive questions: Is Nietzsche a positive or a disruptive force for the modern world and in particular for Europe and Germany? Is it possible to build a real future for the Germans on Nietzschean philosophical theory, or does it lead to Bolshevism?[60] He supplied the answers in his lecture: "Nietzsche did not want to found a new religion. Notwithstanding that, he tried to mask his ideas with the religious language of the Prophets and the Gospel, and to preserve some definite cultic forms. With materialistic and purely natural foundations, Nietzsche hoped to replace the Catholic Church with a presumptuous "cathedral" of a new German national culture, which is destined to end with a Babylonian confusing of the minds [...]."[61] This was said in Vienna in April 1937, a few months after his *Grundlagen* was criticised and censored. This time Hudal wasn't given permission to edit his lecture in Austria. He decided therefore to publish it in Rome, at his own expense, but again certain forces stood in the way: a few months later, on September 27, 1937, the Italian Propaganda Ministry prohibited its publication and it was taken off the market by the Fascists.[62]

VII. Hudal's Action within the Vatican

Also in the spring of 1937, Hudal claims to have written a *votum* for Cardinal Canali of the Congregation of Extraordinary Affairs (today part of the Secretariat of State), in which he argues for an energetic and decisive attitude towards the German problem (he even proposed to recall the Nuncio in Berlin). Hudal states that this *votum* was used in part for the Pope's letter *Mit brennender Sorge* of March 14, 1937.[63] It will be the task of future research to confirm the truth of this claim.

A year later, on April 13, 1938, a rescript was issued by the Congregation for Studies, ordered by Pius XI and signed by Msgr. Ruffini,

---

59. Hudal, *Nietzsche und die moderne Welt*, 49-50.
60. *Ibid.*, 50-51.
61. *Ibid.*, 51.
62. Hudal, *Römische Tagebücher*, 120.
63. *Ibid.*, 121.

Secretary of the Congregation. This condemned Hitler's race ideology, not from a political perspective, but declared it a heresy. Given the involvement of Ruffini, Savino and Carlo Pacelli, all working at the Congregation of Studies at that time and all three acquaintances of Hudal, it would be interesting to investigate the origin of this rescript and a possible connection with Hudal.[64]

It must be recognized, in Hudal's favour, that he was swimming in other waters than the National Socialists and that he never ceased to defend the interests of the Catholic Faith and of humanity in general. This is demonstrated by what Hudal considered to be the conditions necessary to win and secure peace. These conditions are enumerated in Hudal's appendix to a peace plan he was secretly drafting, without the Holy See's knowledge, together with *SS-Obersturmbannführer* Dr. Waldemar Meyer:[65] in addition to the amnesty for imprisoned clergymen, restitution of confiscated ecclesiastical goods, ceasing the leaflet propaganda, ending discrimination against Catholics and Protestants in public service, full freedom for religious education and filling the vacant bishoprics, Hudal proposed the *immediate suspension of the killing of Jews*. Stehle remarks that neither the Pope nor any other Bishop of the Catholic Church ever included this last most astonishing condition in any note of protest.[66] A year later, in October 1943, Hudal contacted the German Ambassador Ernst von Weizsäcker and General Stahel in an attempt to prevent the SS from carrying out Himmler's orders to liquidate the Jews of the Roman Ghetto. His

---

64. Msgr. Ruffini was the Secretary of the Congregation, Paolo Savino an *'aiutante di studio'*, and Carlo Pacelli a Legal Consulent working in the administrative office of the Congregation. (Cf. *Annuario Pontificio* [Città del Vaticano, 1937] 704-706.) For the propositions declared "absurd" by the Rescript, see: *Credere: Settimanale dell'Azione Cattolica*, May 29, 1938, 1, and Georges Goyau, "Un acte décisif et retentissant de Pie XI contre le racisme," *Le Figaro*, May 3, 1938, 1, 3.

65. See Robert A. Graham, "Goebbels e il Vaticano nel 1943: Un enigma risolto," *La Civiltà Cattolica* 125, no. 4 (1974) 130-140; id., "La questione religiosa nella crisi dell'Asse: Il confronto Orestano – Hudal (1942-43)," *La Civiltà Cattolica* 128, no. 1 (1977) 448-451 and Hansjakob Stehle, "Bischof Hudal und SS-Führer Meyer: Ein kirchenpolitischer Friedensversuch 1942/43," *Vierteljahreshefte für Zeitgeschichte* (1989) no. 2, 299-322.

66. Stehle, *Bischof Hudal und SS-Führer Meyer*, 310: "Die erstaunlichste Forderung aber, die so unverblümt anklagend weder Papst noch ein Bischof jemals in eine Protestnote geschrieben hatten, lautete: 'Sofortige Sistierung [Einstellung] der Judenmorde.'" One can remark that for instance also the Dutch bishops protested fiercely against the deportation of Jews; see J. M. Snoeck, *De Nederlandse kerken en de joden 1940-1945* (Kampen: Kok, 1990) and the contribution of Lieve Gevers in this book.

action may not have been the decisive one that halted the deportations,[67] but – as Langer states – at least Hudal did what he could at that moment.[68]

VIII. The Complexity of a Humanitarian

One of the recurrent elements in the literature on Hudal is the help he offered to Nazi criminals after World War II.[69] It is known that Otto Waechter, SS Official and well known for having participated in the murder of the Austrian Chancellor, Engelbert Dollfuß, on July 25, 1934,[70] and other former German and Austrian Nazi's were helped by the Anima Rector, for he openly admitted it.[71] However, one must be very careful not to overestimate or personalize his role in giving aid to such people, and it will take further investigation to evaluate the real dimension of Hudal's activities in this regard. One should not forget that after the liberation, the church and buildings that made up the Anima were under strict surveillance by the liberation forces in Rome, a fact so far ignored by historians.[72] In his memoirs, Hudal, commenting

---

67. Historians take differing positions on Hudal's intervention in this affair. Some deny that he took any action in favour of the Jews, such as Susan Zuccotti, *Under His Very Windows: The Vatican and the Holocaust in Italy* (New Haven, NJ/London: Yale University Press, 2000) 152-170. Others, such as Andrea Tornielli, affirm the veracity of this intervention, *Pio XII: Il Papa degli Ebrei* (Casale Monferrato: Piemme, ³2001) 281-293. I cannot agree with the statement made by Zuccotti that "historians speculate that Bishop Hudal may have been prompted to write by Weiszäcker, or by Weiszäcker's aide Albrecht von Kessel." Hudal's intervention is known and documented by Langer, *Alois Hudal: Bischof zwischen Kirche und Hakenkreuz*, 176-182, and Pierre Blet, *Pio XII e la Seconda Guerra mondiale negli Archivi Vaticani* (Cinisello Balsamo: San Paolo, 1999) 283. Moreover, given Hudal's involvement in the Escape Line, I doubt Zuccotti's statement that "Hudal was apparently not a confidant of the Pope and had little influence in the Vatican" (p. 162).
68. Langer, *Alois Hudal: Bischof zwischen Kirche und Hakenkreuz*, 182. The text of Hudal's intervention in: "Le Saint-Siège et les victimes de la guerre, janvier-décembre 1943," *Actes et documents du Saint-Siège relatifs à la Seconde Guerre Mondiale*, 9, ed. Pierre Blet, Angelo Martini and Burckhart Schneider (Città del Vaticano: Libreria editrice Vaticana, 1975) 373. These facts have recently been confirmed by Adolf Eichmann in his diary distributed in 2000. Cf. Jansen, *De zwijgende Paus?*, 360-361, 627-628.
69. See for instance: Ernst Klee, *Persilscheine und falsche Pässe: Wie die Kirchen die Nazis halfen* (Franfurt am Main: Fischer Taschenbuch Verlag, ³1992) 24-50 and *passim*.
70. Graham, *La questione religiosa nella crisi dell'Asse*, 448.
71. Hudal, *Römische Tagebücher*, 263, 295, 298.
72. See the account of Brigadier John Burns, who himself asked the Intelligence of the Allied Forces in Rome to put the Anima under surveillance. John Burns, *Life Is a Twisted Path: A Time of Imprisonment, Escape, Evasion and Final Refuge with the Mattei*

on the period immediately following Liberation, refers to many visits by the Allied and Italian Secret Services, to the detachment of a Secret Service Agent to the Anima College, to the fact that he was threatened with a warrant to appear before the war tribunal.[73]

Oddly enough, Hudal was put under surveillance not only because the Allied Forces considered him a friend of the Third Reich during the war, but also – and this is new – because of his humanitarian efforts during the war in favour of Allied refugees. This helps to explain why he was the object of so much distrust immediately after the Liberation. The recently published eye-witness record of a New Zealand prisoner of war, who escaped in Italy, depicts Hudal as taking great risks to save the lives of different "enemies,"[74] giving them protection in the buildings of the Anima. As the church was designated as the National Austrian-German Church of Rome and was frequented as such by both German soldiers and civilians living in Rome, this made for an odd situation, with the Germans being under observation by the enemy hidden within the Anima.

The new elements locate Hudal as a key element in the unsolved puzzle of the Vatican Escape Line. They confirm two very important points. In the first place, Bishop Hudal, the so-called "Nazi Monsignore," gave shelter and protected Allied soldiers in his own "German" house, where he often also received SS personnel and German officers. In the second place, the story tells us of clergymen and religious figures, such as Msgr. Hugh O'Flaherty, Father Owen Snedden and Msgr. Edward Flanagan, who were active in the 'Allied Escape Line' through the Vatican, in connection with the Italian resistance and in close contact with the "Brown" Monsignor, without any fear that he would betray them. The episode involving Hudal in resistance actions is in contrast to his post-liberation difficulties and the general opinion of his activities in this regard. It seems that the current historiography has so far only presented a one-sided account of the humanitarian actions of Bishop Hudal, informing the public only of his post-war action, while ignoring his actions during the war. The question of why and by what means historiography developed in this direction seems to be more important than the issue itself.

of Montecelio and Bishop Alois Hudal of Santa Maria dell'Anima, Rome (Rome: Santa Maria dell'Anima, 2002) 129.
    73. Hudal, *Römische Tagebücher*, 295.
    74. According to the New Zealand escapee, besides his fellow Ken Phillips, there were at least three others hiding with them: Bernard Schilling and Franz Kaminski, who presented themselves as Austrians, and an Italian Officer of the Carabinieri, Major Rossi.

IX. Hudal as a Piece of the Vatican Puzzle

According to the New Zealand refugee, the escaped prisoners of war were, while hiding in the countryside, in contact with a person associated with the Vatican. They entered Rome with the assistance of members of the Italian Resistance and were brought into the Vatican. Once arrived there, they were brought into contact with Father Snedden and Msgr. Flanagan.[75] Within a few hours after arriving in Rome the two escapees were transported in a "German car" to the Anima, and placed under the protection of Bishop Hudal where, as they soon discovered, they were not the only ones in hiding. During their stay in the Austro-German Institute, they received regular visits from Snedden and Flanagan.

There are many indications that Hudal's actions were closely connected with his work as a consultor for the Holy Office. Msgr. Hugh O'Flaherty, the well-known Irishman, who appears to have worked in the diplomatic service of the Vatican as an '*Addetto*' to the Papal Nunzio in Haiti until 1938,[76] after a period of absence from papal service, reappears, this time among the '*scrittori*' of the Holy Office, in 1939-1940.[77] The question is, however, what exactly was the nature of O'Flaherty's work for the Congregation. According to H. Jansen, who cites Chief Rabbi Zolli, many refugees found shelter in the Vatican: many of them were lodged in the Vatican Palaces and in the apartments of different Cardinals and Prelates. Jansen remarks that O'Flaherty helped those Jews whose lives were in danger and that the contacts and conversations with those in need of help took place in his office, on the first floor of the Holy Office.[78] As it turns out, O'Flaherty was assigned to the Holy Office only from the beginning of the war and he left – as it seems – no record of any work of a doctrinal or disciplinary nature. Again according to Jansen, both Cardinal Ottaviani

---

75. While Father Owen Snedden was a New-Zealander, Msgr. Edward Flanagan came from Bathurst, Australia. (Cf. *Annuario Pontificio* [Città del Vaticano, 1940] 930.) On the activities of Snedden: Rosaleen Conway, "Dodging the Gestapo in Rome," *The New Zealand Tablet*, Wednesday June 3, 1981, 10-11, who describes the activities of the two clergymen. Snedden apparently lived in the Pontifical Urban College. One of Snedden's "rounds" was Via Firenze and it backed onto Gestapo headquarters. He and Flanagan had over 40 billeting places in Rome and they wrote the names of escapees under their protection on cards packed into biscuit tins which they buried in the Vatican gardens. The two also broadcasted on Vatican Radio the names of the New Zealanders alive in Italy.

76. *Annuario Pontificio* (Città del Vaticano, 1937) 727. In 1936 the Nonciature in Haiti was vacant, and in the *Annuario* of 1938, O'Flaherty is no longer mentioned, thus out of service.

77. *Annuario Pontificio* (Città del Vaticano, 1940) 692.

78. Jansen, *De zwijgende Paus?*, 264.

and Cardinal Tisserant, whose apartments were located in the Palace of the Holy Office, opened their apartments to Jews.[79] Still today the oral tradition of the Holy Office tells of a "domestic animal" being kept in the courtyard of its palace: a cow that served as a source of milk.

Additional circumstantial evidence regarding the very nature of the activity of the Holy See is provided by the fact that, also in 1939-1940, Gianbattista Montini was named Consultor of the Holy Office.[80] As a consequence, the three top men of the Secretary of State, Card. Luigi Maglione, Secretary of State, Msgr. Domenico Tardini, Secretary for the Extraordinary Affairs,[81] and Msgr. Montini, Substitute for the Ordinary Affairs, were all working for the Holy Office, the latter two as Consultors and thus colleagues of Alois Hudal. Furthermore, it is known that Hudal had a close friendship with Carlo Pacelli, the nephew of Pope Pius XII, who occasionally functioned as a messenger to him.[82]

But there is more: the other German foundation, the Campo Santo Teutonico dei tedeschi e fiamminghi, located inside the Vatican, seems to have been even more involved than Santa Maria dell'Anima that is located in the actual city. The Church historian Hubert Jedin states in his memoirs that the British Escape Organization was located in the Campo Santo, where he himself had been hidden.[83] Also interesting in this respect is the case of Karl Bambas.[84] In July 1943, as the German *Wehrmacht* occupied Rome, Bambas, whose wife was of Jewish origin,

79. Jansen, *De zwijgende Paus?*, 264.
80. *Annuario Pontificio* (Città del Vaticano, 1940) 691.
81. See: Carlo Felice Casula, *Domenico Tardini (1888-1961): L'azione della Santa Sede nella crisi fra le due guerre*, Coscienza studi, 18 (Roma: Studium, 1988) 80.
82. Hudal, *Römische Tagebücher*, 215. At least on one occasion this relationship is confirmed by other sources: Jansen, *De zwijgende Paus?*, 628.
83. Hubert Jedin, *Lebensbericht: Mit einem Dokumentenanhang*, ed. Konrad Repgen, Veröffentlichungen der Kommission für Zeitgeschichte: Reihe A, Quellen, 35 (Mainz: Matthias-Grünewald-Verlag, 1984) 124.
84. Born in Vienna in 1896, he studied dentistry in his native city and in Hamburg. In 1921 he settled in Albania with his wife; in 1923 he formed the plan to immigrate to the United States, but a malaria infection caught in Tirana brought him to Italy. He became resident in Rome and set up a dental practice in the Via Gregoriana. Before the war he had founded the Austrian cultural societies 'Oesterreichische Tafelrunde' (1925) and 'Oesterreichische Landsmannschaft' (1925). Both organizations ceased to exist with the Anschluss. The 'Oesterreichische Landsmannschaft' and the 'Deutsche Vereinigung in Rom' worked together quite well until 1933. After Hitler took power, the 'Oesterreichische Landsmannschaft' moved to the College of the Anima, directed by Alois Hudal – according to Schlick "notwithstanding the pan-German character of the Rector of the Anima." We thank Brigitte Schlick, who kindly permitted us to use her yet unpublished thesis on immigration in Italy. Also thanks to Miss Margherita Bambas, always available to give any information in relation to her father's action. Weiland, *Der Campo Santo Teutonico*, 692ff.

had to hide and found shelter in the Campo Santo Teutonico. The dentist Bambas meanwhile took charge of the "printing-office" located in the building of the Holy Office; among other services, the office supplied false identity papers and passports for refugees.

All evidence points to one fact: that the Holy Office played a key role in the Escape Line of the Vatican and that the buildings nearest to the Holy Office, those of the Campo Santo Teutonico, seat of the German Görresgesellschaft,[85] provided accommodation to many refugees, through the intervention of Msgr. Montini and Msgr. O'Flaherty,[86] who took his meals in the Campo Santo.[87] Hudal also was associated with those two institutions[88] and was the rector of Santa Maria dell'Anima.

During the war, Pius XII charged Montini with the ordinary affairs of the Secretariat of State, which was responsible for the *Pontificia Commissione Assistenza*,[89] in which Hudal was responsible for the Austrian division. In the post-liberation period, Hudal continued to work for the Commission and, until 1950, took several personal initiatives to help and comfort his compatriots imprisoned in the camps or living as fugitives in Italy, as well as their relatives.[90] The Allied Forces who liberated Rome kept the Anima under secret surveillance. Indeed, the two allied escapees who were given refuge at the Anima suggested to British Intelligence that a guard be posted, knowing that Hudal would continue to do the same for others after the liberation as he had done for them during the war. In his eyes they were *all* innocent victims of a course of events he had always tried to prevent.[91]

---

85. Erwin Gatz, "Das Römische Institut der Görresgesellschaft 1888-1988," *Römische Quartalschrift* 83 (1988) 3-18; for the wartime-years see 14-15.

86. Erwin Gatz, "Der Campo Santo Teutonico als Helfer: Zu den Möglichkeiten einer deutschen Stiftung im Ausland," *Römische Quartalschrift* 93 (1998) 79-91, especially 89 to 91: "Der Campo Santo als Zufluchtstätte für Verfolgte während des Zweiten Weltkrieges (1943/44)."

87. Jedin, *Lebensbericht*, 103, 121.

88. On his membership of and his activity for the Görres-Gesellschaft, see Rudolf Morsey, *Görres-Gesellschaft und NS-Diktatur: Die Geschichte der Görres-Gesellschaft 1932/33 bis zum Verbot 1941* (Paderborn: Ferdinand Schöningh, 2002) 112, 161-162. Morsey also refers to the Report of the *Sicherheitsdienst* of October 1936 (cf. n. 51), which states that Hudal, until July 1934 was judged to be "schärfster Gegner des Nationalsozialismus." The Report then refers to a series of publications that appear to portray him as a friend and ally of National Socialism. However, it concludes that a more accurate examination of the publications makes it clear that in the end Hudal was opposed to National Socialism and tried to confuse his adversaries by altering the meaning of their terminology.

89. Langer, *Alois Hudal: Bischof zwischen Kirche und Hakenkreuz*, 209-212.

90. For the request for the permission of Pope Pius XII to give such assistance to German prisoners in Italy, see: "Le Saint-Siège et les victimes de la guerre Janvier 1944-Juillet 1945," *Actes et documents du Saint-Siège relatifs à la Seconde Guerre Mondiale*, 10, 435-436.

91. Hudal, *Römische Tagebücher*, 21.

X. Conclusion

Regarding the question which Dicasteries of the Holy See were involved in combating the ideologies of National Socialism and racism, this study has indicated that it was not primarily the Secretary of State, but the Supreme Sacred Congregation of the Holy Office which directed and coordinated the response. Later, in the second half of the 1930's, for strategic and political reasons, the Congregation for Studies was asked to become involved also. A key role of the Holy Office in the organization of an Escape Line of the Vatican, which worked closely with the Italian Resistance and in which Hudal took an active part, is also confirmed. Even on the basis of published sources alone it is no longer possible to doubt the extreme industry of Hudal in the service of the Holy Office and, at the same time, his 'hypothetical' contribution to decisive interventions, especially in the mid-thirties, regarding the totalitarian ideology of National Socialism.

Alois Hudal was certainly attracted to National Socialism, in the same way as many other intellectuals were attracted to communist or capitalist ideas in those years, but he was not a Nazi. It has become clear that Hudal was an orthodox Catholic, a fact especially his Superiors in the Vatican were convinced of, given that he remained in the service of the Holy Office for many years after the War. This means that he can *not* have been a Nazi. In the past, most authors saw Hudal only in the light of his actions in favour of the fascists and Nazi refugees after the War. This approach obscured important aspects of his writings and his humanitarian activity before and during the War, distorting public opinion concerning the truth of his convictions and ideas on different crucial items such as racial theory and the Jewish question. Hudal wrote in defense of the Jewish people on several occasions, and although his work was inspired by different circumstances than that of, for instance, Bishop Clemens August Count von Galen, it is, again, striking that both were zealous opponents of the Nazi Regime.[92]

The 1944 eyewitness account shows clearly that the assistance Hudal offered during the War to Allied soldiers would, once the War ended, easily turn into humane and charitable activity towards

---

92. For the striking similarity of the content of their critiques of the National Socialist regime, see the above-cited paragraphs on Jewish question and Racism: Heinrich Mussinghof, *Rassenwahn in Münster: Der Judenpogrom 1938 und Bischof Clemens August Graf von Galen* (Münster: Regensberg, 1989) 72-77.

German fugitives, be they war criminals or not. On the topic of Hudal's activities to help refugees and his opposition to the Third Reich, much is still to be discovered, but it can already be concluded that his aid was not politically motivated and simply inspired by his Catholic faith.

Related to this topic is Field Marshal Kesselring, whom Hudal considered as a personal friend. Is it possible that Kesselring knew of the actions of Hudal in favour of refugees but said nothing? Did Kesselring in some way support the humanitarian enterprises of Hudal? Having been condemned by the Nürenberg Court, Kesselring was later set free in response to a telegram from the British Prime Minister. Could Kesselring's conduct in Rome during wartime have been (part of) the reason for Winston Churchill's intercession in his favour after the War? All of these questions call for further study.

Robert A. Graham describes Hudal as an individualist. A man who lived in isolation, imposed on him by both sides, by the political establishment of his time and by the Vatican itself, a situation which neither discouraged him nor provided him any insight.[93] It will take other studies to fully understand the nature of Hudal's thinking. For the moment it may be sufficient to state that Hudal was certainly not a 'Nazi' or a blind follower of the 'party'.[94] On the contrary, he continually criticized the ideological and political excesses of the Nazi-regime. Already before the war, the official institutions of the Third Reich were aware of the danger and the 'untrustworthiness' of Bishop Hudal with regard to their line of politics. However, Hudal – like many others – remained strongly convinced of the merits of a 'purer' National Socialism that could serve as a counterforce against Communism, and therefore hoped that a sort of 'purification' of National Socialism, restoring its alleged original purity, was possible. Both this, on a political level erroneous, hope and the decisive defense of the rights of the Catholic faith on an ideological level, place his name among those who were called 'bridge-builders' in the Reich.[95] The

---

93. Graham, *La questione religiosa nella crisi dell'Asse*, 447-448.
94. We refer to the misleading titles of articles, for example, O. Schulmeister, "Der Nazi-Bischof im Beichtstuhl der Zeit," *Die Presse*, October 16-17, 1976, articles that continue to determine the public opinion.
95. On the subject of the 'bridge-builders', see the studies of Prof. Maximilian Liebmann on Cardinal Innitzer and on Johann Ude (1874-1965). Hudal himself speaks of a "modus vivendi zwischen NS und den beiden christlichen Bekenntnissen im Reich" (Hudal, *Römische Tagebücher*, 116).

patriotic and pan-German Hudal[96] never left any doubts about his deep-rooted Catholic faith, living in a very personal way his own motto *Ecclesiae et nationi*, for the Church and for the Nation, but – as the order of the words suggests – with an explicit priority given to the Church. This last statement is confirmed by the words he wrote in a letter to Cardinal Pizzardo, after being forced to resign in 1952, in which he expresses his repugnance for the conditioning of the Church's inner life by any possible worldly power or ideology, even by that of capitalism.[97]

One may wonder why Hudal himself didn't say a word about his helping opponents of the Nazi's. The bitterness and the disappointment related to the final episode in his life, when he was openly disavowed by the Church, provoked deep distress and even affected his deep-rooted faith. Both the personal defeat and the seemingly intentional negative historiography concerning his person overshadowed for half a century the zealous and courageous activity of this Austrian servant of the Catholic Church. Obviously, the basic question now is no longer whether or not Hudal was a 'Nazi', but rather what motivated historians, and what did historiography have to gain, by treating this Bishop as the Nazi-phile he never was, and by neglecting so much historical evidence that would have put him in a different light? Did Hudal simply fall victim to his own ambiguity?

Selective Bibliography

Pierre Blet, *Pio XII e la Seconda Guerra mondiale negli Archivi Vaticani* (Cinisello Balsamo: San Paolo, 1999).

P. Blet, Angelo Martini and Burckhart Schneider, *Le Saint-Siège et les victimes de la guerre, janvier-décembre 1943*. Actes et documents du Saint-Siège relatifs à la Seconde Guerre Mondiale. Vol. 9 (Città del Vaticano: Libreria editrice Vaticana, 1975).

---

96. It is impossible to cite all the quotations that underscore this quality; it is sufficient perhaps to recall M. Langer's words: "Hudal's Vorliebe für alles 'Gesamtdeutsche' war nicht unbekannt," Langer, *Alois Hudal: Bischof zwischen Kirche und Hakenkreuz*, 49.

97. "[…] Nur eine einzige Stelle hat auf meinen Protest, dass ich als Rektor der gesamtdeutschen Pilgerstiftung der Anima von der Betreuung der reichsdeutschen Pilgerorganisation in brüsker Form ausgeschaltet wurde, erklärt, dass es mit Rücksicht auf die Alliierten erfolgen musste, da ich durch meine Stellungnahme zum Dritten Reich nach der Niederlage Deutschlands kompromittiert gewesen sei. Ich habe damals erwidert: 'Seit wann regieren die Alliierten auch in die Kirche Christi hinein?'" Cited in: Langer, *Alois Hudal: Bischof zwischen Kirche und Hakenkreuz*, 19.

John Burns, *Life is a Twisted Path: A Time of Imprisonment, Escape, Evasion and Final Refuge with the Mattei of Montecelio and Bishop Alois Hudal of Santa Maria dell'Anima, Rome* (Rome: Santa Maria dell'Anima, 2002).
Carlo Felice Casula, *Domenico Tardini (1888-1961): L'azione della Santa Sede nella crisi fra le due guerre*, Coscienza studi, 18 (Roma: Studium, 1988).
Wolfgang Dierker, *Himmlers Glaubenskrieger: Der Sicherheitsdienst der SS und seine Religionspolitik 1933-1941*, Veröffentlichungen der Kommission für Zeitgeschichte, Reihe B: Forschungen, 92 (Paderborn/München/Wien/Zürich: Schöningh, 2002).
Erwin Gatz, "Der Campo Santo Teutonico als Helfer: Zu den Möglichkeiten einer deutschen Stiftung im Ausland," *Römische Quartalschrift* 93 (1998) 79-91.
Erwin Gatz, "Das Römische Institut der Görresgesellschaft 1888-1988," *Römische Quartalschrift* 83 (1988) 3-18.
Hans Jansen, *De zwijgende Paus? Protest van Pius XII en zijn medewerkers tegen de jodenvervolging in Europa* (Kampen: Kok, 2000).
Hubert Jedin, *Lebensbericht: Mit einem Dokumentenanhang*, ed. Konrad Repgen, Veröffentlichungen der Kommission für Zeitgeschichte, Reihe A: Quellen, 35 (Mainz: Matthias-Grünewald-Verlag, 1984).
Ernst Klee, *Persilscheine und falsche Pässe: Wie die Kirchen die Nazis halfen* (Frankfurt am Main: Fischer Taschenbuch Verlag, 1992).
Elisabeth Kovács, "Alois C. Hudal, Römische Tagebücher...," *Mitteilungen des Instituts für Österreichische Geschichtsforschung* 4 (1970) 389-390.
Markus Langer, *Alois Hudal: Bischof zwischen Kirche und Hakenkreuz: Versuch einer Biographie*. [Diss.] Wien, 1995.
Josef Lenzenweger, "Hudal, Alois C. Römische Tagebücher," *Theologische Revue* 74 (1978) 96-100.
Rudolf Morsey, *Görres-Gesellschaft und NS-Diktatur: Die Geschichte der Görres-Gesellschaft 1932/33 bis zum Verbot 1941* (Paderborn: Schöningh, 2002).
Ingrid Richter, *Katholizismus und Eugenik in der Weimarer Republik und im Dritten Reich: Zwischen Sittlichkeitsform und Rassenhygiene*, Veröffentlichungen der Kommission für Zeitgeschichte, Reihe B: Forschungen, 88 (Paderborn/München/Wien/Zürich: Schöningh, 2001).
Hans Spatzenegger, "Das Archiv von Santa Maria dell'Anima in Rom," *Römische Historische Mitteilungen* 25 (1983) 163.
Hansjakob Stehle, "Bischof Hudal und SS-Führer Meyer: Ein kirchenpolitischer Friedensversuch 1942/43," *Vierteljahreshefte für Zeitgeschichte* 37 (1989) 299-322.
Hansjakob Stehle, *Geheimdiplomatie im Vatikan: Die Päpste und die Kommunisten* (Zürich: Benziger, 1993).
Wolfgang Stump, "Hudal, Alois C. Römische Tagebücher," *Römische Quartalschrift* 73 (1978) 132-135.
Andrea Tornielli, *Pio XII: Il Papa degli Ebrei* (Casale Monferrato: Piemme, 2001).
Ludwig Volk, "Hudal, Alois C.: Römische Tagebücher," *Stimmen der Zeit* 102 (1977) 789-790.
Franz Wasner, "Torso aus der Anima: Zu Bischof Hudals Memoiren," *Theologisch-praktische Quartalschrift* 126 (1978) 1, 57-67.

Albrecht Weiland, *Der Campo Santo Teutonico in Rom und seine Grabdenkmäler*, Römische Quartalschrift für christliche Altertumskunde und Kirchengeschichte, 43. Supplementenheft, vol. I (Rom/Freiburg/Wien: Herder, 1988).

Susan Zuccotti, *Under His Very Windows: The Vatican and the Holocaust in Italy* (New Haven, CT/London: Yale University Press, 2000).

List of Contributors

Jan Bank, Amsterdam (The Netherlands), 1940 (on May 10, the day of the German invasion in the Netherlands). Ph.D. in History, University of Amsterdam. From 1988 till 2005 professor of Dutch history at the University of Leiden. Main research fields: political, cultural and religious history of The Netherlands in the 19th and 20th century.

Lieve Gevers, Turnhout (Belgium), 1947. Ph.D. Modern History, Katholieke Universiteit Leuven. Professor of the History of Church and Theology, Faculty of Theology K.U. Leuven. Main research fields: History of the Catholic Church, Religion and Nationalism, Catholic education in the 19th and 20th century.

Idesbald Goddeeris, Kananga (Congo), 1972. MA Slavic Languages, MA History, Ph.D. History, Katholieke Universiteit Leuven. Post-doctoral Assistant at the Slavic Languages Department of the K.U. Leuven. Main research fields: History of Central and Eastern Europe, migration history and history of the Cold War.

Tamara Griesser-Pečar, Ljubljana (Slovenia), 1947. Ph.D. History, University of Vienna, Austria. Free historian. Main research fields: Austria-Hungary, History of Slovenia in the 20th century, History of the Catholic Church in Slovenia (Yugoslavia) in the 20th century.

Emilia Hrabovec, Bratislava (Slovakia), 1964. Ph.D. in History at the University of Vienna, Austria. Habilitation in Eastern European History at the University of Vienna. Professor at the Institute for Eastern European History at the University of Vienna and at the Faculty of Philosophy at the University of Trnava, Slovakia. Main research fields: History of the Catholic Church in Central and Eastern Europe and of the Holy See in the 19th and 20th century, Relations of the Holy See to the states in the context of the international relations.

Johan Ickx, Wilrijk (Belgium), 1962. Ph.D. Ecclesiastical History, Pontifical Gregorian University, Rome. Archivist of the Tribunal of the Apostolic Penitentiary; Archivist of the Austrian-German Institute and Pontifical College Santa Maria dell'Anima. Main research fields: 19th and 20th century Church History, with particular emphasis on the presence and activities of Northern European personalities in the Roman Curia.

Jure Krišto, Stipanjići (Bosnia and Herzegovina), 1943. Ph.D. Systematic Theology, University of Notre Dame, USA, Dr. sc. in Modern History, University of Zagreb. Senior Research Fellow, Institute of History, Zagreb. Director of the Project "Croatian Political Ideologies, Parties, Faiths, and Institutions of the XIXth and XXth Centuries". Editor-in-Chief of the *Review of Croatian History*. Main research fields: History of Catholic Movements, Relationship between the Church and Politics, Ideologies and Historiography.

Vilma Narkutė, Kretinga (Lithuania), 1971. Ph.D. Theology, Katholieke Universiteit Leuven. Scientific researcher, Faculty of Theology K.U. Leuven. Main research fields: History of the Catholic Church, Religion and Nationalism.

Patrick Pasture, Leuven (Belgium), 1961. Ph.D. History, 1991. Associate Professor of History, Faculty of Arts, Katholieke Universiteit Leuven. Research and publications on labour history and the social history of modern Christendom (17th-20th century) from a transatlantic and global perspective.

Lieven Saerens, Mechelen (Belgium), 1958. Ph.D. Modern History, Katholieke Universiteit Leuven. Researcher SOMA/CEGES (Centre for Historical Research and Documentation on War and Contemporary Society, Brussels). Main research fields: the Belgian attitude towards the Jews (end 19th century-ca. 1950).

PRINTED ON PERMANENT PAPER • IMPRIME SUR PAPIER PERMANENT • GEDRUKT OP DUURZAAM PAPIER - ISO 9706

N.V. PEETERS S.A., WAROTSTRAAT 50, B-3020 HERENT